COMPUTER-ASSISTED INSTRUCTION, TESTING, AND GUIDANCE

WITH CONTRIBUTIONS BY

J. C. R. Licklider

Frederic M. Lord

Raven I. McDavid, Jr.

Donald Bitzer

Emmanuel G. Mesthene

C. Victor Bunderson

Mona Morningstar

J. G. Castle, Jr.

Carl B. Shelley

Allan B. Ellis

Robert F. Simmons

Robert Glaser

D. Skaperdas

Bert F. Green, Jr.

Richard D. Smallwood

Lee W. Gregg

Donald E. Super

Vaughn Groom

Patrick Suppes

Wayne H. Holtzman

David V. Tiedeman

Joseph J. Lagowski

Gail S. Young

Edward D. Lambe

Karl L. Zinn

COMPUTER-ASSISTED

INSTRUCTION, TESTING,

AND GUIDANCE

Edited by Wayne H. Holtzman

1817

HARPER & ROW, PUBLISHERS
NEW YORK, EVANSTON, AND LONDON

Contributors

DONALD BITZER, Professor of Electrical Engineering; Director, Computer-Based Education Research Laboratory, University of Illinois.

C. VICTOR BUNDERSON, Associate Professor of Educational Psychology and Computer Sciences, The University of Texas at Austin.

J. G. CASTLE, JR., Professor of Physics, University of Alabama at Huntsville.

ALLAN B. ELLIS, Lecturer in Education, Harvard University; Director, The Center for Educational Software Development.

ROBERT GLASER, Professor of Psychology and Education; Director, Learning Research and Development Center, University of Pittsburgh.

BERT F. GREEN, JR., Professor of Psychology, Carnegie-Mellon University.

LEE W. GREGG, Professor of Psychology, Carnegie-Mellon University.

VAUGHN GROOM, Research Associate, CAI Laboratory, The University of Texas at Austin.

WAYNE H. HOLTZMAN, Professor of Psychology and Education; Dean, College of Education, The University of Texas at Austin.

JOSEPH J. LAGOWSKI, Professor of Chemistry, The University of Texas at Austin.

EDWARD D. LAMBE, Professor of Physics; Director, Instructional Resources Center, State University of New York at Stony Brook.

J. C. R. LICKLIDER, Professor of Electrical Engineering; Director, Project MAC, Massachusetts Institute of Technology.

FREDERIC M. LORD, Chairman, Psychometric Research Group, Educational Testing Service.

RAVEN I. MCDAVID, JR., Professor of English and Linguistics, University of Chicago.

EMMANUEL G. MESTHENE, Director, Program on Technology and Society, Harvard University.

MONA MORNINGSTAR, Research Associate, Institute for Mathematical Studies in the Social Sciences, Stanford University.

CARL B. SHELLEY, Chief, Mission Simulation Branch, Flight Control Division, NASA Manned Spacecraft Center.

ROBERT F. SIMMONS, Professor of Computer Sciences, The University of Texas at Austin.

D. SKAPERDAS, Associate Director, Computer-Based Education Research Laboratory, University of Illinois.

RICHARD D. SMALLWOOD, Associate Professor of Engineering-Economic Systems, Stanford University.

DONALD E. SUPER, Professor of Psychology and Education, Teachers College, Columbia University.

PATRICK SUPPES, Professor of Philosophy, Statistics, and Education; Director, Institute for Mathematical Studies in the Social Sciences, Stanford University.

DAVID V. TIEDEMAN, Professor of Education; Director, Information System for Vocational Decisions, Harvard University.

GAIL S. YOUNG, Professor of Mathematics, Tulane University.

KARL L. ZINN, Assistant Professor of Psychology; Research Scientist, Center for Research on Learning and Teaching, University of Michigan.

Contents

Part III. **Optimizing Learning**

Part IV. **Individually Tailored Testing**

Part V. **Language Processing**

Part VI. **Stanford Programs in Arithmetic, Logic, and Russian**

Preface

It has been observed that, over the years, mankind has successfully developed new technologies, as older methods have proved to be insufficient in the face of rising populations, shortages of raw materials, and other fundamental changes in human affairs. The technology of food production has advanced so that the specter of worldwide famine, although still present, seems no closer than it was when Malthus made his gloomy predictions. Similarly, as older sources of energy such as coal and petroleum face predictable depletion, the newer technology associated with nuclear energy arises as a necessary and viable alternative.

Will a corresponding technological advance occur with respect to mass education? And, if so, will that advance also support needed improvement in the quality of the learning experience for each individual? Does the computer as teaching assistant or as teacher constitute a quantum leap in educational practice?

Certainly a quantum leap is needed. The United States public schools are today failing too many of our children. United States colleges and universities are facing great difficulties in managing and expanding the storehouse of knowledge and in making that knowledge available in meaningful and relevant ways to students. Computer technology, perhaps more than any other means visible at present, holds promise that we can deal with the educational problems of today and tomorrow in significant fashion.

The extent to which this may be true is the subject of this book. Its chapters represent a report of progress, problems, and issues in the application of computer technology to educational practice. Some of the authors are specialists who are actively engaged in developing computer applications to instruction, guidance, and testing. Other authors are critics who identify and discuss issues of practice and purpose. The general reader who might otherwise be put off by the technical content of some of the chapters should find the critical chapters a substantial aid to understanding. In particular, Wayne Holtzman's overview of "Computers in Education" and Emmanuel Mesthene's thoughtful discussion of "Computers and the Purposes of Education" should be of interest to the general reader.

The papers on which this book was based were prepared for a conference at The University of Texas in Austin in October 1968. The conference grew out of mutual interests of the Social Science Research Council and the College Entrance Examination Board. From the council's point of view, its Committee on Learning and the Educational Process concluded a year ago that certain major research and development programs had reached the point where the significance of results could be evaluated. From the college board's point of view, its Commission on Tests had concluded about the same time that the implications of new educational technology for college guidance and admission were highly relevant to its review of the board's testing functions. Happily, Wayne Holtzman was a member of both groups and served as chairman of a special joint committee to plan the conference. Other members of the planning committee were C. Victor Bunderson, University of Texas; Philip Jackson, University of Chicago; Robert Glaser, University of Pittsburgh; and Winton Manning, College Entrance Examination Board.

The council and the college board express their thanks to Dean Holtzman, to the members of the planning committee, to the authors, and to the conference participants.

—RICHARD PEARSON, *President*
College Entrance Examination Board

—HENRY W. RIECKEN, *President*
Social Science Research Council

COMPUTER-ASSISTED INSTRUCTION, TESTING, AND GUIDANCE

1

Wayne H. Holtzman

Computers in Education

National concern for the improvement of education at all levels has grown rapidly in recent years. In his provocative book, Keppel (1966) outlines three phases through which education in the United States has been going. First, he points to the reasonably good success we have had in developing a system of universal education, the first stage in the educational revolution. Then he notes the ferment we have been going through the past twenty years concerning the equality of educational opportunity, which represents the second phase of the revolution—a phase that is still not yet won. The current emphasis on quality in education constitutes the third and last phase in the revolution and began in the post-Sputnick period when national concern for quality mounted across the country. When considered in all its aspects, the idea of universal education of high quality for every student is a dream that few of us wish to set aside—a dream that paradoxically seems more remote at the same time great progress is being made in the development of new technology to make it possible.

Central to the realization of quality education on a universal basis is the development of individualized instruction that takes into account the great human diversity in cultural background, styles of life, values, goals, motivation, mental abilities, and personality of students. The keeping track of a person moving at his own pace in a continuous progress environment where the particular branching of the curriculum is tailor-made for his own learning aptitudes and level requires a computer to manage the curriculum and assist with the instruction. Emphasis is on the learner rather than the teacher. The teacher may be necessary for learning under some circumstances and may actually be a hindrance under others. The student begins at that point in the curriculum where he is best capable of learning and moves at his own rate, with knowledge of his results immediately following his answer. The particular sequence of the curriculum may be controlled almost entirely by a computer or it may be completely under the control of the student, depending on the type of material to be learned, the kind of student, and the purposes of the instruction.

An important first step in the development and implementation of new technology is the preliminary sketching of a design for the future. Given existing technology, current trends in society, and probable developments in the near future, what will instruction, testing, guidance, and other aspects of the educational environment look like in ten to twenty years? Even if it is feasible to develop a truly powerful form of individualized instruction, would the cost of its implementation be prohibitive? What technical and scientific problems must be solved before such an educational system can be realized? How would the individual and society be affected by such developments? Would this bring about some features of George Orwell's monstrous society of *1984?* Or would it lead unerringly to the enlightened society of well-educated, free individuals often envisioned by educational planners? Although most such questions remain unanswerable at this stage of development, they must be kept constantly in mind as technology progresses. Let us imagine for a minute what this educational environment of the future might be, given existing technology and likely developments in the next several decades.

A Glance at the Future

Responsive environments for learning will begin at infancy in the home as well as in special day-care centers. Children will be grouped from the age of three on and there will be no sudden entry into school. Most instruction will be individualized with a continuous diagnosis-prescription-evaluation cycle so that the student can gain mastery of basic skills as efficiently as possible. Learning resource centers with computerized libraries and communications controls will be the centers of education just as the library is the center of knowledge within our great universities. Study carrels or teaching terminals, however, will be remotely located for the convenience of students.

The lock-step, self-contained classroom will completely vanish. Although we may still have lectures from distinguished speakers, the current classroom scheduling system and sequence of courses on a semester or quarter basis will be completely replaced as the uniformly prescribed curriculum disappears. Computers will take over most of the drudgery of scheduling, allocating learning resources to individuals and groups, maintaining progress records while preserving their confidentiality where appropriate, compiling and scoring tests, providing easy access to files of information for reference or guidance by students and teachers, and a host of other management activities. For major segments of the curriculum, the computer will also provide direct interaction between the student and the subject matter to be learned, whether the instruction involves drill and practice in arithmetic or foreign language, tutorial interaction and dialogue, or problem solving and simulation of complex phenomena.

Most of the interaction between the computer and the individual will occur at remotely located inquiry terminals or teaching stations. A typical terminal will consist of a visual-display device, perhaps an ordinary television screen, for presenting both moving pictures and still images to the student. In some cases provision will be made for graphic or schematic material to be superimposed locally on visual images received from afar. Video tape recording/playback features will be present at the terminal, making it possible to shift quickly and economically from one segment of the instructional module to another, repeating where necessary. The terminal will also have audio output in the form of segmented speech, probably generated locally from random-access storage in harmony with the visual display. Limited capability will be present for generating short spoken phrases and sentences in a tutorial dialogue with the student.

The student will communicate with the curriculum material by either typing on a keyboard or pressing a pen at the desired location on the face of the visual display. He will be able to draw lines with the pen across the visual image as well as specific points, and the computer will interpret the graphic input before producing an appropriate response to the student. A hard copy of the dialogue or portions of the computer output can be obtained from the typewriter, from a photograph of the visual display, or later from the computer storage unit before it is erased. Although it would be ideal to provide natural conversational capability so that the student and computer could actually talk intelligently to each other, the technology for such capability is still remote.

Many of the hardware components for a prototype terminal similar to the one described are close to completion now, although their cost is still too high to implement. Existing systems for computer-assisted instruction, such as the IBM 1500 Instructional System, already have some of these features. And several major companies are now designing hardware configurations that will eventually have the functional capabilities outlined above. But it is uncertain whether their cost can be sharply reduced by mass production to the point where it is economically feasible to think of large-scale implementation. Certainly more modest terminal configurations can be made cost-effective, as argued by Bitzer and Skaperdas, Castle, and Lambe elsewhere in this book. The most important problems rest not with hardware but with the development of software.

The term *software* is sometimes used to cover everything needed to make a system work except the equipment itself. Here we shall slightly restrict the meaning to one of the three general categories: (1) the operating system of coded information needed to make the computer, its memory banks, registers, arithmetic units, transfer devices, satellites, and input/output terminals function effectively as an information-handling system; (2) the higher-order languages by which the human being communicates with the computer and develops new functional capabilities; and (3) the content to be dealt with, such as the instructional materials themselves, including the branching strategies, learning-reinforcement procedures, diagnostic routines, visual images, audio output, and the content of the subject matter to be learned.

Responsibility for developing a smoothly functioning operating system generally rests with the computer manufacturer, although such has not always been the case. No company today could effectively market its hardware without at least providing a minimum amount of this kind of software. Given the current competition in the industry and the strong demands from consumers for more powerful and efficient operating systems, the manufacturer must produce a good system to survive. Consequently, the state of the art in this kind of software has advanced rapidly and promises to continue to grow vigorously.

The development of higher-order languages for writing useful computer programs has progressed rapidly but in an uncoordinated fashion that threatens to produce a Tower of Babel. Whereas such conventional compiler languages as Fortran, Algol, and Cobol tend to dominate, there are scores of other special-purpose languages that are generally incompatible with each other, making it inefficient and difficult to employ them at the same time on a single system. Whether or not the present attempts to develop a hierarchical system of compatible languages will succeed remains to be seen. Within computer-assisted instruction the situation is even worse. In a review of CAI languages, Zinn (1968) listed over forty different languages that are being used for interactive computing, display, and the writing of instructional programs. Most of these are frequently being revised and patched together in attempts to improve their capability. The number could be expanded greatly if other lesser known variations of these languages were included.

Technology for the third kind of software varies widely with the type of application. Contemporary instructional technology is in its embryonic stages with very little scientific basis as yet for adapting the curriculum materials to the specific motivational, aptitude, and personality patterns of the individual learner. In a highly critical review of educational technology, Oettinger and Marks (1968) stated that only drill and practice for skill training in narrowly defined areas has thus far proved of practical value and even here they question the significance of the work to date. Although few educational technologists would take such a pessimistic view as Oettinger, no one doubts the need for an enormous amount of research and development to create truly effective instructional software for individualized learning, testing, and guidance.

Uses of the Computer in Education

The use of the computer as an instructional tool is only one of many applications of computers in education. Most of the rapid growth of computers during the past ten years can be attributed to the vastly improved administrative services, high-speed numerical calculations, and large-scale file management made possible by the modern computer. Although many of these applications proved their worth initially in solving problems for business, government, military, engineering, and scientific research, their contributions to education are proving just as profound.

The growth rate of the computer industry has been so great, increasing at an annual rate of nearly 40 per cent, that most predictive studies made in the past have been unduly conservative. For example, a careful study by the American Federation of Information Processing Societies used past trends and a 1965 figure of 30,000 computers as a basis for estimating that by 1970 there would be 50,000 computers in the United States. But the 50,000 mark was reached in half the expected time—early in 1968 rather than 1970! Of course, such growth cannot be sustained for many decades without tapering off. Many segments of the industry are predicting continued growth at this level at least through the 1970's, however.

It is estimated that by 1975 the amount of computer power devoted solely to education will be equal to the entire computer output for all purposes in 1968. What are the major uses to which such computers will be directed?

Business administrative services. The most immediate applications in public school systems and higher education involve the simple transfer and adaptation of techniques developed successfully in business and industry. Such daily transactional activities as purchasing, payroll, inventory, personnel records, and auditing are being rapidly computerized. In the larger, more sophisticated systems, operations research and improved methods of forecasting are being developed. Program planning, budgeting, and control, as well as improved estimation of cost effectiveness, require greatly improved processing of information.

Educational management services. In addition to the administrative services typical of any complex organization, educational institutions have unique requirements that are being met by new computer applications. The processing of information for admission of students, continual updating of student records, scheduling of classes, registration of students, and reporting of course grades are but a few of the more important educational management services that are proving amenable to more effective handling by computer. The greatest growth of such educational support services will probably occur in the early 1970's when some of the basic software packages being completed by major companies become generally available at a relatively low cost.

The computer as a problem-solving tool. From its earliest days the computer has proved of greatest value as a high-speed numerical calculator, making it possible to solve mathematical problems that were previously intractable, in educational circles as well as elsewhere. The availability of new languages for nonnumeric information processing and logical problem solving, the development of special sketch-pad devices and computer graphics, and the simulation of complex phenomena by computers represent more recent capabilities of the computer as a problem-solving tool. Such applications are becoming commonplace in leading universities, research centers, and technical institutes throughout the country. Their anticipated extension downward to junior colleges, high schools, and possibly even elementary schools leads directly into the use of a computer for instructional purposes as an aid to the student.

Computer-managed instruction. The use of a computer as a teacher's aid is a relatively new application that has yet to be properly developed. Any form of individualized instruction immensely complicates the life of a teacher because curriculum units must be individually prescribed for each student in accordance with his recent progress and goals. Achievement tests, diagnostic procedures where necessary, and reference information for guidance of the student must also be prescribed, stored, and retrieved on demand. Although clerks or teachers' aides can fulfill these functions to some extent, at least in the early stages of development, it is obvious that a computer support system for instructional management is essential to the eventual success of such programs. Several major experiments already underway are designed to demonstrate the importance of this application. In Chapter 5, Glaser describes some of the features of the IPI (Individually Prescribed Instruction) program underway at Oakleaf Elementary School. During the 1968–1969 academic year, about 100 additional schools initiated similar programs of partially individualized instruction using the IPI materials, and this number may grow to several thousand shortly. A slightly different approach to computer-managed instruction is described by Brudner (1968), who has been working closely with Project PLAN (A Program for Learning in Accordance with Needs). Developed jointly by Westinghouse Learning Corporation and the American Institutes for Research under the leadership of John Flanagan, Project PLAN provides the teacher with programmed instructional units, perhaps 100 units for a given subject, and remotely located computer management of the student's progress. The student interacts with his teacher, the instructional guide units, multimedia materials, and guidance personnel when available.

Computer-assisted instruction. In computer-assisted instruction (CAI) the instructional materials themselves are stored in the computer or at a terminal serving as a teaching machine. The student interacts directly with the material to be learned, providing a highly individualized form of instruction with great potential power. Simple drill-and-practice exercises with highly structured material, as in elementary mathematics and spelling, have been the easiest to develop and implement on existing equipment. Detailed examples of this application are presented by Suppes and Morningstar in Chapter 12. Tutorial interaction is more difficult to program because the student's response can vary so greatly. Nevertheless, considerable advances have been made the past several years, as evidenced elsewhere in this book. Currently available author languages that employ partial answer recognition, when coupled with a clever use of Socratic methods, can yield rather impressive tutorial interaction approaching conversational dialogue for a wide variety of materials. Still more advanced forms of interaction involving complex simulation and problem solving can be employed as CAI. Detailed examples of such uses are given elsewhere in this book by Lagowski, Groom, Shelley, and Licklider. It is likely that by the early 1970's the simpler forms of CAI will be in full operation in many schools. The more highly enriched tutorial CAI will spread more slowly, largely because of the amount of effort needed to develop it properly and the relatively high costs of implementation. By the mid-1970's, however, it should also be fairly commonplace in settings where the effectiveness offsets the cost.

File management for library systems. The rapid accumulation of books, journals, pamphlets, and other reference materials in nearly every library poses an enormous problem for educational institutions, a problem that can be solved only by a different process of storing and retrieving archival materials. Although the document storage and retrieval problem has not yet been solved satisfactorily, computers are on the threshold of providing a library management system that will be invaluable for many educational purposes. Computer programs are being developed to handle all the major activities of a library, from document ordering to file search and revision. Conceptually, the problem is roughly similar to the management of files in the system for guidance of students described by Ellis and Tiedeman in Chapter 18. After a master library, such as the Library of Congress, has been properly computerized, the establishment of the data banks for smaller libraries is a relatively simple matter that will proceed fairly rapidly.

The computer as a subject of instruction. Computers have become so much a part of modern society that they are acquiring a place in the curriculum as a subject matter of general interest, as well as of professional and vocational concern. The most rapidly growing new department in most universities is computer or information science. Among junior colleges, technical schools, vocational institutes, and many high schools, the field of data processing by computers is an attractive opportunity for students. The availability of a computer, even if remotely located, is as essential to instruction in computer sciences and information processing as a teaching laboratory is to instruction in the natural sciences.

After briefly reviewing the numerous significant applications of computers to education, it should be apparent that computer systems will soon be viewed as an essential part of any major educational institution. Because most institutions cannot afford specialized systems for different applications, the multipurpose computer system will probably prevail. Regional networks make it possible for a smaller institution to benefit from large, remotely located central computers of which their own small computer is a satellite. Such a utility network provides modest stand-alone capability plus high power, when needed, at a relatively low cost by time-sharing the more expensive central computer with other institutions.

Individualized Instruction

The concept of individualized instruction is so fundamental to the idea of quality education on a universal basis that it deserves to be examined in more detail. The term itself has been employed in a general way by educators since the time of John Dewey's laboratory school at the University of Chicago before the turn of century. The idea of adapting the curriculum to individual levels of ability and achievement is an enticing one that has eluded precise definition and demonstration. And yet it is obvious to even the casual observer that the opposite concept, the lock-step classroom where every child is doing the same thing at the same time, is clearly unsatisfactory. Most teachers try to compensate for such leveling effects by giving special attention to certain children at the expense of others. Such efforts have only limited success at best, because it is impossible for one or two teachers to give undivided attention to each child. And even if they could, there is serious question as to whether they could keep track of the many details of the child's performance and the branching of curriculum units as they relate to the specific goals of the instruction.

The first and most obvious parameter of learning that must be considered when recognizing individual differences is the rate at which the student moves through the curriculum. Most of the recent experiments involving programmed instruction demonstrate how much more efficiently learning takes place for a group of students when each individual moves at his own pace. Another parameter often considered is the extent to which different instructional objectives may be recognized for different students. In general, the farther along a student is in his education, the more varied are the possibilities for exploring many fields or developing special interests in addition to a certain common core. Still a third parameter to be varied is the degree to which program branching is admitted and the extent to which it is under the student's control as contrasted to the author's or teacher's. Such branching may be relatively simple, determined solely by the degree of difficulty experienced by the student in learning the material. Or it may be fairly complicated, taking into account some combination of the aptitudes, motivational pattern, and learning styles of the student, although little is yet known about how to do this effectively.

When one or more of the preceding parameters is taken seriously throughout an entire educational institution in an attempt to individualize instruction, it is immediately apparent that the task of keeping track of everyone and matching the learning resources with the individual student at the right time and place is immensely complicated. Only the computer provides a reasonable solution to this problem. Let us look more specifically at what is required.

Scheduling. In the traditional school, scheduling does not present a serious problem because children are generally grouped together in similar sized classes doing essentially the same thing. Minor variations from this pattern require a good deal of trial-and-error adjustment or result in inefficient utilization of resources. When fully implemented, a program such as IPI requires daily demand scheduling of both students and resources, keeping in mind the allocation of physical facilities, the assignment of students, the assignment of instructional personnel, and the allocation of any equipment or materials needed. At the end of each day, the teachers and students state their requirements for the following day and the scheduling is worked out in time to implement it the next morning.

Student records. Current student records typically consist of census information, periodic test data, attendance figures, grade reports, and miscellaneous information, all of which are fairly static. After individualized learning programs are established, dynamic student record keeping is essential to keep an accurate accounting of student paths and progress. The constant updating of files requires on-line inquiry capability from a terminal to a computer.

Measurement. In the traditional school the teacher keeps a record of how well each student does on each achievement test for the course, whereas the periodically collected scores from standardized tests are stored centrally. When instruction is individualized, testing must be done more frequently and at different times for each student. In many cases performance testing and instruction are so closely interwoven that they appear as one integrated learning activity. Except for periodic testing at a later date to determine how much a person has retained, even the conceptual nature of measurement shifts from a normative basis, where each person is compared with a general population, to a criterion reference basis, where the only decision made is whether or not the student has achieved the desired objective for a specific instructional module. Not only are more short tests given but many more have to be constructed, again requiring a computer for generating tests from item pools as well as scoring and storing them for each student.

Management of learning resources. For a program of individualized instruction, the different curriculum units or modules for a given school run into the thousands. Each must be stored, inventoried, and retrieved on short notice when needed, much like a large pharmacy or auto parts store. Control information must also be maintained concerning films, audio tapes, laboratory supplies, workbooks, and special equipment so that they can be efficiently scheduled.

Guidance services. After the student is given a wide array of options in an individualized approach, he must also have easy access to information on educational planning and career opportunities. A reference shelf with well-chosen books and pamphlets and a chance to confer with an experienced guidance counselor may be sufficient for most purposes. Nevertheless, there are numerous occasions in the life of a student when he could profit greatly from access to the kind of computerized guidance system with large data files described in Chapter 18 by Ellis and Tiedeman.

Each of the preceding requirements for additional information processing as a result of individualized instruction applies whether or not CAI is added to the repertoire of instructional methods employed. Instructional modules where the actual curriculum is stored in the computer, the distinguishing characteristic of CAI, can be treated like any of the other individually prescribed units in systems for computer-managed instruction. Eventually, however, it is expected that the equivalent of an entire semester course, or more, will be stored within a computer, making it possible for CAI to be the primary mode of instruction for certain subjects.

Computer-assisted Instruction, Testing, and Guidance

The ultimate in individualized instruction becomes possible only when major segments of the curriculum can be stored in a computer where the student can interact in a highly personal manner with the material to be learned. The same computer can be providing CAI for a number of students simultaneously. By partitioning the core memory and employing fast, random-access, high-capacity auxiliary storage, a variety of other educational support activities can also be undertaken concurrently with CAI to provide for the management of instruction, administrative services, and batch processing of larger problems. Such systems are already in operation at the University of California at Irvine (Gordon, 1969) and at The University of Texas at Austin, and a number of others are being installed in universities where there is a strong interest in the development of general educational support systems. Given the current stage of technology, a fairly large computer is needed, one at least the size of an IBM System 360/50, which costs over $30,000 per month for hardware rental alone. If such a system is dedicated solely to CAI, it can support several hundred on-line typewriter terminals simultaneously and a somewhat smaller number of multimedia terminals.

Of course, where a variety of scientific and educational uses are mixed in the same system, queuing and priority problems are bound to arise. These must be anticipated and dealt with at a high level to avoid major conflict. In a large university it is unlikely that one central computer system can serve all purposes. In most educational institutions where major research activities do not exist, a single computer system should be sufficient to meet the requirements for educational support. For smaller schools, where CAI is concerned, the only reasonable solution in sight is the sharing of a computer.

A number of problems must be solved before computer-assisted instruction, testing, and guidance can be properly implemented as an integrated system. Many of these difficulties are discussed in detail throughout this book, together with some suggested solutions. At present the cost of equipment is still prohibitive. The need to regenerate continuously the image on a cathode-ray tube uses up a great deal of capacity that could be better used elsewhere. Interaction involving a light pen on the face of the display device greatly increases the rate of information flow, requiring expensive communication devices when the terminal is remotely located. A high-speed, high-fidelity, random-access audio unit is very expensive at present, although there is hope that within several years a suitable low-cost device will be available. Fortunately, much of the power and flexibility needed now for research and development will be less essential for many direct applications after materials and procedures have been perfected.

Even more important to solve in the long run are the software problems. As indicated earlier, these range from the need for better programming languages to the lack of a sound scientific basis for prescribing specific sequences in the branching of the program. The conceptual approach to instructional design outlined by Bunderson in Chapter 4 and elaborated further by Glaser in Chapter 5 is a major step toward providing such a scientific basis, but a great deal of research is necessary to complete it. As Uttal has pointed out (1968), programming languages should be more than simply compilers for assembling vast dictionaries of canned comments that are needed for matching with the student's response. Elsewhere, Uttal et al. (1969) propose the development of generative languages that use algorithms to generate problems, answers, diagnostics, and remedial materials for transmission to the student based on his current status and recent responses. Uttal and his colleagues present a detailed model of such a language for teaching analytical geometry. A wider variety of functions should also be delivered to the student at the terminal, at least for the more advanced applications of CAI. Language capability for numerical computation, list processing, logical analysis, file management, simple computer graphics, and simulation are all highly desirable, preferably in one general system so that the terminal user can switch quickly back and forth, mixing his functions as needed to solve problems.

The production of high-quality CAI materials is very time-consuming and expensive. The equivalent of a three-semester-hour course in high school mathematics takes many months to develop and the cost may run as high as $500,000 or more. Of course, after it is properly developed and perfected, additional copies can be provided for other users for only a little more than the cost of the raw materials themselves. As in any creative activity calling for a high degree of skill and experience, the development of first-rate CAI materials that properly exploit the unusual capability of a modern computer calls for a rare talent. Given the shortage of highly-gifted authors, the technical difficulties of preparing good audio-visual programs and the limited number of adequate computer systems for CAI, it is apparent that large-scale use of CAI is at least four or five years in the future.

Some limited versions of CAI could be implemented on an operational basis almost immediately, as evidenced elsewhere in this book. Certainly some of the drill-and-practice units and a few of the tutorial programs are already sufficiently successful to warrant their serious consideration, particularly in settings where their cost effectiveness can be justified by the more efficient learning that they make possible. Still other courses should be ready for general use by the early 1970's when many of the educational support systems described will also be ready for implementation on computers.

More than $80 billion per year is spent on all forms of education, most of it in our public schools. At any one time about one of every three individuals in the United States is either a full-time student or teacher. In addition, countless others are engaged in various forms of self-study. Given the great importance of education in our changing society, any improvement in the efficiency of learning by the application of new technology is indeed significant.

Contrary to the skeptical criticism of some alarmists, there is no reason to believe that this new technology will necessarily dehumanize man. There are many things in this world that can be done better by machines than by human beings. The advent of the computer, and the educational technology related to it, clearly points the way to major changes in education that will free the individual, both teacher and student, to interact in more human ways than ever before.

REFERENCES

Brudner, H. J. 1968. Computer-managed instruction. *Science* 162:970–976.

Gordon, R. M. 1969. Computer-assisted instruction: some operational aspects. *Datamation* 15 (Jan.):37–44.

Keppel, F. 1966. *The necessary revolution in American education.* New York: Harper & Row.

Oettinger, A. G., and Marks, S. 1968. Educational technology: new myths and old realities. *Harvard Educational Review* 38:697–755.

Uttal, W. R. 1968. *Real time computers: technique and applications in the psychological sciences.* New York: Harper & Row.

Uttal, W. R., Pasich, T., Rogers, M., and Hieronymus, R. 1969. *Generative computer-assisted instruction.* Communication 243. Ann Arbor: Mental Health Research Institute, Univ. of Michigan.

Zinn, K. L. 1968. Programming conversational use of computers for instruction. *Proceedings of 23rd ACM national conference.* Princeton: Brandon/Systems Press, pp. 85–92.

PART I

System Design

The engineering design aspects of a computer-based instruction system cannot be separated from its pedagogical considerations, as Bitzer and Skaperdas point out in their presentation (Chapter 2). The intended modes of computer use, the areas of study, and the characteristics of students all interact with the hardware design considerations. Such interdependence is apparent throughout this volume. After describing the Plato system that has evolved over the past eight years, Bitzer and Skaperdas outline the requirements of an economically viable system built around a new plasma-display panel. They believe that this system will reduce the direct operating cost of instruction to 25 cents per student hour. The system involves a very large computer with 4000 student terminals that can be located at any distance from the central computer. In addition to a key set, each student terminal would consist of the plasma-display device, which is about twelve inches square and has an advantage over the commonly used cathode-ray-tube display in that the images need not be continually regenerated. A digitally "addressable" slide selector and projector will allow locally stored information to be projected on the rear of the translucent glass-paneled display. In this way projected images, in color, can have alphanumeric or graphic displays superimposed on them. These displays, generated by the control computer, can be transmitted via telephone line.

Bitzer's novel design is reviewed by Castle (Chapter 3), who points out that it is stimulating to have such a complete design made public in its preliminary form. However, in Castle's opinion, insufficient attention has been given to the complicated problems of curriculum and computer system programming and to the logistics of instructional material and scheduling for the proposed system. Many participants in the conference were skeptical of Bitzer's preliminary cost estimates, believing it unrealistic to expect cost per student-hour to drop much below $2 in the near future. Yet, all agreed that the basic idea is promising and may indeed represent the kind of engineering breakthrough essential to progress in this field.

2

Donald Bitzer and D. Skaperdas

The Economics of a Large-scale Computer-based Education System: Plato IV

The University of Illinois[1] has been experimenting with a computer-based educational system (Plato) for the past 8 years. This system has evolved from a single terminal connected to the Illiac I (a medium-speed, 1954-vintage computer) to a computer classroom of 20 graphic-pictorial terminals connected to a Control Data Corporation (CDC) 1604 Computer. Some of the areas in which studies have been conducted are electrical engineering, geometry, biology, nursing, library science, pharmacology, chemistry, algebra, math drill, computer programming, and foreign languages. This material has been presented by use of a variety of teaching strategies, ranging from drill and practice to student-directed inquiry. Based on these experiences and the data gathered over 70,000 student contact hours of credit teaching, this chapter describes the development of an economically viable teaching system. Some of our guidelines for developing the system's software and hardware are as follows.

1. The computer should be used only when it is the best method of presentation. Less expensive methods, such as programmed texts, films, slides, and tape recorders, should be used when appropriate.

2. The computer should be used as much as possible to simulate results in models constructed by the students rather than simply to turn pages.

3. The system must be flexible and adaptable. It must be able to teach

1. The Computer-based Education Research Laboratory (CERL) at the University of Illinois is primarily supported by the following grants: ONR Nonr 3985 (08) from the Advanced Research Projects Agency and NSF GJ-81 from the National Science Foundation.

many subjects and present the lesson materials by a variety of teaching strategies. The system must change to meet the needs of the students and teachers and not be limited to the off-the-shelf items presently available.

4. The method of integration into the educational system must be considered in the system design. For example, a school should be able to start with a single terminal for the incremental terminal cost instead of having to invest large sums of money for an entire system before it has determined if it wants or needs computer-based education (CBE).

5. The cost of CBE should be comparable with the cost of teaching at the elementary grade school level. Cost effectiveness should be determined by an hour-to-hour cost comparison (25–30 cents per terminal hour for use of the computer and terminal).

The Present System: Plato III

A present student terminal consists of a key set and a television monitor, as shown in Figure 2–1. Information viewed on the television monitor is composed of a slide selected by the computer (random-access time is less than one millionth of a second) and a superimposed image of graphs, diagrams, and/or alphanumeric characters drawn by the computer in a point-by-point fashion. The student uses the key set for constructing answers and questions and for setting up simulated or real experiments as well as for controlling his progress through the lesson material. The computer responds to the student's requests within one tenth of a second.

The computer also controls other devices, such as movie projectors and

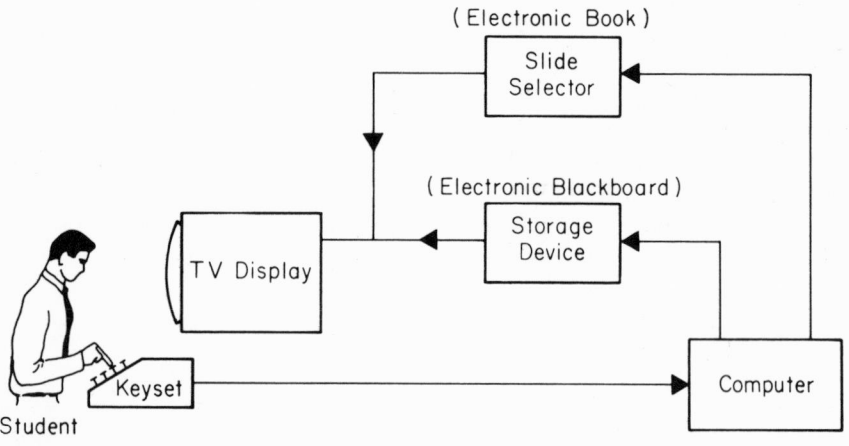

Figure 2–1.
Block diagram of the Plato equipment.

lights. The students at the terminals can interact with each other through the computer, thus permitting games that require communication between the players to be played.

In addition to keeping detailed records of the student's performance, the computer can provide individualized instruction, immediate feedback, and remedial training by the use of complex internal branching and the alteration of presentation or type of material based on the student's past performance. These unique features seem to make the computer an ideal instructional device for developing cognitive skills.

To encourage development of critical thinking skills, the author sets up the teaching strategy and presents the student with questions or problems so that the student must think about what information he needs and about possible solutions to the problems or sources of information, must interpret the data gathered, and must test his solution. The computer immediately provides appropriate feedback to open-ended questions, thus reinforcing a correct approach or, in the case of an incorrect response, encouraging the student to a new approach.

The computational aspects of the computer are used in several ways. First, experiments can be simulated by the computer, immediately providing the student with results he uniquely requested. These same results might require hours or even days to calculate by hand. Second, a large amount of computation is involved in processing student responses. The more flexibility provided for the student to answer a question, the more feedback is needed to inform him of the correctness of his response. When only multiple-choice responses are required, the processing is relatively simple, but when the student is permitted to construct long alphanumeric and graphic responses, the computer must analyze the answer to see if it is equivalent to a correct response, check for spelling and completeness of the answer, as well as inform the student which part of an incorrect answer is unacceptable.

Whenever possible, algorithms are used to determine the correctness of the student's response. For example, when the student is asked to give a positive even integer, the student's answer is checked to see if it is positive and then it is divided by 2 and checked for a remainder. If there is no remainder, the answer is correct. The use of algorithms instead of comparing the answer against a long list of prestored answers not only makes the system more flexible but also saves memory space. In some cases this approach is almost a necessity. For instance, in teaching algebraic proofs, students can prove theorems in any manner as long as their statements follow logically from the available axioms and their previous statements. We have one example in which the author of the material was unable to prove a theorem in the 12 lines provided and thus was unable to supply even one prestored solution. Nonetheless, one student was able to complete the proof in the required 12 lines and was told by the computer he was correct.

A record of each student's request (his identity, the key pushed, and the time to the nearest sixtieth of a second) is stored on magnetic tape. These data are processed by the same computer that is used for teaching. We have used these records for improving course content, designing better teaching strategies, as well as for planning new, economically viable computer-based education systems.

A Proposed New System: Plato IV

On the basis of CERL's experience with early Plato systems, certain design philosophies for the proposed system have been formulated. First, each student terminal requires a key set and a display, both connected to an inexpensive data transmission system, which can also drive optional equipment such as random-access audio devices, reward mechanisms, movie films, and lights. Second, each student terminal must be capable of superimposing randomly accessed color slide images on the computer-generated graphics. Third, the system should be controlled by a large-scale, centrally located computer rather than by many small computers located at the classroom sites. This decision is based on social and administrative factors as well as on system economics. Semiconductor large-scale integration techniques may some day make the use of small computers as effective as large ones, but the added human expense of operating a computer center does not promise to scale as effectively. It is our opinion that the initial low cost of a single terminal will permit tightly budgeted public school systems economically to incorporate computer-based teaching into their programs. The number of terminals could be increased or decreased as the needs of the school system dictate. Fourth, the cost per student contact hour for the proposed system must be comparable with equivalent costs of traditional teaching methods.

Before discussing an economical system design from the technical viewpoint, it is necessary to consider the cost of producing lesson material. Reported costs have ranged over a factor of 10 for producing similar lesson material. The differences in author languages can account for this wide range. The author language must be just as natural for the teacher to use as the teaching strategy is expected to be natural for the student to use. However, in the long run the cost of lesson material should constitute only a small fraction of the educational costs, just as the textbooks and lesson materials represent only a small part of educational costs today.

Preparing a good CAI course is roughly equivalent in effort to writing a good textbook. Most good authors are quite willing to produce textbooks at a 10–15 per cent royalty rate that yields to them approximately 80 cents per student. Most textbooks are used in courses that have at least 40 hours of classroom instruction. The costs of royalties, reproduction, and distribution of lesson material total $1.20 per student and when used for 40 hours of instruction yield an eventual cost of approximately 3 cents per student-hour of instruction. The reproduction and distribution of materials for computer-assisted instruction terminals promises to be very inexpensive (approximately 40 cents per student for visual and audio materials).

Statistical records of over 70 million requests on Plato indicate that the average request rate per student depends on the teaching strategy used, but the product of the average request rate and the average processing time is relatively constant. For example, when using a drill-type teaching strategy, the average request rate per student is one request every 2 seconds and the average processing time is 10 milliseconds. When using a tutorial or inquiry strategy, the average request rate per student is one request every 4 seconds but the processing time is 20 milliseconds. We shall base our calculations on the 20-millisecond processing time, which is equivalent to executing approximately 1000 instructions in the CDC 1604.

The request rate probability density function versus computer execution time is approximately an exponential curve; therefore, student requests requiring the least amount of computer time occur most frequently. For example, the simple and rapidly processed task of storing a student's key push in the computer and writing the character on his screen represents 70 per cent of the requests. On the other hand, the lengthy process of judging a student's completed answer for correctness, completeness, spelling, and so on occurs only 7 per cent of the time.

Several existing large-scale computers can perform about 4 million instructions per second. Even if we double the number of instructions needed, providing 2000 per student request, it is seen that these large-scale computers require an average processing time of only 500 microseconds per request. Allowing a safety factor of 2 to ensure excellent system response time, the system can accept an average of 1000 requests per second. This safety factor implies that the computer will be idle approximately 50 per cent of the time. However, the computer time not utilized in processing the student requests can be effectively used for other purposes such as background batch processing. Because the average student request rate is one fourth of a request per second, the system can handle up to 4000 students simultaneously, allowing 1 millisecond to process a request.

Assume that the student input arrival time is Poisson-distributed (a reasonable assumption for 4000 independent student stations) and that the request rate probability density function versus computer execution time is approximately exponential (Plato statistical records substantiate this).

From queuing theory (Bitzer and Braunfeld, 1962; Goode and Machol,

1957) the expected waiting time $E(w)$ that elapses before the computer (single channel) will accept a given student's request is given by

$$E(w) = \frac{\rho^2 + m^2\sigma_T^2}{2m(1 - \rho)} \tag{1}$$

where

$$m = \text{request rate} = 1000 \text{ requests per second}$$
$$\sigma_T = \text{execution time standard deviation} = 500 \times 10^{-6} \text{ second}$$
$$E(T) = \text{execution time expected value} = 500 \times 10^{-6} \text{ second}$$
$$\rho = mE(T) = 0.5$$

These values yield an expected waiting time $E(w)$ of 500 microseconds. The probability $P(w)$ that a student's request will wait a time w or longer before being served by the computer is given by

$$P(w) = \rho \exp[-w(1 - \rho)/E(T)] \tag{2}$$

The probability that a student must wait for 0.1 second or longer is negligible. Hence the probability of a student's request queue becoming long or of the student experiencing a noticeable delay is very small.

Presently, each student needs to be assigned approximately 300 words of extended core memory to be treated individually. The maximum used in any teaching strategy has been 600 words per student. Let us allow on the average 500 words (50 bits of information per word) for each student for a total of 2 million words for 4000 student terminals. Our data show that 20 per cent of the computer instructions refer to these words of unique student storage. Therefore the system must be capable of rapidly transferring data between the slower extended core storage and the high-speed core memory. Some existing computers are capable of transferring data at 10^7 words per second, requiring only 50 microseconds to transfer the data each way between the memory units. This transfer time is acceptable.

The peak data rate from the computer to each student station is limited to 1200 bits per second to permit data transmission over low-grade telephone circuits, a system feature made possible by the use of the plasma-display panel (discussed later). For 4000 stations the worst case data rate would be about 4.8 million bits per second, well within the present state of the art for buffering data out of a computer.

Summarizing the computer requirements, the central computer requires about 2 million words of extended core memory capable of high-speed transfer rates to the main computer memory; it must have an execution time of approximately 4 instructions per microsecond and be capable of transmitting data at a rate of 4.8 million bits per second. There should be a sufficiently large memory (64–128K words[2]) in the central processing unit

2. Where $K = 2^{10} = 1024$.

for storing lessons (1000–2000 words per lesson) and for the various teaching strategies. Several existing computers meet these requirements.

The economic feasibility of the proposed teaching system is dependent on the newly invented plasma-display panel (or an equivalent device) now under development at the University of Illinois and other laboratories. This device combines the properties of memory, display, and high brightness in a simple structure of potentially inexpensive fabrication. In contrast to the commonly used cathode-ray-tube display, on which images must be continually regenerated, the plasma display retains its own images and responds directly to the digital signals from the computer. This feature will reduce considerably the cost of communication distribution lines. The plasma display is discussed in detail in the listed references. Briefly, it consists of a thin glass panel structure containing a rectangular array of small gas cells (about 0.015 inches in density of about 40 cells per inch—see Figure 2–2). Any cell can be selectively ignited (gas discharge turned on

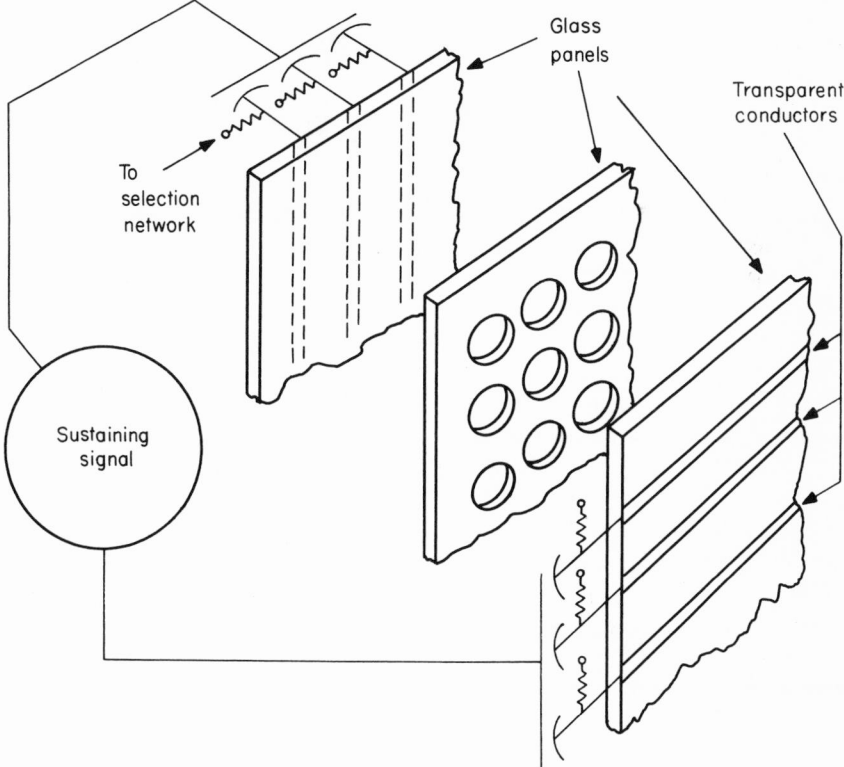

Figure 2–2.
Schematic diagram of the plasma panel.

Figure 2–3.
Small prototype plasma panel.

or turned off by proper application of voltages to the orthogonal grid structures without influencing the state of the remaining cells). Figure 2–3 shows a small, developmental panel displaying two characters. Each of these characters is only ⅛ inch in height. The plasma panel is transparent, allowing the superposition of optically projected images.

A schematic diagram of a proposed student terminal using the plasma display is shown in Figure 2–4. The display will be approximately 12 inches square and will contain 512 digitally addressable positions along each axis. A slide selector and projector will allow prestored (static) information to be projected on the rear of the glass panel display. This permits the stored information to be superimposed on the panel, which contains the computer-generated (dynamic) information. A prototype random-access slide selector for individual use is shown in Figure 2–5. This projector is digitally addressable, pneumatically driven, and contains a matrix of 256 images on an easily removable 4-inch-square plate of film. The film plate is mounted on a Cartesian-coordinate slide mechanism and can be simul-

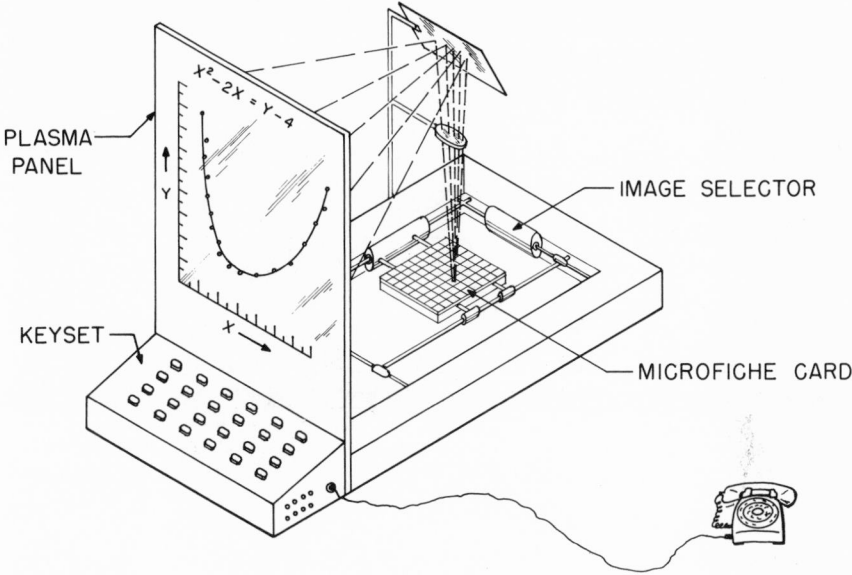

Figure 2–4.
Schematic drawing of the new student terminal.

taneously translated along either of the two coordinate axes to bring a desired image over a projector lens. The positions along each coordinate axis are selected by a set of four pneumatic cylinders mounted in series. The stroke length of each cylinder is weighted 8, 4, 2, 1, the length of the smallest being ¼ inch. Each slide selection requires less than 3 cubic inches of air at 8 pounds per square inch. Based on the prototype model now being tested, a low-cost image selector with approximately 0.2-second random-access time is anticipated.

Data arriving from the computer via a telephone line enter the terminal through an input register. As previously stated, data rates to the terminal will be held to 1200 bits per second. Assuming a word length of 20 bits, the terminal could receive data at 60 words per second, an important design feature when considering standard television tariff for communicating. With proper data formats, data rates will be adequate for the applications envisaged. For example, packing 3 character codes per word will permit a writing rate of 180 characters per second, which is a much faster rate than that of a good reader. Using 18 bits to specify a random point on the 512×512 array, 60 random points per second can be plotted. If the x increment is assumed, such as when drawing graphs, 120 graph points per second can be plotted. In addition, continuous curves requiring only 3 bits to specify

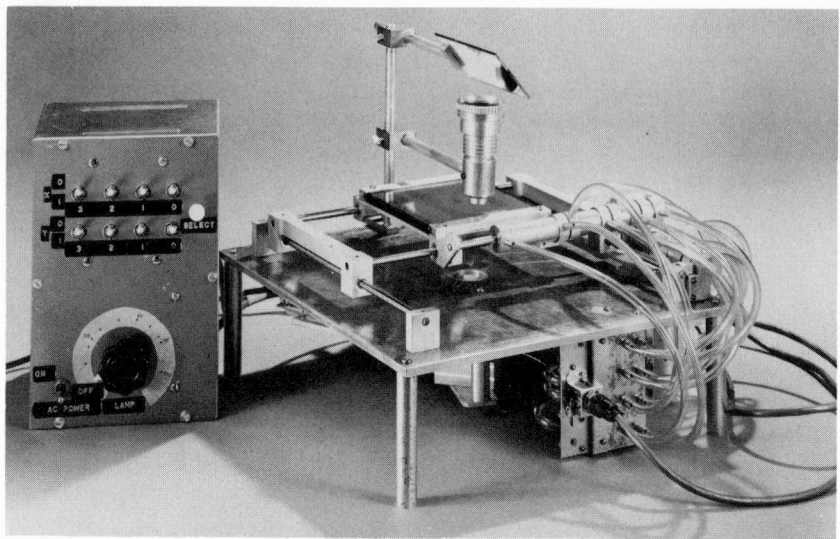

Figure 2–5.
Prototype random-access slide selector.

the next point can be drawn at rates of 360 points per second. The key set will provide the student with a means of communicating with the computer. The problem of converting the fast parallel output data from the computer into serial data for transmission to terminals at 1200 bits per second has been studied. This can be solved by the use of small buffer computers performing the parallel-to-serial data conversion.

In the situation where a large number of students are located at considerable distances from the central computer, costs can be lowered drastically by use of a coaxial line instead of numerous phone lines. For example, the cost of a 4.5-megacycle-per-second television channel is approximately $35 per month per mile, whereas the rate for a 3-kilocycle telephone line is approximately $3.50 per month per mile. Each television channel can handle at least 1500 terminals on a time-shared basis, each terminal receiving 1200 bits per second. Hence, for an increase in line cost of a factor of 10 over that of a single channel, an increase of a factor of 1500 in channel capacity can be obtained. In addition to a coaxial line transmitting 1500 channels at 1200 bits per second from the computer to the terminals, a data line for transmitting the student key-set information back to the main computer center is required. A data channel of 100,000-bits-per-second capacity, available from Bell Telephone, can handle 1500 students, allowing 60 bits per second to each student. The costs for this line are approximately $15 per month per mile. Data to remote locations will be transmitted by a coaxal line to a central point; from this point local telephone lines rented on a subscriber's service basis can transmit the proper channel to each student terminal. A block diagram of a proposed distribution system to several remote points is shown in Figure 2–6.

Over 200 cities, and on a more limited scale many schools, already use community antenna television systems or closed-circuit televison. Because FM radio had already established itself prior to the spread of television, a frequency gap existed between channels 6 and 7, which is greater than eight channels wide. These existing channels can be used to communicate to over 12,000 home terminals.

The main-frame cost of a computer meeting the specified requirements is approximately $2.5 million. The additional cost for 2 million words of memory and other input/output equipment is approximately $2 million. An estimate for the system software, including some course development programming, is another $1.5 million. The total of $6 million amortized over the generally accepted period of 5 years yields $1.2 million per year.

Assuming that the 4000-terminal system will be in use 8 hours per day for 300 days per year, there are approximately 10 million student contact hours per year. The system cost, excluding the terminals, is thus 12 cents per student contact hour. For the equipment cost to be comparable to a conventional elementary school classroom cost of approximately 27 cents

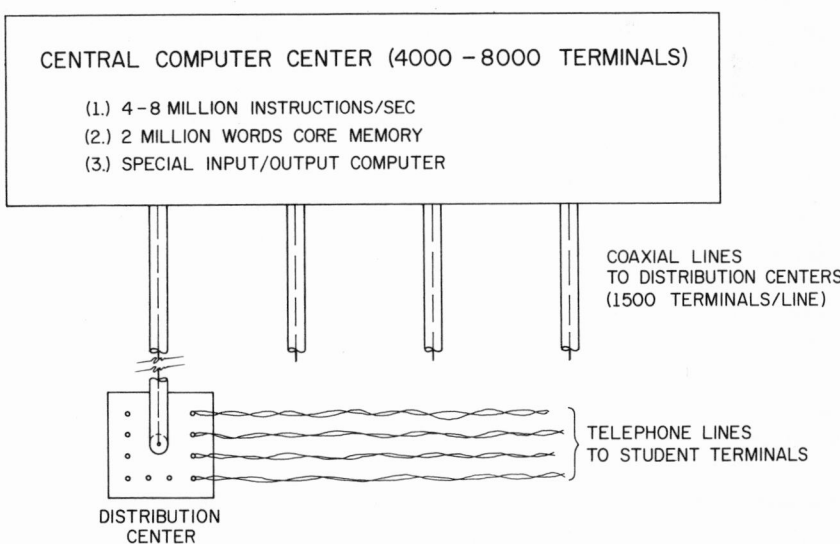

Figure 2–6.
Schematic drawing of communication distribution system for Plato IV.

per student contact hour, the terminal costs must be limited to 15 cents per student contact hour, or to a total cost of about $7.5 million over a 5-year period. The cost for each of the 4000 terminals, which includes a digitally addressed graphic display device and its driver, a key set, and a slide selector must therefore be a maximum of approximately $1900. Present indications are that this cost can be met.

Data distribution costs for a CBE center approximately 100 miles from the main computer are approximated as follows. The coaxial line rental is approximately $3500 per month, or $2.35 per terminal per month, based on 1500 terminals. The 100,000-bit-per-second wide-band data channel line is approximately $1500 per month, or $1.00 per terminal per month. Allowing $3.00 per terminal per month for a private telephone line from the coaxial terminals to each student terminal gives a total data distribution cost of $6.35 per terminal per month, or 4 cents per student contact hour if each terminal is used 160 hours per month. The author costs were discussed previously.

These costs, based on the preceding assumptions, are summarized in Table 2–1. The earning power of the computer for the remaining 16 hours

Table 2–1. Summary of Costs for Proposed System

Item	Total cost, millions of dollars	Cost per year, millions of dollars (5-year amortization)	Cost per student contact hour, cents
Computer and extended memory	4.5	0.9	8
Software	1.5	0.3	4
4000 student terminals	7.5	1.5	15
Subtotal	13.5	2.7	27
Lesson material	—	—	3
Data distribution lines	—	—	4
Total			34

each day and for the idle time between student requests, which would further reduce costs, has not been included.

Conclusion

Using newly developed technological devices, it is economically and technically feasible to develop large-scale computer-controlled teaching systems for handling 4000 teaching stations that are comparable with the cost of teaching in elementary schools. The teaching versatility of a large-scale computer is nearly limitless. Even while simultaneously teaching 4000 students, the computer can take advantage of the 50 per cent idle time to perform data processing at half its normal speed. In addition, 16 hours per day of computer time is available for normal computer use. The approximate computer cost of 12 cents per student contact hour pays completely for the computer even though it utilizes only one-sixth of its computational capacity. The remaining five-sixths of its capacity is available at no cost.

REFERENCES

Bitzer, D. L., and Braunfeld, P. G. 1962. Description and use of a computer-controlled teaching system. In *Proceedings of the national electronic conference,* pp. 787–792.

Bitzer, D. L., and Easley, J. A., Jr. 1965. Plato: a computer-controlled teaching system. In *Computer augmentation of human reasoning,* ed. M. Sass and W. Wilkinson, pp. 89–103. Washington: Spartan.

————. 1968. Plato III: a computer-based system for instruction and research. In *Proceedings of the 16th international congress of applied psychology, Amsterdam.*

Bitzer, D. L., and Skaperdas, D. 1968. Plato IV: an economically viable large-scale computer-based education system. Paper presented at the National Electronics Conference, December 1968.

Bitzer, D. L., and Slottow, H. G. 1966. The plasma display panel—a digitally addressable display with inherent memory. In *Proceedings—fall joint computer conference,* pp. 541–547. Washington: Thompson.

————. 1968. Principles and applications of the plasma display panel. In *Proceedings of the O.A.R. research applications conference.* Arlington, Va.: Office of Aerospace Research. (Also appears in the *Proceedings of the 1968 micro-electronics symposium I.E.E.E., St. Louis,* 1968.)

Bitzer, D. L., Lichtenberger, W., and Braunfeld, P. G. 1961. Plato: an automatic teaching device. *IRE Transactions on Education* E-4:157–161.

Goode, H. H., and Machol, R. E. 1957. *Control systems engineering.* New York: McGraw-Hill, pp. 328–343.

Knight, K. E. 1966. Changes in computer performance. *Datamation* 12 (Sept.): 40–54.

————. 1968. Evolving computer performance 1963–1967. *Datamation* 14 (Jan.):31–35.

Lyman, E. R. 1968. *A descriptive list of Plato programs, 1960–1968.* Computer-Based Education Research Laboratory, University of Illinois, Urbana, CERL Report X-2.

3

J. G. Castle, Jr.[1]

Design of Interactive Computer Systems for Educational Purposes: One View of the Proposal for the University of Illinois

Bitzer and Skaperdas have made a most unusual proposal to deal with an educational need at the University of Illinois, presenting in brief a novel design for computer-based education through the vehicle of 4000 student stations, indicating several engineering advances, and estimating the system costs to be less than 50 cents per student contact hour. It is stimulating to find such a complete design of a new teaching system being made public in preliminary form. However, most readers will probably want more information.

The description of the proposed hardware is reasonably detailed but still incomplete for the reader who wants to evaluate the proposed system for an alternative application. The several engineering novelties presented and implied make controversy easy but constructive criticism difficult. Description of the proposed computer systems software is lacking, except to imply that the Plato IV system will use an executive package similar to the one that has been successful on Plato III. The serious concern that has been expressed over the adequacy of this plan for software control with so

1. The reviewer appreciates the openness and the hospitality of Professors Bitzer and Skaperdas and their staff during his visit to the University of Illinois to discuss Plato systems. Gratitude is also due to Professor R. Glaser, Professor J. G. Holland, Dr. Wilson Judd, W. H. Broadley, R. Fitzhugh, and L. B. Lauffer of the Learning Research and Development Center for their critical discussions. The work reported herein was performed pursuant to Contract OE-3-16-043, with the Office of Education, U.S. Department of Health, Education, and Welfare at the Learning Research and Development Center of the University of Pittsburgh.

many terminals on line might well be alleviated by more information on the proposed systems software. Possibly their comment that all the active code for each student who is on line will be held in core memory rather than on disc or tape files will suffice to remove the doubts expressed over the likelihood of excessive systems overhead such as found in some large time-sharing systems.

Reference to the educational functions to be served by the proposed system seems inadequate. One looks for several features such as widespread student acceptance of the present Plato methodology, a more explicit statement of the flexibility to be allowed at the student stations on the large system, an indication of how the quality of the course programming has been and will be maintained, and a description of the proposed manner for handling the logistics of distribution of course information to the student. Cultivation of course quality and procedures could blunt a possible buildup of student resentment, which seems popular in schools and on campuses these days.

General Considerations

In their introduction Bitzer and Skaperdas point out the extensive experience of some 70,000 student contact hours that has been accumulated on the Plato systems in a variety of courses at the University of Illinois. The authors state three main points in the general guidelines they have adopted to develop the software and hardware of Plato systems: (1) using the system for computer simulation of the results of student choices or of student-built models rather than simply for page turning, (2) using the system only when it is the best method of presentation of any given course material, and (3) keeping the system flexible and adaptable to students' needs.

The Plato experience is certainly extensive, but it is not clear in the author's statements or references whether the results of student progress to date form an adequate basis for such a large expansion. The authors indicate that Illinois students who have taken college courses for credit on the present Plato III system have attained equal performance in fewer hours than were required by other students in normal courses. The list of courses that have been (and presumably are still being) given on Plato III covers a wide variety of topics but gives the impression that they are rather special courses involving selected college students rather than students sampled from the whole range of the student body, which is the spectrum to be served by the proposed system. Possibly evidence on a larger cross section of students will be available soon from current operations of the Plato III system. The intended use of proved computer-based educational techniques is surely an excellent way to obtain effective performance with a new system. The fact that the University of Illinois is using the Plato III system to provide about 1000 student semester hours for credit during the fall term of 1968 will be taken by many as prima facie evidence of its value. It would be interesting to explore this aspect more fully.

The most outstanding feature of Plato III is that the student station responds to each student request within one-tenth of a second. The authors are to be complimented on this accomplishment. The response contingency on Plato III takes the form of adding computer-generated graphic or character information to the visual display within a tenth of a second after the appropriate key push. This rapid contingency management may well account for most of Plato III's success and the student acceptance achieved so far.

The illustrative examples indicate that considerable adaptability to student needs has been achieved on the Plato III system. A personal visit to see course material being constructed and learned at Plato terminals is recommended for those readers who are concerned about the guidelines of flexibility.

The use of a computer-based educational system only when it is the best method of presentation seems fine for a small system where unit costs are high. But when unit costs are estimated to be very low, as in the proposed system, why should not all course material compatible with the operating features of the student stations be placed on the system? In fact, it would seem that the high use rate required for low unit costs on any system would dictate that a large computer system would be used for every compatible course with a large registration until a full schedule of student use (estimated at 2400 student contact hours per calendar year) is attained at each student station.

Bitzer and Skaperdas state that their guidelines for developing a computer-based educational system include a target cost of about 25 cents per student contact hour for use of the terminal and computer system. The 25-cent figure is presumably intended to apply not to the first-generation Plato IV system but to the differential cost figures for a large system of the proposed design when it is manufactured on a mass production basis. Such mass-produced items would probably be available within a very few years after a successful demonstration of the Plato IV system, assuming continued enthusiasm from student and faculty users. The cost goal seems reasonable because the mass market will probably require wide use in schools across the country. Their cost analysis assumes several significant improvements in the engineering design that have been made or are being made by the research and development group at Illinois.

Design of the Plato IV System

The basic design of the Plato IV system features a student station that includes key set, visual display, a data transmission unit, and a facility for optional devices such as an audio record player. The display will have a capability for superimposing static color slide images (available within one-half second) on computer-generated graphics whose increments are available within a tenth of a second.

Four basic requirements must be met if Bitzer and Skaperdas are to come close to their low cost objective:

1. A novel design of their own in the form of a plasma screen for the display of computer-generated information
2. A novel design using pneumatic positioning of a microfiche slide card for the random-access slide projector
3. Educational use of a wide-band communications cable between the computer and groups of student stations
4. Complete control of the system by a large-scale centrally located computer rather than having any computer hardware at the student stations.

Before looking at any details of these novel designs or of the specific cost estimates, let us consider briefly these stated design criteria for a large-scale computer-based educational system. A thorough consideration of the stated criteria could be the main topic for another technical conference.

Maintaining very rapid contingencies for student response—0.1 second for incremental visual display and under 0.5 second for slide change and/or audio playback—at every one of the several thousand student stations while supplying lesson material with the depth and flexibility of the present Plato III system represents the most significant feature of the proposed system. Success in attaining such rapid response to every student request can be expected to lead to continued success with the educational functions. The authors assure us that the large computer used in the manner they have in mind will permit the system response to be essentially that of the student station components. Their demonstration of the several components in prototype form gives ample evidence that their student stations will be able to supply the rapid contingency feature as called for in their design criteria.

The facility for displaying superposed images of two types—one from slides and the other selected under computer control from prerecorded data or generated by computer program from the student's responses—

appears to be a key to flexibility in a system that responds rapidly to student requests. The proposed superposition of images also appears to match well the usual (textbook) manner of presenting information in a college course and to minimize well the logistics of preparing, using, and changing the displayed information at each point in the student's course of learning. Plato III experience has apparently provided the authors with a great deal of information on these issues.

In my opinion, audio playback should definitely be included in the student station. With access times equal to that demonstrated for the slide changes (about 0.2 second), audio playback will extend considerably the utility of the proposed system, whereas it will add only a small amount (probably less than 20 per cent) to the investment cost of the terminal. Audio playback would, for example, extend the system capability to vocabulary acquisition tasks in which aural associations are crucial, such as elementary courses in foreign languages and in many natural sciences.

The choice of one very large central computer, instead of a network system with a satellite computer at each group of student stations, was apparently an economic one. The merits of this decision are not clear. The grouping of student stations in classrooms, dormitory lounges, or study halls, given the modest costs of physical maintenance and security, suggests that there would be very little extra cost in operating a satellite computer for each major cluster of student stations. The increased flexibility of such a satellite network must be balanced against the increased power of one central computer.

The Central Computer

Data collected on the present Plato system have been used to predict the specifications for the central computer of the proposed Plato IV system. When using tutorial strategy, the data show a mean rate of one student request every four seconds and a mean of 1000 machine instructions per student request on the CDC 1604 computer. Seventy per cent of all student requests require computer storage and display of only a single character, while only 7 per cent of the requests ask for the judging of a completed (multiword) answer for such features as spelling, correctness, and completeness. Assuming that these data can be generalized roughly to the larger system, the authors specify the necessary computer characteristics, leaving a modest but reasonable safety factor for the computer speed and volume.

One wonders whether adoption of a more restrictive strategy for display contingency might increase the average figures for the number of machine instructions per student request to the point at which queuing times comparable to the design delay time of 0.1 second might occur frequently. Consider, for example, the strategy applicable to a "spelling" task in which incorrect characters are not displayed but correct ones are displayed promptly.[2] Adoption of this strategy for a large fraction of the course material would increase the mean number of machine instructions per student response. The authors assure us, however, that when the constructed response is singular, as in a given spelling word or a particular arithmetic exercise, the increase in computer load is very slight, probably well under a factor of 2. The load is apparently not heavy until the number of combinations that are acceptable for any class of answer becomes much greater than 1.

At this point it is worth recalling that the hardware design of the large Plato IV system calls for assigning to each student who is on line a large block (about 1000 fifty-bit words) of fast, extended core memory, after the successful pattern of Plato III. It is to be inferred that with transfer of the stored data in fifty microseconds between memory units the system will not experience the excessive systems overhead that has been found on large time-sharing systems that rely on shuffling data on and off disc files.

It still seems questionable to infer that the amount and complexity of systems programming for control of thousands of equivalent but identifiable student stations in a single central computer of the indicated configuration will scale accurately from the present Plato III system. Much of the skepticism concerning the computer aspects of the proposed Plato IV system center on the expectation of excessive systems overhead.

The Student Terminals

The student terminals are not available today in the form proposed. Features required to meet the guidelines stated are under rapid development at the University of Illinois. The authors propose to use a semitransparent plasma screen of their own invention on which to display a high-resolution image of computer-generated information, to store that same image, and to project the slide information. Assuming that the problems of the materials, assembly, and circuitry associated with such a plasma screen have been solved, the 1972 date for the proposed system is almost reasonable. The requisite storage will be available to permit telephone line transfer of visual information and the ultimate cost per display unit can be very low indeed.

2. This strategy has been found useful by O. K. Moore, *On Responsive Environments,* University of Pittsburgh Learning Research and Development Center Working Paper #40, April 1967, and is recommended for computer-based spelling courses by the reviewer (J. G. Castle, Jr., and M. A. Riva, Westinghouse Software Symposium, February 1967).

The positioning of the slide (one microfiche card containing 256 slides) by coded pneumatic drivers as demonstrated by Bitzer and Skaperdas should be at once reliable, quiet, and inexpensive. The logistics of each student carrying one or two microfiche cards with all the slide information for each course seem very reasonable. One expects that adequate mechanical designs of the composite terminal will permit reliable loading of the microfiche card by the student.

The key set will, of course, have a full set of characters—like a typewriter keyboard. Reliable key operations may turn out to be the most expensive component of the proposed student station.

The proposed design of the student station appears to fall short of full utility for the authors' computer-based educational system in two ways. First, audio playback should be a standard feature, with headphones having about thirty-decibel isolation and with pneumatic positioning of the playback heads similar to that demonstrated for the slide projector. Second, the visual display should have a transparent overlay that is touch-sensitive, with the resolution of active areas compatible with finger touching and the number of active areas compatible with keyboard replacement. Then the operation of the touch-sensitive surface in place of the key set for any given station could be under remote control.

The audio playback capability will serve an essential need in those learning tasks that involve vocabulary acquisition, as required in most introductory college courses and in much of the elementary school curriculum. It is for such verbal tasks that the computer-based system appears to have the greatest advantage for the largest number of users.

The function of the low-resolution touch-sensitive surface is to permit more direct association between the learner's visual stimulus and his response. For the sophisticated student the clever key arrangement of the Plato III system is satisfactory, allowing him to "move a bright spot around on the grid" that is displayed. For many students, however, especially young children, the direct selection of a visual choice should reduce ambiguity and improve the instructional process. Useful designs for such a touch-sensitive surface are under development at several places including the Learning Research and Development Center at the University of Pittsburgh. Estimates at the Center indicate that transparent touch-sensitive surfaces made to overlay the visual display and to be electrically interchangeable or compatible with a key set should cost no more than the electric keyboard.

Cost Estimates

The cost projections are given for a large computer with the fastest memory available today, for wide-band transmission cables operated in the fashion prescribed currently for educational uses, for computer systems software presumably operating in a manner similar to that of the current Plato III system, and for several thousand student stations (that are still being invented and developed) out of a sales volume many times larger. The unit costs are based on the expected use of each student station for 2400 hours per calendar year.

The projected use factor seems unduly optimistic. Therefore, the estimated unit costs may be too low. Again, additional experience on Plato III would seem pertinent to the prediction of station use. Significant savings can certainly come from the availability of the central computer for other purposes when it is not completely saturated by management of the 4000 student stations.

The cost estimates may be subject to other minor revision. For the computer, one is tempted to use 3 cents per bit for fifty nanosecond extended core memory, which adds 20 per cent to the investment in the computer itself. The systems software capable of sustaining reliable and adaptable operation of the student stations might, over the five-year span, cost double the estimated figure. The transmission costs are expected to be very low; the full use projected should put data transfer below 3 cents per student contact hour. The student station costs are much more uncertain. But, in a market of mass-produced components such as the television industry, the cost estimate of about $2000 for each terminal seems very reasonable, even conservative. Presumably, maintenance of the hardware would add 10 to 20 per cent per year, which is less than the uncertainty inherent in the preceding estimates.

Assuming the use of the proposed system for 10 million student contact hours per calendar year and the reasonable five-year write-off of the investment, the cost estimate is still well below 50 cents per student contact hour. It remains to be seen whether these estimates are sufficiently pessimistic to be realistic.

It should be noted, however, that costs of administration of the system and cost estimates for course preparation have been omitted. Apparently, preparation of courses on the current Plato III system has proved to be very inexpensive compared to the preparation costs on other systems. For example, a tentative five-year cost of three times that needed recently for all the preparation of one three-semester-hour course on Plato III would still be less than 50 cents per student contact hour if 1000 students use that course each year. More detailed information on course preparation for Plato would be very desirable, especially as it may differ from other kinds of programmed instruction currently being developed for computer-based educational systems.

The problems of excessive systems overhead building up inside the central computer when several thousand users are independently time-shared may require a different network design with different cost factors. One argument advanced for a single central computer is the economy of human management of a single computer installation as contrasted to many installations. Because this argument may have overlooked the need for human supervision of groups of student stations, it would seem that neither the economy nor the software design for a single computer with several thousand independent users on line is clearly established in their proposal. Therefore, a more detailed comparison would be desirable between the proposed centralized computer system and a partially decentralized system in which satellite computers handle all the short requests from groups of student stations—possibly as many as 100 in a group—and the central computer is called on only for handling the occasional requests from the students that require more extensive processing. The data from Plato III should be useful in such a comparison.

Conclusion

Bitzer and Skaperdas are to be congratulated for their developments on the Plato system. Their pioneering designs for student station components offer real hope for reducing the costs of student stations to a level competitive with other forms of instruction.

The most striking feature of the proposed system, aside from the overwhelming number of stations involved, is the maintenance of 0.1-second response contingencies for new inputs on the visual display. The rapid response of the plasma display to each student request, coupled with the flexibility demonstrated by the current Plato system, should bring about adequate student acceptance of CAI while keeping the unit costs very low.

To extend the range of usefulness of the proposed system, it is suggested that the student station should include audio playback with 0.2-second access time, using pneumatic positioning, as demonstrated by the slide projector, and direct selection of visual choices by means of a transparent touch-sensitive surface overlaid on the display. With such features, the proposed system could reach nearly all students effectively.

System Design: Discussion

The adequacy of Plato III can be questioned as a basis for projections of the cost of Plato IV because the two designs are qualitatively different. First, there is the problem of scale in time-sharing and communications. The problems associated with handling 4000 users with one or a small number of computers are of a different kind than those encountered with only 20 learning stations. Present time-sharing systems exceed 100 active terminals only by restricting the mode of use, as in the airline reservation systems or the RCA math drills system for New York City. The problems of general-purpose, multiuser facilities require something more than just a faster computer.

Second, Plato IV will also have to handle increased complexity in computer-based curriculum materials in order that the cost of automated instruction can be justified. Many of the lessons on Plato III could probably be as well presented in a paper-and-pencil format. Rather than use all the key presses ever made on the Plato system, Bitzer and Skaperdas should base their projections on that subset that they believe to be characteristic of future uses. Current applications are using increasing amounts of symbolic and verbal processing. What remains of 1000 operations per key press after the time-sharing overhead is deducted will do very little to recognize student input, manipulate text files, and respond to student constructions. Interesting lessons will also require considerably more storage than typically is used in Plato demonstrations.

A third discontinuity between past and future will occur as a result of the introduction of computer assistance for the designers of learning exercises. Additional processing time and storage will be required to assist the author working on the computer, to maintain records of his own work as well as the performance of test students, and in general to serve as a kind of extension of his span of attention and skill in manipulating the pedagogical concepts.

Two of the major choices made in the design of the Plato IV system were disputed in discussion among the conference participants. Bitzer has proposed that copies of audio and visual supplements to the curriculum be distributed to and stored at each terminal location. Atkinson and Suppes have found centralization of audio to be advantageous in their operations. Some of the considerations are cost of duplication, reliability and maintenance of local equipment, and availability of the current copy of material.

Another disputed decision involves placing most of the computing power and electronic storage at one central site rather than distributed through satellite systems. Bitzer's plan to use video lines reduces considerably the usual cost of communications, so he is less concerned about reducing the transmission load by providing for local decision and reply to the student. An alternative approach exemplified by the Stanford system involves small computers (PDP-8) located across the country operating as satellites of a larger central computer (PDP-1). Bitzer intends to concentrate the lines from the local terminals in each region with an electronic switch connecting to the high-capacity video line and perhaps to provide some stock answers as they are stored in local audio and visual files.

A number of other cost studies are worthy of mention here. Kopstein and Siedel (1968) discussed current systems and a framework in which CAI could be compared with teacher-administered instruction. Randall and Blaschke (1968) analyzed the interdependence of school management practices and educational technology. They concluded that the personnel resources freed by computers are not likely to be available for new tasks such as curriculum preparation for computers. COMPLAN, Inc. (1968) discussed and compared proposals by General Learning Corporation and IBM for design of a regional service center that had somewhat restricted aims but that reached all students. Balough and Purdum (1968) provided a framework in which cost analyses might be done but gave no data to fill out the structure.

A brief list of cost factors for consideration includes

Computer processor and storage
Student learning station and other terminal devices
Financing and maintenance (if purchased)
Operating system for multiaccess, multiprocessing facility

Software packages for educational applications
Maintenance of software
Operations personnel
Communications (including line concentrators or signal distributors)
Curriculum development, distribution, and maintenance
Supervision (proctor, administrator)
Potential use per year
Per cent effective use (loss caused by equipment failure and scheduling
    problem)

Data on these various cost factors will have to be obtained from projects moving into operational stages at universities such as Stanford, Illinois, Penn State, Florida State, and Texas and the secondary school projects in Philadelphia, Pontiac (Michigan), Pittsburgh, Palo Alto, and New York. The large number of interacting variables makes cost estimation a highly complex process.

REFERENCES

Balough, R. L., and Purdum, D. L. 1968. *Computer-assisted instruction*. Feasibility study, NASA CR-917, various pagings. Washington, D.C.: NASA.
Computation Planning Incorporated. 1968. *Functional analysis and preliminary specifications for a single integrated central computer system for secondary schools and junior colleges*. Bethesda, Md.
Kopstein, F. F., and Seidel, R. J. 1968. Computer-administered instruction versus traditionally administered instruction: economics. *AV Communication Review* 16, No. 2:147–175.
Randall, R., and Blaschke, C. 1968. Educational technology: economics, management and public policy. *Educational Technology* 8, June 30:5–13.

PART II

Instructional Design

The authors of Chapters 4 and 5 discuss problems and potentials of instructional design for computer-based systems, with particular attention to psychological research on individual differences and learning strategies that may be relevant. Bunderson outlines a rather detailed plan for the design process, indicating logical interconnections among statement of goals, analysis of tasks, description of learner characteristics, design of materials, and evaluation of outcomes. He is rather optimistic about psychological research providing the needed tools for individualizing learning strategies. Bunderson anticipates that the cross-fertilization among computer science procedure and formalization, programmed instruction, and learning psychology will lead to new methods and standards of instructional design. A detailed analysis of behavioral objectives extending down through the entering behaviors is the most crucial step in instructional design. A flow chart showing how multiple entry points into the hierarchy are to be provided for students differing in attainment of intermediate objectives can be prepared. The modularity provided by the behavioral analysis meets good design standards for computer programs. Using materials recently developed for an IBM 1500 instructional computer system at The University of Texas, Bunderson illustrates in detail the manner in which individualization of instruction can be prescribed and continuously improved, taking into account the learner's aptitudes and the immediate rate of progress.

In the role of critic, Glaser develops further four major issues raised in

Bunderson's chapter: (1) the analysis of the learning tasks and their structure, (2) the difficulty of discovering interactions between individual differences and learning variables, (3) the kind of short-term history variables to measure and the type of learning treatments to employ to individualize instruction, and (4) the potentiality of computer-assisted instruction in giving the student a facility for manipulating, redesigning, and rearranging the elements of the curriculum. To illustrate these points, Glaser draws extensively from his own work in the Learning Research and Development Center at the University of Pittsburgh and at the Oakleaf Experimental School, where a major demonstration of individually prescribed instruction has been under way for several years. His description of the program for individually prescribed instruction at the Oakleaf school is an excellent example of computer-managed instruction within which CAI can be thought of as a special case.

4

C. Victor Bunderson

The Computer and Instructional Design

With each new technological aid to instruction, from the textbook through the video tape, a set of production procedures and design standards had to evolve, and indeed are evolving still. These procedures and standards were conditioned both by the characteristics of the medium and the needs and tastes of the users. CAI can be viewed as a compound resulting primarily from a union of programmed instruction and the use of time-shared, interactive computer systems, although it has other important antecedents. Program design, from this point of view, will be seen to have inherited procedures and standards from each parent discipline. The evolution of these procedures and standards are not likely to result in a product entirely predictable from either discipline alone.

In coming to grips with the computer, the author of instructional materials will find many old problems of structure, organization and sequencing, and display format in only slightly altered form. The existence of exciting computer capabilities will not in itself solve these problems, even if such things as natural language translation and vocal speech detection are achieved tomorrow. The computer, however, brings with it not only specific capabilities but also a host of techniques and formal systems that may be applied to instructional problems. Their application may range from the specific application of formal systems through the intuitive application of the metaphor provided by the methods and findings of computer science.

At The University of Texas Computer-Assisted Instruction Laboratory,

45

procedures and standards for designing CAI programs have been developed as a result of stimulation from curriculum development contracts, efforts to teach students to design CAI programs, and efforts to conduct research in human learning and instruction. The instructional design model described in this chapter was originated to provide management and quality control for curriculum development, to provide a bridge between the curriculum development and basic research activities of the laboratory, and to serve as a focus for teaching students and others how to design quality CAI programs. Its development was influenced by the author's attempts to adjust to a joint appointment between educational psychology and computer science and to communicate with staff members and students from both fields.

Instructional Design in a Computer Programming Context

When the designer of instructional materials confronts the task of preparing a CAI program, he places instructional design in a new context, that of computer programming. This context reveals many points in common with systematic procedures for developing programmed instructional (PI) materials. It brings some new perspectives to instructional design, however, that might have important implications for an emerging discipline of instructional design, especially as it applies to CAI.

Most introductory books on computer programming rapidly plunge the reader in amid the "trees" of binary codes, registers, and input/output devices, neglecting to discuss the outlines and composition of the "forest." Of concern here is not the technical detail, but the problem-solving approach used in programming. Thus the programmer specifies clearly his input and output and then attempts to break the problem down into subproblems, considering any constraints that may limit his possible approaches. He may represent aspects of the solution strategy by means of flow charts, which serve as an aid to design as well as for later documentation. At a later point he codes the solution strategy in a formal language and then debugs the program, revising it on the basis of test runs.

Definitions and descriptions of programmed instruction (PI) have often emphasized the systematic approach used in the design of self-instructional sequences as much or more than the product itself. Systematic procedures for developing PI and multimedia materials have been described elsewhere (Lysaught and Williams, 1963; Thomas et al., 1964; Lange, 1967, p. 58; Briggs et al., 1967). These procedures bear analogy in critical elements to the steps taken by computer programmers.

In PI, the program designer insists on the specification of input and output in terms of entering skills and terminal behaviors to be expected of the learner. He performs a task analysis during which he determines the subproblems or component behaviors and their relationships. He employs the test and revise attitude implicit in debugging both during early test runs with a few students and on the basis of later validation studies.

Despite these surface similarities, there are differences in the task of the computer programmer—some subtle, some obvious—that may have implications for the way an instructional designer conceptualizes his task and proceeds. These differences are revealed against the context of an article by Strachey (1966), who has described the activities of the system analyst and programmer in a manner useful to our present purposes. He illustrated the more important design steps in the development of a computer program to play checkers.

An early step of critical significance is to decide on a representation for the checkerboard. How can the checkerboard be represented as an information structure so that the processing routines of a checker program can easily be described? Strachey selected a useful representation of a board extended one row on each side, so that a move at the edge would have the same characteristics as a move in the middle but could be flagged as illegal. This representation greatly simplified the programming of playing routines.

The analysis of the processes for finding a proper move was so complex that a typical programming strategy was adopted. A hierarchical resolution of the problem was undertaken, defining subroutines, each with well-defined output and input. In essence what was done was to put off the work of solving the major problem of selecting a best move and to go about solving subproblems instead until the major problem itself was incidentally solved. The importance of this procedure to the systems analyst was stressed by Strachey (1966, p. 72): "Since there is a limit to the size and complexity of a problem we can hold in our head at one time, it appears that the best way to extend our capability is to treat relatively large and complex operations as single units and combine these units hierarchically."

The relationships between the various subprograms need to be represented by the systems analyst by means of a flow chart. It may also be appropriate to use a flow chart to represent the processing sequences internal to a subroutine. Flow charts form only one part of the detailed documentation that must accompany a large program.

When the system analysis is complete, coding of the solution strategy in an appropriate computer language is undertaken, sometimes by a person other than the analyst. Work with computers has demonstrated positively that a complex program is almost never right the first time. An error in a program is merely an opportunity, often forceful and explicit, to improve the program. More importantly, the rapid communication from the computer of diagnostics or unexpected results made possible by the requirement that the program be stated in a formal language enables the programmer to focus his revision efforts quickly and effectively.

Consider now the analogue of these steps in the design of programmed instruction. Regarding the selection of a representation, one immediately thinks of the task of selecting the appropriate media displays and response formats. Briggs et al. (1967) have described a procedure for the design of multimedia instruction. In this procedure the logic of a component analysis enables specifications to be made for which a set of media should be used in a particular instructional sequence. The conditions of learning appropriate for different classes of learning objectives, as described by Gagné (1965b), form the basis for this media specification.

By contrast, the advantage of a good representation in computer programming lies in establishing an efficient basis for information processing within the computer program. This can perhaps be generalized to instruction through the notion of displays simplifying and perhaps (through both fixed and dynamic computer graphics) even sharing the learner's information-processing task. A requirement for this function would be an analysis of the learner's task as an information-processing algorithm, which might provide useful detail within Gagné's categories of complex learning: concept learning, principles, and problem solving.

The use of flow charts in instructional design becomes a necessity in design for CAI. Although simple flow charts may be used to describe certain characteristics of intrinsic (branching) PI programs, where a modicum of one type of individualization is allowed, the conditional branching capability of the computer makes complex tree-like or modular instructional programs a reality. The variety of paths for individualization thus provided requires new forms of documentation, both to assist the designer in representing the complexity and in providing permanent documentation. Flow charts, decision tables, and standards of documentation for computer programs go well beyond available procedures in PI for describing the decision logic basic to individualization. On the other hand, certain PI documentation standards (AERA, APA, DAVI-NEA, 1966) will be required when the computer program is an instructional program.

Coding a program in a computer language is another departure from PI. We must wait to see what effect the discipline of coding instructional frames will have on the techniques of frame construction developed in the PI movement. At the least, it is likely to lead to the formalization of researchable teaching logics or interaction paradigms with variables explicitly defined.

It is in the analysis function that a great deal of adjustment must take place between PI and computer programming approaches. A learning hierarchy, as described by Gagné (1968), represents a series of behavioral skills, arranged in hierarchical form to show the patterns by which empirical transfer may occur from a lower to a higher skill. The computer programmer's analysis is based on logical prerequisites of one information-processing sequence on another in solving a complex problem. Analysis serves as an aid to his thinking during the design process. It also serves as the basis for efficient systems architecture.

The implications are that it is enough to have an analysis that is economical, complete, and efficient in regard to the representation selected. Considerations of transfer or of the unique status of behavioral components are less important because the analysis is viewed as a somewhat arbitrary, but useful, invention.

These differences may or may not lead to useful insights into instructional design. When the instructional product is a computer program that teaches, insights that PI brings in terms of a behavioral science foundation consisting of both data and theory will be profoundly important to the CAI programmer. Important also are the quantitative techniques and research models of behavioral science. Notions from both these disciplines are incorporated in the model to be described.

A Prescriptive Model for Instructional Design in CAI

The word *model* is used here in the sense of a pattern or blueprint. It is prescriptive, in a sense, for it prescribes the activities to be performed by the instructional designer, their approximate sequence, and the product of each activity. The model is summarized in Table 4–1 and Figure 4–1. Table 4–1 lists the activities prescribed by the model in one coumn and the product of each activity in the second column. Design activities generally follow the sequence implied by the ordering in Table 4–1, but because the tabular display cannot communicate in detail the dependencies of one design activity on others, the flow chart in Figure 4–1 was prepared.

Figure 4–1 should not be taken to imply a rigid temporal sequence but rather a sequence of logical dependencies. Probably no CAI programs are generated directly from an analysis of needs into goals, and goals into behavioral objectives and subobjectives, any more than axioms preceded theorems in the creation of mathematics. More often, a germinal idea springs up in the mind of an experienced teacher when he observes or considers CAI capabilities. For adequate development, however, such an idea must be operationalized through behavioral analysis and course synthesis, placed in context, and justified through an analysis of and synthesis of needs and goals.

It should also be noted that this model, in all its detail, is most appropriate for extensive (and usually expensive) CAI curriculum development

Table 4–1. Components of a Prescriptive Model for Designing CAI Programs

Design activity	Design product
1. Intent and justification	Description of:
a. Write societal needs	Social context requiring an educational or training program
b. Write institutional need	If a program is already institutionalized, its problems requiring improvement
c. Write program goals	
c.1. Describe job requirements	Situation in which program graduates will find themselves; general skills needed
c.2. Describe student population	General relevant learner capabilities
c.3. Describe institutional constraints	Available time, facilities, and other relevant resources
d. Write justification for CAI	Why the planned CAI mode is more appropriate to goals than other means of presentation
2. Instructional design: analysis	
a. Derive operational requirements from goals	Specification of:
a.1. Derive terminal objectives	Most general behavioral objectives: develop posttest
a.2. Set entering performance standards	Prerequisites: tentative design of pretest
a.3. Consider effect of constraints on program design	Design limitations, if any
b. Behavioral analysis	
b.1. Obtain intermediate objectives through analysis of terminal objectives	What subobjectives are necessary to achieve higher-order objectives
b.2. Construct learning hierarchy	Block or tree diagram showing prerequisite relationships among objectives
c. Analysis of learner traits	List of traits that are implied by behavioral analysis or could interact with different representations
3. Instructional design: synthesis	
a. Specify interface	Written justification of:
a.1. Display and response devices	Devices selected
a.2. Representation; each objective	Conventions and function of representation, if appropriate
b. Construct individualizing flow chart	Gross flow chart showing how individuals are entered into different levels of hierarchy and into alternate routes through any subobjectives
b.1. Hierarchy-based gating mechanisms	
b.2. Trait-by-treatment branches	
b.3. Continuously adaptive mechanisms	Separate flow charts describing computation and use of any adaptive parameters
c. Write working draft	
c.1. Construct curriculum-embedded tests controlling major flow	Tests go in manual, as do instructions for obtaining and inputting trait scores, if any
c.2. Write steps and describe format of steps	Author's draft written according to conventions known to coders and media specialists

Design activity	Design product
4. Produce program materials	
a. Code from author's draft	Program in card, tape, or disk, and listing form
b. Produce media	
c. Debug code and proof media	Filmstrips, audio tape, workbooks
5. Evaluate and revise	
a. Editorial evaluation	
b. Internal empirical evaluation	Item analyses and the like
c. External empirical evaluation	Documentation of revision and validity data in program manual
c.1. Validation testing	
c.2. Longitudinal validation	
6. Use of feedback	
Return to any previous step as indicated by evaluation, revise, and recycle	

projects, especially those involving considerable text and display authoring in connection with the production of tutorial sequences. These projects can require 200, 300, or more hours of work on the part of a team of authors, instructional designers, programmers, and media specialists to produce a sequence that would take an average student only one hour to complete. As CAI languages develop, it will become easier for the individual teacher or professor to generate quickly sets of drill or practice exercises on the one hand or simulation models for laboratory-like activity on the other. Such programs can be prepared in a few hours and may generate from a few minutes to a few hours of useful activity integrated with an ongoing instructional program. The extensive documentation, analysis, and testing prescribed by the model will never be undertaken by such authors, although if they wish to improve the quality of their efforts, or in any way disseminate their programs, they may find some activities and products prescribed by the model to be quite helpful.

Intent and justification, needs. A consideration of the context of an instructional program requires that the program be viewed as a subsystem of a larger whole. The larger system imposes constraints that limit the design of the program and specifies requirements that it must meet. It is not often necessary to write extensively concerning the societal need for a CAI program unless the intent and justification is to be circulated to some funding agency with a proposal for financial support. A publisher may also find such comments useful in the dissemination of a CAI program. Lehman (1968) suggests that the principal pitfall that an analysis of needs avoids

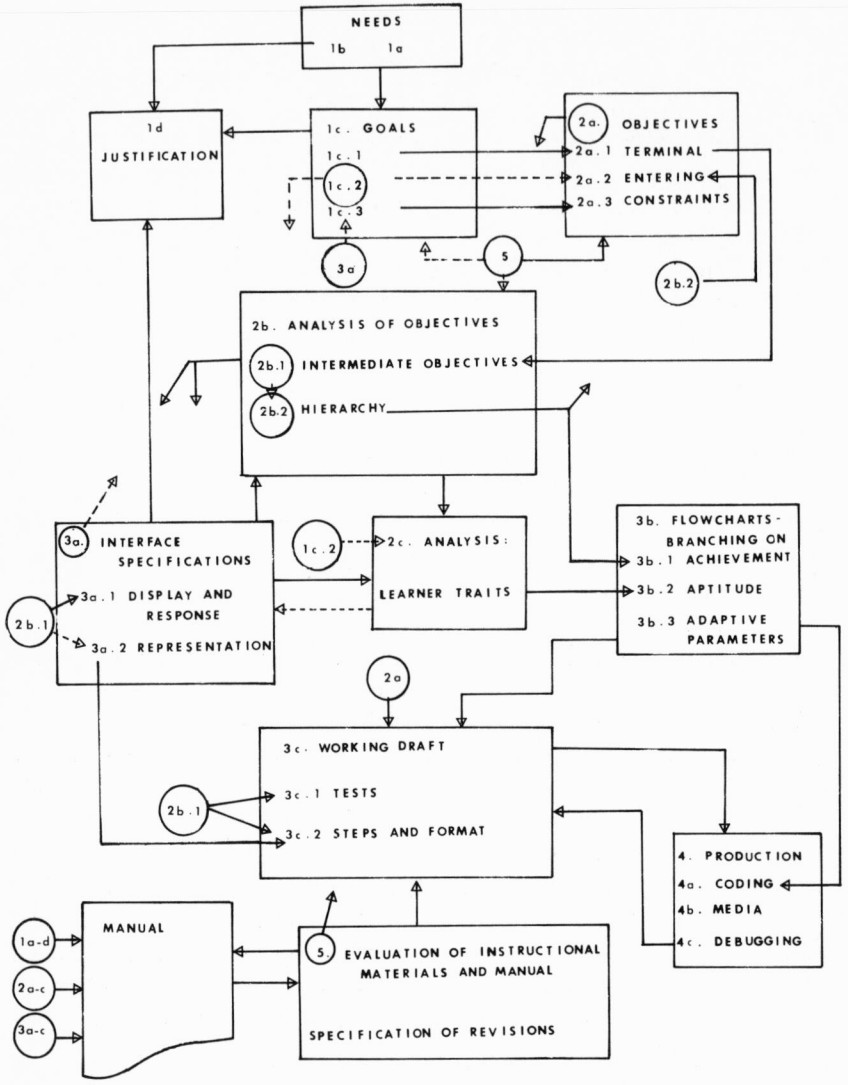

Figure 4–1.
Sequential and dependent relationships among instructional design activities. Solid arrows imply that information from source of arrow is required by indicated subsystem to derive its output. Dotted arrows imply information flow, which is generally useful in deriving output of individual subsystem. Code numbers refer to Table 4–1.

is that of designing instruction to meet a problem for which education or training is not really the most appropriate solution.

The need for most CAI programs is institutional. Examples include inadequate teaching staff or facilities, gross background differences in students, objectives requiring expensive equipment or rare circumstances that suggest the use of simulation, or objectives that are not being achieved by conventional means. As will be discussed, the institutional need often provides a major part of the justification for using CAI, although, as Figure 4–1 implies, the program goals may assist in justifying CAI, as may the interface requirements specified as a result of the behavioral analysis.

Goals. The specification of program goals is a first approximation to the classic problem definition phase of systematic problem solving. Where are the students now, where do we want them to be, and what constraints limit our solution? The specification of *program objectives* answers these questions in operational language. The *goal statement* answers them generally. Users of behavioral objectives have been criticized because it is possible, and indeed easy, to write behavioral objectives that are trivial and that miss important values that presumably are achieved through traditional presentations (Atkin, 1968). To the extent that these criticisms are valid, the writing of program goals in nonbehavioral language is an attempt to assure that the CAI program will indeed enable the student to achieve at least the more important capabilities that will enable him to function on the job or in any later relevant situation. If the derivation of behavioral objectives from the goals suggests that important values cannot be accomplished by CAI, the program manual should describe the possible results of using the CAI program without accompanying instructional activities designed to achieve the balance of the program goals.

The criticism of triviality often leveled at behavioral objectives can also justifiably be raised in regard to experimental hypotheses in a scientific journal. The scientist, especially the behavioral scientist, may be concerned with an important but fuzzily defined problem area. At some point he must become operational. He then runs the risk of choosing operational definitions so narrow as to miss the essence of the problem. In most cases the trivial experimental hypothesis, as any journal editor will testify, is not accompanied by a clear description of the problem area involved in the study. Writing of overall needs and goals provides the same context for the instructional designer as problem development does for the researcher.

Justification. As long as CAI curriculum development remains as expensive as it is, we shall be faced with the salutory discipline of justifying the use of this medium for a given set of instructional goals. Justification is essentially a cost-effectiveness question and cannot be answered precisely at this stage of development of CAI. At a higher level of generality there is something that can be said, however. Too much of the early CAI in this country consisted of the implementation on CAI systems of PI-like materials or, worse, lecture-like materials interspersed with questions. It is doubtful that such programs could show significant gains in either time or achievement to justify the choice of CAI over paper and pencil or cheaper audio-visual materials. It is because of the existence of poorly justified programs such as these that there is often much truth in the comment by Skinner (1968) that "Setting up a computer to teach children is just idiotic . . . a simple programmed workbook will do what the computer can do at one-tenth the cost."

The answer to the justification question may come in two principal forms. It may follow directly from the institutional need, where high costs and/or logistic problems suggest a CAI solution. It may also arise in answer to the question "What does the computer *uniquely* have to offer as an instructional device?" A good CAI program will have elements of both these factors in its justification. It will be a good computer program, exploiting unique machine capabilities and having a clean and efficient architecture as a system, and it will enable students to achieve important objectives more efficiently or more adequately and at costs acceptable to the institution.

Even at today's costs there are applications of CAI that can be justified. This is especially true in higher education and in government and industry. Military training costs average $1.80 per student-hour (Kopstein and Seidel, 1968). Industrial training programs may be very expensive in terms of employee travel and per diem, not to mention costs from lost working time, teachers, and facilities. It has been estimated that the college chemistry laboratory may cost over $2.00 per student-hour (Pierce, 1967). Medical education has laboratory situations even more costly. Regarding programmed instruction, one study suggests that even a relatively inflexible CAI program may enable freshman chemistry students to achieve the conceptual objectives of a portion of the qualitative analysis laboratory as well as or better than students who take the regular "wet" laboratory—and in half the time (Hollen et al., 1968). Chapter 14 by Lagowski provides a detailed justification for CAI in university science education.

Individualized diagnosis and tutorial, drill, or practice units in skills basic to mathematics and language arts may prove to be well-justified uses of CAI from preschool through college. The computer in these cases can serve a management as well as an efficient instructional function. Computer simulation and man-machine problem solving (integrated, perhaps with tutorial sequences) may be justified as *unique* contributions of the computer to instruction. Between these extremes there lies the great majority of courses now taught by the lecture method. The objectives of these courses are to convey a large body of facts, concepts, and principles. In the author's view, it will be difficult to justify tutorial CAI in these areas, except as a recitation-review or testing supplement to textbooks and live or canned lectures or as an information retrieval assistant to individual study. CAI may be used as a means to *develop* textbooks or other materials, however. The computer capabilities of response recording and analysis and rapid revision can lead to a quantum leap in the quality of published instructional products.

All products of the *intent* and *justification* activities become part of the program manual. This part of the manual will function primarily in assisting the author or his agent to sell the idea for a program to officers at various political levels in the system in which he is imbedded. On a broader scale it will assist the publisher to disseminate the program at a profit.

Instructional design: analysis. The need for an operational statement of behavioral objectives as the beginning step in instructional design has been documented elsewhere. An initial statement of the entering skills expected of students should also be made at this point. As Figure 4–1 shows, however, the latter cannot be firm until the behavioral analysis and learning hierarchy are complete so that relevant prerequisites can be specified precisely.

The importance of behavioral analysis is also well established (Glaser, 1965, 1966; Gagné, 1965a), and various techniques for performing it have been described (Gagné, 1962, 1965a; Mechner, 1965, 1967). Gagné's description (1962) of the process as the sequential application of the question "What must the learner be able to do, given only instructions, to achieve the next higher objective?" has proved to be quite useful. This process results in a hierarchy of behavioral objectives having prerequisite relationships to one another. If a transfer study were to be done between any two behavioral tasks having such a prerequisite relationship, empirical transfer would be observed if the analysis were correct (Gagné, 1968).

As Table 4–1 shows, the products of behavioral analysis include a list of intermediate objectives, extending down to and including the entering behaviors. A block diagram similar to those used by Gagné (1965b) and by AAAS, *Science, A Process Approach* (1968), is another product. On this block diagram it is easy to denote those subordinate objectives that will be required as prerequisites to the program. This may lead to a revision of the tentative statement of entering skills and a revision of any pretest used to screen students who do not possess these prerequisites.

Although the importance of analysis has been emphasized repeatedly in PI literature, in CAI it is surely the keystone of system architecture. As Figure 4–1 shows, analysis is the most central of all steps in instructional design. More subsequent steps depend on the adequacy of the intermediate objectives and hierarchy than on any other design products. Further, as the preceding analogy to computer programming implies, the hierarchical resolution of a complex instructional problem can serve the same heuristic and design functions for the instructional programmer as for the computer programmer. The flow chart can be prepared showing how multiple entry points into the hierarchy are to be provided for students differing in attainment of intermediate objectives.

The program architecture can be designed in a modular fashion, letting each subobjective be defined as a module with entry conditions established through diagnostic testing and exit conditions specified in the response measures embedded within the module. Such modules can serve as subroutines in an extensive instructional system, where a module might be called on from many points higher in the course that depend on the objective it teaches. This procedure was used in the design of our Preskills mathematics program. A set of intermediate objectives was obtained through analyses of a smaller set of terminal objectives. These intermediate objectives each defined the output of a module. A learning hierarchy was prepared which showed the prerequisite relationships among modules and points at which subroutine modules could be called. For example, certain basic subroutines dealing with nomenclature and operations involving bases and exponents are called at multiple points by both the scientific notation segments and the logarithm segments. Certain of the scientific notation modules are also called by the logarithm modules. Thus a student who started in the logarithms segments without first having gone through exponentiation could pick up the prerequisite modules at the appropriate points in his instruction on logarithms if his responses indicated such a need.

The modularity provided by the behavioral analysis also meets good design standards for computer programs. Revision is easier when it can be restricted to a single module, rather than reverberating throughout the entire course, and additions can be made easily by adding modules. A higher-order control program will exist in instructional systems with this modular design. Information required at a supramodular level should pass through this program.

The advantages of modular program design are well documented in the computing literature (for example, Greenberger, 1966, pp. 145–146). The design of Preskills is in pleasant contrast to some of our earlier tutorial efforts using the Coursewriter I language. Early courses had a tendency to spread like cancer over the disk, consuming more and more space and becoming less and less comprehensible. This continued until even the author could no longer comprehend or maintain his monster, let alone communicate it to others, and it was abandoned.

The hierarchical analysis procedure seems readily applicable to any cumulative subject matter such as mathematics, much of science, and even music. It seems less applicable in highly verbal areas. Our experience in attempting to design English Preskills programs has shown the analysis procedure described to be useful but much less definitive. Although it is possible to construct hierarchies, they seem somewhat arbitrary, because there are always other ways to reach the same goal. The structure of English may be more net-like than tree-like.

Analysis of learner traits. A giant step toward individualization has been taken when a learning hierarchy is prepared and a diagnostic mechanism implemented to assess the learner's prerequisite and intermediate behaviors. The learner can then be gated to activities that will build his prerequisites, entered into some intermediate point in the program, or gated past the program with a stamp of approval. As pointed out before, however (for example, Glaser, 1966), the task of diagnosing preinstructional behavior must go beyond assessing the status of objectives constituting the hierarchy to a consideration of more enduring traits of the learner. Such traits can interact with treatment conditions within a module in such a way as to make alternative versions of the module pay dividends in learning efficiency and motivation.

Evidence is accumulating in support of this point. Sutter (1967) showed that anxiety interacted significantly in learning from CAI with a partner versus working at the terminal alone. Tallmadge et al. (1968) investigated the relationships of both cognitive and noncognitive abilities to two types of learning tasks, one involving numerical computation and the other involving visual discrimination skills. Two versions of each task were developed so that each task could be taught by either a deductive (expository) or an inductive (guided discovery) instructional procedure. Tallmadge et al. found significant interactions between the instructional method used and certain trait measures, primarily noncognitive. The direction of the interaction was opposite in the two types of tasks. Thus individuals who could be characterized as having technical-quantitative interests did better on the criterion test for the quantitative task after an inductive instructional treatment, whereas individuals who had social-aesthetic interests did better if they learned this task by a deductive procedure. The reverse was true for the visual discrimination task. By predicting criterion scores in the quantitative task for both inductive and deductive modes for individuals based on the related noncognitive measures, Tallmadge et al. estimated that assignment of individuals to the proper instructional condition would yield performance at the seventy-seventh percentile in comparison to performance at the forty-fourth percentile for a mismatched treatment assignment.

King et al. (1969) investigated the interactions between cognitive ability measures and treatment conditions, which they described as verbal deductive (expository), verbal inductive, figural deductive, and figural inductive. No interactions were found with the verbal versus figural variable in the tasks, but the deductive versus inductive treatment differences were found to interact with two cognitive tests. A deductive test was a better predictor of achievement with deductive materials, whereas a verbal inductive test was significantly better for predicting the inductive materials.

It has been demonstrated that a careful analysis of learning tasks can lead to fairly detailed predictions regarding the role of cognitive abilities in learning that task (Bunderson, 1967). The same major abilities were independently selected as relevant and shown to be related to concept learning by Lemke et al. (1967), showing that independent investigators can reliably select the cognitive abilities likely to be relevant in a learning task by logical analysis. Dunham et al. (1968) showed that the characteristics of a variety of concept tasks were shared by tests of cognitive factors. The factors were shown to be related to the concept learning scores obtained from the use of these tasks. One implication of these studies is that stimulus and processing characteristics of a learning task, which can be identified by logical analysis, are related significantly to the abilities called into play during learning. Because these aspects of the task can be manipulated by the experimenter or by the instructional designer, the abilities demanded by a task can be manipulated. Thus learners high on a set of abilities can be helped to succeed in one treatment, whereas those high on a different set might require a different treatment.

Although no trait-by-treatment interactions have yet been designed into curriculum projects at the CAI Laboratory, several of our basic research studies have been motivated by the preceding thinking. Dunham and Bunderson (1969) showed that the variable of rule instruction in solving four-category concept problems produced a significant flip-flop in the ability profile of solvers. Solvers in the no-rule group were high on associative memory, whereas those in the rule group were high on reasoning. Mean performance in both groups was the same, suggesting that gains could be made by assigning those high on reasoning in the no-rule group to the rule group and vice versa.

The implications of this work for instructional design in CAI are clear; if the demand for mental abilities can be brought under stimulus control, and the characteristics of this stimulus control can be specified in advance, then instructional designers can be taught to design treatments in which the representation and processing requirements posed by the treatment exploit the learner's strong abilities. Alternatively, the instructional designer can design treatment options such that memory and processing requirements are minimized by the representation and the instruction, preventing difficulty or failure from students low on otherwise critical abilities. This implication will be considered further.

Instructional design: synthesis. The quality of the analysis and synthesis activities listed in Table 4–1 will in large measure determine whether the CAI program will achieve eminence or become kin to the dozens of hopeful new textbooks that fail each year. One should be able eventually to expect from an instructional design model helpful guidance as to how the activities of course synthesis can be conducted to increase significantly the chance that the products will possess quality as well as producing the behaviors desired. As David Markle (1962) and Susan Markle (1965) have shown, a program with a certain amount of positive validation data may nonetheless be worthless because of poor content and design.

Unfortunately, the design model described here cannot yet prescribe in detail how such quality is to be built in. If the model is at all on the right track, however, it will have described the tangible activities and products that account for a major portion of the variance in such quality. The success of repeated revision cycles on improving the program will be limited if the original synthesis of the course is off-key in harmonizing subject matter structure and representation to learner and computer capabilities. Without the guidance provided by a model such as this, anyone who has assigned the design of a short learning program as a term project—even to bright graduate students and experienced teachers (university colleagues included) —will observe that the architecture of the first draft may be totally inappropriate for the instructional objective. It may hold little or no hope of improvement through revision without major demolition and reconstruction.

In addition to its other advantages, a correct behavioral analysis is the foundation for tasteful and effective course synthesis. As Figure 4–1 shows, it enters importantly into each and every synthesis step. The hierarchy forms the basis for the design of individualization and its description in flow-chart form. The list of objectives is the basis for the specification of interface requirements, the diagnostic and curriculum-embedded tests, and the terminal parts of the sequence of steps for each subobjective.

This multiple usefulness derives from the characteristics of a well-stated operational objective. Each objective, intermediate and terminal, has three parts: (1) a statement defining the stimulus situation to be displayed to the learner, (2) a statement involving action verbs describing the responses required, and (3) a performance standard defining some measurement of response adequacy. The performance standard guides the construction of test items for diagnostic gating past instructional modules or exit from within them. The stimulus and response portions of the objective guide the selection of display and response detection conventions, the representations to be used across or within modules, and consequently the format of actual program steps. They also form the basis for the analysis of learner traits— especially cognitive abilities likely to be of major importance for individualization—for any cognitive ability construct is operationalized in terms of item formats and response requirements in the set of tests defining its factor.

Glaser et al. (1966) have developed the concept of "interface between the student and the subject matter" at some length. They have shown how an analysis of subject-matter competency in different content areas will lead to specifications for display and response detection that differ across subject-matter areas. They stress that characteristics of subject-matter competency should dictate the design of terminal devices rather than available devices constraining the objectives and method of instruction. Unfortunately, their analysis of interface requirements for elementary mathematics and reading yields specifications for audio display and reception not likely to be achieved by manufacturers for many years to come. Other devices they specify as necessary are less esoteric but nonetheless not likely to be readily available in the near future.

When this chapter reaches print, it should be possible to obtain commercially any subset of the following equipment: a typewriter with up and down half-line feed (for graphs, diagrams, and notation), a rapid access image projector with several-hundred slide capacity, an audio tape system with moderately rapid access to prerecorded messages, a cathode-ray tube (CRT) with the capability of presenting stored digital graphics as well as characters, and keyboard and light pen (pointing) response. All these will be controllable either by a tutorial or an algebraic language and will be cost-feasible for a combination of research and instruction in certain areas, especially in higher education, where certain costs per student-hour are currently high. CRT displays with vector-generated graphic capability and light pen for graphic input will be available, but costly, and usable by means of software not specifically designed for CAI. The terminal described by Bitzer in Chapter 2 exemplifies a set of capabilities likely to be available on a wide scale a few years later. It is the capabilities represented by these terminal devices, then, that will probably be the concern of most CAI programmers for several years to come. The approach of Glaser, Ramage, and Lipson to the specification of interface requirements is thus of immediate use to the instructional designer primarily in a negative sense. An analysis of objectives may lead to specifications beyond the capabilities of CAI systems likely to exist during the life of the program. For example, the display aspect of an objective may imply specifications for extremely rapid- and random-access segmented audio. The action verb in an objective might lead to specifications for detecting the manipulation of physical objects or the decoding of vocal speech. In these cases a justification is not possible (note the arrow in Figure 4–1 from interface specifications to justification) and those objectives must be achieved by some other medium within the institutional setting.

One of the positive contributions of the approach of Glaser et al. to the problem of interface will be the design and development of new terminal devices that will open new classes of objectives to adequate instruction by

CAI. For most CAI uses, however, a different emphasis must be taken. The questions "What educational objectives are appropriate to present interface capabilities?" and "For what forms of instructional interaction can existing devices provide a unique contribution?" must be asked instead. The latter question suggests that our ideas about instructional objectives and interaction may change substantially as a result of the confluence of current instructional design procedures, with their PI and audio-visual heritage, and the computer's capabilities for real-time computation, display, and retrieval.

A consideration of these questions is implicit in design activity 3.a, "specify interface." Selection of representations is the most crucial positive contribution to the success of an instructional design in matching computer capabilities and subject-matter structure. Thus it is that solid arrows appear in Figure 4–1 leading from activity 3.a.2, "representation," to the analysis of objectives and of learner traits, to the layout of the steps and step format in the author's draft, and to the justification. These will be explained.

At this stage of development in instructional design, few definitive guidelines can be given to the instructional designer in regard to representation. We can help him to detect conventions for display and response that are poorly justified. We can alert him to possible profound positive effects on the efficiency of learning and transfer of an economical and powerful representation, and we can alert him to the possibility of dramatic interactions with learner traits caused by minor changes in a representation. We cannot, however, tell him how to invent one.

A step in defining a representation has already been taken when the behavioral objectives are written. An objective that includes a statement of "What is given?" or "Under what circumstances will the behavior occur?" has begun to delimit certain aspects of the representation, at least in regard to terminal sequences within a module. In certain cases this early freezing of representation is entirely appropriate. For example, in teaching associations or multiple discriminations, where the stimulus material is fixed, the representation problem becomes one of adopting conventions for display and response detection appropriate to the interface. The major concern is that the conventions selected do not cause inconvenience, confusion, or unnecessary difficulty for the learner. Because students above the elementary grades have well-developed symbol systems, it is possible to inflict on them awkward translation tasks required by a limited student terminal. Examples of this are the special notational systems that have been invented by CAI programmers to accommodate mathematical, chemical, or other notation to a typewriter interface with no reverse index feature (or even no lowercase!). These compromises place an unnecessary information-processing burden on the learner. The use of long, verbose type-outs on a slow teletype device where a graphic on an image projector or in a booklet could communicate the idea quickly is another example. The use of exercises with "easy numbers" when a student computational language is unavailable or not easily accessible from the tutorial language is another bad compromise from the point of view of what CAI should be.

There is still another class of objectives for which the representation should definitely not be fixed prematurely. This class includes concepts, rules, and types of problem solving where the very meaning of the objective lies in its cross-situational applicability. It was perhaps to achieve this generality that the authors of the AAAS *Science, A Process Approach* wrote their objectives using behavioral verbs but did not identify any particular stimulus situation. Performance standards were also handled separately by well-defined competency measures with specified content.

Among psychologists, the importance of the concept of representation to cognitive processing has been most fully developed by Jerome Bruner. Bruner's concern with representation arises in part from his conception of a theory of instruction that, among other things, "must specify the ways in which a body of knowledge should be structured so that it can be most readily grasped by the learner. Optimal structure refers to the set of propositions from which a larger body of knowledge can be generated, and it is characteristic that the formulation of such structure depends upon the state of advance in a particular field of knowledge . . . the goodness of a structure depends upon its power for *simplifying information,* for *generating new propositions,* and for *increasing the manipulability of a body of knowledge.* Structure must always be related to the status and gifts of the learner" (Bruner, 1966, p. 41).

However structured, knowledge becomes internalized in terms of one of three modes of representation, according to Bruner. *Enactive representation* refers to action sequences, *ikonic* to images or graphics, and *symbolic* to linguistic or logical propositions drawn from some symbolic system with its own laws and syntax.[1] Any two representations may differ in *economy,* which refers to the amount of information that must be held in memory and processed to achieve comprehension. They may also differ in *effective power,* which is determined by the generative value of the set of learned propositions.

The influence of particular representations (viewed as an internal cogni-

---

1. It is interesting to note that factor analysts (for example, Guilford, 1967) have found three broad classes of abilities related to the handling of different forms of information: figural or pictorial stimulus content, symbolic content (numbers, letters, and other symbols), and semantic or verbal content. Guilford has added a category for behavioral content that suggests Bruner's enactive representation mode. The analogy of Guilford's symbolic and semantic to Bruner's symbolic and of figural to ikonic is also interesting.

tive structure) on particular aspects of cognitive growth has been documented by Bruner and his colleagues (1966). The influence on instruction of different representations (viewed as ways of presenting or displaying instructional tasks and material to produce internalized cognitive structures) has also been explored (Bruner, 1966), although much remains to be done.

The task of the instructional designer in selecting a representation is a difficult one, for many subject-matter areas lack ready-made representations having both economy and power. The invention of a useful representation may indeed be an important contribution to a field, as, for example, was Kekule's renowned invention of the benzene-ring model. It is not likely that instructional designers will be the source of many major structuring inventions unless they are simultaneously creative scholars of some depth in a field. Teamwork between scholar-teachers and CAI specialists will be required. The former will confirm the analysis, suggest and develop the major representations, and author the basic steps of the program. Instructional designers will help by suggesting representational ideas appropriate to the interface, prompting with heuristic questions suggested by design principles, developing system architecture in close cooperation with the authors, filling in details, and supervising the coding, media preparation, and program documentation and maintenance.

To assist him in this role, the instructional designer should be given guidance from the design model for representations generally useful for different classes of concepts and problems and appropriate to author language and display capabilities. In this task the cross-fertilization from computer science may be of significance. Important progress has been made in computer science in the generation of economical and powerful representations for given problem areas. The operationalizing of problems in terms of a formal computer language is a major reason for this progress. The formalization of display and response elements of instructional interaction in terms of the CAI terminal hardware and tutorial languages that drive it will hopefully lead to the same progress in instructional design for CAI. Stimulation from the metaphor provided by the study of information structures, and their applications in artificial intelligence and computer graphics, may facilitate progress in this area.

In artificial intelligence, the critical importance of an economical representation is well known. The checkerboard representation used by Strachey has been alluded to earlier. Gelernter et al. (1963, p. 155) reported that when a mechanism for constructing geometric diagrams was implemented within a geometry theorem-proving program its efficiency was greatly increased. That the same gain in effectiveness can be achieved when humans use a good representation has been discussed by Newell (1966, p. 180).

Newell also chided the behavioral analysis approach of Gagné (1966) for failure to consider the importance of representation.

The major processes of an artificial intelligence program may serve as models for human thinking, even though the author did not intend the program as a simulation (for example, see Paige and Simon, 1966). Although it may not be very interesting to conduct studies to see if naïve college sophomores use the same economical representations and processes as these programs, it may be of great interest to see if students can be taught to use them.

We have far to go to a point where instructional theory can tell the designer how his choice of representation will interact with differences in learner traits. A study by Blaine and Dunham (1968) illustrates that a minor change in what is represented may react in a major way with cognitive traits and in an unexpected manner. The difference in representation between the two experimental groups was slight. Concept instances were typed out to the learners one at a time. One group had no past instances available other than through recall; the other group had one past instance displayed at the terminal at all times. The obvious prediction is that the one-instance group would have less demand on memory, and hence the memory factor most related to recalling previous instances would show a lesser relationship to learning scores in their group. Although this effect was observed, a more interesting observation was that in the one-instance group learners high on this memory factor were *actually hindered,* as demonstrated by a positive relationship between this memory factor and the number of trials to criterion. Conversely, a second factor, dealing with the ability to cognize and remember concepts, became more strongly related negatively to trials to criterion when one instance was available. This factor could not be interpreted as memory for previous instances as could the first factor. It dealt instead with an ability to cognize and retrieve the concept common to two or more instances.

The positive relationship between the previous instance factor and trials to criterion in the one-instance group indicates that reliance on a strong ability may lead a learner to choose an inappropriate strategy. The choice among variations in a representation gives the instructional designer control over which strategy will be more effective, but he has no way of predicting whether a learner will use that strategy without knowledge of the learner's traits. Research is needed to determine whether sequences can be written to induce a learner, whose traits do not so dispose him, to use a strategy appropriate to an economical representation or whether alternative representation should be available.

Flow chart. That the major patterns of individualization described by the flow chart are based on the learning hierarchy and on predicted trait-by-treatment interactions (if any) has been mentioned previously. Activity 3.b.3 acknowledges a third type of individualizing mechanism that will require its own flow chart for description. This is a continuously adaptive mechanism that adjusts parameters controlling the timing of displays or responses, item difficulty, and other factors that can be measured as continuous, or at least as ordered, variables. Lewis and Pask (1965) have designed adaptive mechanisms of this sort that aim at the goal of maintaining a viable man-machine interaction. Chapter 6 by Smallwood describes a continuously adaptive mechanism for the control of sequence that offers a sharp contrast to the models of Lewis and Pask. Chapter 8 by Lord on tailored testing provides a theoretical basis for adaptive mechanisms for testing.

Author's draft. The nature of the author's draft for a CAI program will differ in many respects from the author's draft for a non-CAI program, even one developed according to the design model described here. The diagnostic and curriculum-embedded tests written for CAI may have a number of novel features. Tailored testing is only one. The capabilities for display and response detection provided by an enriched interface open up many new item formats and perhaps will make possible the measurement of a number of human abilities and achievements not possible heretofore.

Procedures for writing frames for programmed instruction have been described elsewhere (S. M. Markle, 1965; Brethower et al., 1964). These procedures can be of great assistance to the instructional designer if they are placed in proper context with the computer's unique capabilities. If the course synthesis steps of interface specification and flow-chart construction have been taken properly and the justification is clear, there is little chance that an experienced PI author will "do what he knows best" and implement a "digital PI text" on the computer.

Production of program materials. A special skill that will be required of instructional designers will be to write the author's draft according to conventions that can be communicated to coders and media specialists. One procedure that has shown promise at the University of Texas CAI Laboratory is the use of decision tables (Groom, 1968). The rows of the top portion of a decision table are designated by condition stubs, which designate conditions that might or might not prevail at a given point in a program. The rows at the bottom of the table are identified by action stubs, which define the display, timing, and other actions that might be taken. The columns of the table represent decision rules, each of which represents the actions that should be taken when certain of the conditions apply (see Pollack, 1963). Decision tables have an advantage over flow charts in that complex decisions can be documented more easily and altered more easily as logic changes are made. A decision table can be used by an author with great precision, prescribing the instructional interaction for the coder minutely.

Alternatively, the author with a capable and creative coder can block out the steps and step format more generally. In either case the decision table allows the author to write more in his own terms, without learning a CAI language (although he must fully understand its capabilities).

Another advantage of the decision table is that it can serve as permanent documentation of the program. A CAI program is a complex system, and a programmer must be in charge of its maintenance at any institution where it is used. The flow charts and description of tests and steps assist him in this task and enable him to incorporate "updates" as they are received. Decision tables can eliminate some of the flow charts and integrate others. Decision table documentation, supplemented by a listing of the program code, can also assist in the task of translating the program into another CAI language.

The author's working draft, whether in decision table form or not, must be formatted to enable the media specialist as well as the coder to work from it in order to produce any filmstrips, audio tapes, or printed materials to accompany the digital code. Production of images and audio tapes for CAI incorporates a complex technology currently fraught with unsolved problems. Authors cannot afford errors in communication to pass unnoticed through these currently expensive and time-consuming processes.

It is estimated that on large non-CAI computer programming projects design takes 30 per cent of the development time and debugging another 30 per cent (Lecht, 1967). These figures for debugging may be low in CAI program development. The removal of logical and syntactical errors from the program is only the beginning. The tuning of a CAI program to students from the intended population is a time-consuming process. For the first dozen or so students, response listings recorded by the computer during instruction should be scanned individually and modifications in the program made immediately. A number of these modifications will consist of conventions or prompts designed to keep the interaction going as students become more familiar with terminal operation. More basic are modifications in ambiguous items or the construction of remedial sequences when students fail to learn. After the information from a sufficient number of individual students has been processed in this way, it is more economical to list summary statistics from a larger number of students. These item analyses should be designed to focus attention on ambiguities, points of exceptional difficulty, and unnecessary material, so that modifications can be made in the program code and, if necessary, in the audio-visual materials.

Evaluation and revision. In Table 4–1, three evaluation activities are identified. Editorial evaluation refers to the critical review of the products of instructional design. This review is based on subjective but to some extent describable criteria rather than on empirical data. Internal empirical evaluation has been discussed under the topic of debugging, where it appeared to fit most naturally. External empirical evaluation refers to the testing of the revised, finished program with groups of students from the intended population in order to determine the extent to which objectives are met, by which students they are met, and in how much time. Field testing is longitudinal in nature and can yield important data regarding the breadth of applicability of the program and its utility in various institutional settings relative to the goals established early in program design or perhaps other goals that were not anticipated.

As S. M. Markle (1967) has provided an excellent discussion of the empirical evaluation of instructional products, the reader is referred to her discussion. There is a close correspondence between her terms *developmental testing, validation testing,* and *field testing* and design activities 5.b, 5.c.1, and 5.c.2, respectively. The link back to institutional needs through longitudinal (field) testing is not stressed by Markle, perhaps because of the difficulty of showing empirically that the attainment of certain objectives do transfer to program goals. The logic of this design model leads to such an emphasis.

At the beginning of her treatment of evaluation, Markle also touched on the continued importance of nonempirical aspects of quality control such as soundness of subject matter, brilliance of insight, and artistry of presentation. This is part of what is meant by the term *editorial evaluation,* selected here. There has been a serious attempt throughout this chapter to describe a set of standards for the intermediate projects that go into the development of a first-rate CAI program. These include the system analysis aspects, especially the justification, and the technical design standards followed in connection with analysis and synthesis activities. Documentation of these activities in the program manual assures that independent reviewers will be able to comment on the appropriateness of a CAI product and its excellence of design. It may be possible to attain some agreement on a set of standards for CAI programs related to design and documentation, if not justification (the market place will provide a judgment for the latter).

The aesthetic aspects of editorial evaluation are difficult to specify. As S. M. Markle (1967, p. 106) points out, "a brilliant presentation is defined by its impressiveness to colleagues, who can appreciate its artistry, and not by its effect on students, who may not only be unable to see why it is brilliant, but, indeed, may have failed to acquire even lesser behaviors from it." In my judgment the impression of brilliance, style, and taste given by a CAI program will prove to be a joint function of the representation and the individualizing mechanisms adopted. It will be a function of the representation both generally, in terms of the lack of awkwardness of interface conventions adopted, and specifically within modules, where the economy and power of a representation can be enhanced by the computer's dynamic processing and display capabilities. Anyone who has stood by a knowledgeable critic seated at a terminal can attest to the important aesthetic impact of clever individualizing mechanisms or the negative impact of poor ones.

The Instructional Design Model and Research

An instructional design model such as the one described can have an important influence on the direction of basic and applied research. Taking the University of Texas CAI Laboratory as an example, the model has served as more than a management and quality control procedure and as more than a basis for teaching instructional design. It provides a context for basic and applied research, generates questions, and provides an incentive for researchers to seek to develop answers to research questions in a manner that can translate to instructional design practice in actual curriculum projects.

The application of modular programming principles to instructional design is a current interest. The instructional designer needs a rational approach to the analysis and representation of task structures. Gagné's recent discussion (1968) of the confirmation of learning hierarchies as essentially an empirical problem to be answered by a large number of separate transfer studies seems unacceptable for our applied objectives. There must be some rational procedure to enable the designer to describe a task structure in a manner that is economical and powerful. The application of formal languages for the description, manipulation, and documentation of task structures may ultimately provide this power. In the meantime we are operating at a more heuristic level, and our questions are applied questions having to do with how to help the instructional designer perform useful task analyses. Questions of sequence between two subtasks in the representation of a task structure may be less important from this point of view than the manner in which the structure is revealed to the learner.

Ultimately, the question of analyzing and representing task structures becomes a basic question of theoretical importance. In the instructional design model as now developed, the sections dealing with task analysis and program synthesis provide far too little guidance for the instructional designer. Perhaps what the designer ultimately needs is a taxonomy of generalized task structures and a taxonomy of generalized component tasks. In addition, the model should provide guidelines for determining from the analysis those individual difference variables potentially of critical significance relative to the task dimensions of the taxonomy. This would imply that cognitive and affective variables be linked by means of a set of theoretical constructs to the same dimensions used to classify the tasks.

Questions of task structure and sequencing are being studied at the CAI laboratory by means of an abstract hierarchical learning task. This task is composed of a hierarchy of concepts and rules that make up the imaginary "science of xenograde systems" (Merrill, 1964, 1966). A simulation of this "science," adapted from Merrill's task, has been programmed for the IBM 1500 system and a series of studies are under way. Because the task is imaginary, previous learning of the concepts and rules comprising the task is held constant, so that the individual differences are caused by traits and styles the learners bring with them to the task.

In addition, the structure of the task is well defined, and the instructional programs built around the task have been developed according to the design model. The results of studies investigating the interaction of trait patterns with sequencing variables and display variables can lead directly to prescriptive statements usable by the instructional designer. Such studies are under way. Because the task is similar in important ways to actual curriculum materials under development in our science and mathematics projects, the hope is that the transfer of actual instruction of laboratory findings can, through the mediation of the instructional design model, be expedited.

Less obviously tied to our curriculum development efforts are basic studies in the trait-by-treatment interaction related to concept and rule learning. Some of these studies have been described here. Stylized laboratory tasks are used in these studies. Here the hope is that general propositions can be developed relating manipulable task variables to trait patterns. These relationships, in turn, can enable the instructional designer to produce on his first pass more nearly optimal instructional interaction for teaching single concepts or rules.

Looking ahead, the logic of this chapter would lead to the desirability of formalizing interaction paradigms as generalized computer routines in some formal language. Interaction paradigms would exist at two levels.[2] At the task structure level, the paradigm would represent more global individualizing mechanisms concerned with sequence and with the representation of task structure and of cumulative payoffs to the learner. Such mechanisms could be formalized as higher-order control programs. At the lower level the interaction paradigms would be concerned with component tasks such as discrimination learning, verbal learning, and concept learning. These interaction paradigms, which would incorporate in their decision logic complex stimulus-response contingencies, would possibly be easier to teach to instructional designers than the learning theory and research techniques employed in their development. At the same time they would

2. Stolurow and Davis (1965) have identified the need for individualizing mechanisms at two levels. The lower level employs the "teacher function" and the higher level employs the "professor function."

provide a promising communication mechanism between researchers in human learning and instruction, while still being comprehensible to the designers of instruction.

Summary

In his contribution to the study of creativity, Koestler (1966) remarked that "All decisive advances in the history of scientific thought can be described in terms of mental cross-fertilization between different disciplines." The cross-fertilization between system analysis and computer programming, and curriculum design for CAI, may yet produce a decisive advance in education.

This chapter has surveyed some of the results of cross-fertilization as it has been evolving at the University of Texas. An instructional design model was described that represents an attempt to merge procedures and criteria for developing good programmed instructional material with criteria for good computer programs. The model is useful as a management and quality control procedure for large-scale CAI curriculum development projects. It is also useful as curriculum material for the training of a new class of skilled instructional personnel, especially those that will be called instructional designers but also including coders and CAI media specialists.

The model described in this chapter has implications for the direction of basic and applied research. Some implications of the model to research were discussed and illustrated by reference to experience at the University of Texas CAI Laboratory.

REFERENCES

American Association for the Advancement of Science. 1968. *An evaluation model and its applications—second report*. Miscellaneous publications of AAAS no. 68-4. Washington, D.C.

American Educational Research Association, American Psychological Association, Department of Audio-Visual Instruction of the National Education Association, and Joint Committee on PI and Teaching Machines. 1966. *Recommendations for reporting the effectiveness of PI materials*. Washington, D.C.: DAVI of NEA.

Atkin, J. M. 1968. Using behaviorally-stated objectives for designing curriculum: a cautionary note. Paper presented at the meeting of the American Educational Research Association, February 1968, in Chicago.

Blaine, D. D., and Dunham, J. L. 1968. Memory abilities in concept learning. Paper presented at the meeting of the Southwestern Psychological Association, April 1968, in New Orleans.

Brethower, D. M., Markle, D. G., Rummler, G. A., Schrader, A. W., and Smith, D. F. P. 1964. *Programmed learning, a practicum.* Ann Arbor, Mich.: Ann Arbor Publishers.

Briggs, L. J., Campeau, P. L., Gagné, R. M., and May, M. A. 1967. *Instructional media: a procedure for the design of multi-media instruction, a critical review of research and suggestions for further research.* Pittsburgh: American Institutes for Research.

Bruner, J. S. 1966. *Toward a theory of instruction.* Boston: Belknap Press.

Bruner, J. S., Olver, R., and Greenfield, P. M. 1966. *Studies in cognitive growth: a collaboration of the center for cognitive studies.* New York: Wiley.

Bunderson, C. V. 1967. *Transfer of mental abilities at different stages of practice in the solution of concept problems.* Research Bulletin RB-67-20. Princeton, N.J.: Educational Testing Service 1968.

Dunham, J. L., Guilford, J. P., and Hoepfner, R. 1968. Multivariate approaches to discovering the intellectual components of concept learning. *Psychological Review* 75(3):206–221.

Dunham, J. L., and Bunderson, C. V. 1969. The effect of decision-rule instruction on the relationships of cognitive abilities to performance in multiple-category concept learning problems. *Journal of Educational Psychology* 60:121–125.

Gagné, R. M. 1962. The acquisition of knowledge. *Psychological Review* 69: 355–365.

———. 1965a. The analysis of instructional objectives for the design of instruction. In *Teaching machines and programmed learning, II: data and directions,* ed. R. Glaser. Washington, D.C.: Division of Audio-Visual Instruction of the National Education Association.

———. 1965b. *The conditions of learning.* New York: Holt, Rinehart & Winston.

———. 1966. Human problem solving: internal and external events. In *Problem solving: research, method, and theory,* ed. B. Kleinmuntz. New York: Wiley.

———. 1968. Learning hierarchies. Division 15 Presidential Address, Annual Meeting of the American Psychological Association, September 1968, in San Francisco.

Gelernter, H., Hanson, J. R., and Loveland, D. W. 1963. Empirical explanation of the geometry-theorem proving machine. In *Computers and thought,* eds. E. A. Feizenbaum and J. Feldman. New York: McGraw-Hill.

Glaser, R. 1965. Toward a behavioral science base for instructional design. In *Teaching machines and programmed learning, II: data and directions,* ed. R. Glaser. Washington, D.C.: Division of Audio-Visual Instruction of the National Education Association.

———. 1966. The design of instruction. In *The changing American school.* The 65th Yearbook of the National Society for the Study of Education. Chicago: Univ. of Chicago Press.

Glaser, R., Ramage, W. W., and Lipson, J. J. 1966. *The interface between student and subject matter.* Technical Report 5. Pittsburgh: Learning Research and Development Center, Univ. of Pittsburgh.

Greenberger, M. 1966. The uses of computers in organizations. In *Information. A Scientific American Book.* San Francisco: W. H. Freeman.

Groom, V. 1968. *Applications of decision tables in CAI programming.* Austin: Univ. of Texas Computer-Assisted Instruction Laboratory (mimeo).

Guilford, J. P. 1967. *The nature of human intelligence.* New York: McGraw-Hill.

Hollen, T. T., Bunderson, C. V., and Dunham, J. L. 1968. Computer-simulated laboratory exercises in qualitative chemical analysis. Paper presented at the meeting of the American Educational Research Association, February 1968, in Chicago.

King, F. J., Roberts, D., and Kropp, R. P. 1969. Relationship between ability measures and achievement under four methods of teaching elementary set concepts. *Journal of Educational Psychology* 60:244–247.

Koestler, A. 1966. *The act of creation.* London: Pan Books.

Kopstein, F. F., and Seidel, R. J. 1968. Computer-administered instruction versus traditionally-administered instruction, economics. *AV Communication Review* 16(2):147–177.

Lange, P. C., ed. 1967. *Programmed instruction.* The 66th Yearbook of the National Society for the Study of Education, Part II. Chicago: Univ. of Chicago Press.

Lecht, C. P. 1967. *The management of computer programming projects.* American Management Association, Inc.

Lehman, H. 1968. The systems approach to education. *Audiovisual Instruction* 13(2):144–148.

Lemke, F. A., Klausmeier, H. J., and Harris, C. W. 1967. Relation of selected cognitive abilities to concept attainment of information processing. *Journal of Educational Psychology* 58:27–35.

Lewis, B. N., and Pask, G. 1965. The theory and practice of adaptive teaching systems. In *Teaching machines and programmed learning, II: data and directions,* ed. R. Glaser. Washington, D.C.: Division of Audio-Visual Instruction of the National Education Association.

Lysaught, J. P., and Williams, C. M. 1963. *A guide to programmed instruction.* New York: Wiley.

Mager, R. F. 1961. *Preparing objectives for programmed instruction.* San Francisco: Fearon Publishers.

Markle, D. G. 1962. In which it is demonstrated that a program that works may well be worthless. *Programmed Instruction* 2(6): 12–15.

Markle, S. M. 1965. The wastebasket reflex. *NSPI Journal* 4(6): 8–11.

————. 1967. Empirical testing of a program. In *Programmed instruction,* ed. P. C. Lange. The 66th Yearbook of the National Society for the Study of Education, Part II. Chicago: Univ. of Chicago Press, pp. 104–140.

Mechner, F. 1965. Science education and behavioral technology. In *Teaching machines and programmed learning, II: data and directions,* ed. R. Glaser.

Washington, D.C.: Division of Audio-Visual Instruction of the National Education Association.

————. 1967. Behavioral analysis and instructional sequencing. In *Programmed instruction,* ed. P. C. Lange. The 66th Yearbook of the National Society for the Study of Education, Part II: Chicago: Univ. of Chicago Press.

Merrill, M. D. 1964. *Transfer effects within a hierarchical learning task as a function of review and correction on successive parts.* Technical Report No. 5. Urbana: Training Research Laboratory, Univ. of Illinois.

————. 1966. Hierarchical preview versus problem-oriented review in learning an imaginary science. *American Educational Research Journal* 3:251–261.

Newell, A. 1966. Discussion of papers by Robert M. Gagné and John R. Hayes. In *Problem solving: research, method, and theory,* ed. B. Kleinmuntz. New York: Wiley.

Paige, J. M., and Simon, H. A. 1966. Cognitive processes in solving algebra word problems. In *Problem solving: research, method, and theory,* ed. B. Kleinmuntz. New York: Wiley.

Pierce, J. R. 1967. *Computers in higher education.* Report of the President's Science Advisory Committee, February 1967. Washington, D.C.: U.S. Government Printing Office.

Pollack, S. 1963. *Analysis of the decision rules in decision tables.* Memorandum RM-3669-PR. Santa Monica, Calif.: Rand Corporation.

Skinner, B. F. 1968. Ice cream for the right answer. Interview in *Forbes* 102(3):46.

Stolurow, L. M., and Davis, D. 1965. Teaching machines and computer-based systems. In *Teaching machines and programmed learning, II: data and directions,* ed. R. Glaser. Washington, D.C.: Division of Audio-Visual Instruction of the National Education Association.

Strachey, C. 1966. System analysis and programming. In *Information.* A Scientific American Book. San Francisco: W. H. Freeman.

Sutter, E. 1967. Individual differences and social conditions as they affect learning by computer-assisted instruction. Unpublished doctoral dissertation. Austin: Univ. of Texas at Austin.

Tallmadge, G. K., Shearer, J. W., and Greenberg, A. M. 1968. *Study of training equipment and individual differences: the effects of subject-matter variables.* Technical Report: NAVTRADEVCEN 67-C-0114-1. Palo Alto, Calif.: American Institutes for Research in the Behavioral Sciences.

Thomas, C. A., Davies, I. K., Openshaw, D., and Bird, J. B. 1964. *Programmed learning in perspective. A guide to program writing.* Chicago: Educational Methods, Inc.

5

Robert Glaser

Psychological Questions in the Development of Computer-assisted Instruction[1]

Bunderson's article (Chapter 4) has a broad scope and covers the components of instructional design for CAI. He raises many issues and has stimulated me to react by probing a little deeper into certain of the components of his prescriptive model for designing CAI programs. In particular, I have chosen to speak of psychological questions that need to be investigated before developments in CAI proceed much further. I shall consider four of the major areas that Bunderson raises in his chapter: (1) the analysis of learning tasks and their structure, (2) individual difference variables relative to task constraints, (3) individualizing mechanisms, and (4) instructional paradigms.

The Analysis of Learning Tasks and Their Structure

Perhaps more than any other instructional requirement, the analysis of learning tasks poses a new enterprise for the psychologist for which he has few available techniques. However, under the pressures of practical instructional design, there has emerged the concept of task analysis, concerned with techniques for analyzing the properties of behavior to be learned and with the sequencing of the component tasks involved in a particular course of learning. The problem appears to be twofold: We must analyze not only

1. The preparation of this chapter was supported under a contract with the Personnel and Training Branch, Psychological Sciences Division, Office of Naval Research.

the nature of competent performance but also the way in which this performance is learned. Bunderson refers to a general notion of task analysis currently in wide favor. This entails identifying prerequisite skills and knowledge that the learner must command before he can successfully learn a new task or educational objective, so that a hierarchy of competence is identified. I should like to elaborate on Bunderson's remarks on this matter because we have recently had some experience along these lines at our research center (Resnick, 1967). Component task analysis begins with any desired instructional objective, behaviorally stated, and asks in effect, "To perform this behavior what prerequisite or component behaviors must the learner be able to perform?" For each behavior so identified, the same question is asked, thus generating a hierarchy of objectives based on behavioral and testable prerequisites. The analysis can begin at any level and always specifies what comes earlier in the curriculum. The importance of the backward analytic procedure for instruction is that it provides a method for identifying critical prior behaviors—behaviors whose absence not only may be difficult to diagnose but also may be significant impediments to future learning. In practical applications a component task analysis can stop when the behaviors identified are the ones that the course designer believes can be safely assumed in the student population. Thus this kind of analysis attempts to provide ordered sets of tasks for inclusion in a curriculum and also to specify the skills a student needs to enter a curriculum successfully. The skill hierarchies generated through such a process of component analysis are best represented in the form of tree diagrams, such as in Figures 5–1 and 5–2.

What kind of information does such a structure provide for the design of instruction? First, it observes the basic constraint that no objective is taught to the learner until he has, in one way or another, met the prerequisites for that objective. These prerequisite learnings can be attained in a variety of ways; they can be learned one at a time or they can be learned all at once in large leaps. The learning process would seem to be optimized by continuous identification of the skill farthest along the hierarchy that a student can perform at any moment or, if a student is unsuccessful at a particular objective, by determining the most immediate subobjective at which he is unsuccessful. The tree-like hierarchies indicate only the relation of subordination or order of attainment. They specify neither what tasks should be taught at the same time nor how much time should elapse between tasks if there are two branches leading to a combined task or the like. Each analysis says only what tasks and behaviors are to be observed and tested for; nothing is said about how these behaviors are to be taught, even though it may take a significant amount of instruction to get from one component task to another. So, although nothing is said about instructional

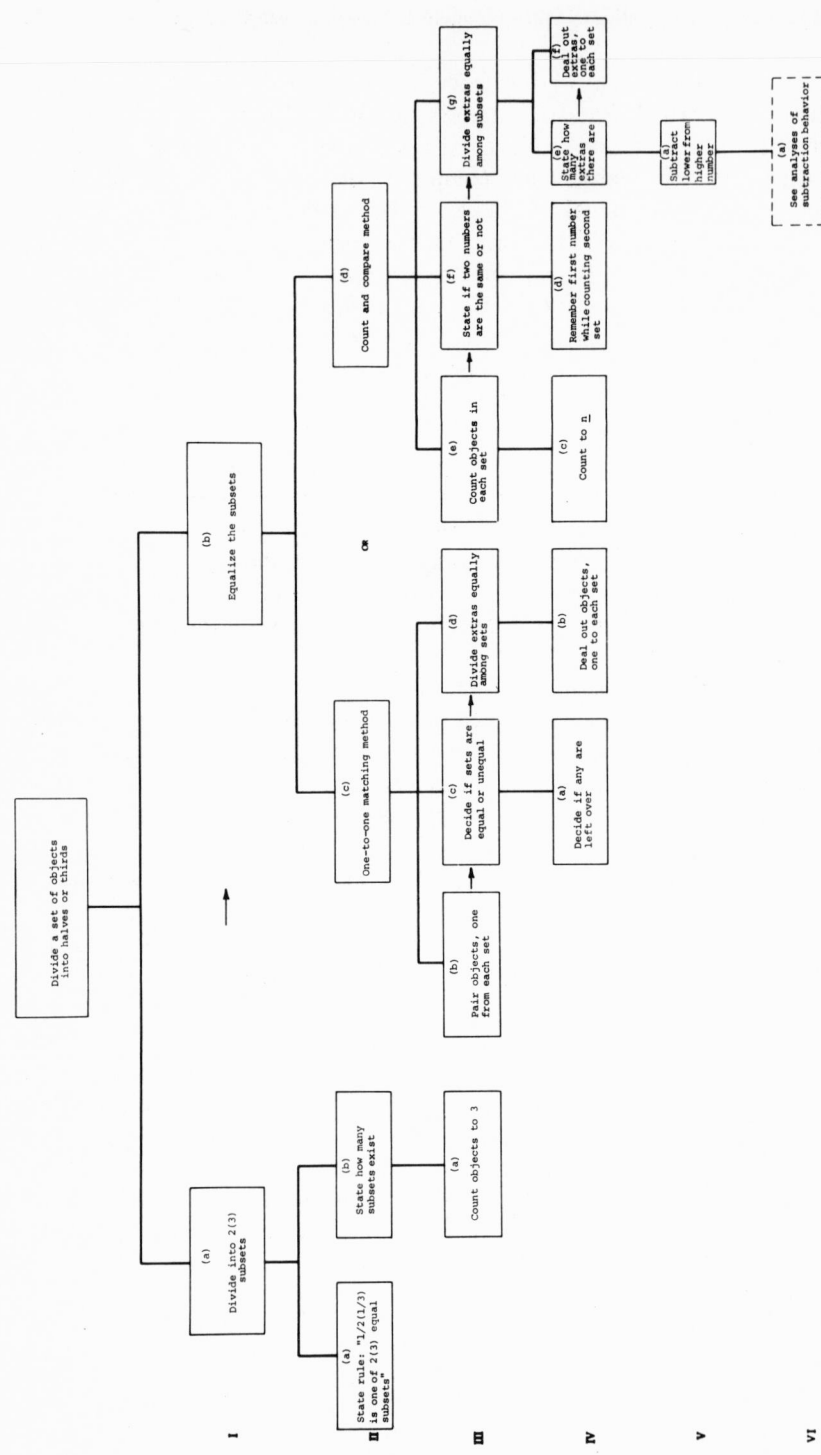

Figure 5–1.
Component task analysis of dividing a set into halves or thirds (from Resnick, 1967).

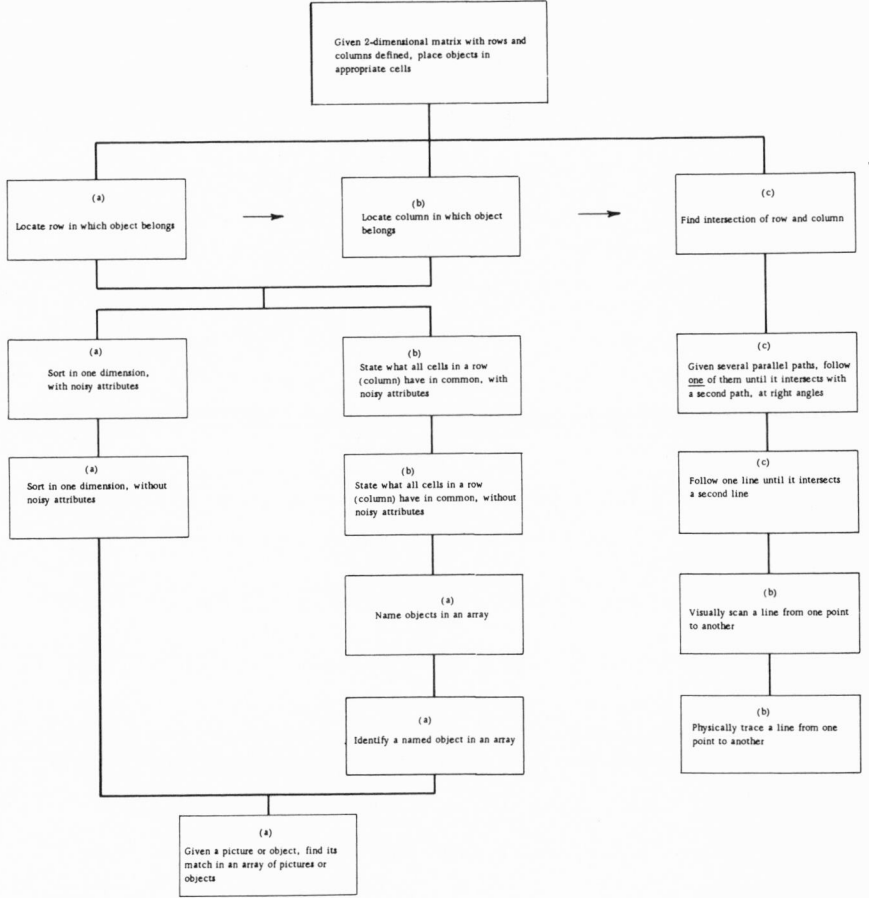

Figure 5–2.
Component task analysis of placing objects into the cells of a two-dimensional matrix (from Resnick, 1967).

method per se, much information related to method is provided, because the instructor or instructional device is told what observations to make in assessing learning. With respect to individualization of instruction, a hierarchical analysis provides a good map on which an individual student may be located.

As these component hierarchies are generated, they essentially stand as hypotheses about how learning can proceed. And they require empirical validation. An initial component analysis may suggest several possible curriculum sequences. It may also have failed to identify all necessary component and prerequisite behaviors. Lauren Resnick is currently directing an effort to validate certain component hierarchies. Tests have been constructed for each component task in a hierarchy, and children are being tested (not taught for this particular purpose) to determine their pattern of performance. Sequential scaling procedures such as Guttman's scale analysis are being used in analyzing the results; the results obtained can lead to redesign of the sequences and to the identification of questions that require experimental study, such as the relationship between hierarchical components and transfer of training.

It is of interest to speculate on the possibility that other procedures for analysis might be employed to generate structures around which instruction could be designed and learning could take place. In the early-learning examples that I have given, there is essentially no subject-matter structure provided by an organized field of knowledge. However, when we teach a recognized subject matter, the organization of knowledge in the field contributes to the structuring of the learning hierarchy. It is difficult to say at this time how close the correspondences are between the knowledge hierarchies and learning hierarchies. It seems that one should influence the other and, in particular, that the empirical data obtained from learning hierarchies might influence the way in which a knowledge structure has, heretofore, been represented. Suppes (1966) has also made this point by saying that a behaviorally oriented way of looking at mathematical concepts may promise a new approach to the foundation of mathematics itself.

Another distinction implied by the technique of task analysis is that a behavioral statement of objectives has both subject-matter-content and psychological implications. It not only tells what needs to be taught in subject-matter terms but also identifies the kind of behavior involved. Is it rote learning, concept learning, a chained procedural sequence? These differences imply different ways in which behavior might be tested and different ways in which it might be taught. The correspondence between behavioral taxonomies and teaching procedures is an additional question for psychological research. [For example, present knowledge of concept learning suggests certain ways in which concepts might be taught (Glaser, 1968; Mechner, 1965).]

Individual Difference Variables Relative to Task Constraints

Bunderson is fairly optimistic that on the basis of a careful analysis of learning tasks, predictions can be made regarding the role of "cognitive abilities" required in learning a particular task. He implies that from a task analysis one can say, for example, that spatial relations aptitude is required for one kind of task or that good associative memory is required for another task. The discovery of the interactions between individual differences and learning variables is perhaps one of the toughest problems the psychologist will have to face in this respect. The kinds of individual differences referred to here are differences that develop from the long-term history of the learner: aptitudes, learning styles (whatever that means), personality characteristics influencing learning, and prior training and knowledge. (I shall refer to short-term history variables, that is, behaviors that are generated in the course of instruction, later.)

There is very little knowledge about the relationship between long-term individual traits and learning methods. Psychologists concerned with individual differences and their measurement have concentrated on the prediction of the outcomes of learning; what has been predicted, with more or less success, has been the end product of learning rather than optimal methods of learning. In contrast to predicting the end result of a course of learning, the requirement in CAI is to predict success in the next instructional step. Experiments suggest that the predictors of the end results of learning and the predictors of immediate instructional success are not the same; this may be especially so if the immediate instructional step is optimized for the learner.

Certain aptitudes have attained fundamental importance as measures of human behavior as a result of their utility in predicting long-range criteria such as school and college success. The task posed in CAI is an additional one in that measures of individual differences must imply decision-making procedures based on the relationships between these individual differences and instructional alternatives. It can be postulated that if the criteria for aptitude test validation had been immediate learning success rather than long-range criteria, the nature of the generally accepted aptitude batteries of today would be quite different. I have reviewed the history of research on learning and individual differences elsewhere (Glaser, 1969). Present types of measured aptitude may be limited insofar as they are operationally designed to predict over the long period, given reasonably nonadaptive forms of instructional treatment.

It is difficult to know where to begin the endeavor that Bunderson suggests for determining information on individual differences relative to the learning requirements for a task. However, Bunderson suggests some leads from his own research and from the research of Guilford (1967). The line suggested by Bunderson is an interesting one. He proposes that the characteristics of a task, identified by logical analysis, are related to the abilities called into play during learning. If aspects of a task can be manipulated by the instructional designer, then the abilities demanded by a task can be manipulated. Thus learners measuring high on a set of abilities can be helped to succeed in one treatment, whereas those high on a different set might require a different treatment. Experiments showing that this occurs are necessary.

A caveat I would introduce here is that it may be the wrong tactic to utilize generally available measures of individual differences and attempt to relate them to learning variables. A sounder approach may be to investigate the different ways in which individuals go through a learning sequence and develop an index of these differences. For example, if one student goes through a hierarchical sequence always covering many steps at a time and another student goes through it covering single steps at a time, we might measure this characteristic and use it to decide on an appropriate instructional alternative. If an individual is one who slowly paces himself and responds correctly, in contrast to one who rushes through his exercises making frequent errors, we might develop a measure of this that could be used for instructional decisions. Measures of these kinds might best be taken in the course of learning and not in advance by global test batteries. The notion of developing measures based on the continuous assessment of learning brings me to the next point.

Individualizing Mechanisms

As a student proceeds to learn, his performance is telemetered, and measures of his performance are summarized and indexed at appropriate intervals. These are short-term history measures in contrast to the long-term history measures used for initial decisions. If instruction is in effect long enough, these two history measures will, of course, fuse into combined indices. The essential problem in setting up individualizing mechanisms is to know what kind of short-term history variables to measure and what kind of learning treatments to use in adapting to the performance indicated by these measures. The kinds of measures one usually obtains in the course of learning consist of information about such things as the frequency of correct and incorrect responses; error analysis as determined by answer processing, for example, what part of a word is misspelled or on what part of an arithmetic problem are errors generally made; and speed of performance, which is easily obtained in CAI, although the implications of performance-time measures are far from clear-cut.

Certain kinds of short-term history characteristics that are easily measured can be thought of in terms of a component analysis diagram. For example, initially one can test to see at what level in the tree a student can be placed. When a student fails at a level (a particular test box), it is assumed either that he has not mastered the necessary prerequisite skills or knowledge, or that instruction is required, or both. A detailed analysis then needs to be made to determine which of these conditions exists, and instruction can proceed on this basis. The power of an instructional procedure would be measured in terms of the number of test boxes that it permits the student to pass without actually being taught. Two measures of teaching power emerge: One is, as I have mentioned, the degree to which instruction permits a far reach for extrapolating learning to higher levels; a second measure of teaching power is, after the terminal behavior is reached, the breadth of the student's knowledge, that is, the number of instances of a class of behavior to which the knowledge learned can be applied.

Of special interest in the assessment of short-term history are measures that are suggested by experimental work on learning. Two examples may give the flavor of this. One comes from the work of Zeaman and House (1963) in which they postulate a chain of two responses for problem solution in discrimination learning: The first is paying attention to the relevant stimulus dimensions, and the second is correct selection of the positive cue of the relevant dimension. They then ask whether individual differences in empirical learning curves are attributable to differences in the speed of acquisition or to some underlying process such as attention. The data they obtain show wide individual differences in learning curves, with higher IQ subjects doing better than the lower; however, the important difference in the curves between the brighter and duller subjects is not the slope of the curve, that is, the rate of learning, but the length of the initial plateau. Thus it is not the rate of improvement, after it starts, that distinguishes bright and dull but how long it takes for improvement to begin. The length of time for improvement to begin is considered an attentional variable and suggests, with respect to the concerns of this chapter, that the measurement of plateau length rather than rate of improvement is a sensitive measure of learning in this case.

A second example is a study performed in my laboratory on paired-associate learning (Judd and Glaser, 1969). The interest here was on response latency as an index of learning. Our study investigated changes in latency over the course of learning from initial learning, through a criterion of near-perfect performance, and then through overlearning. Throughout this course, frequency of correct response increased to criterion and then continued at asymptote through overlearning. In contrast, latency showed no change and remained constant as correct response probability increased from chance to near 1.0; however, during the overlearning period, whereas response probability remained relatively constant, latency showed a significant and sustained decrease presumably related to the consolidation of learning during the overlearning period. The suggestion from this work is that the latency measure, as a short-term learning history variable, seems to detect aspects of learning not detectable from response frequency and may be related to and predictive of future retention.

The main principle of tutorial CAI is that short-term histories during learning and instructional assignment are interlinked in a series of adaptive stages. Two kinds of psychological problems are posed. The first is that the information relevant to this kind of adaptation comes from interaction effects between performance and learning treatments. We shall win the individualization game to the extent that we identify instructional alternatives differentiated in a way to maximize their interaction with performance variables. The experimental task (Bunderson appears to be working on it) is to identify those interactions that are negligible and those that are not in a particular instructional situation.

A second point concerning the continuous pattern of assessment and instructional prescription, and assessment and instructional prescription again, is that this process can be represented as a multistage decision process where decisions are made sequentially and that decisions made early in the process affect decisions made subsequently. The task posed for instruction is to prescribe the most effective sequence. Problems of this kind in other fields have been tackled by mathematical procedures applied to optimization problems. This has been pointed out by Smallwood (1962) and by Groen and Atkinson (1966). Essentially, optimization procedures involve methods of making decisions by choosing quantitative measures of effectiveness and determining the best solution according to these criteria. A quantitative model is developed into which values can be placed to indicate the outcome produced when changes in these values are introduced. For implementing this notion in CAI, two difficult steps are required: (1) obtaining quantitative knowledge of how the variables in the model interact and (2) obtaining agreed-on measures of instructional effectiveness because what is optimized becomes critical.

While on the topic of individualizing mechanisms, it is useful to talk about the instructional decision-making process in our project at Pittsburgh on individually prescribed instruction (IPI), under the general direction of John O. Bolvin. In this project there is an interesting set of evolutionary steps involved in moving individualization into a CAI stage. The math curriculum in the IPI project has a rough hierarchical structure. The kindergarten through sixth grade curriculum has identified 430 specific instructional objectives. These objectives are grouped into 88 units. Each unit comprises an instructional entity that the student works through at any one time; on the average there are 5 objectives per unit, with a range of 1 to 14. A set of units covering different subject areas in mathematics comprises a level; levels can be thought of as roughly comparable to a school grade level. On entering the school, the student takes a placement test that places him in a particular unit. If his profile is scattered, he begins work on the lowest numbered unit. A unit has associated with it a pretest and a posttest, and each objective within the unit has attached to it one or more curriculum-embedded tests. Following placement to a unit, the student takes the unit pretest, which attempts to diagnose the student's profile within the unit. For example, he may have mastered objectives 1, 2, 4, and 5 but not 3, 6, 7, and 8; at this point the teacher prescribes for him work related to the objectives he has not mastered. As a student works through a lesson, he takes, at the teacher's discretion, the curriculum-embedded test, which assesses whether mastery has been attained on the objective and also to what extent some competence has been attained on the next objective. When all objectives have been mastered, the unit posttest is taken. If 85 per cent is attained on this test, the student begins the next unit; if not, he is reassigned to an appropriate objective in the unit until he masters it. Various discretionary powers are left to the teacher about whether to keep the student in a unit or to move him ahead.

In the Oakleaf School, an approximation of this model has been attempted manually for several years (Glaser, 1967; Lindvall and Bolvin, 1967). Teachers are supplied with information on written forms, and on the basis of this information they make instructional prescriptions. The large amount of student information required has been processed by a "simulated computer," that is, a roomful of clerks. We have been observing the kinds of information the teachers require and how they make prescriptions.

After several years of this, we moved up a notch in automation and the use of computers. We began to design a management and information system for individualized instruction that would service both the ongoing school teacher and the researcher seeking to study and improve the system. The clerical operations that had evolved over the three years of nonautomated IPI helped to clarify the nature of the data and the types of questions that are asked of these data. In addition, memoranda have been collected from experienced staff members summarizing the types of questions they wanted to ask of the IPI data base. All this helped us to define the content and the organization of the data files. An analysis of the types of data generated by the operation of IPI and the types of inquiries that teachers, evaluators, and researchers wanted to make of the data determined the design of a first approximation to what we prefer to call a management and information system for individually prescribed instruction, developed under the direction of William Cooley (Cooley and Glaser, 1969).

As an economy measure, the system design also took into account available computer hardware. This included the University of Pittsburgh IBM 360/50, the IBM 1050 terminal with card reader attachment, and three IBM 2741 terminals. The central processing unit has extended core that allows up to 32,000 bytes per on-line terminal. A 250 million-byte disc and six tape drives are also part of the 360 configuration. An IBM 1232 optical reader is used as the basic device for collecting and converting data into machine readable form. The 1050 terminal is located at the school and connected by leased line to the 360 computer on the university campus. The IBM 2741 terminals are located in the researchers' offices.

The major aspects of the system as it is operating today are summarized in Figure 5–3 (more detail is given in Cooley and Glaser, 1969). The basic data are recorded on optical scan forms by clerks scattered throughout the school. These are brought together and processed at the 1232 scanner. The resulting punched cards are then read by the 1050 terminal at the school and the data edited and added to the current student file on disc. If errors are detected in the editing, diagnostics are sent back to the school terminal for correction. The student disc file contains test and prescription data on the unit in which the student is currently working and data on the most closely content-related previous unit. When a student completes a unit, the data obtained are written out on a scratch file on disc. At the end of the day, a program updates the student tape from the scratch file. The student tape contains all the instructional history available for each student. The tape is organized by the student and consists of a variable number of fixed-length records for each student, the number depending on the number of instructional units he has completed. Also included are background data

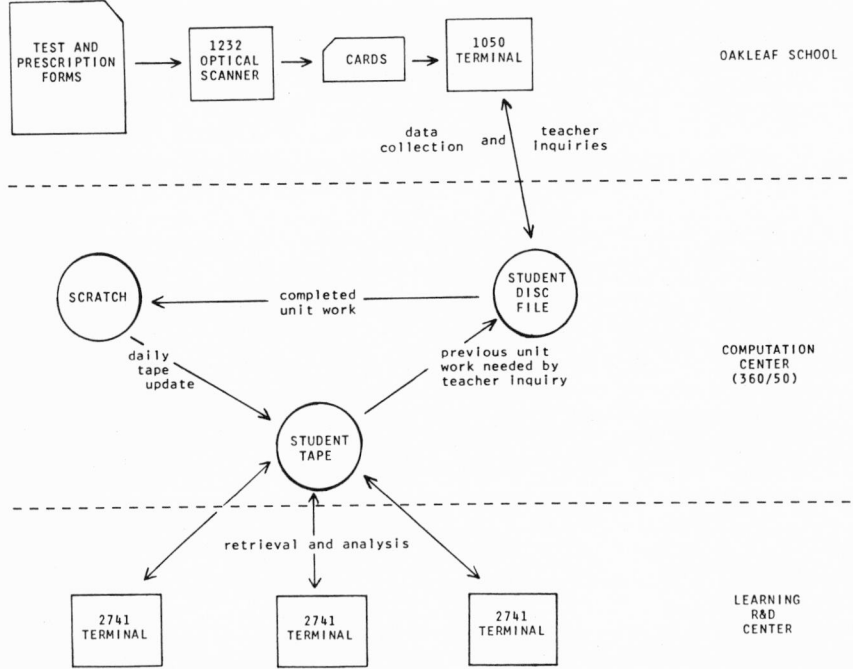

Figure 5–3.
Major components of the IPI management information system (MIS) (from Cooley and Glaser, 1968).

collected at the beginning of each school year, such as standardized test results, home background data, sex, and homeroom. The program that updates the tape also pulls off data summarizing the student's previous work in a unit closely related to the one he is about to begin. This work is then available on the student disc for on-line teacher inquiries.

Illustrative kinds of data that can be obtained with this information system are shown in Figures 5–4 through 5–8. A print out such as shown in Figure 5–4 can be obtained for all units in the program. Figure 5–4 shows

Search Example:*

```
>$$logon e65wwc.
>$$att d stutape as xx.
>$$load d search.

TYPE THE FILE NAME OF THE STUDENT TAPE.

>xx

THE STUDENT TAPE IS DATED 042068.
LIST YOUR SEARCH PARAMETERS.

1. >id.
2. >otis iq!
3. >st acp%ile!
4. >math pret,e4,=1.
5. >math presc,e4,skill 1(1),cet!
6. >math presc,e4,skill 2(1),cet!
7. >math presc,e4,skill 3(1),cet!
8. >math post,e4,=1!
9. >end.

PARAMETER LIST COMPLETE
DO YOU WANT YOUR OUTPUT ON TAPE OR DISC?
>disc

SPECIFY DATASET NAME.
>e4stuff.
COMPILATION BEGINS.
```

(diagnostics printed here if there were errors in the search parameters)

```
COMPILATION COMPLETE
OUTPUT FORMAT:

ONE BACKGROUND RECORD OF 09 BYTES PER STUDENT.
ONE OVERALL RECORD OF 91 BYTES PER STUDENT.
SEARCHING BEGINS

YOUR OUTPUT FILE CONSISTS OF 32 STUDENTS.
THE SEARCH IS COMPLETED

M:  END OF JOB
```

---

*
Lines typed following the > were typed by the terminal user. The other lines were typed under computer program control.

Figure 5–4.
Number of students taking a posttest once, twice, or more times.

the number of students in each unit taking a posttest one or more times; units showing the necessity for students taking more than one posttest are suspect as efficient teaching sequences. Figure 5–5 shows an example of the search program by which the researcher can retrieve data for selected

```
>$$att d stutape1(163rjr) as F8.
>$$load d unidif.
LOADING STARTS AT LOC 058200
EXTERNAL SYMBOL TABLE
    MAIN        058206
    IBCOM       05A1F0
    FIXPI       05B566
FIRST UNUSED LOC IS 05B600
EXECUTION STARTS AT LOC 058206
```

FREQUENCY OF STUDENTS TAKING MULTIPLE POSTTESTS FOR EACH AREA AND LEVEL.

LEVEL	AREA	TEST FREQUENCY 1	2	3	4
2	1	34	10	0	0
2	2	35	3	1	0
2	3	34	6	1	0
2	4	0	0	0	0
2	5	0	0	0	0
2	6	0	0	0	0
2	7	0	0	0	0
2	8	3	0	0	0
2	9	16	2	0	0
2	10	12	1	0	0
2	11	23	5	0	0
2	12	4	0	0	0
2	13	0	0	0	0
3	1	61	26	8	0
3	2	33	3	0	0
3	3	37	16	4	0
3	4	36	6	1	0
3	5	0	0	0	0
3	6	0	0	0	0
3	7	46	11	0	0
3	8	70	12	1	0
3	9	19	2	0	1
3	10	42	6	1	0
3	11	39	6	0	0
3	12	6	0	0	0
3	13	0	0	0	0
4	1	86	24	3	0
4	2	42	16	4	0
4	3	39	5	1	0
4	4	47	13	3	1
4	5	24	1	0	0
4	6	42	9	3	0
4	7	43	25	6	1
4	8	64	17	2	0
4	9	52	17	3	0
4	10	31	7	1	0
4	11	52	23	9	3
4	12	7	1	0	0
4	13	0	0	0	0

Figure 5–5.
Illustrative tape retrieval program for mathematics unit E4 (from Cooley and Glaser, 1968).

student samples or curriculum units, according to search parameters that he types in as verbal requests. The entire student history file can be searched in five to ten minutes, depending on the demands placed on the time-sharing system at the time.

Figure 5–6 shows a data print out of the kind of information about a student's performance that a teacher can use as a basis for instructional prescriptions. This figure shows Robert H's current level and unit of work in mathematics; for each objective in the unit his pretest scores are given

```
   1548          H . . .  Robert          DATE - 016


CURRENT MATH IS LEVEL D MULTIPLICATION

             PRETEST            POSTTEST SCORES
SKILL        SCORES     1ST     2ND        3RD        4TH

   1           99        99
   2           00        99
   3           38        99
   4           75        99
   5           20        99
   6           99        99
   7           20        99
   8           00        99

DATE          004       015


PRESCRIPTIONS AND CETS

DATE    SKILL                    PAGE - SCORE

010      02        01-50    02-90    03-90    04-90    05-90
                   06-90    07-60    09-50    11-90    13-90
                   08-90    12-90
                   CET 17   PART 1-99    PART 2-99

010      03        CET 17   PART 1-99    PART 2-86

011      05        CET 07   PART 1-99    PART 2-83

011      04        CET 08   PART 1-95    PART 2-99

012      06        CET 09   PART 1-89    PART 2-00

013      07        01-90    02-90    03-90    04-90
                   CET 05   PART 1-99    PART 2-50

014      08        CET 08   PART 1-80    PART 2-
```

Figure 5–6.
Unit summary for Robert H.

and also the posttest scores if he has reached that point; below these scores are printed the lesson work pages and the curriculum-embedded tests that were assigned. Figure 5–7 shows another student, John K, in reading. This student's unit pretest scores were high enough so that the teacher moved him along with no prescriptions and considered the unit mastered. Figure 5–8 shows a print out, which a teacher can obtain daily, of a listing of all the students in a class and what they are currently working on.

The next step in the development of this computer-based management and information system is to install a terminal network at the school so that both teachers and students can have convenient access to terminals. At the present time the teacher attempts to diagnose a student's difficulty by examining his record and questioning him on his lessons in a type of clinical branch testing. It is likely that this can be done much more effectively with a student terminal, branch-testing approach. Given the current unit in which the student is having difficulty and given the prerequisite behavior for that unit, items can be presented for on-line student response, which should facilitate the identification of the missing knowledge or skills. Prescriptions can then be written for appropriate lesson units. At the moment the procedure is to print out the information for the teacher and have her

```
  0897              K . . . John           DATE - 022


CURRENT READING IS LEVEL G LITERAL COMPREHENSION

              PRETEST            POSTEST SCORES
  SKILL       SCORES      1ST    2ND       3RD    4TH

    1           80
    2           80
    3           99

  DATE         013



PRESCRIPTION AND CETS

  DATE     SKILLS                        PAGE - SCORE

           NO PRESCRIPTIONS
           UNIT IS MASTERED
```

Figure 5–7.
Unit summary for John K.

GRADE 5   MR. CHARLES BARNHART   DATE - 030   MATH

D NUMERATION
      0795   JANICE C . . .   01
      0853   JAMES I . . .   05
      0909   KATHLEEN L . . .

D PLACE VALUE
      0955   JAMES N . . .   07

D SUBTRACTION
      0842   WILLIAM H . . .
      0886   LOUIS K . . .   05
      0933   KEVIN MCCARTY . . .   02

D COMBINATION OF PROCESSES
      0784   EDWARD C . . .   05
      0977   DAWN R . . .   04

D FRACTIONS
      0829   KIMBERLY D . . .   05

D MONEY
      2063   MICHELE C . . .   06-M

D SYSTEM OF MEASUREMENTS
      0762   JAMES B . . .   01
      0944   PATRICIA M . . .   01
      0966   BRIAN P . . .   04
      1025   KELLY ANN T . . .   01

E NUMERATION
      2119   CHRIS G . . .   08
      0864   KURT K . . .   03
      2122   KATHERINE S . . .   02
      2132   JEANNIE V   07
      1036   SUSAN V . . .   08
      1047   PATRICIA W . . .   06
      1069   SUZAN Z . . .   01

E SUBTRACTION
      0807   SUSAN C . . .   02
      0988   JEFFREY R . . .

E MULTIPLICATION
      0727   DAVID A . . .
      1014   GLEN S . . .   04

E DIVISION
      0749   DAVID C . . .   05
      0773   MICHELE B . . .   03
      1058   KARL W . . .   02

E COMBINATION OF PROCESSES
      0921   JAMES M

E SYSTEM OF MEASUREMENTS
      0716   JOHN A   03
      1003   PATRICIA S . . .   03

F MULTIPLICATION
      0812   LAWRENCE C. . .   10
      0922   TRACY M . . .   03

F FRACTIONS
      0831   JAYME G . . .   12
      0875   CHARLES K . . .   14
      0897   JOHN K . . .

Figure 5–8.
Class list sorting students by units.

use this information to make an instructional decision. As we accumulate information on this prescription procedure, and as the teachers become familiar with the system, it will be possible for us to print out suggested prescriptions that the teacher can then accept, reject, or edit. Further, and to encourage student initiative in the instructional process, it should become possible for the student to work at this terminal to receive his own prescriptions and obtain his instructional materials accordingly.

When we get to this point, we have put testing and decision-making aspects of instruction on the computer. To implement CAI, what remains is to utilize the computer for actual teaching. The progression, then, in launching an individualized program, as we have been working on it, is first a manual simulated-computer operation; second, a computer management and information system that provides a service for the researcher and a terminal for the teacher; third, a terminal for the student at which he can be tested and at which he can receive instructional prescriptions; and, fourth, where appropriate, CAI in which instructional decision-making, student testing, and teaching procedures occur at a student terminal. This progression appears to be one in which aspects of each stage are either retained or incorporated in the next stage as is appropriate to the emerging school design.

Instructional Paradigms

Most discussions of CAI are concerned with computer hardware and software problems. A few are concerned with decision logics and instructional strategies that primarily involve explanation of the functions involved in transferring from instructional block to instructional block. Fewer discussions involve detail about the characteristics of the teaching sequence within these blocks in terms of the stimulus display, the student response, and feedback information required. The amount of space devoted to this topic in Bunderson's chapter also reflects this emphasis. He does, however, refer to his concerns about the console interface and its design. When my colleague and I (Glaser and Ramage, 1967) wrote about the student/subject-matter interface some years ago, we meant to make certain points that still, to my mind, remain significant ones. One point is that possibly the greatest potential of computer-assisted instruction is its capability to provide the student with a facility for manipulating, redesigning, and rearranging the elements of a subject matter. This may be as, or more, important than the capability to adapt to individual differences by accumulating data and switching to new lessons. The two notions, however, are not mutually exclusive.

Let me explain what I mean by manipulating elements of a subject matter. As the negative case, I would point out that much of CAI lesson material is conceived of in terms of putting the tutor into the computer to intervene between the subject matter and the student in the way that a human tutor does. The tutor even says "Good day," "Excellent work," and "You're a nice fellow." In contrast, I would emphasize that the main objective of tutorial instruction via computer is to put the student in contact with the subject matter so that he can work with it directly. Human tutorial functions need be simulated only where they serve this purpose. I have in mind here lessons that are designed so that the student has a great deal of flexibility in working subject-matter problems. Good examples are the capability provided by the Culler-Fried system (Fried, 1967); the Feurzeig and Papert (1968) Logo system, which allows children to manipulate number and symbol strings; and the capability in the Atkinson and Hansen (1966) reading program to manipulate morphemes and the like. There is a rather deep psychological significance behind the necessity for highly manipulative interfaces in which the results of a student's response to a change he makes in a presentation are fed back to him in terms of a re-designed presentation. Psychological experimentation has shown that changes that the learner produces in a stimulus presentation are highly reinforcing and motivating and foster effective learning. There is a great deal of research on the motivating effects of stimulus change and highly responsive environments; such environments can result in highly curious and exploratory individuals.

A second reason for the emphasis on the student/subject-matter interface is to counteract the "myths of multimedia." The point to be made here can be illustrated by saying that there is an apparently undocumented truism among educators, especially those concerned with elementary and high school education, that multimedia stimulation enhances learning by virtue of the fact that the learner experiences the same thing through different sensory channels. Although there may be good reasons for presenting a subject matter in a variety of ways, sheer multiple bombardment is not enough. In fact, there seems to be some evidence to the contrary. Also, I know of no systematic research that allows us to predict that some students will learn best by reading, some by listening, and so on, unless obvious visual or auditory defects exist. Further, the indiscriminate use of available media devices—television, film projectors, slide and transparency projectors—causes some worry about the possible uncritical use of available terminal hardware. I am aware of the difficulties of console design, but in the course of the development of CAI a significant amount of attention is required to match the properties of console displays and controls to the properties of subject matter in order to design relevant conditions for learning.

In the writing of lessons, there are things to be learned from the original notions of programmed instruction. These notions concern (1) the sequencing of events to set up the increasingly precise forms of response defined as subject-matter competence, (2) the significant process of the sequencing of instruction to establish and transfer stimulus control (the expert in a subject matter makes precise responses to fine discriminations, and he is, in this sense, much more under the control of the nuances of his subject matter than is the novice), and (3) sequences that involve the systematic withdrawal of the learning supports required by the novice so that the behavior of the expert becomes increasingly self-sustaining and is maintained for long periods of time without the external support of aids and references required by the novice.

Finally, it seems useful to say that in the back of some people's minds is adaptation to something generally called learning style. This appears vaguely related to the fact that there are differences in the way people learn that are difficult to pin down operationally—analytical versus synthetic types, impulsive versus reflective types, intuitive leapers versus systematic plodders, and so on. The existence of these individual differences and kinds of instructional sequences that must be designed for them can be discovered on the basis of CAI experience—but only if instructional sequences are set up in a fashion experimental enough to allow these differences to emerge.

REFERENCES

Atkinson, R. C., and Hansen, D. N. 1966. Computer-assisted instruction in initial reading: the Stanford project. *Reading Research Quarterly* 2:5–25.

Cooley, W. W., and Glaser, R. 1968. *An information and management system for individually prescribed instruction.* Working Paper 45. Pittsburgh: Learning Research and Development Center, Univ. of Pittsburgh (in preparation).

Feurzeig, W., and Papert, S. 1968. Programming languages as a conceptual framework for teaching mathematics. Paper presented at a NATO Conference on Major Trends in Programmed Instruction Research, 13–17 May, 1968, at Nice, France.

Fried, B. D. 1967. Solving mathematical problems. In *On-line computing*, ed. W. Karplus. New York: McGraw-Hill, pp. 131–175.

Glaser, R. 1967. Adapting the elementary school curriculum to individual performance. In *Proceedings of the 1967 invitational conference on testing problems.* Princeton, N.J.: Educational Testing Service, pp. 3–36.

———. 1968. Concept learning and concept teaching. In *Research approaches to school-subject learning,* ed. R. Gagné. Itasca, Ill.: F. E. Peacock (in press).

———. 1969. Learning. In *Review of Educational Research,* 4th ed. New York: Macmillan (in press).

Glaser, R., and Ramage, W. W. 1967. The student-machine interface in instruction. *1967 IEEE International Convention Record, Part 10.* New York: Institute of Electrical and Electronic Engineers, pp. 52–59.

Groen, G. J., and Atkinson, R. C. 1966. Models for optimizing the learning process. *Psychological Bulletin* 66:309–320.

Guilford, J. P. 1967. *The nature of human intelligence.* New York: McGraw-Hill.

Judd, W., and Glaser, R. 1969. Response latency as a function of training method, information level, acquisition, and overlearning. *Journal of Educational Psychology* (in press).

Lindvall, C. M., and Bolvin, J. O. 1967. Programmed instruction in the schools: an application of programming principles in "individually prescribed instruction." In *Programmed instruction,* ed. P. Lange. The 66th Yearbook of the National Society for the Study of Education, Part II. Chicago: Univ. of Chicago Press, pp. 217–254.

Mechner, F. 1965. Science education and behavioral technology. In *Teaching machines and programmed learning, II: data and directions,* ed. R. Glaser. Washington, D.C.: Division of Audio-Visual Instruction of the National Education Association, pp. 441–507.

Resnick, L. B. 1967. *Design of an early learning curriculum.* Working Paper 16. Pittsburgh: Learning Research and Development Center, Univ. of Pittsburgh.

Smallwood, R. D. 1962. *A decision structure for teaching machines.* Cambridge, Mass.: MIT Press.

Suppes, P. 1966. Mathematical concept formation in children. *American Psychologist* 21:139–150.

Zeaman, D., and House, B. J. 1963. The role of attention in retardate discrimination learning. In *Handbook of mental deficiency,* ed. N. Ellis. New York: McGraw-Hill.

Instructional Design: Discussion

Some of the participants expressed concern about the dangers of over-systematizing instructional planning by using the detailed procedures discussed by Bunderson and Glaser. Operating strictly within their development strategies, a curriculum designer might be inclined to rule out organizations of the subject matter potentially useful for some students. Perhaps more important, the careful attention to analysis in behavioral terms may cause one to overlook vague but significant objectives. But Bunderson has allowed for creative hunches and intuitive leaps in the loose applications of his scheme. That is, the designer who has faith in an ill-defined plan may work outside the framework of the procedure described by Bunderson. And yet eventually he will have to come around to a more careful behavioral analysis when he chooses to conduct an evaluation.

Many restrictions are imposed on instructional strategies by the programming language and other aspects of the particular computer system that is available. In a given system, for example, the data available for use with instructional decision rules may be limited to a few markers, counts, and character strings and even then only for the current student. Decisions in such a limited system have to be based on relatively terse descriptions of student performance. Any actions depending on the performance of two or more students will have to be extracted by the author from a listing of performance data and entered manually into the strategy description.

For some time the facility of the computer for generating problems and other instructional material from a general rule had been excluded by the most common programming languages for CAI. Recently it is being considered seriously again. A discussion of the implications of programming languages for instructional strategies is included in the report of a recent study in which languages and supporting systems were compared (Zinn, 1969).

One of the major problems with instructional strategy is the lack of prescriptions for instructional design. Some of the participants pointed out that there is no adequate data base from which to derive prescriptions in any one curriculum area and that no generally useful prescriptive rules are found in instructional theory. Glaser has said that the prospects are poor for a major breakthrough from psychological research in the near future. For some time, curriculum designers will continue operating with the trial-and-error, cut-and-fit approach of programmed instruction. Perhaps there is some hope in the additional power provided by generative techniques, because designers will then be more likely to identify and manipulate significant parameters.

It is very interesting to explore the interaction between analysis of the instructional material and the organization or content of the subject being taught. Bunderson's comments in this regard are supported by anecdotes about instructional design influencing the content of science teaching at the University of Michigan. Some professors highly regarded in their subject areas have organized materials for teaching, have uncovered inconsistencies in the standard textbook presentations of research findings, and have then returned to the laboratory or literature to discover new information and organizations. These fresh approaches turn out to be interesting to their colleagues as well as helpful to their students by simplifying constructs for the learning tasks. When the task analysis or other steps in the design procedure fail to confirm a meaningful organization, new data are required. When the pedagogical game or simulation derived from current knowledge does not appear adequate to the students or the professor and his colleagues, the additional work necessary to improve the model constitutes an original contribution to the research literature.

Student manipulation of the subject matter recommended by Glaser certainly is an attractive approach to using the computer in teaching. It is more likely to be of immediate success because the author gives up control where he is not sure of his prescription for the student. In the best of worlds, a rather rich environment would be provided on an expensive terminal for each student, although such power is not necessary in all subject areas or with all students. Administrators should consider carefully the cost of giving these computer-based learning tools to the individual student in spite of any apparent face validity they may have for modeling and problem-solving uses.

In some situations, programming the computer to respond to the initiative of individual learners may be the best strategy. Given the ambitious objectives, the risk to personnel, and the large budget of the space program, the best strategy for ground-controller training may be to simulate with as much fidelity as possible the environment in which personnel are expected to work (see Chapter 16). Another instance that may be justified within Bunderson's category of "institutional need" is the simulated laboratory activity described by Lagowski and Lambe in Part VIII. An argument can also be made for learning tools that would not be available to students otherwise; modeling techniques and other instances of procedure writing are currently promising. Feurzeig and Papert (1968) have demonstrated that elementary school children can use programming languages effectively in mathematics and science courses where testing procedures and manipulating symbols are an essential part of the subject matter.

Participants discussed different approaches to sorting out computer and noncomputer contributions to the total learning environment. Within Bunderson's framework a justification is required but not necessarily before materials are produced for the computer. At the end of the development and evaluation one can better decide if the computer should be used instead of less expensive and more convenient modes of instruction. For example, the mathematics skills course, which was designed very carefully on an expensive computer system, perhaps now could be shifted to a noncomputer mode for more convenient use by intelligent and motivated college students. The computer contribution was mostly in materials development and testing; perhaps some of the less able and interested students benefit from computer pacing and prodding.

Glaser began in a noncomputer mode some years ago, in part for reasons of economy but also to assure that the major responsibility would remain with the classroom teacher and curriculum supervisor in the elementary school setting. As strategies for sequencing segments of material were derived from the judgments of teachers and supervisors, they were implemented on a computer as an aid to the teacher. As new procedures are understood and appear suitable for automatic processing, they are programmed for the computer. Only after this computer-aided management stage has been successful are selected exercises given to the computer for interactive instruction on line.

Using a third approach, one introduces the computer into regular course work when the expenditures appear justified among the costs of other resources such as libraries and laboratories. At the University of Michigan computer resources are allocated to schools and departments for those teaching and research activities that are ordinarily supported from general funds. Deans, chairmen, and faculty committees are deciding when and how much to spend on student learning exercises and whether to give a request for additional computer funds priority over other categories of learning resources. One participant pointed out that these decisions should have the benefit of the careful analysis and evaluation techniques described by Bunderson and Glaser; another remarked that the decisions will be made nevertheless.

REFERENCES

Feurzeig, W., and Papert, S. A. 1968. Programming languages as a conceptual framework for teaching mathematics. Paper presented at a NATO conference on major trends in programmed instruction research, 13–17 May 1968, at Nice, France.

Zinn, K. L. 1969. *Comparative study of languages for programming interactive use of computers in instruction.* Research memorandum 1469. Boston: Educom.

PART III

Optimizing Learning

An important problem in computer-assisted instruction is the development of a theory and accompanying mathematical models for optimizing learning on the basis of the student's past history. Such a theory should not rely on standard teaching heuristics but on a quantitative description of learning. Chapter 6 by Smallwood presents an optimization procedure for a general class of learning models. The major objective is to design a decision (branching) logic so that the available past history of the student, particularly his immediate past performance, can be used in some meaningful way to influence the future course of his instruction. In the particular learning model employed by Smallwood, an optimization procedure in which the minimum presentation-cost alternative is always chosen at each sequence in the instruction represents a decision policy that would be nearly 80 per cent more efficient than a fixed sequence for all students. Smallwood's procedure overcomes a serious computational obstacle in former optimization schemes.

In Chapter 7 Gregg acknowledges the importance of formalizing the decision-making procedure and making explicit just what it is that must be optimized when dealing with individualized learning. But as a critic of Smallwood's approach, he is concerned about what he regards as the inappropriateness of the learning models that are used by Smallwood. These models do not reflect the internal states of learners as revealed by information-processing analyses. Indeed, the way in which the student organizes information in short-term memory depends heavily on the way he conceives information, which differs from one learner to another. Gregg presents several examples of how the internal representation of the learning process within the individual might be formulated as an alternative approach to optimizing learning.

6

Richard D. Smallwood

Optimal Policy Regions for
Computer-directed Teaching Systems

In the past few years several significant advances in computer-aided instruction have opened the way for an evolution toward more sophisticated educational systems. Perhaps this is the time for some consideration and reappraisal of the direction for this evolution. As I see it, the primary direction for much of the current work in computer-aided instruction is toward the provision of tools that will permit the implementation of essentially classic teaching heuristics. The end result of this line of research will be a set of tools that allow the construction of computer-based teaching systems that provide a faithful mimicry of classic teaching methods.

On the other hand, we might look to the physical sciences and technologies for another possible tack to take in this evolution of educational systems. For example, we could view the past advances in CAI as individual contributions to an expanding technology, that is, as incremental advances to a cohesive set of theoretical concepts, experimental methodologies, and practical tools that together add up to an educational technology. Thus we can view the evolution of educational systems as centered about an educational technology with each new contribution having for its foundation the distilled essence of previous contributions and in turn adding its own contribution to the state of the technology. If this technology is to grow and flourish, then it must be founded on a quantitative science similar in substance to the scientific bases of other technologies. This implies the development and utilization of classes of mathematical models, optimization techniques, and other theoretical structures necessary for the growth of the technology.

The development of a technology typically arises from the repeated application of the experimental-theoretical cycle. That is, experiments to test and extend the present theoretical status of the technology are planned and conducted, and then these are followed by modifications to the theoretical structure based on the results of the experiments. This chapter will present a potential contribution to the theoretical side of this educational technology.

One of the crucial questions to be considered in the future development of computer-aided teaching systems is the extent to which the latent computational power of the machine can be used to make rational decisions on the course of the instruction. A system that included such a decision process in its operation might be termed *computer-directed* rather than *computer-aided* instruction. This discussion will focus on the development of a method for implementing such a decision process in a teaching system.

One of the discouraging problems encountered in a theoretical formulation of the decision process in a computer-directed teaching system has been the excessive computation required. If the decision process is to consider any significant number of future trajectories that the student might experience, then the computation time can become a significant limitation in operating the system. This chapter describes a technique that involves a very small amount of computation time for implementing a truly optimal decision policy in a computer-directed teaching system. Furthermore, the results are applicable to a very large class of models of human learning. As mentioned, these results represent only a theoretical contribution to the educational technology. The experimental testing and validation of these theoretical results are equally important—and much more difficult to achieve; this, then, represents only the first step toward the solution of the problem.

Decision Making in CAI: A Formulation

This section presents a general formulation of the decision problem in a tutorial computer-directed computer system. This formulation is not new; it has been described in one form or another previously (Groen and Atkinson, 1966; Smallwood, 1962, 1967). It is presented here to provide a general perspective for viewing the results of succeeding sections.

The first question we should ask is "Why should decision processes be incorporated into CAI systems?" The answer to this question follows from the natural desire to develop a teaching system that will detect and respond to the differences exhibited by individual students. Thus we should like to design a decision logic (sometimes called a branching logic) into our CAI system so that the available past history of the student can be used in some meaningful way to influence the future course of the student's instruction. To begin then, let us imagine a hypothetical student with a particular history for whom a decision policy is required. This decision policy will be encoded into the computer teaching system and will prescribe for the system what alternative instruction should be provided for this student and for other students with different past histories. The role of the past history in the decision process is extremely critical, for this quantity represents a parameterization of the available information about the student that will determine how well the system adapts to the individual learning characteristics of the student. We shall denote the past history of our hypothetical student by h and shall have more to say on this subject later.

The existence of the decision process within the teaching system implies that there must be a set of alternative courses of action available for dealing with our hypothetical student. Because this set of instructional alternatives will typically be dependent on the student's current status and, furthermore, because we have agreed to represent the student's current status in the form of his past history h, then the set of available instructional alternatives for the student will be denoted by $A(h)$.

For each of the alternative presentations of the material there will typically be a question or set of questions to test the student's comprehension of the material. The student's responses to these questions provide additional information that we must incorporate into his past history to guide the future course of the instruction. Because each of the possible responses that might be elicited from the student will have a different impact on the student's updated history, it is necessary to consider all possible responses explicitly. Thus we shall assume that for each possible instructional alternative there is a finite set of possible student responses, and we shall denote this set of responses by $R(a)$, where a is the particular instructional alternative from $A(h)$ that has been presented to the student.

With this representation of the instructional alternatives and student responses we can illustrate the complete decision problem with the decision tree shown in Figure 6–1. As shown in the figure, for a student with a past history h there is a set of instructional alternatives, each of which may produce a sample from the set of possible student responses. At the conclusion of this response there will be a new past history h' and a new decision to be made, and this decision-response cycle may extend a considerable distance into the future until the instruction is terminated. The problem then is to calculate the optimal instructional alternative at each decision node, taking into account the possible effects that this may have on the future course of the instruction. A brief look at Figure 6–1 will show the tremendous number of possible student trajectories through the

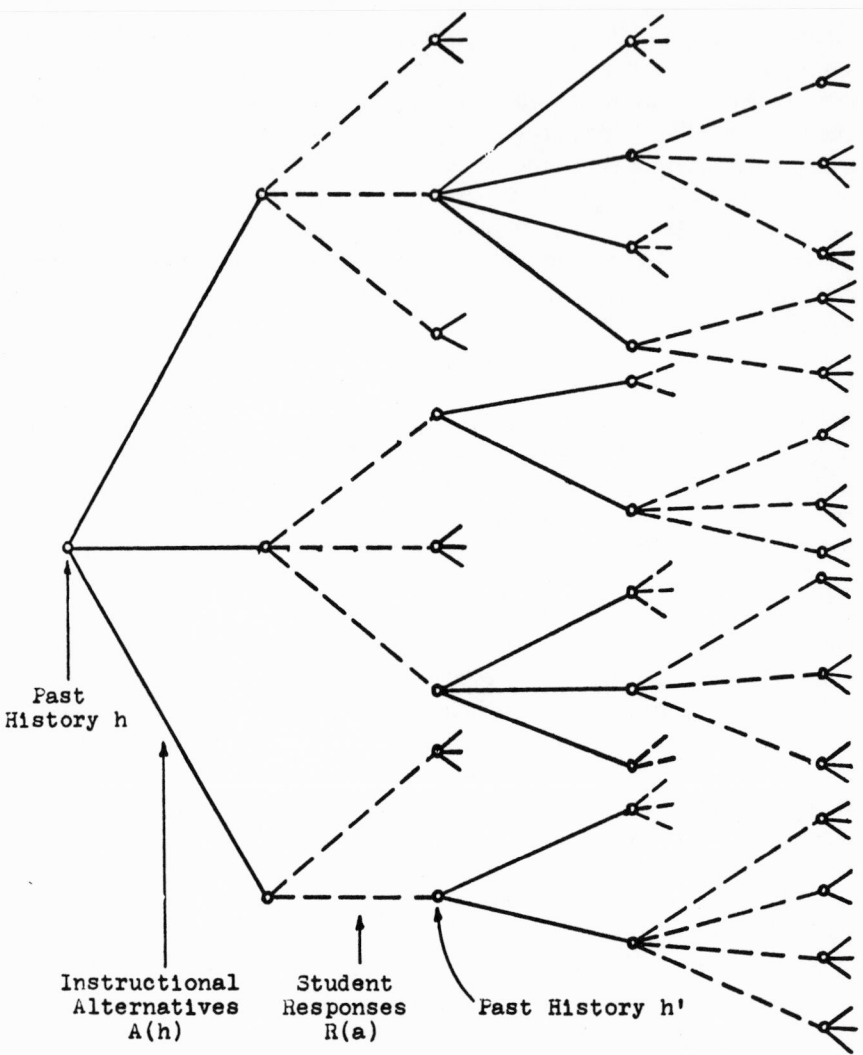

Figure 6–1.
Decision tree.

decision tree that must be considered if all possible paths are to be accounted for in the calculation. For example, if there are five instructional alternatives at each decision node in the tree and if there are two possible responses by the student for each instructional alternative, and if we desire to calculate the optimal instructional alternative based on those paths by the student that extend ten presentations into the future, then this will require the consideration of 10 billion possible student trajectories for each decision. This is clearly an infeasible solution to the problem. This chapter will propose an alternative way of viewing this decision problem that will eliminate all but the most trivial of calculations for each decision in the course of a student's instruction.

To continue with the formulation of the decision process, the selection of one of the instructional alternatives at a decision point requires a criterion for appraising the relative value of each alternative. More explicitly, we shall need a quantitative representation of the purposes of the instruction as well as the relative costs of alternative presentations. For our purposes here we shall assume the existence of an utility function $u_a(k,h)$ that specifies the immediate value that is accrued if alternative a is presented to a student with past history h and the kth response is elicited. This function describes the immediate rewards (or costs) that are associated with each particular stage in the decision tree of Figure 6–1. There is the additional question of the terminal rewards (or costs) that are accrued by terminating the instruction with the student in a particular status. For this purpose we assume the existence of a terminal utility function $u_o(h)$ that describes the utility associated with terminating the instruction for a student with a past history h. A particular example of such a utility structure will be illustrated in a later section.

In considering the different possible student trajectories in Figure 6–1, we must weight the utilities associated with each trajectory by the probability that the student will in fact traverse that path in the decision tree. This requires a model of student behavior that allows the calculation of the probability that a student will produce a particular response to the presentation of an instructional alternative. Thus we assume the existence of a mathematical model for calculating the probability $p(k|h,a)$ that a student with past history h who has been presented instructional alternative a will respond with the kth response [where $k \in R(a)$ and $a \in A(h)$].

These definitions lead directly to an equation that defines the maximum expected total utility $v(h)$ that can be achieved for a student with a particular past history h. To write this equation, consider all possible responses that a student might produce for a particular instructional alternative. For each such response there will be an immediate utility that is accrued plus the contribution from all future instruction that will follow with the updated past history h'. Thus a recursive equation for the expected total utility is

$$v(h) = \max_{a \in A(h)} \left[\sum_{k \in R(a)} p(k|h) \, [u_a(k,h) + v(h')] \right] \qquad (1)$$

In this equation we assume the existence of a rule for updating the student's past history; that is, h' represents the past history associated with the student who had a past history h, who was given alternative a, and who responded with the kth response.

The formulation of the decision problem represented by Equation (1) is a typical dynamic programming recursive equation. Previous works have formulated the decision process in a computer-directed teaching system in a similar way (Suppes, 1964; Groen and Atkinson, 1966; Smallwood, 1967). In particular, the reader is referred to the excellent review article by Groen and Atkinson (1966).

The implementation of an actual teaching system with a decision process based on this formulation was attempted in 1961 (Smallwood, 1962). For this simple system the number of instructional alternatives at each decision point ranged from one to four, while the number of possible responses ranged from two to five. In terms of the decision tree in Figure 6–1, the calculation of the optimal alternative at each decision node was carried out by extending the calculations in Equation (1) three stages into the future. The weakest component in that early system was the mathematical model used for the calculation of student response probabilities. Also, the particular choice of past history parameterization for the student was very simple and did not realize the full capabilities of the system. In the next section we shall consider a very general class of models that might be used for describing student learning behavior. The incorporation of this class of models into the decision process will alleviate many of the shortcomings of that earlier system.

A Class of Models

The first step in formulating a model is to attempt an explicit description of our intuitive understanding of the phenomenon. One such description of the instructional process defines it as the systematic attempt to change the student's internal state of knowledge about the material being presented. Suppose now that it were possible to describe these internal knowledge states as a finite number of entities, each of which represents one possible internal state of knowledge that a student may occupy during his course of instruction on the subject material. We shall refer to these entities as states, and it seems reasonable at this point to assume that they are mutually exclusive and exhaustive.

Within the limits of this representation, the instructional process can be viewed as the selection of alternative mechanisms for causing a student to make transitions from one internal state to another. These transitions will seldom be deterministic; that is, a particular instructional alternative will generally cause only a transition from one state to another state with a certain probability. Thus we define as a parameter of the model the quantity

$t_{ij}(a)$; this is the probability that a student occupying the ith state will make the transition to the jth state if he is presented with the material associated with instructional alternative a.

With this description for the influence of instructional material on a student's internal state of knowledge, the question arises, "How can we gain access to information concerning the internal state of the student?" The mechanism for accomplishing this, of course, is to ask the student questions, the answers to which will depend on the student's internal state of knowledge about the material. Thus if we assume that there is a discrete set of responses that a student will give for a particular instructional alternative a, then we can model the relationship between the student's internal state and his response. For this purpose we define the probability $r_{jk}(a)$ that a student who is presented instructional alternative a and who is presently occupying the jth internal state will give the kth response to the question associated with the presentation of the material. In this definition there is the explicit assumption that the student's response is dependent only on his internal knowledge state. Figure 6–2 is a graphic representation of this class of models.

Now we must consider what additional parameters of the student's past history should be incorporated into the decision process as a result of this model. If we somehow were given access to information concerning the true state of the student, then this would be a very valuable component in the parameterization of the student's past history. Because we seldom, if ever, have perfect information about the student's state, the logical component for the student's past history is the current state of information about the student's internal knowledge state. We can represent this state of information as a set of probabilities $[\pi_1, \pi_2, \ldots, \pi_i]$, where π_i is the probability that the student presently occupies the ith state. If this set of probabilities is included as a parameter of the student's past history, then we can visualize this set of numbers changing as the student is presented with various instructional alternatives throughout the course of his instruction and as his responses to various questions are used to update the state of information about his progress.

If a model of the type presented here is to be used in the decision process in a teaching system, that is, if a model of this type is to be used in calculating $v(h)$ in Equation (1), then two analytical results are required from the model. The first of these is a procedure for calculating the response probability $p(k|h,a)$, and the second is the mechanism for updating the past history $h = [\pi_1, \pi_2, \ldots]$ as a result of presenting an instructional alternative and observing a particular student response.

To describe the answers to these two demands, let us assume that for a particular student with past history $h = [\pi_1, \pi_2, \ldots]$ we are considering

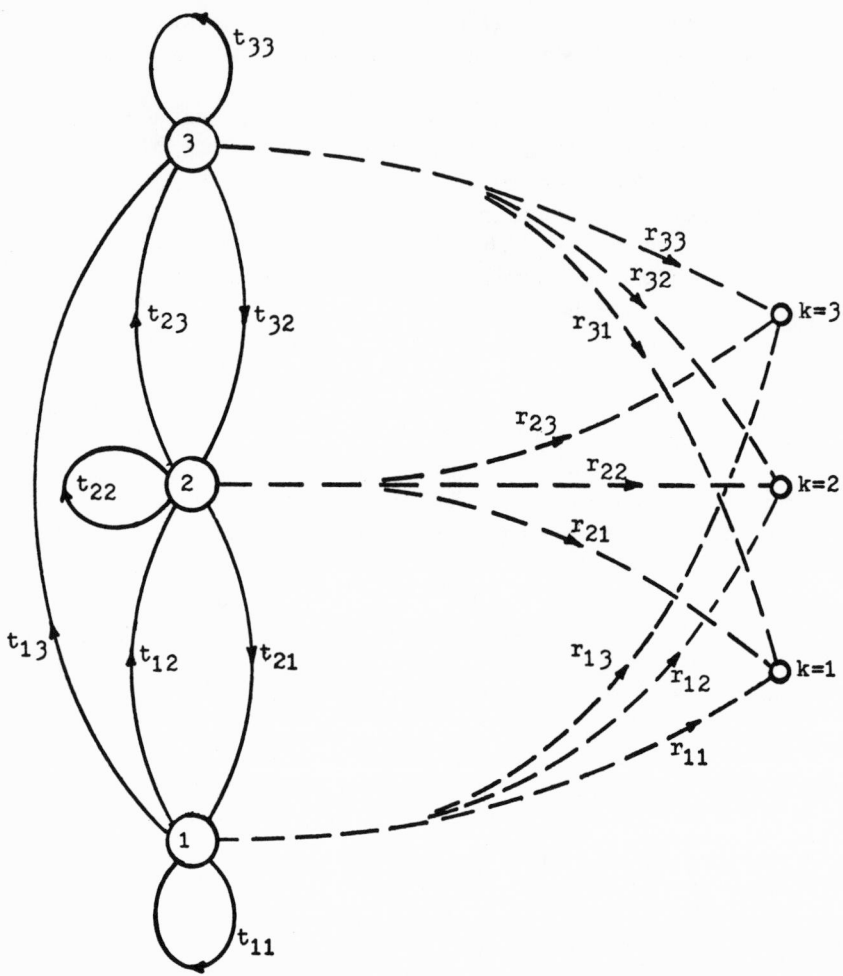

Figure 6–2.
Three-state/three-response model.

presenting instructional alternative a. This instructional alternative will consist of some simple textual material followed by a question to test the student's comprehension of the material. We shall further assume that any transitions of the student's internal state occur prior to his response.[1]

We shall consider the response probability $p(k|h,a)$ first. This quantity can easily be calculated by considering all possible states that the student

1. This is the so-called preresponse transition case (Smallwood, 1967). Similar results can easily be calculated for the postresponse transition case where state transitions occur after the student's response.

might occupy after presentation of the textual material. For this quantity the application of elementary probability operations yields

$$p(k|h,a) = \sum_i \sum_j \text{Pr } \{\text{prior state} = i, \text{ succeeding state} = j, k\text{th response}|$$
$$h, \text{ give alternative } a\}$$
$$= \sum_i \sum_j \pi_i t_{ij}(a) r_{jk}(a) \tag{2}$$

The procedure for calculating the updated state probabilities $[\pi'_1, \pi'_2, \ldots]$ can be derived in a somewhat analogous way. Let us suppose that a particular student with a past history $h = [\pi_1, \pi_2, \ldots]$ has been given instructional alternative a and has given the kth response to the question associated with that alternative. The updated state probability, π'_j, can be written through a simple application of Bayes' rule plus some elementary operations as

$$\pi'_j = \sum_i \text{Pr } \{\text{prior state} = i, \text{ succeeding state} = j|k\text{th response}, h,$$
$$\text{give alternative } a\}$$

$$= \frac{\sum_i \text{Pr } \{\text{prior state} = i, \text{ succeeding state} = j, k\text{th response}|h, \text{give alternative } a\}}{p(k|h,a)}$$

$$= \frac{\sum_i \pi_i t_{ij}(a) r_{jk}(a)}{\sum_{i,j} \pi_i t_{ij}(a) r_{jk}(a)} \tag{3}$$

Thus this class of models provides a very simple mechanism for calculating the response probabilities as well as updating the past history. In the next section we shall show how this model can easily be incorporated into the optimal decision calculation of Equation (1).

The Optimization Problem

In a tutorial computer-aided teaching system it is often desirable that each student be exposed to certain basic information even though the actual presentation of this information may take on many forms. The general branching network shown in Figure 6–3 illustrates a very general and flexible technique for achieving this result. In the general branching network each student starts the instruction at the first level. On the basis of the initial evaluation of the student's past history, one of the instructional alternatives leaving the first level is presented to the student. Each of these instructional alternatives will be assumed to consist of a presentation of some textual material followed by a question designed to test the student's

LEVEL

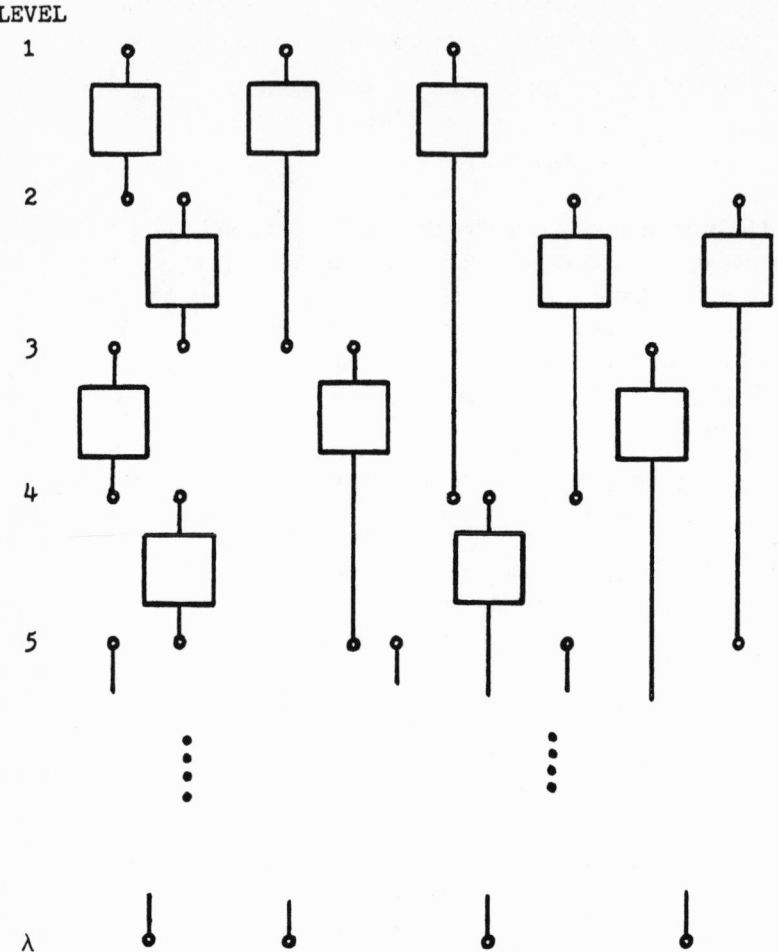

Figure 6–3.
General branching network.

comprehension of the material. If the student responds with the correct answer to this question, then he is placed at the final level corresponding to that alternative. On the other hand, if the student's response is not correct, then we shall assume the existence of some assignment rule that places the student at some level appropriate to that response. In other words, we shall assume the existence of a function $l(m,n,k)$ that determines the next level for a student who responded with the kth response to the nth instructional alternative leaving the mth level. After the student has been assigned this new level, then, of course, a new decision calculation must be carried out to determine which of the instructional alternatives leaving the student's level should be presented next.

Given such a general branching network for a set of subject materials, it seems feasible that one of the models discussed in the preceding section might very well describe the student's learning dynamics while progressing through the instruction defined by the various alternative presentations in the branching network. Thus let us assume that such a model does indeed exist and that there is a set of transition probabilities $t_{ij}(a)$ and response probabilities $r_{jk}(a)$ for each of the instructional alternatives in the branching network, that is, for each of the blocks in Figure 6–3. The problem then is to use the optimization procedure in Equation (1) with this formal structure to calculate, on the basis of the student's past history, the optimal alternative at each level in the branching network.

To accomplish this task, we must define the student's past history. For the general branching network of Figure 6–3 and a mathematical model of the form in the preceding section the appropriate parameterization of the student's past history is his current level in the general branching network and the current state probabilities. In other words, we let $h = [m, \pi_1, \pi_2, \ldots]$, where m is the student's current level in the general branching network. For a student at the mth level who has been presented the nth instructional alternative leaving that level and who has responded with the kth response, the updated past history is $h' = [l(m,n,k), \pi'_1, \pi'_2, \ldots]$ where π'_j is calculated according to Equation (3).

The one remaining component for the optimization is the utility structure. One reasonable description of a utility structure, and the one that will be used here, defines a presentation cost for each of the blocks in the general branching network and also defines a terminal cost that is dependent on the student's terminal state when he finishes the instruction at the last level. Thus we define the presentation cost for the nth instructional alternative leaving the mth level as c_{mn}.[2] The terminal cost at the conclusion of the instruction is just $\sum_i \gamma_i \pi_i$, where γ_i is the cost of terminating the instruction with the student in the ith state. Because this utility structure has been postulated in terms of cost rather than values, we must transform the value formulation of Equation (1) into a cost formulation. This is easily done by multiplying Equation (1) by (-1) and replacing the max by min. For this cost formulation we can define the quantity $w_m(\Pi)$ as the total expected optimal cost for a student who is at the mth level and whose vector of state probabilities is $\Pi = [\pi_1, \pi_2, \ldots]$. The substitution

2. This presentation cost can also be made dependent on the student's response with no loss in applicability of the results. This generality will not be included in this section for the sake of notational convenience.

of these definitions into the general formulation of Equation (1) yields the following recursive equation for this more specific problem:

$$w_m(\Pi) = \min_n \left[\sum_k p(k|h,n) \left[c_{mn} + w_l(\Pi') \right] \right]$$

$$= \min_n \left[c_{mn} + \sum_k p(k|h,n) w_l(\Pi') \right] \qquad (4)$$

where m denotes the mth instructional alternative leaving the mth level.

In Equation (4) the subscript l is the assignment function $l(m,n,k)$ and the elements of the updated probability vector Π' are calculated from Equation (3). The cost associated with the terminal level in the branching network is, of course, just

$$w_\lambda(\Pi) = \sum_i \gamma_i \pi_i \qquad (5)$$

where λ is the last level in the branching network.

Appendix A uses the formulation in Equations (4) and (5) to show that the quantity $w_m(\Pi)$ can have the following relatively simple form:

$$w_m(\Pi) = \min_n \min_i \left[\sum_j \alpha_{nij}^{(m)} \pi_j \right] \qquad (6)$$

where n ranges over the set of instructional alternatives leaving the mth level and i is simply an integer valued index for each instructional alternative. With this simple expression for the minimal expected cost, the optimal decision policy for all student past histories can be written very simply:

Select the instructional alternative n for which the

quantity $\min_j \left[\sum_j \alpha_{nij}^{(m)} \pi_j \right]$ is minimum $\qquad (7)$

After the values for $\alpha_{nij}^{(m)}$ have been calculated, the implementation of this decision policy is very simple. The extensive searches throughout the decision tree have been eliminated through the prior calculation of a set of optimal policy regions that uniquely determine the optimal policy as a function of the student's past history.

Appendix B describes an iterative technique for calculating the values of the α coefficients in Equation (6).

To test these ideas, a simple but nontrivial example was constructed and the iterative technique of Appendix B was used to calculate the optimal policy regions. The mathematical model that was used is the simple two-state model shown in Figure 6–4. As can be seen, this model has only two parameters associated with it, the single transition probability t and the single response probability r. This is the simple one-element model that has

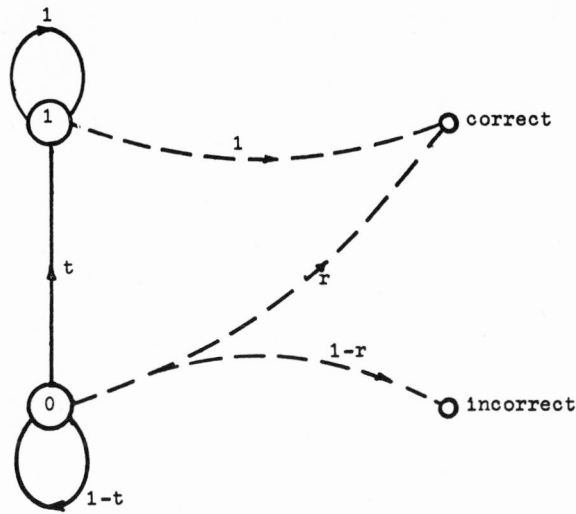

Figure 6–4.
One-element model.

been considered so extensively in the literature (Atkinson et al., 1965; Karush and Dear, 1966, 1967; Matheson, 1964; Smallwood, 1967). The zero state in this model is generally associated with the unconditioned or unlearned state, and the "one" state with the conditioned or learned state. There are two parameters for this model: The transition probability t is the probability that a student in the zero state will make the transition to the one state on a particular presentation of the instructional alternative, and the response probability r is the probability that a student in the zero state will still respond with the correct answer (this is often referred to as the guessing probability).

Figure 6–5 shows the sixteen-level branching network that was used for the example. In Figure 6–5 the values for the transition probability t and the presentation cost c_{mn} are shown within the rectangle representing that instructional alternative. The outputs from each block that exit from the side of the rectangle represent the level assignment function for incorrect responses to the question associated with that instructional alternative. The response probability r was equal to 0.2 for all the alternatives. The terminal costs γ_0 and γ_1 were set equal to 30 and 0, respectively. (There is an interesting physical interpretation for the quantity γ_0 in this formulation of the problem. This quantity is simply the maximum amount that we are willing to pay in order to achieve the transition of a student from the zero state to the one state.)

LEVEL

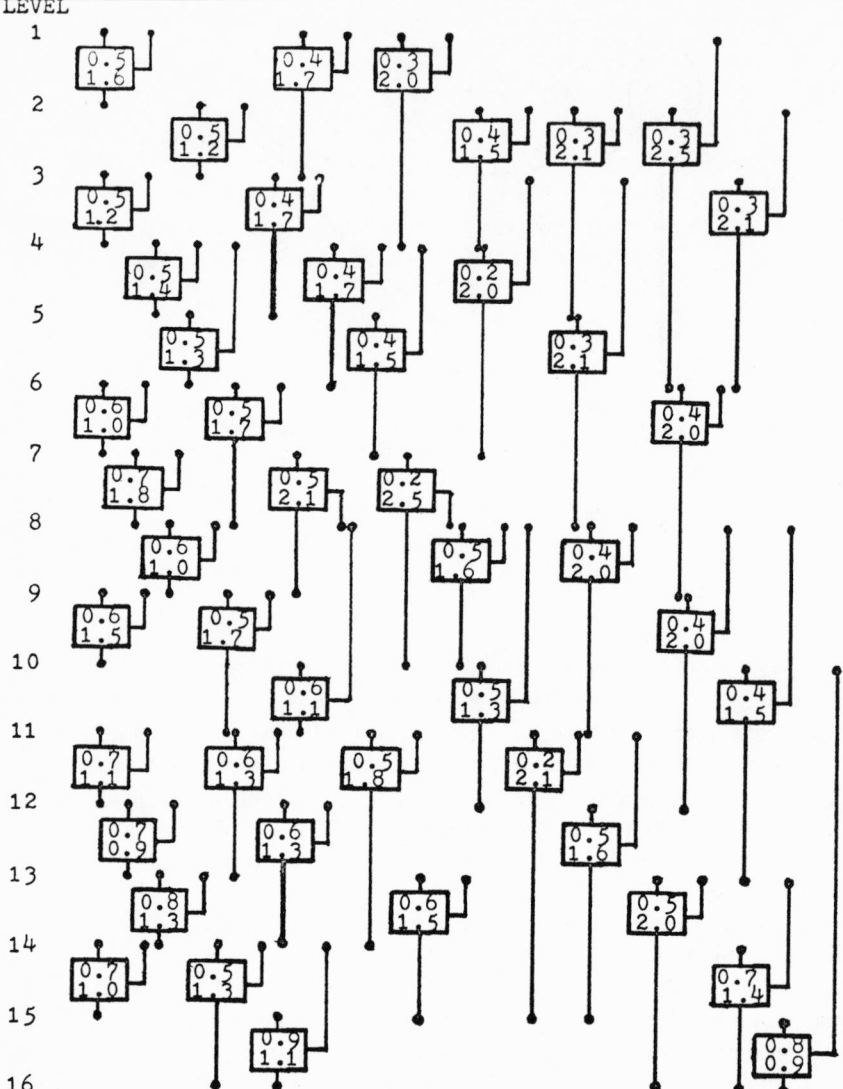

Figure 6–5.
Branching network for the example.

When the iterative procedure described in Appendix B was applied to this problem, approximately eleven iterations were necessary for convergence of the optimal policy regions. This optimal policy is shown in Figure 6–6. The optimal policy region for each of the instructional alterna-

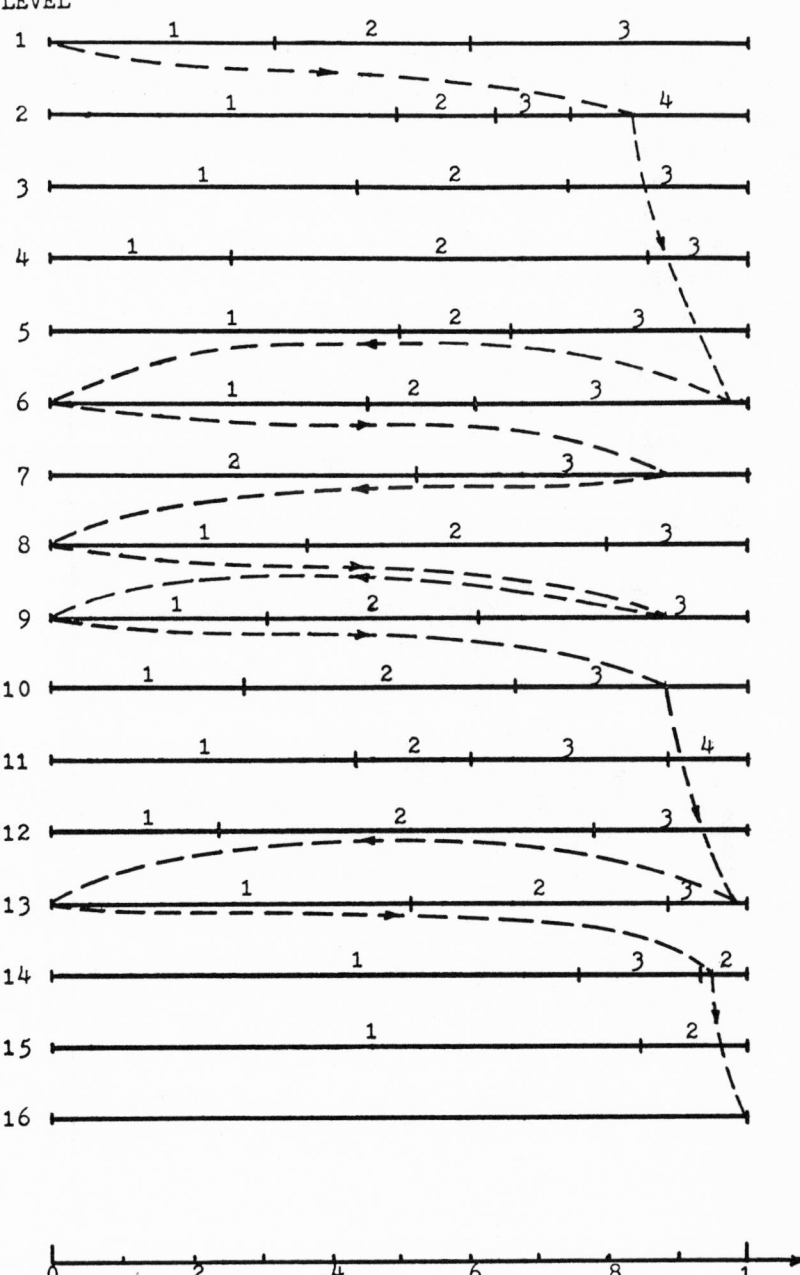

Figure 6–6.
Optimal policy regions for the example.

tives is plotted as a function of the state probability π_1. Some typical trajectories that students might take through the general branching network are also plotted.

It is interesting to consider the speed of convergence of the iterative process. Figure 6–7 shows the total expected instructional cost starting at the first level for several of the decision policies that were calculated during the eleven iterations. As can be seen, the iterative process converges quite rapidly in terms of the total expected cost function. As an illustration of the efficacy of such an optimization procedure, Figure 6–7 also shows the total expected cost for a student for whom the minimal presentation cost alternative is always chosen. As illustrated in Figure 6–7, this policy results in a total expected instructional cost that is 60 to 80 per cent higher than the optimal policy.

Summary and Conclusions

As indicated in the introduction to this chapter, the results presented here represent only the first (and probably the easiest) step in an evolutionary sequence of theoretical-experimental advances to the educational technology. This chapter presents an optimization procedure for a general class of learning models; the procedure essentially eliminates the tedious costly calculations associated with a straightforward decision-tree optimization calculation. Hopefully, later contributions to the educational technology will explore some of the experimental implications of these results. Specifically, much work remains to be done on the validation of models and more experiments must be conducted to test the efficacy of optimal decision processes in computer-directed teaching systems. The potential benefits of educational systems that truly adapt to the individual learning characteristics of the students will justify the allocation of future research resources toward these goals.

Appendix A: *The Optimal Policy Cost Function*

The following recursive equation was derived for the optimal policy cost function for a student with past history $h = [m, \pi_1, \pi_2, \ldots]$:

$$w_m(\Pi) = \min_n \left[c_{mn} + \sum_k p(k|h,n) \, w_l(\Pi') \right] \qquad (4)$$

where n is the number of the instructional alternative leaving the mth level. This appendix will show that Equation (4) is consistent with a solution of the form

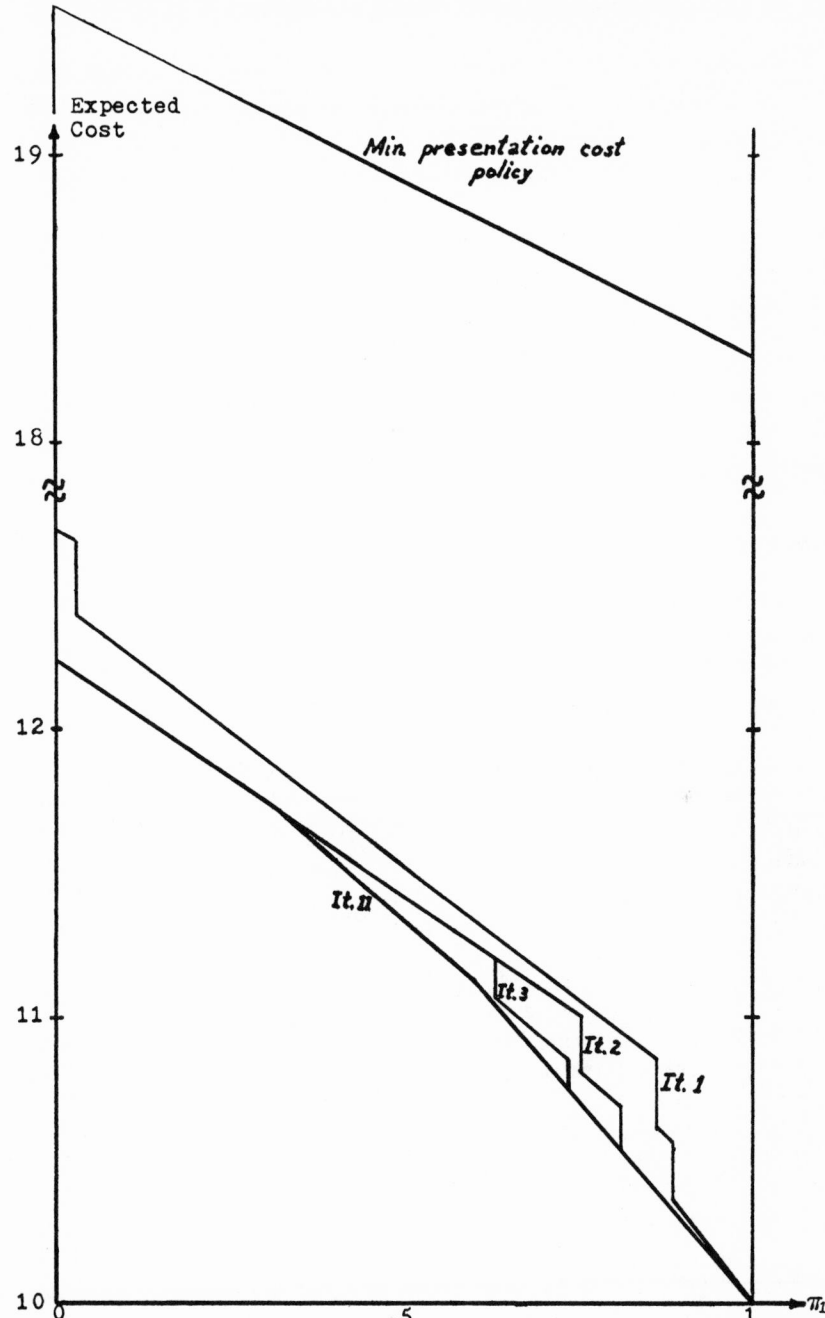

Figure 6–7.
Expected first level instructional cost for several iterated decision policies.

$$w_m(\Pi) = \min_n \min_g \left[\sum_j \alpha^{(m)}_{ngj} \pi_j \right] \tag{8}$$

First of all, the two quantities $p(k|h,n)$ and π_j' in Equation (4) can be written directly from Equations (2) and (3):

$$p(k|h,n) = \sum_i \sum_j \pi_i t_{ij}(a) r_{jk}(a) \tag{9}$$

$$\pi_j' = \frac{\sum_j \pi_i t_{ij}(a) r_{jk}(a)}{\sum_{i,j} \pi_i t_{ij}(a) r_{jk}(a)} = \frac{1}{p(k|h,n)} \sum_i \pi_i t_{ij}(a) r_{jk}(a) \tag{10}$$

where a represents the nth instructional alternative leaving the mth level. Now if we assume that $w_l(\pi')$ on the right-hand side of Equation (4) is of the form shown in Equation (8), then the substitution of π_j' and $w_l(\pi')$ into Equation (4) yields

$$w_m(\Pi) = \min_n \left[c_{mn} + \sum_k p(k|h,n) \min_{n'} \min_g \sum_j \alpha^{(l)}_{n'gj} \frac{\sum_i \pi_i t_{ij}(a) r_{jk}(a)}{p(k|h,n)} \right] \tag{11}$$

where n' refers to the n'th instructional alternative leaving the new level $l(m,n,k)$. Now, because the response probability $p(k|h,n)$ is independent of n' and g, this quantity can be canceled in the final term of Equation (11) to give

$$w_m(\Pi) = \min_n \left[c_{mn} + \sum_k \min_{n'} \min_g \sum_j \alpha^{(l)}_{n'gj} \sum_i \pi_i t_{ij}(a) r_{jk}(a) \right]$$

$$= \min_n \left[c_{mn} + \sum_k \min_{n'} \min_g \sum_i \pi_i \sum_j \alpha^{(l)}_{n'gj} t_{ij}(a) r_{jk}(a) \right] \tag{12}$$

For each set of state probabilities $\Pi = [\pi_1, \pi_2, \ldots]$ there will be a set of indices $S(\Pi) = [n_1', g_1, n_2', \ldots, n_k', g_k, \ldots]$ that satisfy the last two minimizations in Equation (12). In other words, for each value of Π we define n_k' and g_k as the two indices that satisfy the minimizations in Equation (12) for the kth response, and $S(\Pi)$ is the set of these indices. Furthermore, the number of possible such index sets will be finite; and so if we were to investigate the space of possible values for the state probabilities, we would find this space divided into regions, each with its own value for the index set $S(\Pi)$. For the sake of this development, we shall define an index over these regions; that is, we shall let b denote the bth region in the space of state probabilities and $S_b(\Pi)$ the set of indices corresponding to this region.

Now, by the definition of this index set, we can rewrite Equation (12) as

$$w_m(\Pi) = \min_n \left[c_{mn} + \min_b \sum_i \pi_i \sum_k \sum_j \alpha^{(l)}_{n_k' g_k j} t_{ij}(a) r_{jk}(a) \right] \tag{13}$$

where n_k' and g_k are elements of the bth index set and h ranges over the possible index sets S_b, corresponding to the various regions in the space of state probabilities.

And finally, by using the fact that the sum of the state probabilities must be unity we can move c_{mn} inside the summation to give

$$w_m(\Pi) = \min_n \min_b \left[\sum_i \pi_i \left(c^{mn} + \sum_k \sum_j \alpha^{(l)}_{n'g\ j}\ t_{ij}(a) r_{jk}(a) \right) \right] \quad (14)$$

Equation (4) is of the same form as Equation (8), with

$$\alpha^{(m)}_{nbi} = c_{mn} + \sum_k \sum_j \alpha^{(l)}_{n'g\ j}\ t_{ij}(a) r_{jk}(a) \quad (15)$$

Thus we have shown that an optimal policy cost function of the form shown in Equation (8) is consistent with the recursive equation of Equation (4). Of course, the terminal cost function in Equation (5) is also in this form, and so the argument is complete.

Because the optimal instructional alternative is just the one that minimizes the cost function, it follows that the α's that determine $w_m(\Pi)$ can also be used to prescribe the optimal policy as described in Equation (7).

Appendix B: *The Calculation of Optimal Policy Regions*

This appendix describes an iterative scheme for calculating the optimal policy cost function $w_m(\Pi)$. The basic equation defining the iterative process is very similar to Equation (4): If $w^{(z)}_m(\Pi)$ is the optimal policy cost function after the zth iteration, then we define the process by

$$w^{(z+1)}_m(\Pi) = \min_n \left[c_{mn} + \sum_k p(k|h,n) w^{(z)}_l\ (\Pi') \right] \quad (16)$$

for $z \geq 0$. The process is started by assuming an initial value for $w^{(0)}_m(\Pi)$:

$$w^{(0)}_m(\Pi) = \sum_j \alpha^{(m)}_{oj} \pi_j \quad (17)$$

where the $\alpha^{(m)}_{oj}$'s are to be specified later. Of course, the terminal cost function will always be equal to

$$w^{(z)}_\lambda(\Pi) = \sum_i \gamma_i \pi_i \qquad \text{for all } z \quad (18)$$

where λ is the terminal level of the branching network.

According to the form for $w_m(\Pi)$ shown in Equation (6), a convenient method for specifying the function is by several sets of α's—one set for each possible combination of n and g in Equation (6). Each iteration then amounts to using the previous sets of α's to calculate new sets of α's for each level. The complete iteration process thus consists of the following steps:

1. Set up the initial values of the α's for each level.
2. For each level m search through the space of possible state probabilities Π and find all those sets of α's that, on the basis of the α's calculated on the previous iteration, determine the value of $w^{(z)}_m(\Pi)$.

3. Check to see if the new values of the α's are sufficiently close to the previous ones to justify stopping the iteration process; if not, return to step 2.

One possible method for carrying out step 2 is first to find the sets of α's at several points throughout the space of state probabilities, for example, at the points defined by $\pi_1 = 1$, $\pi_2 = 1$, $\pi_3 = 1$, ... The intersection of the hyperplanes defined by these sets of α's, $\sum_i \alpha_{ngi}^{(m)} \pi_i$, will generally determine one or more additional points in the space of state probabilities, and the α's for these additional points can be added to the list of α's for the level under consideration. This process continues until there are no intersections of the hyperplanes that yield a new set of α's for the level under consideration.

This process of finding a new set of α's for a particular point Π in the state probability space is not a difficult one. Equation (12) can be used to find the appropriate values of n, n'_k, and g_k, and then Equation (15) can be used in the actual calculation of the α's.

The proof of convergence for this iteration process proceeds by induction. Suppose that $w_m^{(z)}(\Pi) < w_m^{(z-1)}(\Pi)$ for all $m < \lambda$ and all Π. Then, because $p(k|h,n) \geq 0$, from Equation (16) we have

$$w_m^{(z+1)}(\Pi) < \min_n \left[c_{mn} + \sum_k p(k|h,n)\, w_m^{(z-1)}(\Pi') \right] = w_m^{(z)}(\Pi) \qquad (19)$$

Thus, if we can find an initial set of α's such that $w_m^{(1)}(\Pi) < w_m^{(0)}(\Pi)$, then the sequence of iterations will yield a monotonically decreasing sequence $[w_m^{(1)}(\Pi),\ w_m^{(2)}(\Pi),\ .\ .\ .]$ bounded below by $\min_n [c_{mn}]$, and this will prove convergence.

The first iteration of the process yields

$$w_m^{(1)}(\Pi) = \min_n \left[c_{mn} + \sum_k p(k|h,n) \sum_j \alpha_{oj}^{(l)} \pi'_j \right] \quad \text{for } 1 \leq m < \lambda \qquad (20)$$

where we have substituted Equation (17) into Equation (16) with $z = 0$. The problem now is to find a set of values for the α_{oj}'s such that the expression in Equation (20) is less than $\sum_i \alpha_{oi}^{(m)} \pi_i$ for all Π.

If we substitute π'_j from Equation (10) into Equation (20), we have

$$w_m^{(1)}(\Pi) = \min_n \left[c_{mn} + \sum_i \pi_i \sum_{j,k} \alpha_{oj}^{(l)} t_{ij}(a) r_{jk}(a) \right]$$

$$= \min_n \left[\sum_i \pi_i \left(c_{mn} + \sum_{j,k} \alpha_{oj}^{(l)} t_{ij}(a) r_{jk}(a) \right) \right] \qquad (21)$$

Now $w_m^{(1)}(\Pi)$ will be less than $\sum_i \alpha_{oi}^{(m)} \pi_i$ for all Π if there is some instructional alternative, n, for which

$$\alpha_{oi}^{(m)} = c_{mn} + \epsilon + \sum_{j,k} \alpha_{oj}^{(l)} t_{ij}(a) r_{jk}(a) \tag{22}$$

where $\epsilon > 0$. Thus, if Equation (22) is satisfied for some $\epsilon > 0$, the condition $w_m^{(1)}(\text{II}) < w_m^{(0)}(\text{II})$ will be true, and convergence of the iterative process is proved.

It can be shown that the set of simultaneous linear equations in Equation (22) will always have a positive solution as long as the quantities $(c_{mn} + \epsilon)$ are positive. Thus we can be assured of convergence of the iteration process if we select for each level m an instructional alternative with $c_{mn} > 0$ and then solve Equation (22) for the starting α's. Of course, in most practical situations the solution of these equations will not be necessary; some reasonable set of initial α's will usually suffice.

In practice there is a slight modification of step 2 in the iterative process that yields somewhat faster convergence. For this modified version of step 2, we start with the next to last level $(\lambda - 1)$ and work backward. In addition in the calculations of $w_m(\text{II})$, we use the values of the α's *already calculated during the present iteration when calculating* w_l (II') for any l greater than m.

REFERENCES

Atkinson, R. C., Bower, G. H., and Crothers, E. J. 1965. *An introduction to mathematical learning theory*. New York: Wiley, Chap. 3.

Groen, G. J., and Atkinson, R. C. 1966. Models for optimizing the learning process. *Psychological Bulletin* 66:309–320.

Karush, W., and Dear, R. E. 1966. Optimum stimulus presentation strategy for a stimulus sampling model of learning. *Journal of Mathematical Psychology* 3:19–47.

———. 1967. Optimal strategy for item presentation in a learning process. *Management Science* 13:773–785.

Matheson, J. E. 1964. *Optimal teaching procedures derived from mathematical learning models*. Report CCS–2. Stanford, Calif.: Department of Engineering-Economic Systems, Stanford Univ.

Smallwood, R. D. 1962. *A decision structure for teaching machines*. Cambridge, Mass.: MIT Press.

———. 1967. *Quantitative methods in computer-directed teaching systems*. Stanford, Calif.: Department of Engineering-Economic Systems, Stanford Univ.

Suppes, P. 1964. Problems of optimization in learning a list of simple items. In *Human Judgment and Optimality,* eds. M. W. Shelly and G. L. Bryan. New York: Wiley, pp. 116–126.

7

Lee W. Gregg

Optimal Policies or Wise Choices?
A Critique of Smallwood's Optimization
Procedure

An exciting prospect for the field of computer-aided instruction is envisaged in Smallwood's formulation of a tutorial, computer-directed teaching system. The computer's role as a decision maker selecting alternative items to create an optimal pathway for individualized learning is a demanding part for the ingenue to play. Yet this is the direction that seems right if we are to realize the potential of the computer as a tool in educational practice. In formalizing the decision-making procedure and making explicit just what it is that he wishes to optimize, Smallwood has provided a basis for examining the feasibility of using computers in more powerful and responsible ways.

The issues center on the use of learning models and the description of past histories in terms of internal states of the learner. If there is any objection to the strategy implied by Smallwood's proposal, it is only that a disproportionate amount of research time might be spent in developing optimization methods for a restricted class of presentation methods at the expense of efforts to understand those issues that appear to be more fundamental. Certainly research necessary to test the efficiency of various presentation strategies will very quickly point up the strengths and weaknesses of the dynamic programming optimizations. There are, however, several results already available that suggest potential hazards in attempting to apply the methods. Groen and Atkinson (1966) showed that the single-operator linear model makes the entire response history redundant because response probabilities are completely determined by the number of times items are presented. The optimal presentation strategy is to present items an equal number of times in a random order, the standard procedure in a paired-associate learning experiment. If differential costs are associated with the presentation of different items and if there is a constraint on the total time available for presenting items, this result seems to say that we teach whatever is cheapest to teach—hardly a useful basis for establishing educational goals. Groen and Atkinson go on to consider the one-element, all-or-none model and to demonstrate the application of dynamic programming techniques in a multistage process of the same sort proposed by Smallwood. These authors comment on the problems that arise when the internal states are not observable. In general, the analytical methods lead very quickly to formidable difficulties in obtaining solutions to the resulting equations.

In a recent paper, Calfee (1968) reviewed and extended the Groen and Atkinson findings. He compared the efficiency of the strategies implied by the incremental and all-or-none assumptions by a Monte-Carlo simulation and showed that if learning occurs in an all-or-none fashion the dropout procedure is more efficient than the standard procedure, provided that learning is carried to a criterion. Relative efficiency of the dropout procedure depends only on the criterion chosen. Once again, if differential costs are associated with item presentations, there is little basis for guaranteeing that any particular information will be transmitted to the student.

Thus a cursory examination of the current simplified models of learning shows that an incremental assumption leads to a presentation strategy that selects the item with the fewest number of presentations, whereas the all-or-none assumption selects the item with the fewest number of successes, that is, a dropout procedure. Only if markedly different costs are associated with the presentation of particular items could a change in the selection occur, and this seems unlikely when dealing with a homogeneous set of learning materials. The paradoxical aspect of the problem is that our teaching goals seem to require that the student learn certain information, but the method for controlling the learning sequence precludes our knowing just what is learned.

The Role of Learning Models

Basic to the optimization procedure is the requirement for stating quantitatively the effect of presenting a particular instructional alternative on the student's behavior. Although Smallwood's worked example takes the form of a simple two-state all-or-none learning model, his approach and notation imply a generalization of the simplified form of the model. The transition probabilities and response probabilities are uniquely associated with the student's internal states of knowledge and with the particular alternatives for presentation. This means that complete knowledge of observable states of the individual learner must be available prior to the application of the analytical methods.

In a realizable system the learning model must prescribe the states as a function of the characteristics of the subject matter area and some initial conditions specifying the current state of the individual. The reverse cannot be true. We cannot arbitrarily choose a two-state or three-state or n-state model because values of transition probabilities can change depending on how one chooses to aggregate over states. How somewhat different interpretations can result depending on which states are collapsed or expanded was demonstrated in Gregg and Simon's discussion (1967b) of the all-or-none model applied to simple concept identification. For the present the question is how realistic is it to expect that a precise enumeration of states of the learners and their transition probabilities can be derived from a characterization of the subject matter? I believe that the answer is that only for a set of homogeneous materials, where the states are "unlearned" and "learned," can an approximation to a solution be found.

Even here we face the problem of estimating for individual students the transition probabilities, the $t_{ij}(a)$. The usual interpretation of the single parameter t is the learning rate parameter. Estimation typically is based on group data, although there is no reason for not obtaining an individual estimate, presumably in some preliminary fashion with the particular materials. There are, however, no reported data on the stability of learning rate parameters for a single individual in repeated exposures to the same materials. However, there is a great deal of evidence on learning-to-learn phenomena, which would suggest major difficulties in this approach.

The other explicit contribution of the learning model seems rather less feasible. Response probabilities, the $r_{ij}(a)$, might be assumed equally likely in a multiple-choice test question and take on values $1/n$, where n is the number of choices. Quite clearly this kind of assumption would hold only for homogeneous materials and highly sophisticated preliminary item analyses. It would appear that the virtues of proposing a more complex model of the learning process are lost in any attempt to implement a practical teaching system. Moreover, for the very specialized set of conditions so far considered, it seems unlikely that presentation costs would vary because the items are presumably homogeneous. The need for optimizing based on a concern for reducing computer decision time has little overall importance when, in fact, only a limited range of educational materials and objectives—learning vocabulary items, arithmetic drill and practice—can be handled.

The sequence of events in Smallwood's formulation is common to a traditional format in CAI where (1) some instructional materials are presented to the student; (2) after, or perhaps during, the presentation a test item is administered; (3) the student responds at his own rate; and (4) the computer evaluates the response, provides feedback, and performs the decision-making act. The outcome of the decision is the selection of the next item or instructional alternative. Implicit in this CAI sequence is a time scale of the order of a few minutes for completing the cycle. The need for reducing the calculations carried out by the computer to manageable size stems not only from the costs associated with the search through the decision tree but from the fact that the system must operate in the real-time environment of the student user.

If we view the decision-making role of the computer on a somewhat different time scale, we can conceive of quite a different set of requirements. Suppose that the time scale between decisions was to be hours or days instead of minutes. What kinds of decisions might we expect the computer to make? What kinds of models of learning might apply?

An old-fashioned model of learning, going back to John Dewey, but one that is nevertheless intuitively appealing, states that "we learn by doing." This is hardly a precise, programmable theory. However, it does suggest that the essence of the learning process is in the sequence of behaviors the student performs and that finding appropriate ways of describing the outcomes of these with respect to the student's acquisitions of skills and knowledge is our first order of business.

Suppose that in the more relaxed time scale the major task of the computer were to assess individual students in terms of rates of performing certain tasks and to create a model or description of the state of student— not quite as a vector space but rather in terms of how the student structured the learning environment. To be concrete, the computer administers tests from which it estimates parameters for a learning model.

Suppose further that the computer had available a model of an expert in the subject-matter area—perhaps a professional person or a teacher, perhaps one of the better students or a more advanced student, however selected. By comparing an individual student's current model with the desired model, finding one or more differences, the computer decision process could be a wise choice among global instructional alternatives.

The role of a learning model in this context is to derive predictions about the expected learning rates and performance levels of the student. As in Smallwood's generalization, this function will be intimately tied to content. Questions the model must be prepared to answer are typical of questions asked in research on teaching and learning. For example, how much time is required to learn a set of vocabulary items; how much to master the concept of a logarithm, given that the student is already familiar with the use of exponents? What distribution of errors might be expected in repeated drills, for example, in arithmetic, as a function of amount of practice? In the acquisition of novel materials, what is the expected vocabulary size after a given number of completed lessons? The emphasis on time as a dependent variable reflects a bias that human information processing consumes time and that the phrase "to let each student proceed at his own rate" provides a crucial basis for describing the nature of an individual's learning processes.

This emphasis is lacking in the most current research and theory, partly because of the behavioristic traditions of the discrete trials in verbal learning experiments and partly because of the difficulty in trying to make sense out of data obtained in the more informal presentations. It is far easier to time what the experimenter does than to classify a wider range of subject behaviors that may or may not be observable. Yet there is a growing awareness of the need to state propositions in just these terms (Waugh, 1967).

What should be "optimized" is the use of time by the student. It is probably not sensible to think of minimizing the amount of time required to assimilate information; rather the problem is to find effective ways of using the time available for learning. Empirically, fixation times of five to ten seconds per chunk (where a chunk is considered a familiar, primitive unit such as a letter of the English alphabet) are found in paired-associate learning. This range of values has served well for a variety of experimental predictions generated by the EPAM model (Feigenbaum, 1959; Simon and Feigenbaum, 1964; Gregg and Simon, 1967a). However, for serial learning of similar materials, the values appear to be much higher, twenty to thirty seconds per chunk for lists of twelve to fourteen items. The major difference in the experimental paradigms is in the degree of organization that the learner must impose on the materials in order to retrieve the information learned. The paired-associate task provides a specific cue, the stimulus item, for recall of an integrated, but usually small, response string. The serial task requires the subject (S), particularly in the learn-recall variant, to construct an integrated representation of the entire list when retrieval cues for the substrings are generated from features of the list items and hierarchically related.

In one experiment (McLean and Gregg, 1967) subjects learned lists of twenty-four letters under "whole-part" conditions where items were presented either one at a time or spatially grouped by three, four, six, or eight. The grouping conditions provided stable, unambiguous substructures of the lists so that potential retrieval cues in the form of ordinal names of the groups would be used. For example, subjects in the recall phase mentioned the *first, last, middle,* and *next* groups and then recited the list elements of the group. Given this more accessible and stable organization, fixation time per chunk fell from twenty-nine seconds for the one-at-a-time condition to about fifteen seconds as an average over the grouped presentation.

One interpretation of this result, generally confirmed by the differences in variability of the terminal grouping patterns, is that S's who learned the items in the ungrouped condition constructed identifiable substructures that were later "written-over." For example, there was a very strong tendency in these S's to produce longer than average substrings of the initial list items; that is, these were overlearned relative to later items in the lists. For optimal learning a more evenly distributed effort was possible for S's in the grouped conditions.

A learning model must be rich enough to provide estimates of the times required for assimilating the various subject-matter materials—rich enough to permit diagnostic aid in the decision process.

States and Internal Representations

How does one approach the task of parameterizing the past history of a student? Smallwood argues within a framework of achievement testing that it is possible to determine the student's "comprehension" of some instructional alternative by asking one or more questions about the material. Unfortunately, the relationship between responses and states will be a difficult one to map—except in the trivial case of a very few, finite states where interchangeable, homogeneous items produce interchangeable, hence additive, responses.

If any subject-matter area can be structured, that is, arranged in a logical sequence, placed in a preferred order, or dimensionalized in any way, the learning will exhibit hierarchical properties, and alternative items will be heterogeneous in the sense that different sequential arrangements will lead to differential effects in subsequent item learning. Actually, I believe that transfer effects and similar interactions will result even with very homogeneous, restricted sets.

The states through which a learner passes in acquiring cognitive skills seem more aptly described by the stages of a house under construction than the mere piling up of lumber, bricks, and mortar. Early in learning the space may be uniform and quite empty, and later subparts of the structure appear in skeleton form shored up by temporary props. Only much later does the structure assume an integrated balance where functional units are identifiable and related in useful ways. Any body of knowledge consists of clusters of interrelated parts. The systematic knowledge comprising the basic data of an academic subject-matter area has both formal and informal structural properties: formal, in the sense that classification rules and logical hierarchies are imposed by precedence or current pedagogical theory; informal, in that ideosyncratic outcomes may be expected in attempting to communicate the corpus to a learner.

When such a body of knowledge is large, that is, consists of many facts, only a relatively small proportion of the formal relationships can be acquired as explicit connections. Most of the learning process is a matter of developing ways of generating implicit relationships that have the property of being "legal" associations within the factual space.

It is the existence of such implicit relationships that points both to the need for determining the decomposable subcomponents of states during acquisition (a model of the learner) and for defining a desired terminal state (a model of the "expert").

In his exploration of internal representation of associative data networks, Michon (1968) presents an experimental paradigm of how such state descriptions may be made explicit. Michon had his S's learn three-letter words, which were "understood" to be arranged in the following matrix:

1	2	3	4
Dad	Fan	Cap	Bat
Lad	Man	Gap	Fat
Mad	Pan	Lap	Hat
Sad	Van	Tap	Rat

The presentation of the items was serial, however, so that in one condition the order of the words was Dad, Lad, Mad, .Sad, Van, . . . , Fan, Cap, . . . , Tap, Rat, . . . , Fat, Bat.

After S had mastered the list, Michon tested for both explicit and implicit connections. A cell in the matrix was specified by naming the word the cell contained. The S was to respond as quickly as possible with the word contained in a cell designated by directional symbols relative to the named cell. For example, if the named cell were Pan and the symbols ↗2 were shown on the oscilloscope, S should have responded with the word Bat. A variety of connections was explored and, in general, the results demonstrated shorter latencies for searches "on the path" of original learning and longer latencies in retrieving items off the path, in reverse direction, on diagonals, and so on. However, edge effects were noticed because of the limited size of the matrix. These and other implicit connections were detected in the data.

A general notion of internal representations for such materials is shown in Figures 7–1 and 7–2. In Figure 7–1 a hypothetical tree structure is shown for free recall of items of the serial list after a single presentation of the list. The hypothetical S recalls the items in order but with omissions. The time intervals between items increase as a function of serial position.

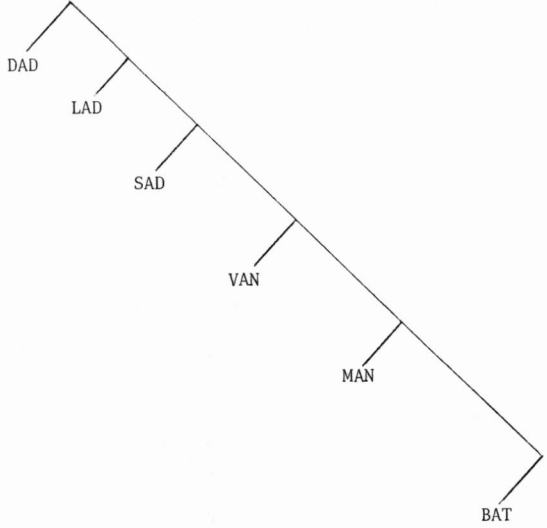

Figure 7–1.
Hypothetical memory tree after a single presentation of the items in serial acquisition of the matrix described in the text. Items recalled are the first, second, fourth, fifth, seventh, and sixteenth. Levels of the items correspond roughly to increasing interitem intervals.

And for such a representation, no obvious clustering or grouping of substrings is apparent. The internal representation of the list is just a linear stringing out of the items in order.

The tree structure of Figure 7–2 is quite different. It was obtained from one of Michon's S's two years after the original learning, although intermediate recall of the items had occurred on two earlier occasions. The S had learned the original list in one self-paced trial lasting approximately ten minutes, and the learning was planned. The strategy used by the S was to remember the sixteen items in pairs and to form visual images for each pair. The Fat-Bat is an easy picture; Van-Pan became a French bread truck with the word Pan written on its side panel. The order of recall and reconstruction is approximately that of the word arrangements from top to bottom.

Quite clearly what is needed to capitalize on such a view of the learning process is a notational system for state descriptions. At least for one class of learning materials—letter-number series and other sequential concepts—such a notation exists (Gregg, 1967; Simon and Kotovsky, 1963). Less obvious are ways of handling very complex semantic relationships, but here too initial results are encouraging (Quillian, 1967).

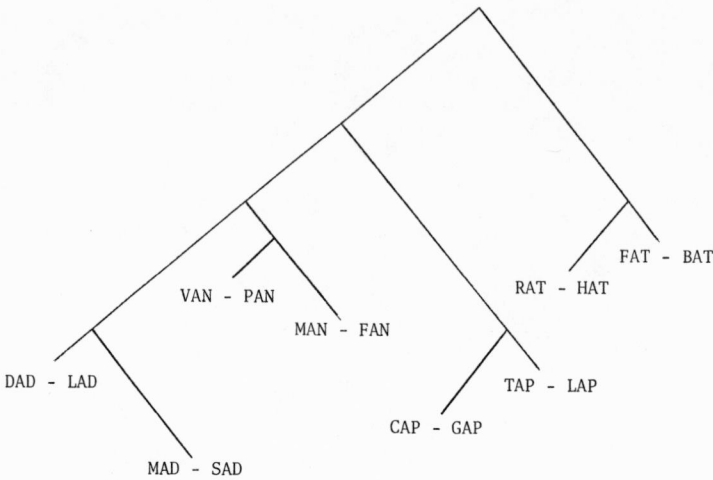

Figure 7–2.
A hierarchical memory tree two years after original learning. Levels of the terminal response images represent the approximate rank order of latencies in desired recall of the pairs (after Fig. 13 in Michon, 1968).

In short, the possibility of adequately describing the internal states of a student's knowledge is within our current capabilities. It is, in fact, precisely what the good teacher tries to do—everyday. It is the key to a teacher's ability to communicate with students and the basis for selecting meaningful examples. And given an extended time scale for the interaction between student and the computer-directed teaching process, it seems feasible at this time to construct, perhaps not an optimal set of decisions, at the least a program of instruction that wisely chooses among alternatives. The alternatives in this case are not individual presentations of verbal materials that might better be presented by a programmed or unprogrammed text but rather more global instructions—perhaps to contact the human teacher for specific help; perhaps to review general assignment areas or to go on to new assignments; or perhaps to prepare for further testing and evaluative tasks to be performed under computer direction.

Implications for Computer-based Testing

There are several techniques, primarily research tools, that have potential value as the basis for identifying the organizational structure of memory. The reaction time methods used in the McLean and Gregg (1967) experiment and in the Michon (1968) matrix learning studies seem particularly promising. These methods in combination with the kinds of analyses suggested by Tulving (1962, 1966) to detect subjective organization in free verbal recall suggest a feasible approach to the complex problem of identifying internal representation.

Suppose, for example, that the student was asked to recall in any order he chose as many new words as he could from a particular lesson. Appropriate content might include subjects in elementary science, languages, history, or mathematics. An analysis of the temporal relations is an easy task for the computer and the word groupings identified by examining the interitem intervals have been shown to reflect reasonably stable units in memory.

A variety of testing methods based on similarity ratings or degree of association are possible. Recent advances in the ability to analyze these in meaningful ways offer further possibilities for identifying clusters of objects, for example, words. A particularly clear example is the hierarchical cluster scheme proposed by Johnson (1967). Under the assumption of the *ultrametric inequality,* on distance measures of pairs of objects

$$d(x,z) \leqq \max[d(x,y), d(y,z)] \tag{1}$$

a simple replacement algorithm can be defined to produce unambiguous "strong" or "weak" hierarchical clustering, two tree structures like the tree of Figure 7–2. Close agreement between the two trees would tend to confirm that the underlying data do in fact reflect real structural properties.

The content of the groups or clusters would be assessed by identifying for the subject-matter material key words. Presumably the teacher would perform this function and could create "desirable clusters" of related words of higher or lower priority. This is just the selective process a teacher now uses in creating examination items.

Where repeated trials are given, the subjective organization score might be modified and used for cluster matching rather than for its metric properties, although the subjective organization score could serve a useful purpose in its own right to indicate over- or underorganized learners.

Conclusions

If individualized instruction is the goal of a computer-directed teaching system, the fact that states of knowledge vary in complex, topographic ways must be recognized and techniques discovered to give meaning to the notion of updating past histories. These techniques require a great deal more than observations of correct and incorrect responses on single test items. The suggestions for testing are not radically new nor especially innovative. They do, however, capitalize on the specialized power that computer technology has produced. The burden of carrying out complex scoring procedures to obtain subjective clusters student by student would be impossible for an elementary school teacher, and only with the computer is routine recording of latencies of individual responses possible. Computers were made to compute. It seems a waste to use them simply as glorified memory drums.

Smallwood expressed the hope that others will explore the empirical implications of his results. I hope so, too, but with the reservation that the focus of effort be on making explicit the processes by which learning occurs. This effort is inevitably tied to detailed study of content, which in turn may dictate methods of presentation that are quite different from what appear to be traditional practices in CAI.

REFERENCES

Calfee, R. C. 1968. *Further analyses of optimal procedures for associate learning.* Madison, Wis.: Cooperative Research Program Report, Univ. of Wisconsin.

Feigenbaum, E. A. 1959. An information-processing theory of verbal learning. Unpublished doctoral dissertation. Pittsburgh: Carnegie Institute of Technology.

Gregg, L. W. 1967. *Internal representations of sequential concepts.* In *Concepts and the structure of memory,* ed. B. Kleinmuntz. New York: Wiley.

Gregg, L. W., and Simon, H. A. 1967a. An information-processing explanation of one-trial and incremental learning. *Journal of Verbal Learning and Verbal Behavior* 6:780–787.

———. 1967b. Process models and stochastic theories of simple concept formation. *Journal of Mathematical Psychology* 4:246–276.

Groen, G. J., and Atkinson, R. C. 1966. Models for optimizing the learning process. *Psychological Bulletin* 66:309–320.

Johnson, S. C. 1967. Hierarchical clustering schemes. *Psychometrika* 32:241–254.

McLean, R. S., and Gregg, L. W. 1967. Effects of induced chunking on temporal aspects of serial recitation. *Journal of Experimental Psychology* 74:455–459.

Michon, John A. 1968. On the internal representation of associative data networks. *Netherlands Journal of Psychology* 23:428–457.

Quillian, M. R. 1967. Word concepts: a theory and simulation of some basic semantic capabilities. *Behavioral Science* 12(5):410–432.

Simon, H. A., and Feigenbaum, E. A. 1964. An information-processing theory of some effects of similarity, familiarization, and meaningfulness in verbal learning. *Journal of Verbal Learning and Verbal Behavior* 3:385–396.

Simon, H. A., and Kotovsky, K. 1963. Human acquisition of concepts for sequential patterns. *Psychological Review* 70:534–546.

Tulving, E. 1962. Subjective organization in free recall of "unrelated" words. *Psychological Review* 69:344–354.

———. 1966. Subjective aspects and effects of repetition in multitrial free-recall learning. *Journal of Verbal Learning and Verbal Behavior* 5:193–197.

Waugh, N. C. 1967. Presentation time and free recall. *Journal of Experimental Psychology* 73:39–44.

Optimizing Learning: Discussion

Smallwood's contribution may be taken as a general structure for looking at optimization. However, participants could not agree on what models would be most useful. Optimization is pointless and even of negative effect if the measures implied by the model are not relevant to the educational goals. Successful application of these techniques assumes that a psychologist can accurately represent the state of knowledge of a student at a given time and that instruction will influence the transition from a faulty state of knowledge to a more desirable one.

Some models of learning may be too simple to be helpful. The corresponding procedure for optimization in such models will not take into account important factors of motivation, context, previous learning, or learning style. Other prescriptions for learning, some of which are called models, do not make sufficiently specific reference to the initial or interim observable behavior of the learner and therefore are not useful for managing instruction.

Some basic issues in behavioral science accounted for much of the discussion. Is a model derived from a conception of stimulus and response adequate to describe the learning of complex skills and changes in an individual's organization of information? Can the maps and lists and other structures of a more cognitive view of human learning and memory be used to derive prescriptions for optimizing learning experiences? Can complex problem solving be quantified at all, and is quantification essential to research and model building?

That instructors and writers of instructional materials will try to optimize content and sequence for individual students is assumed. Whether psychological models and mathematical tools can be applied is the question. Today it is difficult to do much better than the a priori analysis by an experienced teacher of the subject, especially if this technique is further supported by strategies derived empirically for the particular subject area and topic of study. When all potentially relevant factors are considered, the situation becomes rather complex: a model of the learner, including his motives and study habits; a representation of the knowledge and skills to be acquired; a description of the present state of knowledge of the learner; and the interactions among all components, which change with time.

Agreement on models and representations is a difficult problem. Even if one could obtain some agreement among subject experts, one would expect to find considerable variety in the way individual students organize knowledge. Furthermore, it cannot be assumed that all students should be brought to the same representation of knowledge.

Exploration of optimization is one way to bring the tools of rigorous science to bear on the development of theories of instruction. However, the various efforts at present are too far away from finding real solutions to make a choice among them; there is no "best" way to proceed at this time.

PART IV

Individually Tailored Testing

In the near future many mental tests presumably will be administered and scored by computer. Not only can the computer test many individuals simultaneously with the same or different test items, but each subject can be allowed to answer test questions at his own speed. Given a pool of precalibrated items to choose from, the computer can design a different test for each person. In a major theoretical contribution, Lord (Chapter 8) considers problems of test theory for tailored testing in which each item is selected for administration on the basis of the subject's responses to previous items, with a view toward optimal measurement of his aptitude. Restricting attention to tests used for measurement rather than for instructional purposes, Lord discovered that, for a large class of problems and for individuals of average ability, the conventional test and the best individually tailored procedure are about equal in efficiency, but that for high- or low-scoring subjects the conventional peaked test is only about 30 per cent efficient compared to tailored testing. Drawing heavily on bioassay theory and the theory of stochastic processes with particular reference to Markov chains, Lord offers some tentative answers to important questions.

In his review, Green (Chapter 9) extends Lord's work by replotting selected curves from Lord's graphs to illustrate more clearly situations in which tailored testing might be preferred to conventional testing. He also explores in more detail the interaction between testing and instruction and shows that for certain instructional decisions tailored testing provides a potentially significant economy over conventional tests. He directs attention

137

to measures of performance other than gross right or wrong item scores, measures that would be more appropriate to the powerful capabilities of a computer. Because in regard to measurement tailored testing appears to offer little advantage over the best that can be done with conventional testing, the interplay between instruction and evaluation and new possibilities for measurement that are provided by computer-based testing represent potentially more fruitful areas for research.

8

Frederic M. Lord

Some Test Theory for Tailored Testing[1]

It seems likely that in the not too distant future many mental tests will be administered and scored by computer. Computerized instruction will be common, and it will be convenient to use computers to administer achievement tests also (Turnbull, 1968).

The computer can test many examinees simultaneously, with the same or with different tests. If desired, each examinee can be allowed to answer test questions at his own rate of speed. This situation opens up new possibilities. The computer can do more than simply administer a predetermined set of test items. Given a pool of precalibrated items to choose from, the computer can design a different test for each examinee.

An examinee is measured most effectively when the test items are neither too difficult nor too easy for him. Thus for any given psychological trait the computer's main task at each step of the test administration might be to estimate tentatively the examinee's level on the trait, on the basis of his responses to whatever items have already been administered. The computer could then choose the next item to be administered on the basis of this tentative estimate.

Such testing has been called branched testing, programmed testing, sequential item testing, and computerized testing. Clearly, the procedure

1. This work was supported in part by contract Nonr-2752(00) between the Office of Naval Research and Educational Testing Service. Reproduction, translation, use and disposal in part by or for the United States Government is permitted.

could be implemented without a computer. Here, emphasizing the key feature, we shall speak of tailored testing.

It should be clear that there are important differences between testing for instructional purposes and testing for measurement purposes. The virtue of an instructional test lies ultimately in its effectiveness in changing the examinee. At the end we would like him to be able to answer every test item correctly. A measuring instrument, on the other hand, should not alter the trait being measured. Moreover, as already noted, measurement is most effective when the examinee knows the answers to only about half of the test items. The discussion here will be concerned exclusively with measurement problems and not at all with instructional testing.

Sections 3–6 contain necessary technical preliminaries for formulating and dealing with the problem. Section 8 discusses key questions in evaluating different testing procedures. Sections 7, 10, 12, 17, and 19 derive and present mathematical formulas necessary for describing and evaluating various tailored-testing procedures. Sections 9 and 12–19 present some of the numerical results obtained for various testing procedures in various situations. Sections 2 and 11 are devoted to general discussion. A partial summary is given in Section 20.

It is a fortunate fact that most of the problems dealt with here closely parallel similar problems in bioassay. Much fruitful work has been done on the bioassay problems. This provides the inspiration, the background, and indeed the backbone of this chapter. A brief discussion of this bioassay work is given in Section 11 at a point where the similarities and differences with tailored-testing problems can be discussed intelligibly.

1. A Statement of the Problem

When the frequency distribution of the relevant psychological trait in the group to be tested is well known from previous testing of similar groups, a Bayesian analysis, using group statistics, is appropriate. Such an analysis would reach different conclusions depending on the frequency distribution of the trait. The present exploratory treatment will not use Bayesian analysis. Here we shall be concerned throughout with the problem of "measuring" a single examinee with respect to one psychological dimension. Because each examinee is to be considered by himself, group statistics (for example, test reliability coefficients) will play only a very marginal role.

The notion of measuring an examinee implies that there is some numerical value θ, for example, characterizing him that we wish to determine or estimate. The data available for making this estimate will be the examinee's responses to whatever test items are administered to him. The basic problem is to choose n test items for administration so that his n responses will enable us to estimate θ as efficiently as possible.

The optimum set of n items for this purpose depends on the unknown value of θ. Because of this fact, it is not clear that an optimal strategy exists, independent of the unknown θ, for choosing the desired n items. In any case, we shall not even attempt here to find an optimal strategy. Instead, we shall try to evaluate certain available simple strategies with a view to learning which of these are superior to others and what considerations seem relevant for determining their various virtues.

2. Some Strategies

Current research in tailored testing (see Linn et al., 1969 for references; also Hansen and Schwarz, 1968) is typically built on the following rule. If the examinee answers an item correctly, the next item administered should be more difficult; if he answers it incorrectly, the next item should be easier. This will be referred to as the *branching rule*. An obvious question to be answered here is how much the item difficulty should be varied from item to item. A second question of strategy is how to score the responses after the items have been administered. Various scoring methods have been tried, as will be seen.

Suppose for the moment that n, the number of items to be administered, is indefinitely large and that the branching rule is used. Suppose further that at the start large differences in difficulty are used from item to item and that these differences are gradually reduced until ultimately successive items are of nearly equal difficulty. Will such a strategy allow us to pinpoint the item difficulty level at which the examinee answers exactly half the items correctly, in the long run? If so, we can characterize the examinee's ability level in terms of this difficulty level.

The process just described is a Robbins-Monro process (Robbins and Monro, 1951). Conditions for its convergence to the desired value can be approximated in practice. The entire process will be discussed in Section 19.

The point to be made here is that the practical use of the branching process to estimate the examinee's ability does not require strongly restrictive assumptions. It is not necessary for this purpose to know the exact mathematical form of the dependence of item response on examinee ability θ and on parameters, such as item difficulty, describing the item.

If we wish to evaluate and compare the efficiency of different methods for estimating examinee ability, however, it becomes necessary to have some further information. In any one particular case this information could be gathered by exhaustive testing of the particular examinee, provided this testing could be done without changing him in the process. For purposes of this chapter, in order to generalize our conclusions to as yet untested populations of examinees, we shall instead make assumptions about the characteristic curves of the test items.

3. Item Characteristic Curves

An *item characteristic curve* (ICC) represents the probability of a correct answer to an item as a function of the trait θ being measured. If the item is scored zero or 1, this curve is automatically also the regression of item score on θ. ICC's are important, first of all, because they enable us to quantify important characteristics of individual test items, and, second, because they enable us to predict, probabilistically, how the examinee will respond to any chosen item.

Estimated characteristic curves are shown in Figure 8–1 (reproduced from Lord, 1968a) for five actual test items. All these curves have the typical *ogive* shape with an upper asymptote at P_i (probability of a correct answer) equaling 1.0 and a lower asymptote at $P_i = c_i$, $0 \leqslant c_i \leqslant 1$, where c_i is a parameter characterizing item i.

The solid curves shown are all logistic functions. When $c_i = 0$, the *logistic function* is simply

$$P_i == P_i(\theta) = \frac{1}{1 + \exp[-1.7a_i(\theta - b_i)]} \qquad (-\infty < \theta < \infty) \quad (1)$$

where a_i and b_i are parameters describing the test item. (The symbol $==$ is used here and elsewhere to indicate a definition.)

When test items can be answered correctly by random guessing, then $P_i > 0$ for all θ and $c_i > 0$. In this case we sometimes use the *three-parameter logistic function:*

$$P_i(\theta) = c_i + \frac{1 - c_i}{1 + \exp[-1.7a_i(\theta - b_i)]} \qquad (-\infty < \theta < \infty) \quad (2)$$

This is the function shown by the solid curves in Figure 8–1. Logistic ICC's are discussed in detail by Birnbaum (1968).

The logistic function in Equation (1) is in some ways a close approximation to the *normal ogive:*

$$P_i(\theta) = \Phi[a_i(\theta - b_i)] == \int_{-\infty}^{a_i(\theta - b_i)} \phi(u)\, du \qquad (-\infty < \theta < \infty)$$

$$(3)$$

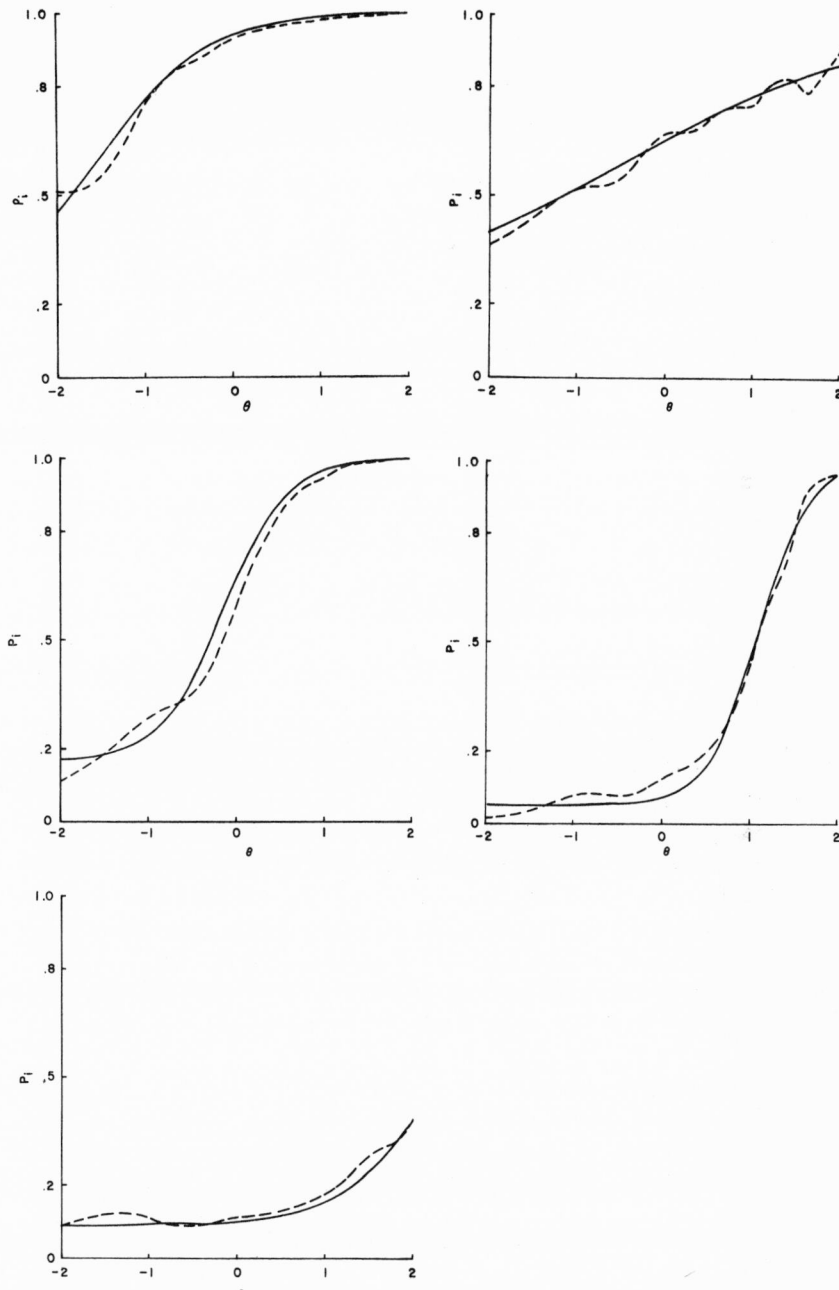

Figure 8–1.
Five item characteristic curves estimated by two different methods.

where Φ is defined by Equation (3) and

$$\phi(u) = = \frac{1}{\sqrt{2\pi}} \exp(-\tfrac{1}{2}u^2) \qquad (4)$$

Equations (1) and (3) do not differ by as much as 0.01 for any value of θ [the ratio of Equation (1) to Equation (3) is large in the tails, however]. When guessing occurs, Equation (3) is replaced by

$$P_i(\theta) = c_i + (1 - c_i)\,\Phi[a_i(\theta - b_i)] \qquad (-\infty < \theta < \infty) \qquad (5)$$

We assume here that Equation (1), (2), (3), or (5) holds true for a given examinee regardless of any knowledge that may be available about his performance on items other than item i. This means that when θ is fixed, the probability of the examinee answering a fixed set of n items correctly is simply

$$\prod_{i=1}^{n} P_i(\theta)$$

the product of the separate probabilities.

A common question is whether it may be possible by empirical studies to establish the superiority of either the logistic or the normal ogive model for ICC's. The appropriate answer to this question is probably that if an empirical study could be made sensitive enough to discriminate between these two models, it would almost surely be sensitive enough to prove that neither model was strictly correct.

Except where otherwise noted, this chapter assumes that all ICC's are of the form of Equation (3) or (5). Similar assumptions have proved to be very valuable in bioassay work. The reader who feels uncomfortable with such assumptions should consider the report by Lord (1968b), in which Equation (2) was found to agree closely with other estimates of ICC's obtained without prior assumption regarding their mathematical form. The latter estimates are shown in Figure 8–1 by the curved dashed lines.

4. Item Parameters

The parameters a_i, b_i, and c_i will be used to describe items. In this chapter we are primarily concerned with the problem of selecting items to be administered. This will be done on the basis of their parameters, determined in advance by pretesting. Thus it will be worthwhile here to examine the meaning of these parameters.

As already noted, c_i determines the lower asymptote. Accordingly, $0 \leq c_i \leq 1$. Any examinee, however low his θ, has a chance $> c_i$ of answering the item correctly. Thus c_i will here be thought of as the probability of chance success on item i as a result of random guessing.

All the curves of Equations (1), (2), (3), and (5) have an inflexion point, which is also a center of symmetry for the curve. The parameter b_i gives the abscissa of the inflexion point, which is at $\theta = b_i$. We shall allow b_i to assume any value in the range $-\infty < b_i < \infty$. It is clear that b_i represents the *difficulty* of the item. The larger the value of b_i, the less likely an examinee is to answer the item correctly.

The value a_i is closely related to the slope of the ICC at the inflexion point. For the three-parameter logistic, this slope is $0.425(1 - c_i)a_i$; for the three-parameter normal ogive, it is $0.3989(1 - c_i)a_i$. The parameter a_i is spoken of as representing the *discriminating power* of the item. For $a_i \geq 0$, the larger the value of a_i, the more the item discriminates between examinees with high θ and examinees with low θ. We plan to use items that are positively correlated with θ; consequently we shall restrict a_i to the range $0 < a_i < \infty$.

In this chapter we assume that all items have been calibrated—the item parameters estimated—by pretesting in advance of any use we make of them. How this is done is not our problem here, but we shall glance at it briefly. Presumably, over a period of years or decades, a large pool of items with accurately estimated parameters will gradually be accumulated.

The item parameters apparently can be estimated by maximum likelihood (Lord, 1968b; Bock, 1967; Birnbaum, 1968, Section 17.9). This is at present a costly and hazardous operation. The parameters can be approximated by more familiar procedures, which we shall mention. These approximations are based on the assumption of normal ogive ICC's with $c_i = 0$ and on the rather unlikely assumption that θ is normally distributed in the group tested. Because the unit of measurement used to express θ is arbitrary, we shall choose it so that $\sigma_\theta = 1$.

Under the assumptions stated, the parameter a_i can be estimated with the help of the relation (Lord and Novick, 1968, Section 16.10)

$$a_i = \frac{\rho'_{\theta i}}{\sqrt{1 - \rho'^2_{\theta i}}} \tag{6}$$

where $\rho'_{\theta i}$ is the biserial correlation of item response with θ. To estimate $\rho'_{\theta i}$ from observable quantities, we can use the fact that it is also the loading of item i on the common factor of the tetrachoric item intercorrelation coefficients ρ'_{ij}. We note that a_i is a monotonic increasing function of $\rho'_{\theta i}$, and also that

$$\rho'_{\theta i} = \frac{a_i}{\sqrt{1 + a_i^2}} \tag{7}$$

$$\rho'_{ij} = \frac{a_i}{\sqrt{1 + a_i^2}} \qquad \frac{a_j}{\sqrt{1 + a_j^2}} \tag{8}$$

Under the same assumptions b_i can be estimated by using its relation to π_i, the proportion of correct answers to item i (Lord and Novick, 1968, Section 16.9):

$$b_i = -\frac{1}{a_i}\sqrt{1 + a_i^2}\,\Phi^{-1}(\pi_i) \tag{9}$$

where Φ^{-1} is the inverse of the normal ogive function defined in Equation (3).

To keep matters simple in this preliminary survey, we shall assume throughout the remainder of this chapter that all items available for a particular test or testing have the same value of a_i and that all have the same value of c_i. Thus items will be chosen for administration solely according to their difficulty, as represented by the parameters b_i. It will be found that this simplification does not by any means make our problem a trivial one.

Before proceeding, let us write a formula that will help us to interpret a_i in terms of more familiar test-theory statistics. Suppose all items are *equivalent*—that is, all items have the same ICC; then all interitem tetrachoric correlations ρ'_{ij} are the same. If also all $b_i = 0$ and all $c_i = 0$, then, assuming a normal distribution of θ and a normal ogive ICC, the interitem phi coefficient ρ_{ij} (product moment correlation between dichotomously scored items) can be expressed as follows (Lord and Novick, 1968, Equation 15.9.3):

$$\rho_{ij} = \frac{2}{\pi}\arcsin \rho'_{ij} \tag{10}$$

the angle being expressed in radians. By Equation (8), because the items are equivalent,

$$\rho_{ij} = \frac{2}{\pi}\arcsin \frac{a_i^2}{1 + a_i^2} \tag{11}$$

By the Spearman-Brown formula the reliability of the number-right score on a test composed of n equivalent items is

$$\rho = \frac{n\rho_{ij}}{1 + (n - 1)\rho_{ij}} \tag{12}$$

If $a_i = 0.333$, under the assumptions already made this reliability for a 60-item test will be 0.80; if $a_i = 0.5$, this reliability will be 0.90; if $a_i = 1.0$, this reliability will be 0.97. In view of this we shall choose $a_i = 0.5$ as a typical value and shall address most of our attention to it.

The following will help the reader to reinterpret the meaning of b_i. If θ is normally distributed with a mean of zero and a standard deviation of 1, then, under the normal ogive model, the proportion of correct answers given by the group of examinees to an item with $a_i = 0.5$ is

$b_i =$	-3.0	-2.0	-1.0	0	1.0	2.0	3.0
$c_i = 0$	0.91	0.81	0.67	0.50	0.33	0.19	0.09
$c_i = 0.2$	0.93	0.85	0.74	0.60	0.46	0.35	0.27

5. Stochastic Processes and Random Walks

As foreshadowed earlier, all the testings to be considered in this chapter proceed one item at a time, as follows. After administration of the first item, each subsequent item is picked for administration by some predetermined rule, solely on the basis of the examinee's response to the preceding item. The choice among items is made entirely in terms of item difficulty b. Let the superscript $v = 1, 2, 3, \ldots$ refer to the order in which the items are administered, so that item $v + 1$ is the item administered immediately after item v.

Now, the origin and unit of measurement in which b and θ are expressed is purely arbitrary—it is easily seen, for example, that adding a constant to b in Equation (1), (2), (3), or (5) while subtracting the same constant from θ will have no effect on the ICC. Because we are free to choose an origin, we shall place it at $b^{(1)}$ so that hereafter

$$b^{(1)} \equiv 0 \qquad (13)$$

unless specifically stated otherwise.

In general, after a successful response we shall want $b^{(v+1)} \geq b^{(v)}$; after an unsuccessful response, $b^{(v+1)} \leq b^{(v)}$. (Conceivably, blocks of items may be substituted for single items in this scheme, with some elaboration of the rule for choosing each successive block.)

Clearly, after the first item, the value of $b^{(v+1)}$, $v = 1, 2, 3, \ldots$, is a chance variable. The frequency distribution of $b^{(v+1)}$ depends, in accordance with Equation (1), (2), (3), or (5), on the value of $b^{(v)}$ and on the examinee's value of θ (considered as fixed). Such a sequence of random variables is called a *stochastic process*. Furthermore, this process has the *Markov property:* After $b^{(v)}$ is known for a given θ, the probability of any value of $b^{(v+1)}$ is independent of the values of $b^{(1)}, b^{(2)}, \ldots, b^{(v-1)}$. Thus for a given examinee the random variable $b^{(v)}$ constitutes a *Markov process*.

By what rule should the successive values of $b^{(v)}$ be chosen? A plausible branching rule would be the following. After administering item v, compute the maximum likelihood estimate of θ. Choose $b^{(v+1)}$ equal to this estimate. Do this for $v = 1, 2, 3, \ldots .$

For a fixed set of items, it is not difficult (at least not for a computer) to obtain a maximum likelihood estimate of θ from the likelihood function

$$L(u_1, u_2, \ldots, u_n) = \prod_{v=1}^{n} P_v(\theta)^{u_v} Q_v(\theta)^{1-u_v} \tag{14}$$

where $P_v(\theta)$ is given by Equation (1), (2), (3), or (5) and $Q_v(\theta) = 1 - P_v(\theta)$. Now for a fixed set of items the values of the item difficulties are fixed and known, but for any stochastic process they are random variables. This complicates the problem to such a point that we shall not attempt to evaluate the results obtained when the stochastic process itself depends on successive maximum likelihood estimation.

At this point let us consider just one very simple kind of Markov process. This process is well known in bioassay work as the *up-and-down method*. In our terms, if the examinee answers item v correctly, then we choose $b^{(v+1)} = b^{(v)} + d$, where d is some *step size* that we pick in advance; if he answers item v incorrectly, then $b^{(v+1)} = b^{(v)} - d$. It is apparent that in the up-and-down method, the random variable $b^{(v)}$ can take on the values

$$b^{(v)} = jd \tag{15}$$

where j is an (possibly negative) integer. Actually, j equals the number of correct responses minus the number of incorrect responses for the first $v - 1$ items. We see that

$$b^{(v+1)} = \begin{cases} b^{(v)} + d & \text{with probability } P(\theta - b^{(v)}) \\ b^{(v)} - d & \text{with probability } Q(\theta - b^{(v)}) \\ \text{any other value} & \text{with probability } 0 \end{cases} \tag{16}$$

where the notation $P(\theta - b^{(v)}) == P_v(\theta)$ is used to display the role of the item parameter $b^{(v)}$.

A Markov process in which the random variable can take only a denumerable set of values [as is the case here; see Equation (15)] is called a *Markov chain*. A Markov chain satisfying Equation (16), for specified values of P and Q, is a *random walk*. The P's and Q's are called *transition probabilities*. The fact that $P(\theta - b^{(v)})$ for fixed $\theta - b^{(v)}$ does not depend on v is customarily described by saying that the transition probabilities are *stationary*.

Now,

$$b^{(v)} = b^{(1)} + d \sum_{r=1}^{v-1} (2u_r - 1)$$

Let us note in passing that the likelihood function of the item responses u_g under the up-and-down method is

$$f(u_1, u_2, \ldots, u_n)$$
$$= \prod_{v=1}^{n} P^{u_v} \left[\theta - b^{(1)} - d \sum_{r=1}^{v-1} (2u_r - 1) \right] Q^{1-u_v} \left[\theta - b^{(1)} d \sum_{r=1}^{v-1} (2u_r - 1) \right]$$

6. Scoring Methods

To set up a tailored-testing operation, we must, in effect, choose not only a stochastic process but also a scoring procedure. For the most part we shall consider just three simple possibilities, all of which have been used in experimental work on tailored testing. Any one of the different scores will be denoted by x. The total number of items to be administered to a given examinee is denoted by n; this is assumed fixed in advance of the testing. Let $u_i = 1$ denote a "correct" response to item i, and let $u_i = 0$ denote an incorrect response.

1. This score is the number of items answered correctly:

$$x = \sum_{v=1}^{n} u_v \tag{17}$$

This is the conventional *number-right score*.

2. This score is the difficulty of the item that would have been administered to the examinee after the nth item:

$$x = b^{(n+1)} = \begin{cases} b^{(n)} + d & \text{if } u_n = 1 \\ b^{(n)} - d & \text{if } u_n = 0 \end{cases} \tag{18}$$

It will be referred to as the *final difficulty score*.

3. This score is the average of the item difficulties, excluding $b^{(1)} = 0$ but including $b^{(n+1)}$ [as defined by Equation (18)]:

$$x = \frac{1}{n} \sum_{v=2}^{n+1} b^{(v)} \tag{19}$$

It will be called the *average difficulty score*.

To start with, let us consider the situation in which we use the simplest of these scores, the final difficulty score, in conjunction with the up-and-down method of selecting items.

7. Up-and-Down Method with Final Difficulty Score

Because $b^{(v)}$ forms a Markov chain under the up-and-down method, standard formulas are available for finding the sampling distribution of the score $x = b^{(n+1)}$ for any specified n. These are outlined in the Appendix. For the present purpose of evaluating this particular tailored-testing procedure, we shall not need the entire frequency distribution of $x = b^{(n+1)}$, but we shall need its expectation and sampling variance.

We need to improve our notation at this point. Let us write $X_v(b,\theta)$ to denote the score after administering v items when the difficulty of the first item administered is b and when the ability level of the examinee is θ. The score $X_v(b,\theta)$ is a random variable whose distribution depends on v, b, and θ. The distribution also depends on d and on the item parameters a and c, although these are not explicit in our notation. In actual practice the first item administered has $b = 0$, as already explained in Section 5. For the derivation, however, we shall need to consider different possible values of b.

If the first item administered is answered correctly, the second item in the up-and-down method is picked to have a difficulty of $b + d$. By virtue of the Markov property, after $X_1(b,\theta)$ is fixed, subsequent performance does not depend on the examinee's response to item 1. Thus when the first item is answered correctly, $X_{v+1}(b,\theta) = X_v(b + d,\theta)$ for $v = 1, 2, 3, \ldots$.

A similar analysis can be made for the case where the first item is answered incorrectly. Thus we can write for $v = 1, 2, 3, \ldots$

$$X_{v+1}(b,\theta) = \begin{cases} X_v(b + d,\theta) & \text{with probability } P(\theta - b) \\ X_v(b - d,\theta) & \text{with probability } Q(\theta - b) \end{cases} \quad (20)$$

Equation (20) and similar ones derived by the same line of reasoning are fundamental to most of our practical results. It provides a relationship connecting the random variable X_{v+1} with the random variable X_v, allowing us to compute necessary quantities for X_n recursively.

Let

$$G_v(b,\theta) == X_v(b,\theta) - \theta \quad (21)$$

denote the error in the score X_v, and write $t == \theta - b$. Then, from Equation (20) for $v = 1, 2, 3, \ldots$,

$$G_{v+1}(b,\theta) = \begin{cases} G_v(b + d,\theta) & \text{with probability } P_t \\ G_v(b - d,\theta) & \text{with probability } Q_t \end{cases} \quad (22)$$

where we write P_t instead of $P(\theta - b)$. The values of P and Q are, as always, to be computed from Equation (1), (2), (3), or (5). In particular, we see from Equation (20) that

$$G_1(b,\theta) = \begin{cases} d - t & \text{with probability } P_t \\ -d - t & \text{with probability } Q_t \end{cases} \quad (23)$$

The bias of X_v is the expectation of G_v for given v and θ, which we denote by

$$E_v(b) == \mathcal{E}G_v(b,\theta) \tag{24}$$

Although $E_v(b)$ is a function of θ, we shall omit the symbol θ to keep the formulas simple. From Equation (22), for $v = 1, 2, 3, \ldots,$

$$E_{v+1}(b) = P_t E_v(b + d) + Q_t E_v(b - d) \tag{25}$$

From Equation (23),

$$\begin{aligned} E_1(b) &= (d - t)P_t - (d + t)Q_t = d(P_t - Q_t) - t(P_t + Q_t) \\ &= d(1 - 2Q_t) - t \end{aligned} \tag{26}$$

The bias of X_n for given n and θ can be computed recursively using Equations (26) and (25).

To obtain the sampling variance of $X_n == X_n(b,\theta)$, we start by defining W_v as the expected mean-square error of X_v for a given θ:

$$W_v == \mathcal{E}G_v^2 = \mathcal{E}(X_v - \theta)^2 \tag{27}$$

where for convenience we omit the arguments in parentheses. Thus, by Equation (22),

$$W_{v+1}(b) = P_t W_v(b + d) + Q_t W_v(b - d) \tag{28}$$

Also, by Equation (23),

$$W_1(b) = (d - t)^2 P_t + (d + t)^2 Q_t \tag{29}$$

The sampling variance of X_n is given by

$$\sigma^2_{X_n|\theta} == \mathcal{E}X_n^2 - (\mathcal{E}X_n)^2 = \mathcal{E}G_n^2 - (\mathcal{E}G_n)^2 = W_n(b) - [E_n(b)]^2 \tag{30}$$

For future use, let us write here one more recursion relation, enabling us to find

$$D_v(b) == \frac{\partial}{\partial\theta} \mathcal{E}X_v(b,\theta) \tag{31}$$

From Equation (20),

$$\mathcal{E}X_{v+1}(b,\theta) = P_t \mathcal{E}X_v(b + d,\theta) + Q_t \mathcal{E}X_v(b - d,\theta)$$

so that

$$\begin{aligned} D_{v+1}(b) = P_t D_v(b + d) &+ Q_t D_v(b - d) + [E_v(b - d) \\ &- E_v(b + d)]\frac{\partial Q_t}{\partial\theta} \end{aligned} \tag{32}$$

Also, from Equations (20) and (13),

$$\mathcal{E}X_1(b,\theta) = P_t(b + d) + Q_t(b - d)$$

so that

$$D_1(b) = -2d\frac{\partial Q_t}{\partial\theta} \tag{33}$$

If the ICC is a normal ogive as in Equation (3), then

$$\frac{\partial Q_t}{\partial\theta} = -a_i\phi[a_i(\theta - b_i)]$$

8. Evaluation of Estimates of θ

Before giving numerical results evaluating the up-and-down method with final difficulty score, it is necessary to consider at some length just how such results should be evaluated. This is not a trivial matter.

Empirical research studies (see Linn et al., 1969, and other references given there; also Hansen and Schwarz, 1968) have often used the correlation of tailored-test score x with some outside criterion to evaluate the effectiveness of testing and scoring procedures. If a particular examiner has repeatedly tested similar groups, he may know approximately in advance the distribution of θ in the next group he plans to test; such an examiner may well use group statistics and Bayesian methods. Although these kinds of evaluation have obvious face validity, they will not be used here for at least two reasons:

1. The correlation coefficient is a group statistic, whereas the problem here is to determine the accuracy with which we can measure a single individual. Important information about the accuracy obtainable for specific individuals is lost when this information is pooled over individuals to get a group statistic.

2. To obtain a group statistic, we would have to make some assumption about the frequency distribution of θ in the group studied. Such an assumption would prevent easy generalization of our results to groups with substantially different distributions of θ. [The few results available to date (see Lord, 1968b) run against the convenient assumption that θ is likely to be approximately symmetrically distributed, at least in the case of highly selected groups such as college students.]

The gain to be hoped for from tailored tests arises entirely (or nearly so) from tailoring the item difficulties to the ability of the examinee. But *in a typical test that is not too heterogeneous in item difficulty most of the items are already well tailored to the abilities of most of the examinees. Thus tailored testing cannot provide greatly improved measurement for most examinees. The value of tailored tests is primarily for those examinees for whom the conventional test would be too easy or too difficult.* The correlation coefficient over the entire group of examinees is not a good index for judging the improved measurement gained by a minority.

One way to describe the measurement properties of the score x is by giving its standard error [the square root of the sampling variance $\sigma^2_{x|\theta}$ of Equation (30)]. It is no surprise to find that the standard error depends on the unknown value of θ. The measurement properties of the score x cannot be summarized by a single number but must be represented by a curve—a function of θ. Thus we might find, for example, that score x_1 provides more accurate measurement than score x_2 for a certain range of values of θ, whereas score x_2 is more accurate for examinees outside this range.

In bioassay work (for example, Brownlee et al., 1953) $E_n(b)$, the bias of x, must be taken into account. This is done by using the *expected mean-square error* $W_n == \mathcal{E}(X_n - \theta)^2$ to describe the accuracy of measurement. As shown in Equation (30), the expected mean-square error exceeds the sampling variance by the square of the bias.

In mental testing, on the other hand, the scale in which θ is measured has an arbitrary origin and unit of measurement. Thus a constant bias in the score x, or even a bias that changes linearly with θ, would not impair the value of x at all. To carry matters further, the scale for θ that yields Equation (2) or (5) is highly arbitrary. Any monotonic transformation of this scale would be defensible for measuring the examinee. *In comparing different tailored-testing procedures, we must use an index of effectiveness that always leads to the same conclusion no matter what monotonic transformation of the θ scale is chosen.*

To describe the effectiveness of the score x for measurement purposes, we shall use

$$I_x(\theta) == \left[\frac{(\partial/\partial\theta)\mathcal{E}(x|\theta)}{\sigma_{x|\theta}} \right]^2 \tag{34}$$

(The reader may wish at this point to glance at Figure 8–3, which shows $\sqrt{I_x(\theta)}$ for certain testing procedures.) This is the quantity recommended by Birnbaum (1968, Equation 17.7.10) to measure the "information" in the score on a conventional test. The use of $I_x(\theta)$ was also recommended by Lord (1952, Equation 57) and, in a very different context, by Mandel and Stiehler (1954). We shall call $I_x(\theta)$ the *information function for the score x*.

As Birnbaum shows, in large samples $I_x(\theta)$ is inversely proportional to the square of the length of the confidence interval for estimating θ from the score on a conventional test. Birnbaum uses this information function for small as well as large samples, and we shall do so here. The meaning and justification of this index in small samples are well described by Mandel, whom we paraphrase closely here: If it is desired to differentiate between two nearby values θ' and θ'' by means of the corresponding measurements x' and x'', it is apparent that the success of the operation will depend on two circumstances: (1) the magnitude of the difference $\mathcal{E}'' - \mathcal{E}' ==$ $\mathcal{E}(x''|\theta'') - \mathcal{E}(x'|\theta')$ for a given difference $\theta'' - \theta'$, that is, the magnitude of the slope $(\mathcal{E}'' - \mathcal{E}')/(\theta'' - \theta')$; and (2) the precision of measurement $\sigma_x|_\theta$. These two desiderata can be combined in a single criterion, the information function, defined as the square of the ratio of the slope to $\sigma_x|_\theta$. It is helpful to visualize the situation with the aid of a diagram (Figure 8–2). A more formal discussion of the small-sample interpretation is given by Lord (1952).

It is important to note that $I_x(\ )$ is an operator, not a function. This means that $I_x(a\theta)$ must be found from the definition in Equation (34), *not* by writing down $I_x(\theta)$ and then substituting $a\theta$ for θ.

It is apparent from Equation (34) that any change in the unit used to measure θ does change $I_x(\theta)$. Thus $I_x(\theta)$ is not a pure number. In fact, $1/\sqrt{I_x(\theta)}$ is expressed in the same score units as θ.

Suppose that a monotonic increasing transformation is made on θ so that $\theta^* == \theta^*(\theta)$ replaces θ. Then the denominator of Equation (34) remains unchanged, but the numerator must be multiplied by $(\partial\theta/\partial\theta^*)^2$ to find $I_x(\theta^*)$. Because $\partial\theta/\partial\theta^*$ may have any form, it is possible to make $I_x(\theta^*)$ assume any shape desired, within the restriction $I_x(\ ) > 0$, simply by a suitable choice of the transformation θ^*.

The conclusion to be drawn is that unless we are willing to assert that we have used a uniquely appropriate scale for measuring θ, we cannot draw conclusions from the shape of the information function. This drastic limita-

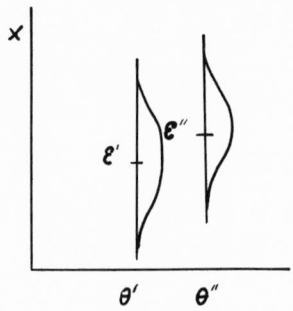

Figure 8–2.

tion leads to no difficulties in this chapter because we shall always be comparing two or more information functions, all based on the same scale for θ. The ratio between the information function for x_1 and the information function for x_2 measures the *relative efficiency* of x_1 and x_2 for estimating θ. *The relative efficiency is unaffected by any differentiable monotonic increasing transformation of θ*, because the factor $\partial\theta/\partial\theta*$ appears twice and cancels out.

In studying the effectiveness of tailored-testing procedures, it will be helpful if we can compare them to more familiar procedures. To keep matters simple, we shall compare the information function of the tailored-testing procedure with the information function of the number-right score on a conventional test composed of n equivalent items with normal ogive ICC and with all $b_i = 0$. This test will hereafter be referred to as the *standard test* (use of number-right score is to be understood). The information function for (number-right score on) this standard test is (Birnbaum, 1968, Equations 20.2.2 and 20.5.1)

$$I(\theta) = \frac{nP'_\theta(\theta)^2}{P(\theta)Q(\theta)} \tag{35}$$

where $P'_\theta(\theta)$ is the derivative of $P_i(\theta)$ with respect to θ. The subscript x has been dropped on the left-hand side of Equation (35) because for tests composed of equivalent items the number-right score is a sufficient statistic for estimating θ (Birnbaum, 1968, Section 18.3.1); consequently, Equation (35) represents the maximal information that could be obtained from the responses to the n items by any scoring method.

Because these n items are ideally suited for an examinee at $\theta = 0$, it follows that no information curve can ever be higher at any value of θ than the value given by Equation (35) when $\theta = 0$. *This provides a horizontal line at or below which all information curves must fall*. Note that this limit is a result of the assumption that a_i is the same for all items. It might well be found in practice that the more difficult items tend to have higher or lower a_i than the easier items, in which case the limit would no longer be a horizontal straight line. The limiting curve can still be computed from Equation (35) if the a_i are known.

It is worth mentioning that the information function for the number-right score on any conventional test is proportional to n, the length of the test. Thus *a per cent increase in any information function, achieved by whatever means, can be understood as an increase in information equivalent to that obtained for a number-right score on a conventional test by increasing the number of test items by the same percentage.*

9. Information Functions for the Up-and-Down Method with Final Difficulty Score

Even when we restrict attention just to the up-and-down method with final difficulty score, there is still quite an assortment of possibilities to be investigated. Here, we restrict our attention to items with normal ogive characteristic curves (for some results under the logistic model, see Section 13). In the next several sections, we shall consider only the case where $c = 0$.

This still leaves us with four parameters to take into consideration: a, n, d, and θ. Figure 8–3 shows information functions for the up-and-down method with final difficulty score, computed from Equations (34), (32), and (30), for $n = 10$ and $n = 60$. Figure 8–3 is appropriate for any value of a_i in a wide range. This is possible because dividing a_i by a constant does not change the value of the ICC in Equation (3) [or in Equation (1), (2), or (5) for that matter] provided b_i and θ are multiplied by the same constant.

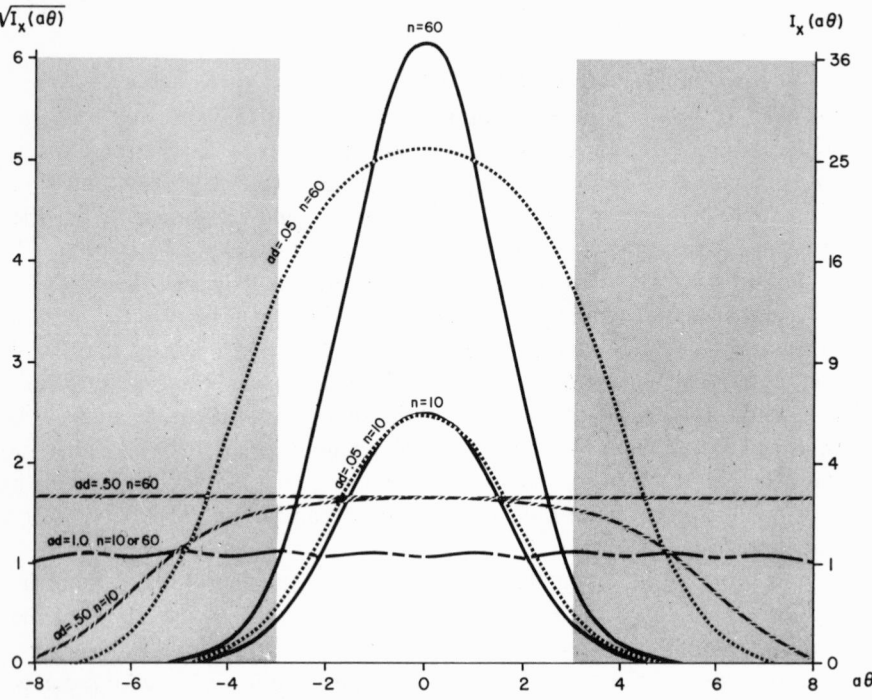

Figure 8–3.
Information functions for the up-and-down method with final difficulty score (solid lines are for the standard tests).

If $a_i = a = 1$, we are likely to be interested in the range of θ between $\theta = -3/a = -3$ and $\theta = +3/a = +3$. Because we have set $\sigma_\theta = 1$ (see Section 4), we may expect that not too many people will lie outside some range such as $\pm 3\sigma$. That part of Figure 8–3 beyond $a\theta = \pm 3$ is shown here for completeness; however, it has been shaded to indicate that it is probably only rarely of interest.

If we consider items with $a_i = a = 0.50$ instead of 1.0, then, if other things are the same as above, since $\sigma_\theta = 1$ always, we shall be interested in the range from $\theta = -1.5/a = -3$ to $\theta = +1.5/a = +3$. When we halve the value of a_i, we must double the value of b_i (as well as of θ) if P_i is to remain unchanged. This means that for $a_i = a = 1$ the curve labeled $ad = 1.0$ represents a random-walk procedure with step size $d = 1.0/a = 1.0$; but when $a_i = a = 0.5$, the step size is now $d = 1/a = 2.0$.

Vertical distances in Figure 8–3 and in all similar figures are proportional to the square root of the information function. Thus *vertical distance is inversely proportional to a large-sample approximation for the length of the confidence interval for estimating θ from a test score.* The vertical scale on the right, however, is numbered to show the information function, not its square root. Thus the numbers given on the scale on the right are proportional to the number of test items required to produce a corresponding amount of information by conventional testing methods.

The two solid lines labeled $n = 10$ and $n = 60$ represent the information functions of a 10- and 60-item standard test (see Section 8), as given by Equation (35). If we read the heights of these curves on the right-hand scale, we can confirm that the 60-item standard test gives exactly 6 times as much information as the 10-item standard test, regardless of the value of θ.

The numerical results shown in Figure 8–3 and in subsequent figures were obtained by programming a computer to evaluate Equations (25), (28), and (32) recursively for $v = 1, 2, \ldots, 59$. All results obtained recursively, both here and in later sections, were independently checked up through $n = 10$ (thus checking the formulas also) by an entirely separate computer program that computed the probability of each of the 2^{10} possible patterns of response to $n = 10$ items, computed the score for each pattern, and then computed the mean and the variance of these scores over all possible patterns, and also the derivative $D_n(b)$. The latter method of computing results cannot be extended much beyond $n = 10$ or 12.

The details of interpreting Figure 8–3 are considered at some length here because most subsequent numerical results will be presented in a similar manner. Hereafter, the verbal interpretation will be for the most part limited to the case where $a_i = a = 0.50$ in order to keep the presentation from getting out of hand.

The scalloped effect when the step size is 2.0 (when $ad = 1.0$) is caused by the fact that when n is even, the difficulty of the $(n + 1)$th item must be an odd multiple of 2.0. Thus examinees at $\theta = \pm 2.0$ or at $\theta = \pm 6.0$ are measured more accurately than those at intermediate levels. Actually, all curves shown here and in subsequent figures should be scalloped. However, the effect is hardly noticeable for smaller values of d and has been ignored in drawing the figures.

When step size is $d = 2.0$, the amount of information obtained within the range $-8 \le a\theta \le +8$ is not appreciably increased by additional testing after the first 10 items—the same curve adequately represents the information functions for both $n = 10$ and $n = 60$. Clearly, the step size is too large to provide accurate measurement. The same is true for $d = 1.0$ $(ad = 0.5)$ within the range $-3 \le \theta \le +3$ but not outside this range.

When step size is reduced to $d = 0.10$ $(ad = 0.05)$, the information obtained near $\theta = 0$ is greatly increased, but less so for θ at ± 3.0 $(a\theta = \pm 1.5)$.

For $a = 0.5$, the 10-item tailored-testing procedure with $d = 0.10$ is better than the standard test for almost all θ. For $n = 60$, the standard test is better at $\theta = 0$, but its effectiveness falls off, so that at $\theta = \pm 3.0$ $(a\theta = 1.5)$ it provides only about 80 per cent as much information as does the tailored test with $d = 0.10$. We see here the broad outlines of a basic problem in tailored testing. *We need a small step size to compete with the accuracy of measurement provided by the standard test for typical individuals* (near $\theta = 0$), *but we need a large step size in order to obtain accurate measurement of atypical individuals* (at $\theta = \pm 3$, for example). The optimal step size in any situation of course depends on a_i, n, and the accuracy of measurement required at different levels of θ.

Note that *no information curve can ever be higher at any value of θ than the maximum of the information curve for the standard test.*

10. The Up-and-Down Method with Number-Right Score

Keeping the same random-walk method of sequencing items, let us see to what extent we get effective measurement when we change the examinee's score from $b^{(n+1)}$, the difficulty of the $(n + 1)$th item, to $\sum^n u_v$, the total number of items answered correctly. This number-right score has been used in experimental studies of tailored testing. Denoted by X_n or by x, it is the score referred to throughout this section, unless otherwise specified. The reader may wish before reading further to form his own judgment as to the relative effectiveness of the scores $b^{(n+1)}$ and $\sum^n u_v$.

Let $X_v(b,\theta)$ now denote the score $\sum_{r=1}^{v} u_r$ obtained in the up-and-down method when the difficulty of the first item administered is b and when the ability of the examinee is θ. As in Section 7, we have a recursion equation for the random variable X:

$$X_{v+1}(b,\theta) = \begin{cases} X_v(b + d,\theta) + 1 & \text{with probability } P(\theta - b) \\ X_v(b - d,\theta) & \text{with probability } Q(\theta - b) \end{cases} \quad (36)$$

for $v = 1, 2, 3, \ldots$. From this we can derive equations for $\mathcal{E}X_{v+1}(b,\theta)$, $\mathcal{E}X^2_{v+1}(b,\theta)$, and $D_{v+1}(b)$ similar to Equations (25), (28), and (32). The error variance $\sigma^2_{X_n|\theta}$ can be computed from the first line of Equation (30). The information function can be computed from Equation (34).

We find that the bias, the mean-squared error, and the sampling variance of $\sum^n u_v$ are (not surprisingly) very different from the corresponding quantities for $b^{(n+1)}$. But we find that the information functions for the two scoring methods are exactly the same!

This result leads us to examine more closely the relation between $b^{(n+1)}$ and $\sum^n u_v$. If an examinee starts at $b^{(1)} = 0$ and finishes at $b^{(n+1)}$ after n steps each of length d, it is clear that for $d > 0$ his number of right answers exceeds his number of wrong answers by $b^{(n+1)}/d$. Because the number of right answers plus the number of wrong answers equals n, we have for $d > 0$

$$\frac{b^{(n+1)}}{d} = \sum_{v=1}^{n} u_v - (n - \sum_{v=1}^{n} u_v)$$

or

$$b^{(n+1)} = d(2 \sum_{v=1}^{n} u_v - n) \quad (37)$$

In the up-and-down method there is a linear relationship between final difficulty score and number-right score. Thus, although the scores show very different biases and sampling variances, they are equally effective for measurement purposes.

11. Bioassay

In bioassay work the average difficulty score

$$\frac{1}{n} \sum_{v=2}^{n+1} b^{(v)}$$

is commonly recommended for the up-and-down method. A considerable amount of theoretical work has been done for this method: Tsutakawa (1967a, 1967b, 1963) was primarily concerned with asymptotic results. Wetherill (1963) used Monte-Carlo methods to investigate a wide variety of branching and scoring methods empirically. Dixon (1965), Cochran and Davis (1964), Brownlee et al. (1953), Dixon and Mood (1948), and others have derived useful large- and small-sample formulas. They also obtained numerical results, mostly for $n = 10$ or 12.

The method of approach and most of the equations of Section 12 are simple extensions of those in the cited work of Brownlee et al. The same general approach is used in several other sections, including Section 7.

It will be worthwhile to point out some of the similarities and differences between our problem and the bioassay problem, as commonly formulated. The bioassayist typically starts with Equation (1) or (3), just as we have here. Whereas we control a_i and b_i while trying to estimate θ, the bioassayist controls θ while trying to estimate the value of b and (sometimes) the value of a. For him θ might be the dosage of the insecticide applied, for example, in which case b would be the LD_{50}, the dosage at which 50 per cent of the treated insects die. The bioassayist chooses the dose $\theta^{(1)}$, administers it to one insect (or to several), and observes the response: survival ($u_g = 0$) or death ($u_g = 1$). He then chooses a dose, $\theta^{(2)}$, administers it to another insect, and continues in this way.

Whereas we are usually interested only in the *relative* values of θ for different examinees, and often only in the rank order of these values, the bioassayist must estimate the absolute value of b for a single given insecticide. Thus the bioassayist uses the mean-squared error as a criterion of effective estimation, whereas we use the information function. Bias is a serious problem for the bioassayist, whereas it is usually of no concern to us.

The fact that the bioassayist has two unknown parameters, a and b, creates a very serious problem. He must choose a step size d without knowing a. If he picks d too large, the sampling error of his estimate of b will be excessive, even for sizable n. On the other hand, if d is small and a happens to be small also, the true value of b may be so far from the value $\theta^{(1)}$ at which the bioassay is started that $\theta^{(n)}$ can never reach the value b in n steps of length d. This results in an unacceptable bias in the estimate of b. Without some knowledge of a, there is no entirely safe way of choosing d. It is possible to estimate a from the observations themselves as they accumulate, but these estimates are very unreliable for the values of n frequently used in bioassay.

Most work on the up-and-down method assumes that a is known or else that a can be bounded (from previous experience) within certain limits. In the latter case the step size must be chosen uncomfortably high to allow for the possibility that a may be small. Here, we have assumed that in mental testing the necessary item parameters all have been determined by pretesting, with good accuracy. The result of all this is that we shall be able to use a smaller step size in mental testing than is commonly recommended for the up-and-down method in bioassay. This, together with the fact that bias is usually of no concern to us, will allow us to obtain better results from the up-and-down method than are usually possible in bioassay.

12. The Up-and-Down Method with Average Difficulty Score

Dixon and Mood (1948), starting with the normal ogive model for bio-assay, derived approximations to the maximum likelihood estimators for a and b. Brownlee et al. (1953) proposed using $1/n \sum_{v=2}^{n+1} \theta^{(v)}$ to estimate b in the bioassay problem, pointing out that this estimator is asymptotically equivalent to the one recommended by Dixon and Mood. Our average difficulty score $1/n \sum_{v=2}^{n+1} b^{(v)}$ corresponds directly to the estimator used by Brownlee et al. For the most part we shall study exact small-sample properties of the average difficulty score rather than asymptotic properties. The development given here for $H = L = 1$ is essentially the same as that of Brownlee et al., except that they are not concerned with $\sigma_{x|\theta}$, nor with quantities analogous to $D_v(b)$, nor with the information function $I_x(\theta)$.

In this section x will always refer to the average difficulty score. By definition the random variable $X_v(b,\theta) == \sum_{r=2}^{v+1} b^{(r)}$ will be the sum of item difficulties obtained under the up-and-down method when the first item is of difficulty b and the examinee is at ability level θ. The basic recursion, corresponding to Equation (20) for the final difficulty score, is seen to be

$$X_{v+1}(b,\theta) = \begin{cases} b + Hd + X_v(b + Hd,\theta) & \text{with probability } P_t \\ b - Ld + X_v(b - Ld,\theta) & \text{with probability } Q_t \end{cases} \quad (38)$$

where $H = L = 1$ (the symbols H and L are not needed here but will be useful in later sections).

Because X_v is a sum, not an average, let us define $G_v(b,\theta)$ by

$$G_v(b,\theta) == X_v(b,\theta) - v\theta$$

Then, by the same reasoning used in Section 7,

$$E_{v+1}(b) = P_t E_v(b + Hd) + Q_t E_v(b - Ld) + E_1(b) \quad (39)$$

$$E_1(b) = (Hd - t)P_t - (Ld + t)Q_t \quad (40)$$

Similarly, the mean-squared error is found from

$$W_{v+1}(b) = P_t W_v(b + Hd) + Q_t W_v(b - Ld) + W_1(b) \\ + 2P_t(Hd - t)E_v(b + Hd) - 2Q_t(Ld + t)E_v(b - Ld) \quad (41)$$

$$W_1(b) = (Hd - t)^2 P_t + (Ld + t)^2 Q_t \quad (42)$$

Finally,

$$D_{v+1}(b) = D_1(b) + P_t D_v(b + Hd) + Q_t D_v(b - Ld)$$

$$+ [E_v(b - Ld) - E_v(b + Hd)] \frac{\partial Q_t}{\partial \theta} \tag{43}$$

$$D_1(b) = -\partial(H + L) \frac{\partial Q_t}{\partial \theta} \tag{44}$$

If the ICC is a normal ogive with or without $c = 0$, as in Equation (3) or (5), then

$$\frac{\partial Q_t}{\partial \theta} = -a_i(1 - c_i)\phi[a_i(\theta - b_i)] \tag{45}$$

Figure 8–4 compares information curves for some final difficulty scores (marked F) with those for the corresponding average difficulty scores

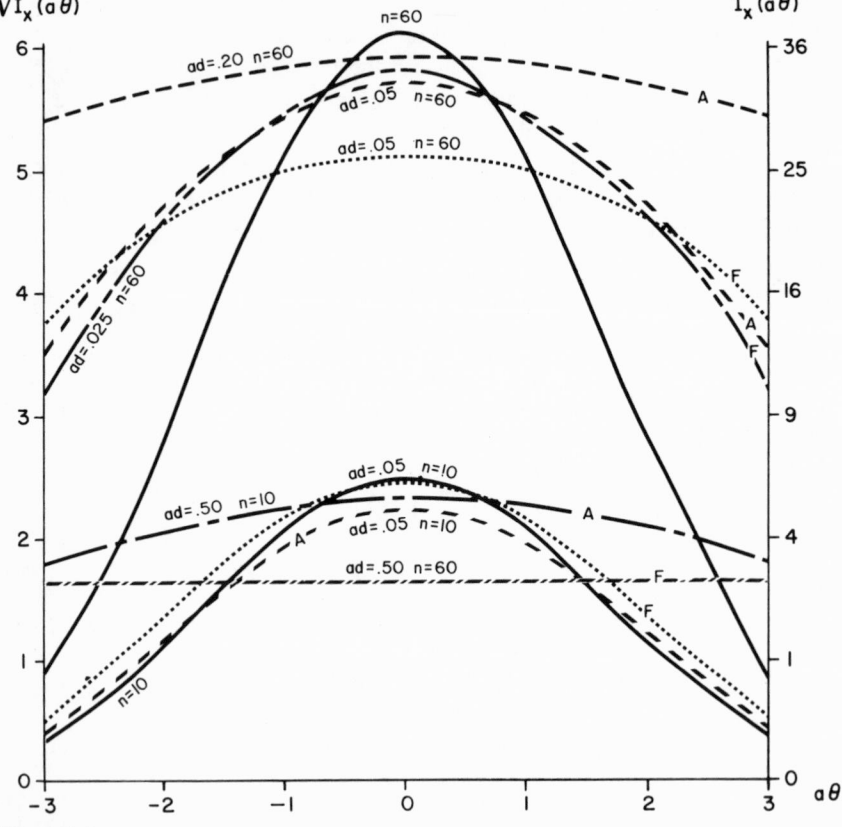

Figure 8–4.
Information functions for the up-and-down method with average difficulty score.

(marked A) both when $n = 10$ and when $n = 60$. When $n = 10$, the final difficulty score with $ad = 0.05$ is best when $\theta = 0$; however, effectiveness has fallen off when $a\theta = \pm1.5$. The average difficulty score, $ad = 0.50$, with $n = 10$, is not quite as good when $\theta = 0$ but is distinctly better when $a\theta = \pm1.5$.

When $n = 60$ and $ad = 0.05$, the average difficulty score is better than the final difficulty score throughout the range $-2 \leqq a\theta \leqq 2$. The final difficulty score can be made to provide more information near $\theta = 0$ by shortening the step size (the curve for $ad = 0.025$ is shown). However, as the step size is shortened, the information curve for the final difficulty score must approach the curve for the standard test, shown as a solid line. This is so because final difficulty score is perfectly correlated with number-right score [Equation (37)]. Thus shortening the step size produces only small gains near $\theta = 0$ and ultimately leads to a serious loss of accuracy for final difficulty score at more extreme values of θ.

The average difficulty score with $ad = 0.20$ is better than any of the other tailored procedures throughout the entire range shown. It is almost as good as the standard test near $\theta = 0$ and is better for other values of θ. This result cannot be improved by shortening the step size. It will be seen that when the average difficulty score is used, too short a step size causes loss of accuracy throughout the entire range of θ.

We conclude tentatively that for the up-and-down method the average difficulty score is preferable to the final difficulty score, at least whenever we want good measurement throughout a range of θ, not just at $\theta = 0$. There may be some exceptions to this in the case of very short tests. Our further investigations of the up-and-down method will be directed principally at 60-item tests and will be based entirely on average difficulty scores.

All the information curves in Figure 8–5 relate to the up-and-down method with average difficulty score, except for the solid curves, which show the information produced by the standard tests. When $n = 10$, the best step size seems to be between $d = 0.2/a$ and $d = 0.5/a$. With this step size the tailored test is 85 per cent efficient at $\theta = 0$ compared to the standard test and is more efficient than the standard test for extreme values of θ. When $n = 60$, the best step size seems to be roughly $d = 0.2/a$. With this step size the tailored test is more than 90 per cent efficient at $\theta = 0$ compared to the standard test. At $a\theta = \pm1.5$, the standard test is only 48 per cent efficient compared to this tailored test (that is, the standard test would have to be more than twice as long as the tailored test to produce the same amount of information for examinees at $\theta = \pm1.5/a$).

It is no surprise that step size can be too small for effective measurement of examinees at extreme values of θ; n cumulated steps may never reach the item difficulty level appropriate for the examinee. It may well seem

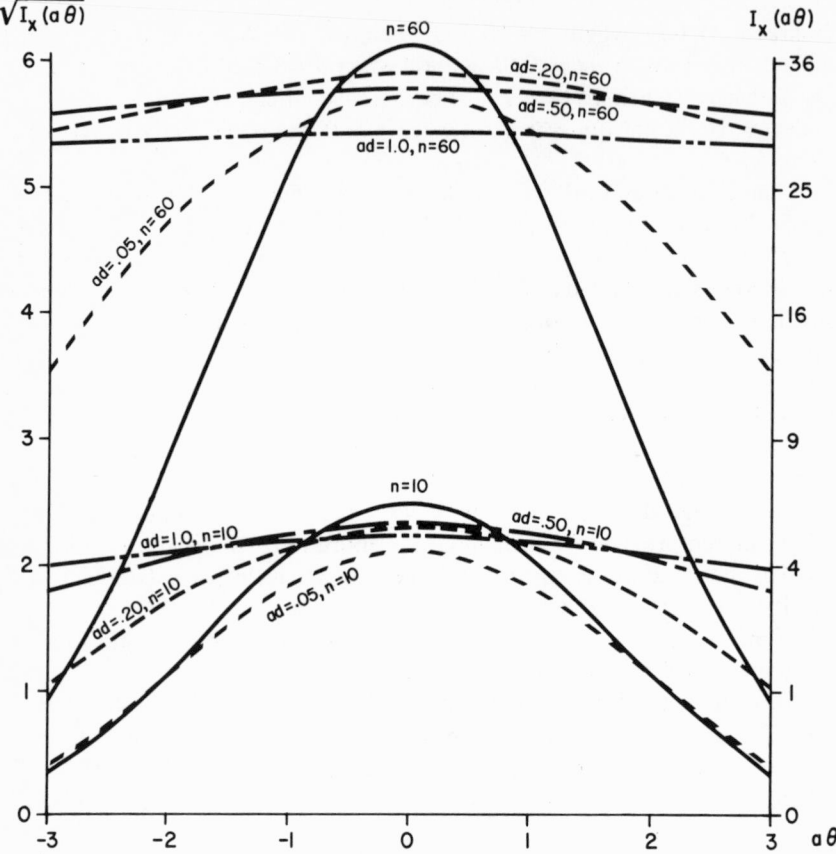

Figure 8–5.

surprising, however, that when average difficulty score is used, step size can be too small for measuring examinees at $\theta = 0$, as shown in Figure 8–5. After all, the most effective measurement for such examinees in conventional testing is obtained when $b_i = 0$ for all items.

Consideration of a limiting case of the up-and-down method, the case where the step size is zero, may throw some light on the apparent paradox. If the step size is zero, all examinees will have the same average difficulty score, regardless of their θ. In this limiting case it is clear that number-right score can provide a good measure of θ, whereas average difficulty score cannot. This suggests that the effectiveness of average difficulty score at $\theta = 0$ falls off when step size becomes too small, as illustrated by Figure 8–5.

13. A Comparison of Logistic and Normal Ogive Item Characteristic Curves

Except for this section, all information functions given in this chapter were calculated under the normal ogive model given by Equation (3) or (5). Here, in Table 8–1, we compare information functions obtained from

Table 8–1. A Comparison of Information Functions for Normal Ogive and Logistic ICC's

Step size ad	Test length n	ICC	Information function $I_x(\theta)$ at			
			$\theta = 0$	± 1	± 2	± 3
1.0	60	Normal	5.45	5.45	5.40	5.37
		Logistic	5.44	5.43	5.38	5.34
	10	Normal	2.22	2.21	2.10	2.00
		Logistic	2.23	2.20	2.07	1.97
0.05	60	Normal	5.73	5.48	4.72	3.53
		Logistic	6.10	5.60	4.41	2.97
	10	Normal	2.27	1.97	1.20	0.45
		Logistic	2.42	1.87	0.98	0.44

Equation (3) for normal ogive ICC's with those obtained from Equation (1) for logistic ICC's.

The numerical differences between the two models are not wholly negligible. However, it does not seem necessary to compute all information functions under both normal ogive and logistic models.

14. The Effect of Chance Success

Common sense and also empirical data tell us that even examinees at the lowest θ levels have a chance considerably greater than zero of getting correct answers to multiple-choice questions. Clearly, this will result from guessing, whether random or nonrandom (if there is such a thing as non-random guessing).

The three-parameter models (2) and (5) were designed to fit this situation. The parameter c_i represents the probability of success for low-level examinees. There is no need to specify any particular relation between c_i and the number of possible responses to a multiple-choice item. With 5-choice items, practical experience indicates that most items will be fitted by values of c_i between 0.10 and 0.20. There is no need to assume that all items in a test have the same c_i. However, for simplicity, we here assume that all items have $c_i = 0.20$. We shall investigate whether or not this has any clear-cut implications for tailored testing.

Figure 8–6 compares information functions for $c_i = 0$ with those for $c_i = 0.20$ for all items. As always, the standard tests are shown by solid lines. All other curves are for the up-and-down method with average difficulty score, $n = 60$.

Figure 8–6 confirms that chance success in answering items seriously reduces measurement efficiency. The loss is, of course, greatest at low θ levels, but in tailored testing it is substantial at all θ levels. The loss in information at $\theta = 0$ is 33 per cent for the standard test, 38 per cent for $ad = 0.05$, 46 per cent for $ad = 0.20$, and 68 per cent for $ad = 1.0$. It appears that the larger the step size, the greater the loss caused by guessing.

The simple up-and-down method as described here is designed to move towards a situation in which about half the items administered to an ex-

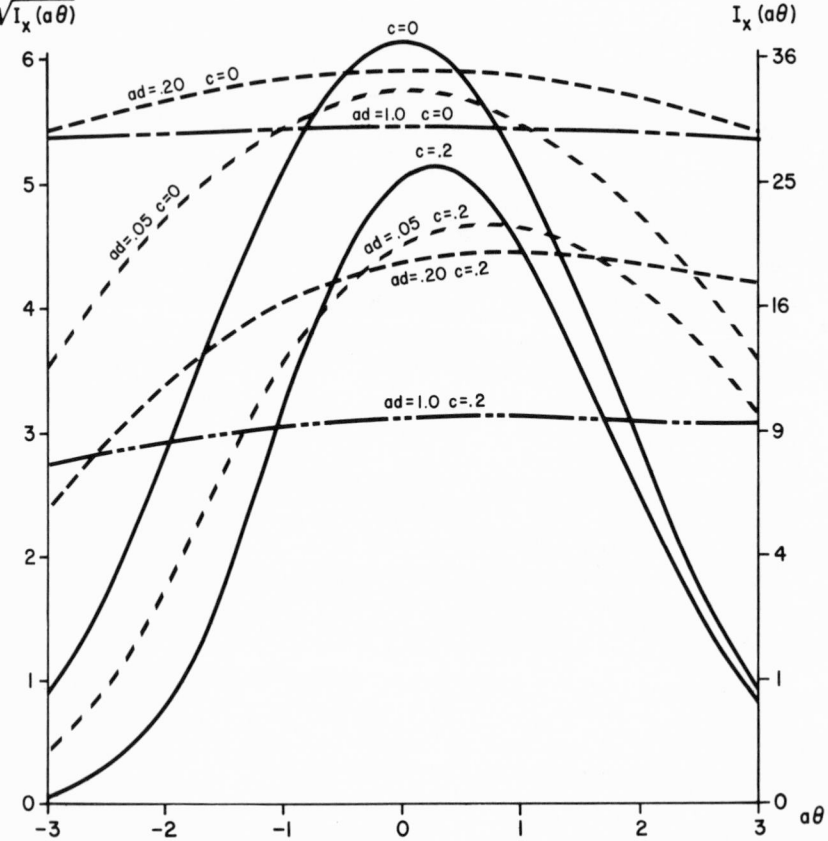

Figure 8–6.

aminee will be answered correctly and about half incorrectly. This is the proper ratio when there is no chance success, but it has long been recognized that easier items are preferable when chance success occurs. This conclusion is particularly obvious when $c_i \geqq 0.5$, so that 50 per cent success is at or below the chance level. It used to be thought that for optimal measurement the examinee should answer $(1 + c)/2$ of the items correctly. This would be 60 per cent of the items, for our case where $c = 0.2$.

Lord (1953, pp. 67–69) found that still easier items than this would be preferable. A formula provided by Birnbaum (1968, Equation 20.4.22) for the logistic model shows that for optimal measurement we should have

$$b_i - \theta = - \frac{1}{1.7a_i} \log_e \frac{1 + \sqrt{1 + 8c_i}}{2} \tag{46}$$

When $a_i = 0.5$ and $c_i = 0.2$, we find that $b_i - \theta$ should be -0.314, in which case, by Equation (2), $P_i(\theta) = 0.653$.

How shall we arrange matters so that on a sufficiently long test the examinee will eventually be answering 60–70 per cent of the items correctly? One possibility is to make the step size in the positive direction smaller than the step size in the negative direction. We shall investigate specifically the branching rule that positive steps be of size Hd and negative steps be of size Ld, for $H = 2$ and $L = 3$. Also for $H = 1$, $L = 2$. Also for $H = 1$, $L = 3$. Although these are still up-and-down methods, we shall also call them *H-L methods*. For convenience we shall speak of the up-2-down-3 method, the up-1-down-2 method, and so on.

15. *H-L* Methods

Unless otherwise stated, subsequently reported results deal with the case in which chance success occurs, with $c_i = 0.2$ for all items.

The *H-L* methods are random-walking methods designed to administer items at a difficulty level appropriate for the examinee. This should reduce the asymmetry of information curves such as those shown for $c = 0.2$ in Figure 8–6.

The chance nature of success introduces a random element into our measurements that necessarily must reduce their accuracy. We cannot hope to regain the lost information by tinkering with item difficulty levels. All we can hope to accomplish is to find a way of determining what items to administer that is better than the simple up-and-down method of previous sections, which we can now describe as the method with $H = L = 1$.

We shall continue to use the average difficulty method of scoring. The necessary recursion equations are again (38) through (45), this time with H and L free to assume any integer values.

For fixed a and for large n, the quantity $d(H + L)/2$ is in practice roughly inversely proportional to the total number of items that will be prepared and stored in the computer (see Section 20). Figure 8–7 compares for $H\text{-}L$ methods, each of which has $d(H + L)/2 = 0.25/a$. The up-1-down-2 method and the up-1-down-3 method seem superior to the others. The up-1-down-1 method is the simple up-and-down method discussed in earlier sections. It is clearly inferior to the other $H\text{-}L$ methods, all of which tend to favor easier items.

To avoid crowding, curves with shorter and longer average step size

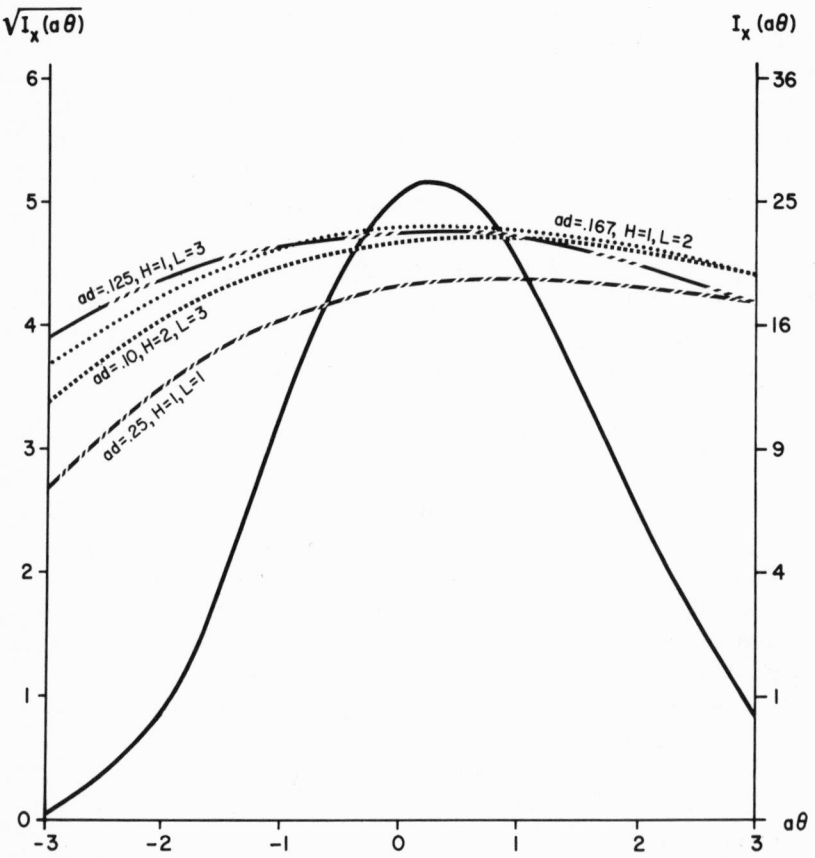

Figure 8–7.
Comparison of various *H-L* methods.

are not shown in the figure. On the basis of numerical comparisons it was found that substantially reducing the step size gave poorer measurement for $\theta = \pm 2$, for example, without improving matters at $\theta = 0$. Increasing the step size gave poorer measurement for $-2 \leqq \theta \leqq +2$ without much gain outside that range. Thus the curves shown seem to be near-optimal for the *H-L* methods.

16. Block Up-and-Down Methods

Let us consider other ways of modifying the simple up-and-down method so as to administer somewhat easier items in situations in which answers may be correct because of chance success. If the score on a single item were polychotomous instead of dichotomous, it might be easier to arrange an up-and-down procedure under which the examinee will get about two thirds of the items right. This suggests combining items of equal difficulty into blocks. After a block has been administered, the score on the block is used to determine which block shall be administered next.

In bioassay the block up-and-down method often has great advantages. For example, it may be convenient to treat several insects at once rather than one at a time. The blocking method has been investigated by Tsutakawa (1967a, 1967b, 1963), Wetherill (1963), Cochran and Davis (1964), and Brownlee et al. (1953). It is not clear that blocking items adds any convenience in computerized testing. It does, however, make possible more complicated branching processes than the usual random walk.

Only one block up-and-down method is investigated here. The blocks contain two items each. If the examinee answers both items at difficulty level b_i correctly, the next block will have items of difficulty $b_i + d$. If he answers only one correctly, the next two items will be at difficulty level b_i. If he answers neither correctly, the next block will be at difficulty level $b_i - 3d$.

If average difficulty score is used, the basic recursion equation for this method is

$$X_{v+2}(b,\theta) = \begin{cases} 2b + 2d + X_v(b + d,\theta) & \text{with probability } P_t^2 \\ 2b + X_v(b,\theta) & \text{with probability } 2P_tQ_t \\ 2b - 6d + X_v(b - 3d,\theta) & \text{with probability } Q_t^2 \end{cases} \quad (47)$$

where the random variable $X_v(b,\theta) \sum_{r=2}^{v+1} b^{(r)}$ is the sum of the b_i values of the items administered to an examinee at ability level θ under the specified block up-and-down method with $b^{(1)} = b$. The other necessary equations can be derived from Equation (47) but will not be written out here.

Results of the calculations showed this particular method to be inferior to a variety of the simple H-L methods described in Section 15. Many other block methods could be tried out. This will not be done here, however.

17. Plicate Methods

When $c \neq 0$, we need to produce an asymmetry, so that the examinee is more likely to give a right answer than a wrong one. An obvious device is to rule that a correctly answered item need not always be followed, as in the simple H-L methods, by a more difficult item.

Here we investigate a *two-ply method,* defined as follows. Whenever the examinee's number-right score on the items already administered is an odd number, the next item is assigned by the H-L method with $H = 1$ and $L = 1$ (this is the simple up-and-down method). Whenever the examinee's number-right score on the items already administered is an even number, we assign the next item by setting $H = 0$ and $L = 1$.

We shall also investigate a *three-ply method:* When the examinee's number-right score is not a multiple of 3, $H = 1$ and $L = 1$; when it is a multiple of 3, $H = 0$ and $L = 1$. These and other similar methods will be called *plicate methods.* The examinee's final score need not be his number-right score. Here in all cases his final score will be his average difficulty score.

The necessary basic equations for the two-ply method, again derived by the same line of reasoning used in Sections 12 and 7, will be given. The extension to the three-ply and to other patterns is straightforward. The average item difficulty

$$x = \frac{1}{n} \sum_{v=2}^{n+1} b^{(v)}$$

is the examinee's score. The random variable $X(b,\theta) = \sum_{r=2}^{v+1} b^{(r)}$ is the sum of the item difficulties when the two-ply method is used with $b^{(1)} = b$, the examinee being at ability level θ.

To start with, we shall need to consider the alternate two-ply method in which $H = 0$ and $L = 1$ when the number-right score is odd and $H = 1$ and $L = 1$ when the number-right score is even. A complete set of equations will be needed for this alternate pattern as well as for the original pattern. A prime will be attached to all quantities computed under the alternate pattern. Thus the random variable $X'_v(b,\theta)$ is the sum $\sum_{r=2}^{v+1} b^{(r)}$ obtained by an examinee at ability level θ when the alternate pattern is used to pick the items administered.

The basic recursions are given by two formulas:

$$X_{v+1}(b,\theta) = \begin{cases} b + d + X'_v(b + d,\theta) & \text{with probability } P_t \\ b - d + X_v(b - d,\theta) & \text{with probability } Q_t \end{cases} \quad (48)$$

$$X'_{v+1}(b,\theta) = \begin{cases} b + X_v(b,\theta) & \text{with probability } P_t \\ b - d + X'_v(b - d,\theta) & \text{with probability } Q_t \end{cases} \quad (49)$$

We can halve the number of equations that must be written by using the superscripts * and ° with the understanding that either one of these is to be omitted while the other is to be replaced by a prime. Then, letting $H = 1$ and $H' = 0$, the following equation can represent both Equations (48) and (49):

$$X^{\circ}_{v+1}(b,\theta) = \begin{cases} b + H^{\circ}d + X^*_v(b + H^{\circ}d,\theta) & \text{with probability } P_t \\ b - d + X^{\circ}_v(b - d,\theta) & \text{with probability } Q_t \end{cases} \quad (50)$$

From this we can derive

$$E^{\circ}_{v+1}(b) = E^{\circ}_1(b) + P_t E^*_v(b + H^{\circ}d) + Q_t E^{\circ}_v(b - d) \quad (51)$$

$$E^{\circ}_1(b) = (H^{\circ}d - t)P_t - (d + t)Q_t \quad (52)$$

$$\begin{aligned} W^{\circ}_{v+1}(b) = {} & W^{\circ}_1(b) + P_t W^*_v(b + H^{\circ}d) + Q_t W^{\circ}_v(b - d) \\ & + 2P_t(H^{\circ}d - t)E^*_v(b + H^{\circ}d) \\ & - 2Q_t(d + t)E^{\circ}_v(b - d) \end{aligned} \quad (53)$$

$$W^{\circ}_1(b) = (H^{\circ}d - t)^2 P_t + (d + t)^2 Q_t \quad (54)$$

$$\begin{aligned} D^{\circ}_{v+1}(b) = {} & D^{\circ}_1(b) + P_t D^*_v(b + H^{\circ}d) + Q_t D^{\circ}_v(b - d) \\ & + [E^{\circ}_v(b - d) - E^*_v(b + H^{\circ}d)]\frac{\partial Q_t}{\partial \theta} \end{aligned} \quad (55)$$

$$D^{\circ}_1(b) = -d(1 + H^{\circ})\frac{\partial Q_t}{\partial \theta} \quad (56)$$

Figure 8–8 compares the best results obtained with the H-L method, the two-ply method, and the three-ply method. The three-ply curve for $ad = 0.2$ is almost the same as the two-ply curve shown, but slightly lower. It appears that the two-ply method is slightly superior when $c = 0.2$ to the three-ply method. The main conclusion is that all the methods shown in Figure 8–8 are almost equally good when the proper step size is used.

Figure 8–8 has been shaded for $\theta > 2$ and $\theta > -1$ to call attention to a way of improving measurement that has not been mentioned up to now.

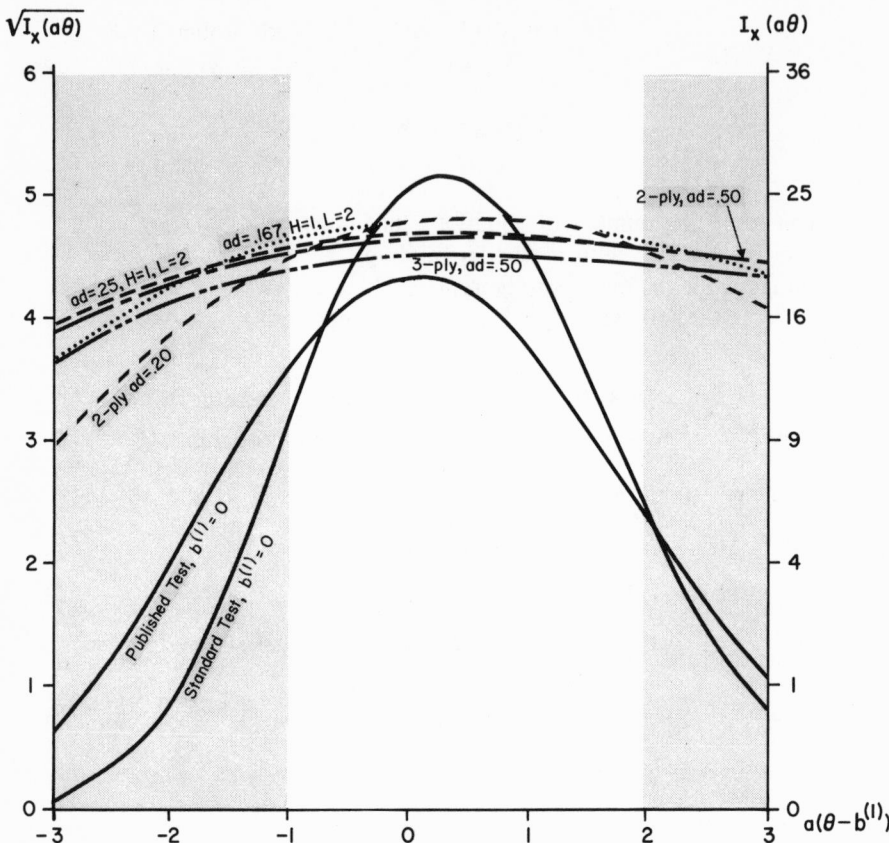

Figure 8–8.
Comparison of *H-L* methods with plicate methods.

Given the items $(a_i, b_i,$ and $c_i)$, the information function does not depend at all on the nature of the group tested. In particular, the information curve depends on θ and $b^{(1)}$ only through their difference $\theta - b^{(1)}$. This has been indicated in Figure 8–8 by labeling the base line $a(\theta - b^{(1)})$. In looking at earlier results (see discussion in Section 11), we have frequently evaluated them for a group of examinees in the range $-1.5 \leq a(\theta - b^{(1)}) \leq +1.5$. Suppose we keep the same group of examinees and the same tailored-testing procedure except that the first item administered is taken at difficulty level $b^{(1)} = -0.5$ instead of at $b^{(1)} = 0$. The examinees now fall in the interval $-1 \leq a(\theta - b^{(1)}) \leq +2$.

Figure 8–8 shows that we get better measurement in this interval than in the other one. The information function is nearly the same from one end of the interval to the other. This is the result achieved by choosing the first item administered at an easier difficulty level than we have used up to now. The two-ply method with step size $d = 0.5/a$ is 86 per cent efficient at $\theta - b^{(1)} = 0.5/a$ compared to the standard test. That is, it produces as much information with $n = 60$ items as would a standard test, $b_i = 0$, with $n = 52$ items. Here we have assumed, as in the last several sections, that all ICC's are normal ogives and that all c_i's $= 0.2$. Except at $\theta - b^{(1)} = 0.5/a$ the two-ply test is more than 86 per cent efficient compared to the standard test. At $\theta - b^{(1)} = -1/a$ the standard test is only 49 per cent efficient compared to the two-ply test. At $\theta - b^{(1)} = +2/a$, the standard test is only 30 per cent as efficient.

The standard test is a peaked test with all items of equal difficulty, $b_i = 0$. This produces unusually accurate measurement around one value of θ (near $\theta - b^{(1)} = 0.3/a$ in our case) at the expense of less accurate measurement at extreme values of θ. The typical published test has a wide range of b_i values (partly because it is easier to produce such a test and partly because most people believe a range of item difficulty is necessary to secure good measurement. Actually, for typical groups and typical values of a_i, the peaked test would usually provide better measurement for all except the most extreme examinees in the group tested, as is illustrated in Figure 8–8). Actual b_i values, estimated for a well-known published test, were used to compute the information curve labeled "published test" in Figure 8–8. The curve shown was computed from Birnbaum's equation (1968, Equation 20.2.2)

$$I(\theta, x) = \frac{[\sum_{i=1}^{n} P_i'(\theta)]^2}{\sum_{i=1}^{n} P_i(\theta) Q_i(\theta)}$$

under the assumption that a_i was the same for all items and also that $c_i = 0.20$ (the actual published test does not satisfy this assumption). The 60 values of b_i ranged from -2.5 to $+1.5$. We note that the tailored tests all measure more accurately at all values of θ than does such an unpeaked test.

18. Item Economy

The theory up to this point has assumed that items were available at whatever difficulty level was required by the random-walk procedure. In principle this would require for the H-L or plicate methods a total of

$n(n + 1)/2$ items, regardless of step size. When $c = 0$, there is usually a vanishingly small probability of needing items with $b_i > 5$, for example. If we supply all the items that theoretically might be required in the range $-5 \leq b_i \leq +5$ and no items outside this range, the simple up-and-down method will require, depending on the details of the random walk, about $(1 + 5/d)(n - 5/2d)$ items, assuming d is a submultiple of 5. For sizable n, this quantity is roughly inversely proportional to the step size d. For $n = 60$, $d = 0.50$, the number of items required would be about 600.

Presumably this number could be considerably reduced without much loss of accuracy of measurement. Whenever items are in short supply (many shortages should disappear, given enough time), practical applications of tailored testing will have to consider which shortcuts will cause the least loss of efficiency. Much light could be thrown on this question by Monte-Carlo studies of different possible procedures.

It would be desirable to assign a cost to items, a cost to computer storage space, and a loss function to errors of measurement. One could then investigate the economic efficiency of various tailored-testing procedures under various cost conditions. Something of this sort will have to be done, whether formally or informally, before tailored testing comes into widespread use. Nothing like this has been attempted for this chapter.

19. Robbins-Monro Processes

It will have occurred to the reader that a large step size is needed for the first few items so that the item difficulty can be rapidly adjusted to suit an extreme examinee. After this has been done, progressively smaller step sizes are needed in order to "zero in" on the best value. Probably considerable gain could be achieved simply by choosing $d = 1$, for example, for the first three or four items and thereafter proceeding with a smaller but fixed d by any of the methods of the preceding sections. This rule has not yet been investigated for tailored testing.

Carrying this idea to its logical conclusion leads to a Robbins-Monro type of process. Let $P(b,\theta)$ denote any monotonic increasing ICC, satisfying certain regularity assumptions. An important advantage of the method is that we do not have to know the mathematical form of $P(b,\theta)$. We wish to find the value of b for which $P(b,\theta)$ equals some chosen constant, α [under the normal ogive model of Equation (3), α is usually chosen as $\frac{1}{2}$, because $P(\theta,\theta) = \frac{1}{2}$].

In a Robbins-Monro process we choose a decreasing sequence of positive constants $A_1, A_2, A_3, \ldots$, to be discussed later. We choose a trial value of b for the first item—let this be $b^{(1)} = 0$. We administer the item and observe the response $u_1 = 0$ or 1. Then we choose all subsequent values of $b^{(v)}$ by the rule

$$b^{(v+1)} == b^{(v)} + A_v(u_v - \alpha) \tag{57}$$

This leads to an *H-L* method with continually shrinking step size. Robbins and Monro (1951) showed that under suitable conditions $b^{(v)}$ converges in probability to θ as $v \to \infty$, that is, $b^{(v)}$ *is a consistent estimator of* θ.

Chung (1954) and Hodges and Lehmann (1956) showed that under certain conditions, satisfied for our problem, if the A_v's are determined from

$$A_v == C/v \tag{58}$$

where C is a constant to be determined, the asymptotic sampling variance of $b^{(v)}$ will be minimized. Hodges and Lehmann (1956, Section 3) show that for our kind of quantal response problem the value of C minimizing the asymptotic sampling variance is

$$C = - \left. \frac{1}{\partial P(b,\theta)/\partial b} \right|_{b=\theta} \tag{59}$$

Of course, this value cannot be determined without knowing the nature of $P(b,\theta)$. In our case this optimal value for the normal ogive model of Equation (5) is

$$C = \frac{\sqrt{2\pi}}{a_i(1 - c_i)} \tag{60}$$

If $c_i = 0.2$ and $a_i = 1.0$, then the initial step size under Equations (58) and (60) is $A_1 == C = 3.1$. If $a_i = 0.333$, then $A_1 = 9.4$; if $a_i = 0.10$, then $A_1 = 31.3$, and so on. However, we have been assuming that almost all our examinees fall within some roughly known interval centered about the origin of our θ scale. If we have such information (obtained from previous testings) and if we are willing to forego accurate measurement of the very rare examinee who falls outside the interval, then we probably do not need to use an initial step size greater than about half the width of the interval.

It would be very desirable to obtain information functions for the test scores $b^{(n)}$ produced by the stochastic approximation method outlined. Unfortunately, there appears to be no available method of doing this precisely for a test longer than a dozen or so items. Recursion formulas cannot be worked out by the methods used in earlier sections.

Asymptotic formulas are available, but these would produce information functions that are horizontal straight lines. Previous sections indicate that optimal step size is found by reducing step size as far as possible without making the information curve fall off too sharply on both sides of the maximum. Asymptotic results would be useless for this purpose.

One way to deal with this problem would be by using Monte-Carlo procedures. For various reasons we have not used any Monte-Carlo procedures for this study. Wetherill (1963) made extensive Monte-Carlo investigations of the Robbins-Monro method from the bioassay point of view. He found that the method was not sensitive to mischoice of C. The method was "extremely satisfactory" in the case where $P_i(b^{(n)},\theta) \to 0.50$ as n becomes large (we have this case when $c_i = 0$), but "of little use," "unsuitable," or "hopeless" in the case where $P_i(b^{(n)},\theta) \to 0.75$ (we have this case when $c_i = 0.5$).

The main trouble in the latter case ($P_i \to 0.75$) is the large bias produced by the Robbins-Monro method. As already pointed out in Section 11, bias is a serious matter in bioassay work but usually of no concern in mental testing. For this reason, and for other reasons indicated in Section 11, it is difficult to apply many of Wetherill's reported results to the purposes of this chapter. (Wetherill also tried many promising up-and-down methods, which could not be evaluated by the techniques used for this study. These could and should be investigated for tailored-testing purposes by use of Monte-Carlo methods.)

The use of Equation (58) for deciding step size is practical in bioassay but is not practical in tailored testing. In principle, use of Equation (58) would require that almost 2^n different items be available to the computer—an impossible requirement if $n = 60$. An obvious modification is to classify all items on b_i into class intervals of width d and then pick a sequence of class intervals corresponding as closely as possible to the sequence specified by Equation (57).

This modification destroys all the asymptotic virtue of the Robbins-Monro process, because the use of fixed class intervals prevents convergence of $b^{(n)}$ to θ as $n \to \infty$. However, this difficulty need not impair the information actually produced by a test of fixed length. If a psychometrician is going to administer a test of fixed length n, there is no good reason he should use a consistent estimator of θ.

The way of choosing items outlined above was tried for this study for short tests with $n = 10$ and $c_i = 0.20$. With $n = 10$ it was possible for the computer to deal individually with each of the 2^{10} possible patterns of examinee response. Average difficulty score was used, not final difficulty score, as in the standard Robbins-Monro process.

No choice of C was found that yielded information curves as good as those obtained by the better up-and-down methods. Detailed results will not be given here.

Another possibility for improving the estimation of θ is to use a weighted rather than an unweighted average of item difficulties for the examinee's score. The difficulty $b^{(1)}$ of the first item has always been omitted from the average difficulty score [Equation (19)] because it is the same for all examinees and thus cannot carry any information about θ. If step size is small, the same objection applies to a lesser extent to $b^{(2)}$. Clearly, the item difficulties for the earlier items are not expected to be as close to θ as those for the later items. This suggests that the later items should receive more weight in determining final score than the earlier items.

Two systems of weighting were tried here:

$$x = \sum_{v=2}^{n+1} \sqrt{v} \, b^{(v)} \tag{61}$$

$$x = \sum_{v=2}^{n+1} v b^{(v)} \tag{62}$$

The weighted score (61) with weights proportional to the square root of the item serial number v was found to be a little better than the unweighted average difficulty score. The weighted score (62) with weights proportional to item serial number was still better than (61).

It would be desirable to have results for $n = 60$ as well as for $n = 10$. In view of the incomplete nature of presently available results, no information functions will be displayed here. There is clearly a need for extensive studies to investigate further the methods already outlined and the numerous possible recombinations and mutations of these methods. Most of these methods may have to be studied by Monte-Carlo procedures. The simpler Robbins-Monro methods can be evaluated for $n = 60$ by a recursive procedure involving numerical interpolation, devised by Cochran and Davis (1965). (Investigations using this procedure are currently in progress.)

20. Summary and Conclusions

When computers are used extensively for instruction, it will be convenient to use them to administer tests for measurement purposes as well as for instructional purposes. We restrict attention here to tests used for measurement. Given a supply of pretested items, the computer can individually design a test for each individual examinee. How can it secure the most accurate measurement?

The question falls into two parts: What items shall be administered to a particular examinee? How shall his responses be scored? We do not find optimal procedures. We compare various simple procedures and answer a number of primitive but previously unanswered questions.

A number of empirical studies of tailored tests have been carried out using an external criterion to evaluate the results. Here we have no external criterion. Our purpose is to measure, not to predict.

The examinee can be measured by the following simple *branching rule:* Administer a harder item after each correct answer and an easier item after each wrong answer. Start with large changes in item difficulty (b) and then use smaller and smaller steps, so as to zero in on the difficulty level at which the examinee answers correctly 50 per cent (for example) of the time. This final difficulty level, $b^{(n+1)}$, is a measure of the examinee's standing on the trait measured by the test.

This is the Robbins-Monro stochastic approximation process. Asymptotically optimal details for the procedure are known. The investigation of its efficiency in subasymptotic situations requires Monte-Carlo methods or special methods involving interpolation recently devised by Cochran and Davis (1965). We do not use these methods here. Instead we investigate various branching rules that do not shrink the step size as testing progresses. We also investigate three different scoring methods. We evaluate the efficiency of these procedures for short, medium, or long tests, as desired. Our problems are found to be very closely related to certain problems in bioassay. Many important results obtained for the bioassay problems are of direct use to us here.

To keep matters simple, we assume that available items differ only in difficulty (b_i). To compare the efficiency of various branching and scoring procedures, we often assume that the probability of a correct answer to an item is a normal ogive function of θ, the examinee's standing on the trait measured. Alternatively, a logistic function is assumed. Both assumptions are generalized to cover the case where correct answers may be caused by guessing.

Conventional tests ordinarily provide good measurement for the middle three quarters, for example, of the group tested. The tailored test cannot hope to provide much improved measurement for these examinees, but it can provide better measurement at higher and lower levels of θ. In view of this picture, we are not satisfied to use an overall group statistic to describe the effectiveness of measurement; instead, we use an *information function* to tell us the accuracy of measurement at each level of θ.

We compute and compare information curves for a variety of procedures. Some of the conclusions tentatively reached for a certain specified, presumably typical,[2] tailored test using a simple *up-and-down* branching rule are listed below. This rule increases (decreases) item difficulty by an amount d after each correct (incorrect) response.

2. The conclusions given are for items with $a_i = 0.5$.

1. If the test score is $b^{(n+1)}$ and the step size d is 0.50, increasing the number of test items beyond $n = 10$ does not appreciably increase the accuracy of measurement.
2. The number of items answered correctly is perfectly correlated with the score $b^{(n+1)}$.
3. When the foregoing scores are used, decreasing the step size increases the accuracy of measurement near some one value of θ and decreases it elsewhere.
4. The average difficulty of all items administered is a score providing better measurement of the examinee than either $b^{(n+1)}$ or the number of right answers.

In the conclusions that follow, the score used is always average difficulty.

5. For $n = 60$ a step size of approximately 0.40 seems best and for $n = 10$ a step size of approximately 1.0. Either shortening or lengthening the step size decreases the accuracy of measurement throughout the range of θ that interests us.
6. When items can be answered correctly by chance success, the accuracy of measurement is sharply reduced. Also, the information curves become asymmetrical.
7. When there is chance success, the accuracy of measurement can be considerably increased by certain asymmetric modifications of the step size used in the simple up-and-down method. Two such modifications are found to be almost equally good.
8. When there is chance success, the first item administered should be easier than that specified by a common rule of thumb.
9. These improvements produce nearly symmetrical and reasonably flat information curves.
10. When these tailored-testing procedures are compared with a "standard" conventional peaked test, also with a conventional unpeaked test, both scored by the number of right answers, we see that the best tailored-testing procedure is nowhere less than 86 per cent efficient compared to the peaked test. For high-level examinees, the peaked test is only about 30 per cent efficient compared to the tailored testing. The tailored procedure gives more accurate measurement than the unpeaked conventional test for all examinees, regardless of level.

Before closing, let us note some of the limitations of tailored-testing procedures and of the theory given here.

1. Suppose a pool of test items can be grouped into subtests measuring substantially different psychological dimensions. Without such group-

ing into subtests, tailored testing based on such a pool cannot produce accurate measurements with a clear meaning.

2. The theory given here assumes that items differ from each other only on difficulty level. In practice they differ also on a_i (discriminating power) and on c_i (see Section 4). It is an open theoretical question how tailored testing should be modified to deal with this more general situation.

3. Accurate estimation of the item parameters necessary for tailored testing is at present a difficult, expensive, and hazardous operation.

4. If there is any doubt about the accuracy of the estimated values of the item difficulties b_i, there will be doubt about the accuracy and fairness of the final scores given to the examinees.

5. If, for example, 500 items are available for tailored testing, better measurement will often be obtained by selecting, for example, the $n = 60$ most discriminating items (highest a_i) and administering these as a conventional test, rather than by using all 500 in a tailored-testing procedure. *This may actually prove to be a fatal objection to any general use of tailored testing.*

Until now, even some very primitive questions about how to carry out tailored testing did not have even vague answers. Granted certain assumptions, we now have tentative answers to some of these questions. More important, we have a theoretical approach, drawing heavily on bioassay theory and results and on the theory of stochastic processes with particular reference to Markov chains. This theory shows how we can go ahead to evaluate the endless variety of different possible combinations of branching processes and scoring procedures available for tailored testing. Perhaps in due course some direct way of finding truly optimal tailored-testing strategies will be found.

The theory in this chapter is based on certain rather technical and specialized assumptions. Most of the conclusions reached are, hopefully, of more general validity. The tailored-testing procedures themselves can provide accurate measurements without any need for many of these assumptions.

We have rigorously evaluated numerically for tests of 60 items a number of tailored-testing procedures with fixed step size. Up-and-down item-selection methods with continually shrinking step size (Section 19) should be able to produce more accurate measurement than is obtained by methods without a shrinking step size. There is a clear need for studies to evaluate various possible shrinking-step-size procedures for tests much longer than $n = 10$ or 12.

Small sample properties of the maximum likelihood estimator of θ

(Tsutakawa, 1967a, 1967b; Billingsley, 1961; Dixon, 1965; Dixon and Mood, 1948) should also be investigated. Another estimation method requiring further study by Monte-Carlo methods is the Spearman-Kärber method (Spearman, 1908; Kärber, 1931). This method has been described and favorably evaluated for bioassay purposes by Tsutakawa (1967a).

Appendix

This appendix outlines one or two results from the theory of Markov chains that are relevant for evaluating tailored-testing procedures.

We are concerned (as in Section 5) with the random variable $b^{(v)}$, the difficulty of the vth item administered to a given examinee. The possible values of $b^{(v)}$ are [see Equation (15)] $b^{(v)} = jd$, where d is some prespecified step size and j is an (possibly negative) integer with $|j| \leq n$. There will be no loss of generality for the purposes of this appendix if we rescale $b^{(v)}$ so as to set $d = 1$, in which case $b^{(v)}$ takes on integer values only between $-n$ and $+n$, inclusive. Denote such integer values by either j, k, or i.

Define the *transition probability*:

$$p_{ij} == \text{Prob}(b^{(v+1)} = j | b^{(v)} = i) \qquad v = 1, 2, \ldots \qquad (63)$$

By the Markov property this does not depend on $b^{(1)}, \ldots, b^{(v-1)}$. We shall consider only *stationary transition probabilities*, which means that p_{ij} does not vary with v (this rules out all branching methods with shrinking step size).

Define the *r-step transition probabilities*:

$$p_{ij}^{(r)} == \text{Prob}(b^{(v+r)} = j | b^{(v)} = i) \qquad r, v = 1, 2, \ldots \qquad (64)$$

It is easily seen that

$$p_{ij}^{(2)} = \sum_k p_{ik} p_{kj}$$

If the $p_{ij} == p_{ij}^{(1)}$'s are written as the elements of a square matrix $P = ||p_{ij}||$ of order $2n + 1$, then the $p_{ij}^{(2)}$'s are elements of $P^2 = PP$. Similarly, the $p_{ij}^{(r)}$'s are elements of P^r:

$$||p_{ij}^{(r)}|| = ||p_{ij}||^r \qquad (65)$$

For any given examinee the nonzero elements of the matrix P are the $P_i(\theta)$'s and $Q_i(\theta)$'s of Equation (1), (2), (3), or (5) (or simple functions of them, depending on the branching process chosen).

Let p_{oi} denote the probability that $b^{(1)} = i$ and let p be the vector $\{p_{oi}\}$. If we choose our origin so that $b^{(1)} = 0$, then p_{oi} is zero, except that when $i = 0$, p_{oi} is 1.

The final frequency distribution of $b^{(n+1)}$ for a given examinee is thus the vector $P'^n p$:

$$\{\text{Prob}(b^{(n)} = i|\theta)\} = P'^n p \tag{66}$$

The mean and variance of this distribution are important quantities related in a simple way to those computed recursively by Equations (25) and (30). These quantities could be computed directly from $p'P^n$. The matrix P^n may be computed from the latent roots and vectors of PP' and $P'P$ (Feller, 1959, Chapter 16, Equation 1.12).

As already noted in Section 19, asymptotic results are of marginal interest for present purposes. Asymptotic properties of $b^{(n+1)}$ can be found from Chung (1960, Part 1, Section 12). Although the $b^{(v)}$'s form a Markov chain, the average difficulty scores do not. The average difficulty score is a *functional of the Markov chain*. Asymptotic properties of such functionals have been treated by Chung (1960, Part 1, Sections 14–16). An asymptotic formula for the error variance of the average difficulty score has been given by Tsutakawa (1967a, Equation 5).

REFERENCES

Billingsley, P. 1961. *Statistical inference for Markov processes.* Statistical Research Monographs, vol. II. Chicago: Univ. of Chicago Press.

Birnbaum, A. 1968. Some latent trait models and their use in inferring an examinee's ability. In *Statistical theories of mental test scores,* ed. F. M. Lord and M. R. Novick. Reading, Mass.: Addison-Wesley, Chaps. 17–20.

Bock, R. D. 1967. Fitting a response model for n dichotomous items. Paper read at the Psychometric Society Meeting at Madison, Wisconsin.

Brownlee, K. A., Hodges, J. L., Jr., and Rosenblatt, M. 1953. The up-and-down method with small samples. *Journal of the American Statistical Association* 48:262–277.

Chung, K. L. 1954. On a stochastic approximation method. *The Annals of Mathematical Statistics* 25:463–483.

——. 1960. *Markov chains with stationary transition probabilities.* Berlin: Springer-Verlag.

Cochran, W. G., and Davis, M. 1964. Stochastic approximation to the median effective dose in bioassay. In *Stochastic models in medicine and biology,* ed. J. Gurland. Madison: Univ. of Wisconsin Press.

——. 1965. The Robbins-Monro method for estimating the median lethal dose. *Journal of the Royal Statistical Society, Series B* 27:28–44.

Dixon, W. J. 1965. The up-and-down method for small samples. *Journal of the American Statistical Association* 60:967–978.

Dixon, W. J., and Mood, A. M. 1948. A method for obtaining and analyzing sensitivity data. *Journal of the American Statistical Association* 43:109–126.

Feller, W. 1959. *An introduction to probability theory and its applications,* vol. I, 2nd ed. New York: Wiley.

Hansen, D. N., and Schwarz, G. 1968. An investigation of computer-based science testing. Tallahassee, Fla.: Institute of Human Learning, Florida State Univ.

Hodges, J. L., Jr., and Lehmann, E. L. 1956. Two approximations to the Robbins-Monro process. In *Proceedings of the third Berkeley symposium on mathematical statistics and probability,* vol. 1, ed. J. Neyman. Berkeley: Univ. of California Press.

Kärber, G. 1931. Beitrag zur kollektiven Behandlung pharmakologischer Reihenversuche. *Archiv fur experimentelle Pathologie und Pharmakologie,* 162:480–487.

Linn, R. L., Rock, D. A., and Cleary, T. 1969. The development and evaluation of several programmed testing methods. *Educational and Psychological Measurement* 29:129–146.

Lord, F. M. 1952. A theory of test scores. *Psychometric Monograph* No. 7.

———. 1953. An application of confidence intervals and of maximum likelihood to the estimation of an examinee's ability. *Psychometrika* 18:57–76.

———. 1968a. An analysis of the verbal scholastic aptitude test using Birnbaum's three-parameter logistic model. *Educational and Psychological Measurement* 28:989–1020.

———. 1968b. *Estimating item characteristic curves without knowledge of their mathematical form.* Research Bulletin 68-8 and ONR Technical Report, Contract Nonr 2752(00). Princeton, N.J.: Educational Testing Service.

Lord, F. M., and Novick, M. R. 1968. *Statistical theories of mental test scores.* Reading, Mass.: Addison-Wesley.

Mandel, J., and Stiehler, R. D. 1954. Sensitivity—A criterion for the comparison of methods of test. *Journal of Research of the National Bureau of Standards* 53:155–159.

Robbins, H., and Monro, S. 1951. A stochastic approximation method. *The Annals of Mathematical Statistics* 22:400–407.

Spearman, C. 1908. The method of "right and wrong cases" ("constant stimuli") without Gauss' formulae. *British Journal of Psychology* 2:227–242.

Tsutakawa, R. K. 1963. Block up-and-down method in bio-assay. Unpublished doctoral dissertation. Chicago: Univ. of Chicago.

———. 1967a. Random walk design in bio-assay. *Journal of the American Statistical Association* 62:842–856.

———. 1967b. Asymptotic properties of the block up-and-down method in bio-assay. *The Annals of Mathematical Statistics* 38:1822–1828.

Turnbull, W. W. 1968. Relevance in testing. *Science* 160:1424–1429.

Wetherill, G. B. 1963. Sequential estimation of quantal response curves. *Journal of the Royal Statistical Society* 25:1–38.

9

Bert F. Green, Jr.

Comments on Tailored Testing[1]

Lord has provided an excellent basis for theoretical explorations of tailored testing. He has taken the necessary first step of studying tailored tests in the context of measurement theory. His studies were thorough and insightful, and his conclusions are sound. In this critique I shall first discuss the salient results of Lord's investigations and comment briefly on some technical aspects. This, however, will be rather like attacking the Surgeon General's report on *Smoking and Health*. One can always find a nit to pick at, but the weight of the evidence is overwhelming. The facts are clear. From the point of view of measurement, tailored testing offers little, if any, advantage over the best that can be done with conventional testing. Being unable to attack the fact, I shall resort to attacking the viewpoint.

Lord has examined the theory of tailored testing for measuring abilities and aptitudes. He has confined his remarks to situations in which tests are used to measure some aspect of human ability or performance, apart from any other purpose. That is, he seems to be thinking about computers giving college entrance examinations. In this restricted context, test theory supposes that each student has a definite amount of the ability being tested. Each can be placed on a single underlying, hypothetical dimension. The purpose of testing is to place each student as accurately as possible.

This restricted view of testing is certainly the place to start, but the computer's failure to improve on conventional testing in this situation does not

1. This work was supported by a research grant, GB 7605X, from the National Science Foundation.

foreclose the possibility of computer advantages in other cases. For example, Lord explicitly omits the interplay between instruction and evaluation in computer-based learning situations. An adequate discussion of instructional testing by computers would seem to depend on the specific nature of the instruction. So, apart from saying that it is a separate and exceedingly important problem, I shall join him in ignoring it. Lord also ignores situations in which the purpose of giving the test is to make some decision about the individual. This omission is unfortunate, because tailored testing offers important advantages in decision procedures. A simple example will be presented. Finally, I shall argue that computer-based testing is valuable because it offers new possibilities for measurement, releasing us from the confinement of individual items scored right or wrong. Latency measures, more extended responses, and sets of related items provide ways of breaking out of the traditional mold of one-zero item scores.

Lord's Findings

When a test is used to place students on a hypothetical ability dimension, a tailored test would seem preferable to a conventional test because each student can be given just those questions that are most informative about his ability level. The technique, borrowed from bioassay and psychophysics, is to present an easier item whenever the student fails an item and to ask a more difficult question after each success. The process of stepping up and down the difficulty scale automatically seeks the level of each student. Each examinee is equally challenged, which is impossible when everyone takes the same items. Nevertheless, Lord finds that a conventional test is superior to any tailored test except for the very poor and the very good students.

Lord's conventional test, which he calls the *standard* test, contains items all having the difficulty level that is optimal for the average student. For comparison he also includes a conventional test with items of varying difficulty, which he labels the *published* test. It is a well-known (but little believed) result of test theory that the standard test will be better than the published test except for the extremes. It is, therefore, not surprising that the tailored test, which by definition has items of differing difficulty, is inferior to the standard test for the average student. There is bound to be some wasted motion in trying to tailor the difficulty level; some steps will be taken in the wrong direction, because test items are not infallible. Still, the extent of the loss is surprising.

Lord studied many possible rules for difficulty stepping and many different step sizes. The best procedure of those he tried is, for five-alternative multiple-choice items, to choose a small step size ($d = 0.167/a$) and to step up 1 for a success and down 2 for a failure. This asymmetry makes up for the imbalance caused by the possibility of guessing. For this case Lord found that the standard test is better in the middle third of the interesting range of ability, with the tailored test better in the upper and lower thirds. With the constants Lord used, we would normally expect 70 per cent of the people to concentrate in the middle third of the distribution, with 30 per cent in the extremes. Our problem then is to decide whether the loss in the midrange is overbalanced by the gain in the extremes and whether the net gain, if we think there is one, is worth the cost of tailoring.

Lord evaluates the tests by an information function I, much like Fisher's concept of information. Information is a function of the ability level. The square root of information is directly proportional to the change in average test scores per unit change on the ability scale and inversely proportional to the standard deviation of expected test scores for fixed ability level. Consequently, the square root of information is inversely proportional to the length of the confidence interval for estimating the ability level from the test score. The confidence interval for a given ability level corresponds to a standard error of measurement for a given test score. Because the standard error of measurement is the usual way of evaluating errors of measurement, it would seem more natural to display the lengths of confidence intervals rather than their reciprocals. Consequently, selected curves from Lord's graphs have been replotted, using reciprocals, because Lord's ordinate is the square root of information.

Figure 9–1 shows the measurement errors for three curves: the standard test, the best tailored test ($ad = 0.167$, $H = 1$, $L = 2$), and the published test, all taken from Lord's Figure 8–8. The effect of taking reciprocals is a lessening of the differences in the interval of interest. The tailored test is very nearly as good as the standard test throughout the midrange. Only at the positive extreme is there a pronounced superiority for the tailored test. Note also that the published test is not much worse than the standard test.

The choice between tailored testing and conventional testing depends on how important it seems to measure well in the extremes of the ability continuum. If the main goal of the test is to place people in the right rank order, then more effort needs to be concentrated where there are more people to tell apart. The extremes deserve less accuracy because there are fewer people there, so they are more easily differentiated. On the other hand, if the main goal is to place each person accurately on the scale of ability, then the fact that there are many people in the middle is irrelevant. If those in the middle are not very different, there is no point in amplifying the small differences just because of the weight of numbers.

If tailored testing is no more costly than standard testing, I would be inclined to favor it, because of its nearly constant precision and its clear advantages at the positive extremes. Moreover, the Robbins-Monro modifi-

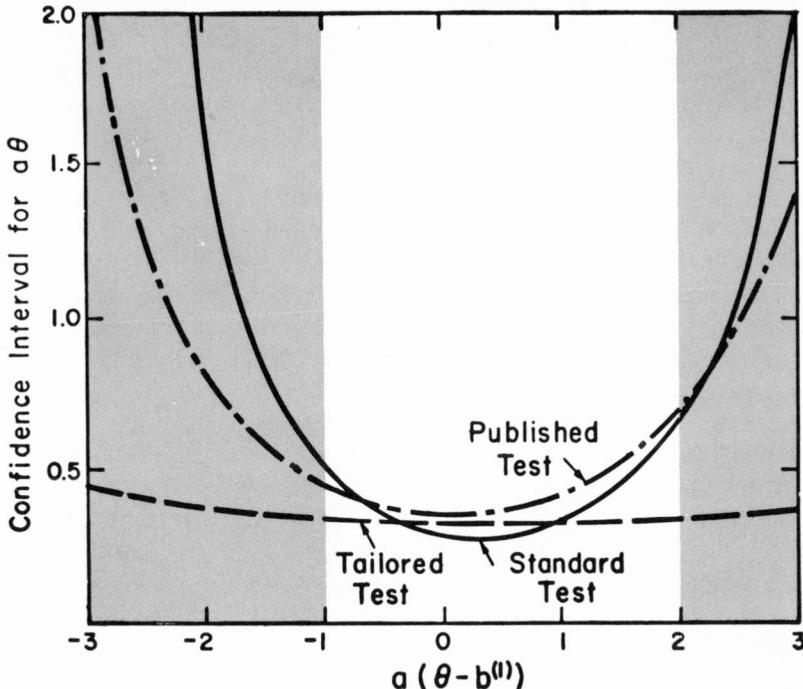

Figure 9–1.
Precision of tailored and conventional tests, shown by the length of 95 per cent confidence interval for a $(\theta - b^{(1)})$, after Lord, Figure 8–8. The tailored test has parameters $ad = .167$, $H = 1$, $L = 2$. The unshaded portion indicates the ability range for 99.7 per cent of a typical population.

cation of the stepping procedure that Lord mentions, and is currently studying, seems likely to improve the tailored test, so that it becomes nearly as good as it can hope to be. (The limit for a tailored test with as many items as the standard is a horizontal line on either graph at the level of the standard test when $\theta = 0$.)

Note that in the shaded portion of the graph, tailored testing is very much better than conventional testing. To arrive here, however, we need more discriminating items or more extreme populations. (Lord's standard conditions are a 60-item test with reliability of 0.90, indicating that $a = 0.5$, with an item-ability biserial correlation of 0.44 and a population with mean $\theta = 0$, standard deviation = 1. In Figure 9–1 the population limits of $\pm 3\sigma$ are indicated by the unshaded portion of the figure.) Better items are unlikely. We are seldom able to make a 60-item test with a reliability exceeding 0.90. If our 60-item test had a reliability of 0.95, a_i would be 0.75, and we could consider the range from -1.75 to $+2.75$. Then we would definitely need the tailored test to do justice to the upper and lower extremes. Tailoring is also needed if the population is unexpectedly good (or bad) so that the standard test is way off target. Put another way, if the potential ability range is large, tailored testing is an alternative to several conventional tests of different difficulty levels.

Lord, in his summation, raises a final devastating objection to tailored testing. His results all assume equally discriminating items. In practice some items are better than others. Assume that at each difficulty level there is a pool of items, the best of which have $a_i = 0.5$ and the worst $a_i = 0.3$. Lord suggests that a conventional "published" test made up of the best items at each level will be better than the tailored test. The tailoring process forces the use of poorer items, because for each student the difficulty will hover around two or three levels so that the item supply at those levels will be depleted. The bottom of the barrel will be scraped. Further, tailored testing is quite sensitive to step size, and using items of varying difficulty may lead to suboptimal stepping. To evaluate this situation, we need to compare Lord's published test, which contains good items of varying difficulty, with some reasonable guesses about the tailored test. The tailored test can do no worse than if it had nothing but the poorer items, and it cannot do as well as if it had all the best items. Estimating $a = 0.45$ and $a = 0.3$ as the upper and lower limits for the average a and ignoring the effect of suboptimal stepping leads to a band of possibilities, as shown in Figure 9–2. We are forced to conclude, with Lord, that unless the items are *all* very good a conventional test using the best of them will usually be better than the tailored test except for extremely able students.

Scores for tailored tests. A minor technical matter deserves comment, partly for its practical consequences. Most of Lord's results are for the *average difficulty score,* which is the average difficulty of all items presented to the subject, that is, the average difficulty of all items *attempted.* This makes perfectly good sense in bioassay, and in a way it is sensible in tailored testing. What the subject cannot do is just as informative as what he can do. Early in his chapter Lord considers the *final difficulty score,* which is equivalent to the number of items answered correctly. The average difficulty score turns out to yield slightly more information, but I would not want the job of defending it at a PTA meeting. An alternative that actually is a compromise between the two is the average difficulty of items answered correctly, which might be called *weighted number right.* There is ample precedent for such a score. The man in the street knows about the $64 question and understands that some questions ought to be worth more points than others. Further, the weighted number right has intuitive appeal. It does not depend so directly on the test-theory model as either of the

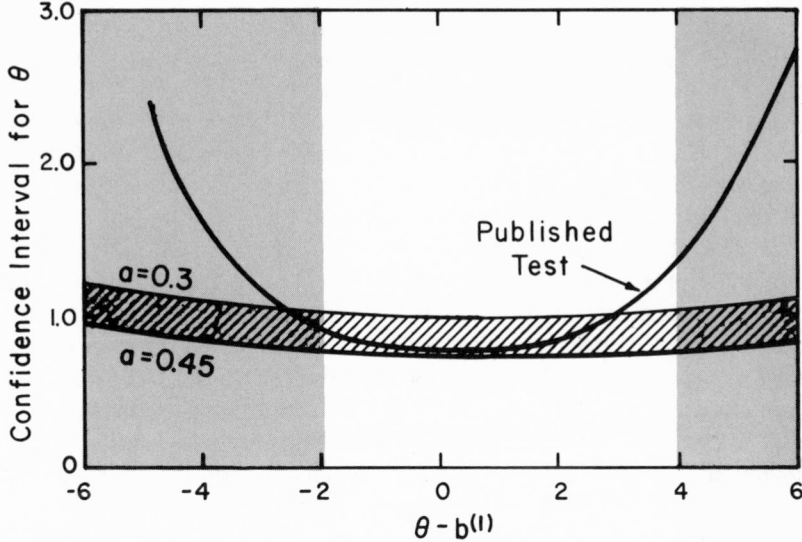

Figure 9–2.
Precision of tests based on items of differing quality, as shown by the length of 95 per cent confidence interval for $(\theta - b^{(1)})$ for a conventional test containing the best items at each difficulty level and a band of possible outcomes for a tailored test using items of varying discrimination.

other scores. Mathematically, the weighted number right can be expressed as a weighted average of *final difficulty* and *average difficulty,* with average difficulty weighted more heavily in the midrange and final difficulty weighted more heavily in the extremes (see the Appendix). This would seem desirable theoretically and should be studied further.

Tailored Testing and the Decision Process

Lord's gloomy conclusions about tailored testing arise from considering measurement per se rather than any use to which the measures are put. This restricted outlook is in tune with our current wasteful decision-making procedures in education, industry, and the military establishment. We typically measure first and decide later. There is very seldom any interplay between measurement and decision. No allowance is made for a decision to collect more data. Cronbach and Gleser (1965) have argued forcibly that this procedure wastes information and ignores many aspects of the decision problem. Both selection and placement problems, they argued, need to be integrated with the measurement process in an overall decision procedure that includes a consideration of costs and values. Although many measurement experts, including Lord (1962), are sympathetic with Cronbach and Gleser's thesis, practical matters have so far interfered with any serious attempt at implementation. Until now it has been impractical to obtain some measures, consider their implications, and then possibly obtain further measures. The computer-controlled test overcomes the practical difficulties, and serious thought can now be given to an integrated decision system.

When the same test information is to be used by many different organizations with different decision criteria, an integrated decision system seems impossible. That is, I see no good way of coupling the college entrance examination board testing to the decision processes of the member colleges without jeopardizing the freedom of the individual or the freedom of each college to use its own jealously guarded subjective criteria. Here there may be no alternative to accurate measurement at every point on the scale.

But whenever the information is to be used by only one decision system, coupling of the testing to the decision scheme is not only possible but extremely desirable. As simple examples, consider advanced placement decisions for college freshmen or foreign language proficiency examinations for graduate students. Here a criterion level is set, and the test is used to decide whether the student is above or below the criterion.

In this simple decision process the best conventional test must be centered at the criterion level. That is, students on the borderline should have a 50 per cent chance of answering each item correctly (in this analysis we shall ignore guessing). Matching the item difficulty to the student will be no advantage here. We do not need to know his score very accurately if he is well above or well below the criterion. We need only a few items to make the appropriate decision for such a student. The advantage of tailored testing, then, will be found in stopping the testing as soon as a decision is reached. We shall tailor the number of items, not their difficulty. For most students many fewer items will be needed than on a comparable standard test. Furthermore, we can set reasonable limits on the needed accuracy by specifying the test's operating characteristics.

Figure 9–3 shows the operating characteristics for conventional standard tests of 10, 20, 30, and 60 items. The calculations are based on the results and methods reported by the Statistical Research Group of Columbia University (1945). The operating characteristic shows the possibility of rejecting a student (by saying that he is below criterion) as a function of the student's probability of answering a single item correctly. The corresponding ability scale (assuming $a_i = 0.5$, as Lord does) is also shown. Figure 9–3 shows that the difference between the 30- and 60-item curves is about the same as the difference between the 10- and 20-item curves. There is a strong law of diminishing returns from more items. Indeed, for the decisions in our examples we would be well satisfied with 30 items or

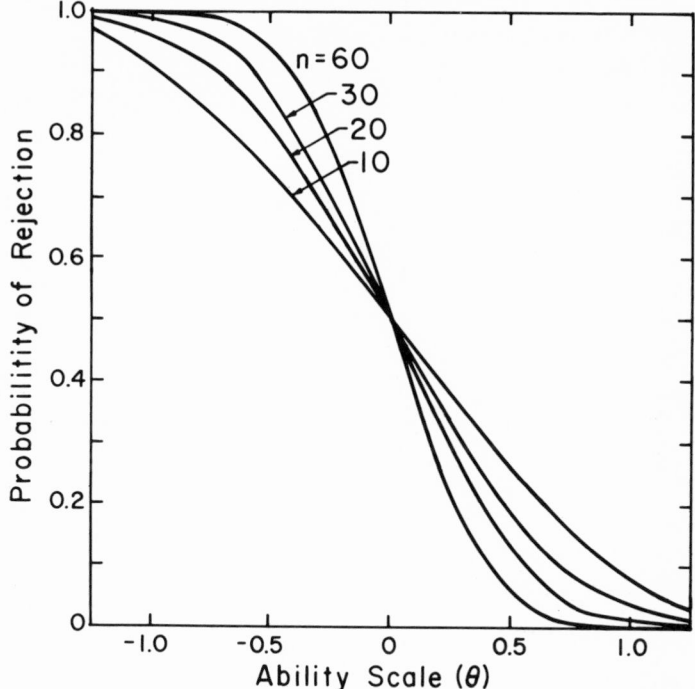

Figure 9–3.
Characteristic curves for standard tests of various lengths. The probability of rejecting a student (saying he has $\theta < 0$) is shown as a function of θ.

perhaps even 20 items. If we turn the decision over to a computer that gives successive items until a decision can be reached, the computer can be set to match any of these operating characteristics. Corresponding to each characteristic curve, Figure 9–4 shows the average number of items needed at each ability level. Although some students will need more than the average number of items, the chances are very small that more than three times the average will be needed. In principle the decision process could go on forever for some students. In practice it can be truncated at some fixed n, for example, $n = 60$ for the 60-item equivalent. This flattens the operating characteristic slightly but not substantially.

It is plain that much testing time can be saved by a sequential decision procedure. To achieve the same operating characteristic as a 30-item standard test, a sequential test will use about 17.5 items, averaging across the whole population. In terms of testing time, sequential testing has nearly a 2 to 1 advantage.

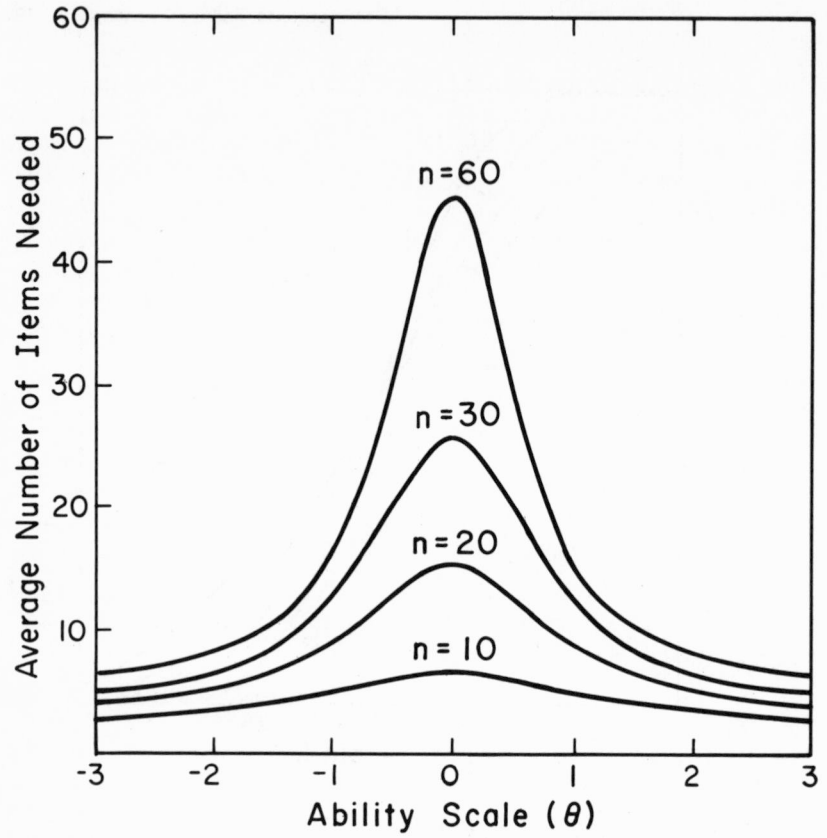

Figure 9–4.
Average number of items required at each ability level to obtain correponding characteristic curves.

The savings in the simple one-dimensional case will surely be amplified when more complex decisions are to be made based on several different tests. Nonlinear procedures also become possible. In many cases students near the borderline of some decision criterion may be qualitatively different from those for whom the decision is easy. Very possibly more attention needs to be paid to other variables, such as motivation, in deciding the borderline cases.

In general, then, computer-controlled sequential testing for decisions has great potential value. This is a fertile field for study.

Other Measurement Possibilities

So far we have been working with the traditional right or wrong scores, which give only one bit of information per item. This seems a rather slim output from the elaborate mental process that must be required to respond to an item. If the items are tapping important aspects of ability, then something more than right or wrong ought to be useful. In computer-aided instruction additional information is customarily collected. Test theory is challenged to make use of this information.

Some CAI systems respond to a wrong response by saying, "Wrong, try again." The sequence of selections of alternatives should provide additional information about the student's understanding of the question. Of course, the distractors must be carefully designed and they must be calibrated. But this should not be too difficult.

Another piece of useful information is the time required to answer the item. One of the main values of computer-controlled experiments in psychological laboratories is the availability of latency measures. Latencies have turned out to be very revealing in the study of perception and memory (for example, Sternberg, 1967). Processing times play an important role in information processing models of problem solving (Dansereau and Gregg, 1966). Again, CAI measures response times.

The value of item response latencies is hard to predict from the psychometric literature. When traditional speed and content scores have been analyzed separately, speed scores tend to define a separate speed factor or even a general second-order speed factor. These studies, however, use number-right scores on speeded tests, not time per item or time per correct item. The relevant research on item response latencies remains to be done. (An incidental advantage of latency measures would be helping to screen out guesses. Any response that is made too quickly can immediately be labeled a guess and not be credited.)

Having admitted latencies, we might even get down to psychological business and find out what goes on when a student is answering an item on an aptitude test. Elaborate factorial theories of intelligence are based on gross right or wrong item scores and have nothing to say about the details of item responding. Current research in the computer simulation of cognitive processes attempts a finer-grain analysis of problem-solving behavior. This research has some close parallels with factorial theories of intelligence (Green, 1964) based on gross right or wrong scores but has much greater potential value. If we knew what students were doing, we might be better able to devise means of measuring it. It may be that the only significant part is the final one-bit result, but I strongly doubt it. More and more, experimental psychology is becoming interested in process. So should aptitude testers!

For example, there has been considerable interest in the details of students' behavior in solving number series and letter series tasks (Simon and Kotovsky, 1963; Bjork, 1968). One straightforward implication of this work is that the response to number series or letter series should not be simply the next element in the series but the next complete period. (Given 1, 4, 7, 2, 5, 8, 3, 6, 9, the student should respond 4, 7, 10, not merely 4.) Partial credit can easily be given. For items of the sort, "Which group doesn't belong—HAXH, DRBD, BXWB, MLPD," the student should be required to generate another set that fits or to alter the bad one so it does fit. In general, any item requiring the student to construct a response, rather than select one, provides more information.

No doubt there are many other novel types of items or groups of items that are uniquely suited to computer-controlled testing. Computers have a reputation for inundating investigators with data, and there is no reason to think that testing will escape the flood.

Conclusion

Lord has shown that there is not much to be gained in the typical testing situation by the use of computer-controlled or tailored tests. Only the best and worst students would be measured much more precisely by tailored testing. But there are many other areas in which computer-controlled testing is worthwhile. As an example, the integration of testing in a complete computer-controlled decision system is shown to save substantial testing time.

Other applications could have been mentioned. In achievement testing a combination of broad-gauge and narrow-gauge questions can be used to probe for general areas of knowledge and then to examine the depth of understanding in each area. In personality testing the computer can function as a clinician, following up interesting leads based on the student's answer to initial probe questions (for example, Kleinmuntz and McLean, 1968). Of more theoretical interest, the computer enables consideration of more complex models of test behavior, involving compensatory or hierarchical ability concepts.

At a more fundamental level the computer offers the possibility of better ways to examine the student's ability. Complicated item responses, sequences of responses to sequences of items, and item response latencies are a few of the possibilities. This approach leads to a more detailed analysis of behaviors in answering test items. A better understanding of cognitive processes seems likely to indicate new ways to measure individual differences in cognitive functioning.

The computer has barely started to establish itself in the testing business. As experience with computer-controlled tests accumulates, we can expect important changes in the technology of testing. Most of these changes lie in the future. Lord's results, clear-cut and devastating as they are, will in the end seem a minor skirmish in the inevitable computer conquest of testing.

Appendix: *Relation of Weighted Number Right to Final Difficulty and Average Difficulty*

Any sequence of item responses in tailored testing (for fixed d) can be sorted into a set that comprises the shortest possible trip from $b^{(1)}$, the initial difficulty, to $b^{(n+1)}$, the final difficulty, and a balanced set of plusses (+'s) and minuses (−'s) that get nowhere. That is, for $H = 1$, $L = 1$, every incorrect answer at level b_i in the balanced set is matched by a correct answer at $b_i - d$, whereas for $H = 1$, $L = 2$, every incorrect answer at level b_i is matched by two correct answers—one at level $b_i - d$ and the other at level $b_i - 2d$.

Let n_t and n_f be the number of items in the shortest trip set and the balanced set, respectively $(n_t + n_f = n)$. Let b_t and b_f be the average difficulty of all items in the respective sets. Then the average difficulty score $\bar{b}$ is

$$n\bar{b} = n_t b_t + n_f b_f + (b^{(n+1)} - b^{(1)}) \tag{1}$$

where the last term corrects for the Lord formula limits. The final difficulty score, $b^{(n+1)}$, is related to b_t by

$$b_t = \tfrac{1}{2}(b^{(n+1)} + b^{(1)}) \tag{2}$$

Since $b^{(1)}$ is constant, b_t is a linear function of $b^{(n+1)}$. It is also true that n_t is a function of $b^{(n+1)}$ because

$$n_t = \pm \frac{b^{(n+1)} - b^{(1)}}{d} \tag{3}$$

$$n\bar{b} = n_t b_t + n_f b_f \pm dn_t \qquad \begin{matrix} + \text{ when } b^{(n+1)} > b^{(1)} \\ - \text{ when } b^{(n+1)} < b^{(1)} \end{matrix} \tag{4}$$

The sum of the item difficulties in the balanced set $n_f b_f$ is the sum of the difficulties of the items answered correctly $(\sum_+)$ plus the sum of the difficulties of the items answered incorrectly $(\sum_-)$:

$$n_f b_f = \sum_+ + \sum_- \tag{5}$$

We need $\sum_+$ and shall calculate $\sum_-$ in terms of it. The balance rule says that, for $H = 1$, $L = 1$,

$$\sum_- = \sum_+ + d\,\frac{n_f}{2} \tag{6}$$

Substituting and simplifying,

$$\sum_+ = \tfrac{1}{2}n_f b_f - d\,\frac{n_f}{4} \tag{7}$$

For $H = 1$, $L = 2$, we have, similarly,

$$\sum_- = \tfrac{1}{2}\sum_+ + d\,\frac{n_f}{2} \tag{8}$$

$$\sum_+ = \tfrac{2}{3}n_f b_f - d\,\frac{n_f}{3} \tag{9}$$

The formula for weighted number right (G) depends on whether the initial set is a run of $+$'s or a run of $-$'s. Thus for $H = 1$, $L = 1$, we have for $(d^{(n+1)} > d^{(1)})$

$$G = \frac{1}{n_t + \dfrac{n_f}{2}}\,(n_t b_t + \sum_+) \tag{10}$$

Using Equation (7), we obtain

$$G = \frac{2}{n + n_t}\left(n_t b_t + \tfrac{1}{2}n_f b_f - d\,\frac{n_f}{4}\right) \tag{11}$$

Using Equation (4), we obtain

$$G = \frac{2}{n + n_t}\left(\tfrac{1}{2}n_t b_t + \tfrac{1}{2}n\overline{b} - \tfrac{1}{2}dn_t - d\,\frac{n_f}{4}\right) \tag{12}$$

$$G = \frac{n}{n + n_t}\,\overline{b} + \frac{n_t}{n + n_t}\,b_t - \frac{d}{2} \tag{13}$$

For $(d^{(n+1)} < d^{(1)})$ we have

$$G = \frac{2}{n_f}\,(\textstyle\sum_+) \tag{14}$$

$$G = \frac{n}{n - n_t}\,\overline{b} - \frac{n_t}{n - n_t}\,(b_t - d) - \frac{d}{2} \tag{15}$$

For reference we shall write comparable formulas for $H = 1$, $L = 2$:

$$d^{(n+1)} > d^{(1)} \qquad G = \frac{2n}{2n + n_t}\,\overline{b} + \frac{n_t}{2n + n_t}\,(b_t - \tfrac{1}{2}d) - \frac{d}{2}$$

$$d^{(n+1)} < d^{(1)} \qquad G = \frac{n}{n - n_t}\,\overline{b} - \frac{n_t}{n - n_t}\,b_t - \frac{d}{2}$$

Clearly, G is a combination of $\overline{b}$ and b_t.

REFERENCES

Bjork, R. A. 1968. All-or-none subprocesses in the learning of complex sequences. *Journal of Mathematical Psychology* 5:182–195.

Cronbach, L. J., and Gleser, G. C. 1965. *Psychological Tests and Personnel Decisions*. 2nd ed. Urbana: Univ. of Illinois Press.

Dansereau, D. F., and Gregg, L. W. 1966. An information-processing analysis of mental multiplication. *Psychonomic Science* 2:71–72.

Green, B. F., Jr. 1964. Intelligence and computer simulation. *Transactions of the N.Y. Academy of Sciences, Series II* 27(1):55–63.

Kleinmuntz, B., and McLean, R. S. 1968. Diagnostic interviewing by digital computer. *Behavioral Science* 13:75–80.

Lord, F. M. 1962. Review of H. Solomon, ed. *Studies in item analysis and prediction*. *Psychometrika* 27:207–213.

Simon, H. A., and Kotovsky, K. 1963. Human acquisition of concepts for sequential patterns. *Psychological Review* 70:534–546.

Statistical Research Group of Columbia University. 1945. *Sequential Analysis of Statistical Data*. New York: Columbia Univ. Press.

Sternberg, S. 1967. Two operations in character recognition: some evidence from reaction-time measurements. *Perception and Psychophysics* 2:45–53.

Individually Tailored Testing: Discussion

Disagreements about the benefits of tailored testing can easily become clouded by confusion of the purpose of large-group achievement testing with the means for individualized instruction. On the one hand are arguments about the cost and social value of improving the accuracy of measurement for examinees at the extremes of the distribution, the prospects for increasing the relative advantage of tailored tests through more precise measures, and the advantages of motivating students by adjusting test difficulty. On the other hand are promises of somehow improving instruction through use of diagnostic sequences embedded in tutorial material, whether by providing better data for decision rules in the teaching strategy, more direct instruction via self-diagnosing test sequences, or improved learner attitudes through responsiveness of the examination material to individual performance. Very little can be added to what has already been clearly stated by Lord.

Green points out that in a specific situation in which a standard test (all items of about the same difficulty) missed the average performance level of the students a tailored test would have been more successful. Social conditions determine the importance of obtaining reliable information about examinees in one or both extremes. Unless it is more economical (and politically feasible) to write and administer separate tests for students at the extremes of the ability distribution, tailored testing (or very long published tests) should be employed; determination of the best strategy requires quantification of the "loss" associated with making errors about students who should be scoring very high or very low and the personal and institutional costs of alternative modes of testing.

It may be important to investigate the interaction of personality and situational factors with tailored testing. The motivational impact on the student when he discovers that most of the items are at a certain level of difficulty (or uncertainty) is unknown. Such contextual factors could have important effects on the performance of some students. The optimal level (or mixture of levels) for a given student will not be derived from test theory alone; information about student anxiety and motivation may also be relevant. For example, does the student feel the examiner is passing over areas in which he has little or no knowledge and permitting him to prove himself on topics of greatest familiarity?

There are other tasks for the computer that are worth at least some attention in the exploration of computer-based testing. Important information about student performance may be derived from the number and sequence of (wrong) alternatives chosen (Coombs et al., 1955), the expressed confidence of the responder (Shuford et al., 1966), the latency of response,[1] or the sequence of steps used in problem solution. Some of these factors were discussed at a conference on computer-assisted instruction held at Educational Testing Service in 1966 (Harman et al., 1968).

The promise of contingent testing sequences for individualized instruction is attractive but yet unproved after ten years of prophesy. Computer-based procedures should improve the depth as well as the economy of testing. A curriculum designer should be able to program better decisions during (or between) instructional sequences because of more reliable and relevant data than available otherwise. However, elegant testing sequences and curriculum decision rules seem always to be just beyond his reach.

Perhaps instruction is in an equally poor state for lack of models on which to base optimization procedures. It is difficult to prepare a sequential strategy that is superior to a linear one determined in advance for the average of a reasonably homogeneous population. Modularity of instructional units is one means proposed to facilitate individualization of each learner's goals without determining rules for individualizing the microstructure of instruction. Perhaps the computer will be just as important as an aid in the preparation of testing and instructional modules as it is in the presentation of modules to learners.

1. See page 81 in Chapter 5 by Glaser and p. 260 in Chapter 12 by Suppes and Morningstar.

REFERENCES

Coombs, C. H., Milholland, J. E., and Womer, F. B. 1955. *The assessment of partial knowledge in objective testing.* PRB Technical Research Note 33. Ann Arbor: Department of the Army, Engineering Research Institute, Univ. of Michigan.

Harman, H. H., Helm, C. E., and Loye, D. E., eds. 1968. *Computer-assisted testing: proceedings of a conference, November 18–19, 1966.* Princeton, N.J.: Educational Testing Service.

Shuford, E. H., Albert, A., and Massengill, H. E. 1966. Admissible probability measurement procedures. *Psychometrika* 31(2):125–145.

PART V

Language Processing

The more powerful applications of computers for instruction, testing, or guidance require some form of natural language processing by the computer. Problems in the linguistic analysis of constructed student responses are examined in Chapter 10 by Simmons, who describes a simplified decision model for a tutorial instructional system. He analyzes a set of actual student responses to demonstrate the methods by which the language processor can "understand" the meaning of constructed responses and generate minimally appropriate tutorial interaction. The tutorial model described requires the capability to recognize and measure the extent to which any two English statements are equivalent paraphrases of each other. Moreover, it must be able to generate English statements that express the meaning of any student response or canonical answer. To satisfy these requirements, the language processor that Simmons has programmed uses syntactic and semantic analysis functions to read and transform the text into a deep structure of concepts where transformational equivalence can be established.

Quite a different approach to the analysis of natural language is taken in Chapter 11 by McDavid, who first discusses some other ways in which computers may eventually prove useful in dealing with speech. He then comments on Simmons' model, arguing that true equivalence of the nuances of meaning cannot be achieved even with use of deep-structure analysis of the language. Nevertheless, a close approximation to natural language processing could be of great value in developing tutorial interactions for computer-assisted instruction, but its implementation is several years away.

10

Robert F. Simmons

Linguistic Analysis of Constructed
Student Responses[1]

Recently, the Systems Development Corporation has been engaged in a research program aimed toward the development of an experimental version of a computer-aided instructional system that can interact with students in a subset of natural English. The basic requirement of such a CAI system is a natural language processor that can successfully generate and semantically interpret a wide range of natural English constructions including sentences, fragments of sentences, questions, and responses to questions. So far a complete though shaky system for syntactic and semantic analysis, paraphrase, sentence generation, and question answering with respect to English sentences has been developed on the project. Detailed descriptions of the syntactic, semantic, and logical approaches used in the language processor are to be found in Simmons and Burger (1970), Simmons et al. (1968), Burger et al. (1968), and Schwarcz et al. (1970). The overall research plan and design for the instructional system was described in Simmons and Silberman (1967).

In this chapter, following a brief exposition of the notion of a natural language CAI system, the initial simplified decision model for the tutorial instruction system is described and a set of actual student responses is

1. Supported by Contract Number F33615–67–C–1968, U.S. Air Force Human Resources Laboratory, Training Research Division at Wright Patterson AFB, toward the development of a Natural Language CAI System. Project members have included John Burger, Robert Schwarcz, William Schoene, Fred Bennik, Harry Silberman, Marianne Celce, Jack Tanaka, and the author.

analyzed to demonstrate the methods by which the language processor can "understand" constructed responses of the student and generate minimally appropriate tutorial interaction.

The Notion of CAI in Natural Language

Various recent CAI systems, typified by System Development Corporation's Planit (Feingold and Frye, 1966), offer some capability for dealing with responses constructed by the student as answers to system problems or queries. Constructed responses have been found to be particularly useful for teaching such formalized disciplines as logic, mathematics, or programming. In these areas variations in form and content of the constructed response can usually be dealt with by using an algebraic evaluation system that can successfully recognize algebraic equivalents of the required answer. However, if the constructed response is allowed to be in the form of an English phrase, the problem is vastly complicated by the lack of any comparable English evaluation system for recognizing every meaning-preserving paraphrase of an answer.

The difficulty in dealing with English paraphrases arises from the basic flexibility inherent in natural languages. It is generally the case that for any word or phrase in a natural language expression another sentence, word, or phrase can be substituted to express almost exactly the same meaning without changing the meaning of the larger expression. With such a wide variety of expressive potential available, the lesson designer who tries to predict all correct variations for a prescribed short English answer is doomed to failure.

Current systems recognize this difficulty and provide a few aids for the lesson designer. Planit offers a logic for detecting and ignoring misspellings, a root-form procedure to account for some variations caused by inflectional suffixes, and a keyword facility for ignoring all but significant content words in a student's response. Eliza, which has recently been used as a CAI system (Taylor, 1968), includes a pattern-operation logic. If a certain ordered pattern of words is present, with or without regard for intervening words, control is passed to a given operation such as the presentation of additional material or the asking of further questions. If these approaches were further augmented by the use of synonym dictionaries or thesauri, another step could be taken to ease the handling of constructed English responses. However, our own experience with such nonanalytic approaches to dealing with English meanings leads inescapably to the conclusion that they are and will remain hopelessly inadequate for the task. The lesson designer who wants constructed English responses—short or long—still requires a complete language-processing system to recognize alternative expressions of the same meaning.

But if he had a powerful language-processing system in conjunction with his CAI machinery, he could do much more. He could develop a radically different concept of a CAI system, one that would minimize lesson programming requirements while it maximized individualized interactions with the student. The reason for this is that a language processor, in order to recognize acceptable paraphrases of an answer, must deal successfully with meanings rather than with words. If it can deal with meanings, it can represent a lesson content as a set of meanings to be communicated to a student and it can measure the student's progress in terms of the amount of meaning that the student has absorbed from the lesson. If it could manage paraphrases, answer questions, and generate English statements, then it could also interact with both student and lesson designer in relatively free English. Such a system could answer questions regarding lesson content whether they came from the student or from the instructor. It could generate English statements representing meanings in the lesson content. In evaluating student responses to questions, it could measure the student's knowledge of lesson content with regard to its own representation and use the discrepancy between the two as a basis for generating statements that the student could learn until the discrepancy disappeared.

In short, a CAI system based on a powerful language processor would soon lead to the design and construction of an automated tutor that could measure the position of a student with respect to the lesson content and use the discrepancy to generate materials that would allow the student to close the gap in a manner fitted to the student's own learning pattern. What we are suggesting is that an adequate language processor must include many of the important symbol-meaning-processing capabilities of a human. If these are available to a computer, they can be used in the manner that a human tutor uses them.

This line of thought and our research program leading to the eventual design of an automated tutorial CAI system have been described in detail elsewhere (Simmons and Silberman, 1967). We have made appreciable progress in the development of a language-processing system that can serve as an experimental vehicle for testing some of these ideas in a CAI environment. This vehicle, Protosynthex III, has also been described previously (Simmons et al., 1968; Schwarcz et al., 1970). Protosynthex III (PSIII) is by no means the powerful language processor that would be required at the base of an automated tutor, but it is at least minimally sufficient to experiment with some actual student responses and so help develop additional knowledge for the eventual construction of an automated tutor.

As a first step in this direction, a version of the Planit system has been modified to use a live tutor to make instructional decisions in response to the students' constructed answers to questions presented by Planit. Protocols of interactions between human tutors and students have been collected to serve as samples of language exchanges that the language processor must eventually be able to encompass. A considerably simplified decision model of a tutorial system has been designed that uses the language processor to recognize discrepancies in student responses and to generate English statements that can help him to correct his errors. As this simplified model of the tutor is perfected, it can be embedded in Planit so that each time a verbal response is constructed by the student Planit can use the tutorial decision system to understand, evaluate, and shape the student response.

The Tutorial Decision Model

Our first approximation to an automated tutor requires the lesson designer to present his material as a sequence of text interspersed with or followed by queries to the student. These queries require short constructed responses from the student. For each query the designer formulates a complete correct answer that contains only the necessary and sufficient information to answer the query. This complete answer is called the canonical answer (CA). The student response (SR) is taken by the language processor and tested to determine if it is an equivalent paraphrase of the CA. The SR is expected to vary widely in choice of vocabulary and phrasing from the CA, and the language processor has the function of determining in what ways the meaning content of the SR corresponds to and differs from the content of the CA.

The five possible relations between the SR and the CA, exemplified by SR1 through SR5, are illustrated in the Venn diagrams of Figure 10–1. In case 1, shown by the exact coincidence of a dashed outline with the solid outline representing the CA, there is no difference between SR1 and CA. SR1 is complete and correct. Case 2 is illustrated by SR2, where the dashed SR and the solid CA are completely disjoint. For this case the student response is completely incorrect and irrelevant. SR3 shows the case of a partially correct answer that also contains some incorrect or irrelevant information. Case 4, illustrated by SR4, is another example of a partially correct response, but without any incorrect or irrelevant information. The final case, SR5, includes the entire correct answer along with some additional irrelevant material.

Our use of correct, incorrect, and irrelevant is strictly with reference to the canonical answer, which is defined as the only correct and complete (that is, necessary and sufficient) information to answer the query. The categories of correctness and relevance into which an SR is classified dictate

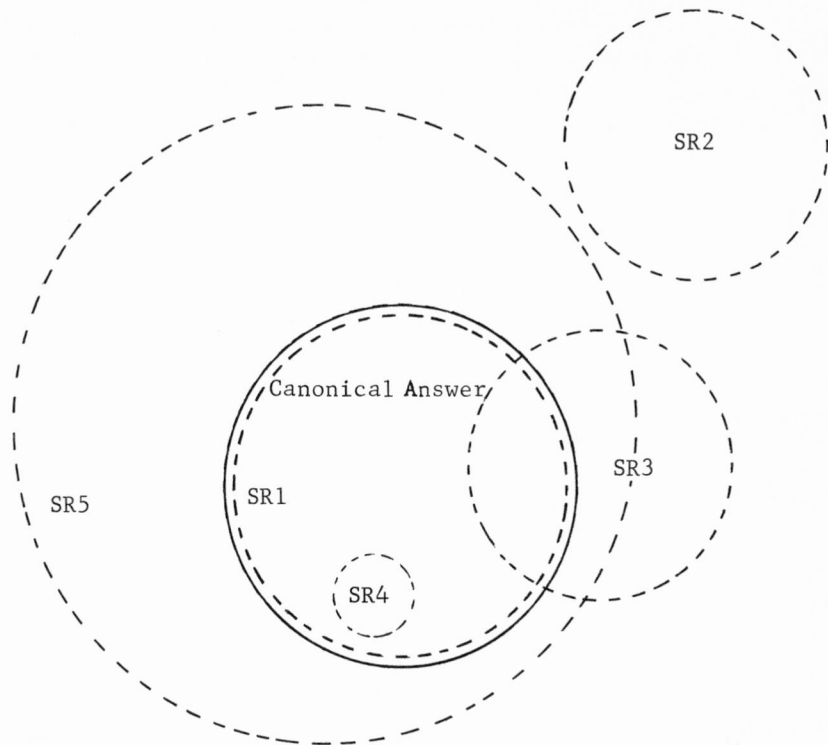

Figure 10–1.
Comparison of student responses (SR) with canonical answer (CA).

the tutorial decisions that the model makes. Table 10–1 summarizes these decisions, showing the types of positive and negative reinforcement given to the student and the subsequent lesson materials provided for him.

For the completely correct and relevant case 1, one of the positive feedback messages, such as "OK," "That's completely right," and so on, is generated and the next frame of the main sequence is presented. For SR3 and SR4, which are partially correct, the feedback tells the student that his answer is partly right and the language processor generates a new query from the part of the CA that the student has missed and uses that part as the new CA. For case 2, where the SR completely misses the CA, the feedback is a negative statement such as "No, that's not at all correct," followed by a paraphrase of the original query. If case 2 occurs twice in sequence, the relevant lesson information is presented again by the same query. For case 5, which includes the complete CA but also some irrelevant material, the feedback is a positive message such as "This is the correct part of your

Table 10–1. Summary of Decision Model

Case	Correctness	Relevance	Feedback type	Decision
1	Correct	Relevant	Positive	Continue lesson
2	Incorrect	Irrelevant	Negative	Generate Do you remember SUBJ
3	Partially correct	Partially irrelevant	Positive Incomplete	Generate Do you remember (omitted SUBJ)
4	Partially correct	Relevant	Positive Incomplete	Generate Do you remember (omitted SUBJ)
5	Correct	Partially irrelevant	Positive Redundant	Generate This part of your answer is enough: (CA)

answer; the rest is irrelevant." This message is followed by an English statement representing the CA.

In cases 2, 3, and 5 the incorrect content of the answer is generally ignored and the student is brought back to the lesson content by generating new statements from the untouched portion of the canonical answer. We made the decision to ignore most incorrect content both because it simplified the tutorial model and because we believe that in most cases working with incorrect content may have the effect of confusing the student. In this first tutorial model our goal is to shape the student's responses toward the desired content by using positive and negative reinforcement supported by partial repetitions primarily in the form of hints generated from the CA.

It can be seen that this model greatly reduces the effort required from a lesson designer. Instead of having to predict for each query all categories of possible responses from the student and to decide in advance what to do for each, he is able to produce a main line of lesson content and allow the tutorial system to deal with individual variations in the student's response patterns. Although the tutorial system assumes a single main line of lesson content, after it is sufficiently developed to be embedded in a general purpose CAI system, there is no reason the designer cannot include branching lessons at a level above the tutorial system. As the tutorial system is further developed, it will probably also be possible for the lesson designer to program appropriate branchings depending on the categories of discrepancy between SR and CA.

The preceding description of the tutorial model is based on two assumptions that are still untested. Perhaps the more important of these has to do with the effectiveness of the model as a teaching instrument. Our faith in its eventual effectiveness is based on the belief that constructed responses demonstrate a greater mastery of subject content at a higher level of understanding than rote learning and that consequently the material learned will transfer more easily to various applications. Certainly, the constructed response requires of the student not only that he remember the text that he has read but that he also be able to generate English statements of his own that reflect the same content. The extent to which such a tutorial model may in fact improve the effectiveness of CAI systems is one that can eventually be answered only by experimental comparisons. But such comparisons depend on the validity of the second assumption, which is that the tutorial model can actually be constructed as a working computer system.

It is with the achievability of the natural-language-based tutorial system that our present line of research is mainly concerned. Many major linguistic and logical problems must be defined and resolved before our present language processor, PSIII, becomes an adequate vehicle to serve as a basis for the tutorial system. Several versions of the tutorial decision model will probably have to be programmed before any useful system is developed. However, the line of development will be seen to be fairly clear as we show in the next section the linguistic and logical analyses that are made in order to represent the meanings that underly the phrases and fragments of English used in student responses.

Analysis of Student Responses

The tutorial model imposes two difficult requirements on a language processor. These are, first, that it be able to recognize and measure the extent to which any two English statements are equivalent paraphrases of each other and, second, that it be able to generate English statements that express the meaning of any student response or canonical answer. To meet these requirements, a language processor must be able to analyze an English phrase or sentence into an underlying logical structure of nonverbal objects that represent concepts or ideas. In conjunction with the analysis process, it must also have the capability of synthesizing, that is, generating, English statements from these underlying structures to represent their meaning in English. A third, implied requirement is that if two underlying logical or conceptual structures are equivalent in meaning, there should be rules of inference that can be used to transform one into the other.

To attain these requirements, a language processing system uses syntactic and semantic analysis functions to read and transform text into a deep structure of concepts whose defining attributes and whose relations with other concepts are made explicit in a well-defined, quantified logical structure. The deep conceptual structures we are using in our most recent versions of PSIII represent the meaning of an English statement as a verb or relational concept in various case relations to the nominal concepts of the sentence. In using this structure, we are indebted to ideas developed by Fillmore in his recent papers (Fillmore 1966, 1967), but we have modified his structure both for convenience in programming and to obtain consistency with our conceptual model as described elsewhere (Simmons et al., 1968a).

The resulting structure can be understood with reference to the example sentence, "The old man bought a boat from Tom." The main verb idea of the sentence is a buying, so this is the head structure. "The old man" is not only the subject of the sentence but an animate, active person and is thus in the agentive case; "a boat" is the direct object of the verb; and the indirect object, "Tom," is technically in the dative case. However, because the preposition "from" carries more information than the case *dative,* we mark the case relation as "from." The general idea behind this approach of case relations is that in most natural languages nominal concepts can be considered to be the objects of prepositions that mark their case relations to verbs. In English such case relations as subject, agent, object, dative, and instrumental are frequently not marked by an explicit preposition, but the information is carried instead by a term's position with relation to the verb or by characteristics (that is, semantic features) of its meaning. (In some languages, for example, Japanese, subject and object are explicitly marked by pre- or postpositional words.)

After analysis, the example sentence has the following structure:

Buy TENSE Past, AGT((Man MOD old) Q 1), OBJ (Boat Q 1), FROM (Tom Q All).

A particular man, distinguished by the MODifier "old" and the article "the," is the subject and agent. The nominal "boat" is quantified (Q) by the article "a" as one of a class of such concepts.[2] The proper name "Tom" is considered (in this example) as signifying all of the concept of *Tom* as a particular person. Several alternative sentences would all have been analyzed to result in the same structure. For example,

1. A boat was bought from Tom by the old man.
2. From Tom, the old man bought a boat.
3. The man who was old bought a boat from Tom.

---

2. In most of the following examples we shall ignore quantification, which is a most difficult aspect of natural languages and one for which we are still attempting to work out a satisfactory approach. Also, the actual representation of a concept is a pointer to a particular sense of meaning for a word. However, to keep our exposition clear, we shall continue to use words to represent concepts in all examples.

Language processors based on this idea of structure may be weak or powerful depending on the depth of the conceptual structure and the generality of the rules for deduction. One structure is deeper than another if the first is able to assign identical structural descriptions to two English statements that mean the same thing when the other cannot. Let us consider two sentences that most people would agree are equivalent paraphrases of each other:

1. Mary bought a boat from Tom.

and

2. Tom sold a boat to Mary.

One system might compute the following conceptual structures:

1a. Buy TENSE Past, AGT Mary, OBJ boat, FROM Tom.
2a. Sell TENSE Past, AGT Tom, OBJ boat, TO Mary.

A second might compute

1b. Exchange TENSE Past, TO Mary, FROM Tom, OBJECT boat, FOR value.
2b. Exchange TENSE Past, TO Mary, FROM Tom, OBJECT boat, FOR value.

Because the second system analyzes the two sentences into identical structures, 1b and 2b, the second type of analysis results in a deeper structure than that of the first system that produced nonidentical structures 1a and 2a. Because the identity of meaning of the two sentences is immediately apparent in the 1b-2b analysis, the second language processor can be said to be more powerful than the first (that is, it accomplishes more work in its analysis than the first).

However, the first system can be made quite as effective for answering questions as the second by adding deduction rules such as the following:

D1. Buy AGT X1, OBJ X2, FROM X3 = Sell AGT X3, OBJ X2, to X1.
D2. Buy = Exchange FOR value, TO <AGT>.
D3. Sell = Exchange FOR value, FROM <AGT>.

Rule D1 is a transformation of one structure pattern into an equivalent one that rearranges the variables X1, X2, and X3 in accordance with the rule. D2 and D3 define *buy* and *sell* in terms of the more abstract verb *exchange,* differentiated by the qualification "FOR value" and the substitution of a prepositional relation for the agentive noun. Thus by operating the rules D1 through D3 on structures 1a and 2a, the deeper structures of 1b and 2b result.

It is apparent that even deeper structures than 1b and 2b can be derived by the use of additional deductive rules. For example, *buy* and *sell* imply not just an exchange of objects but an exchange of the property of ownership of the objects. Thus a deeper structure for the example sentence is as follows:

1c. Exchange FOR (Value ATTRIBUTE ownership)
     OBJ (Boat ATTRIBUTE ownership)
     TO Mary
     FROM John

Even deeper structures defining exchange in terms of two reciprocal changes in ownership from time 1 to time 2 between Mary and John can be developed. Each such deeper structure makes more explicit the inferences that can be made from the sentence. In human thought patterns there is probably no deepest structure, but for any computer system there is probably an optimal depth for any given purpose.

Optimization of depth of structure for a computer language processor depends on how frequently questions that require subtle inferences are to be asked. If they are frequent, the deeper structure is desirable to avoid frequent and redundant application of the rules of inference. If, on the other hand, few deep inferences are required (as might be the case in a document retrieval system), a much shallower structure supported by many rules of inference will suffice. In either case, however, because there is no apparent limit to depth of structure, deductive inference rules that transform one structure into another are required by a language processor.

This apparent digression into an examination of depth of conceptual structures actually shows that equivalent paraphrases are statements that either have the same deep conceptual structure or that can be transformed into each other by some set of deductive rules. If two statements are not equivalent paraphrases, the extent to which they agree can be measured by the degree of similarity and difference in their conceptual structures and in terms of the proportions of those structures that can be transformed into each other.

Thus for the tutorial model the language processor can measure the paraphrastic equivalence of the student response and the canonical answer in terms of the similarity of their respective deep conceptual structures. The portion of the CA that is not equivalent or transformable (hence transformationally equivalent) to the SR then serves as a basis for generating an appropriate hint or new query.

The syntactic and semantic processes the language processor uses to transform from English into the deep conceptual structure are quite complex and a detailed description would require more space than is available in this chapter. We shall, however, attempt to describe briefly the essence of the process for generating English from the conceptual structures, allowing the interested reader to consult previous descriptions (Simmons et al., 1968) for detailed treatment.

Generation from structure to English string is accomplished by taking each triple of structure as a possible left half of a generation rule. Let us consider example 1a again:

1a. Buy TENSE Past, AGT Mary, OBJ (boat Q 1), FROM Tom.

Structure triples are "Buy TENSE Past," "Buy AGT Mary," "boat Q 1," and so on. The first and third terms in each triple are expressed by a word or a morpheme, whereas the middle relational term may be expressed as a word or a function to accomplish a combination of morphemes or to translate a first or third term into a word. Associated with each element of structure is an appropriate syntactic class—thus Buy-VP, TENSE-function, Past-ed, AGT-O, Mary-NP, Q-function, 1-determiner, and so on.

A subset of generation rules sufficient to transform this structure into an English sentence is

NP Q Det   — (TMOD(C,A))NP = a boat
VP TENSE Past — (TENSE(A,C))VP = bought
VP Prep NP   — (A B C) VP = bought from Tom
VP OBJ NP   — (A C) Pred = bought from Tom a boat
Pred AGT NP   — (C A) Sentence = Mary bought from Tom a boat.

Terms such as TMOD and TENSE are functions that are applied to the arguments in the following parentheses. Abbreviations such as Q for quantifier, Det for determiner, NP for noun phrase, VP for verb phrase, and Pred for predicate are common linguistic usage. The letters A, B, and C refer, respectively, to the first, second, and third terms of the left half of the expression. The phrases following the equal sign after each rule show the result of the system's applying the rule and its functions to the structure to produce a string of English words.

The generator that applies these rules is a fairly simple routine that takes first the most deeply nested triple; derives its syntactic form, for example, "NP Q Det" from "boat Q 1"; looks it up as a left half of the rule; applies the rule to convert the structure; and then continues from left to right with the remainder of the structure until the structure is completely expressed in English or it fails for lack of an appropriate rule. If a rule contains a function such as TMOD or TENSE, this generation routine operates the function to obtain its result, which then becomes part of the English string.

Given any set of structures, the generator will produce one or more English sentences to communicate its meaning. With the use of certain introductory phrases that can be elements in rules and the appropriate choice of structures, this generator is an adequate first approximation to what is needed for the tutorial model.

Some Example Analyses of Student Responses

As mentioned earlier, a version of Planit was modified to allow a human tutor to accept free English responses from students and to make instructional decisions. Preliminary experiments with this system have given us a number of protocols that show the text that was presented, the canonical answer, and various student responses. Several CA's and SR's so obtained will be analyzed in this section to illustrate particular aspects of the logic used by the language processor for determining the extent of paraphrase and for generating an appropriate instructional response.

Following the presentation of appropriate text material concerning the anatomy of the eye, the first query in the lesson was

The primary image-forming function accomplished by the cornea and aqueous humor working together is to . . . ? (COMPLETE THE SENTENCE)

The canonical answer (CA1) was

The function is to . . . bend light to form an image on the retina.

The student response (SR1) was

(The function is to) . . . bend light rays for focusing on the retina.

The CA and SR are quite similar to a human reader, but even after analysis the concept structures, as diagrammed in Figure 10–2, do not precisely match.

First, however, a few remarks to explain Figure 10–2. The CA contains three embedded sentences that can be expressed roughly as follows:

1. Function is to bend, etc.
2. Bending of light is to form, etc.
3. Forming of image is on retina.

The SR contains the following four embeddings:

1. Function is to bend, etc.
2. Light rays are bent to focus, etc.
3. Rays are associated with light.
4. Focusing is on retina.

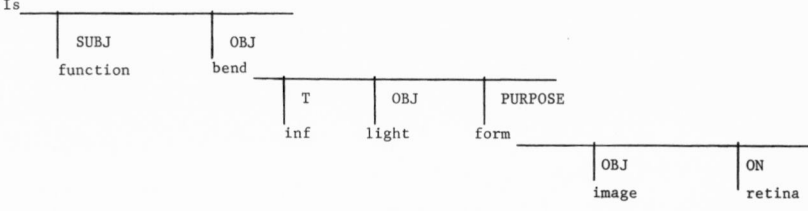

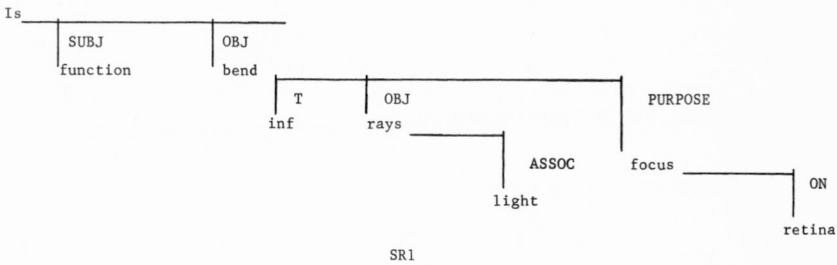

Figure 10-2.
Diagrammatic comparison of canonical answer and student response.

Each of these embeddings corresponds to a downward step in the diagrams of Figure 10–2. With the exception of "Rays ASSOC light" each is headed by a verb. Relational terms such as SUBJ, OBJ, T (for TENSE), PUR-POSE, and so on are labels for the vertical lines in the diagrams. The diagrammatic presentation is exactly equivalent to the previous notation, which used commas, parentheses, and semicolons to show the nested nature of the relationships. For example, CA1 can also be expressed in that nota-tion as

> Is SUBJ function, OBJ (Bend T inf, OBJ light) PURPOSE (Focus OBJ image, ON retina).

A different arrangement using the same notation but eliminating parentheses is as follows:

> Is SUBJ function,
>   OBJ bend
>
>   T inf
>   OBJ light
>   PURPOSE form
>
>   OBJ image
>   ON retina

These various forms of notation are all equivalent expressions of the structure and will be used where appropriate as we continue the illustration.

The reader should especially note in Figure 10–2 that where an embedded sentence is signified by a downward step (or by a parenthesis or a shift right in the other notations) everything in that embedding is an argument of the relation. Thus "bend" and the entire remaining structure of CA1 is in an OBJ relation to "Is."

Comparison to determine if SR1 is an equivalent paraphrase of CA1 is accomplished by examining each embedded structure as a subunit from the most deeply embedded structure up to the top structure. Table 10–2 shows the comparisons to be made.

Table 10–2. Comparison of Embedded Structures in CA1 and SR1

Depth	CA1	SR1
3	Form OBJ image, ON retina	Focus ON retina
2	Bend OBJ light, PURPOSE 3	Bend OBJ 2a, PURPOSE 3
2a		Rays ASSOC light
1	Is SUBJ function, OBJ 2	Is SUBJ function, OBJ 2

Starting with depth 3, the language processor compares the two structures, "Form OBJ image, ON retina" and "Focus ON retina." Because they do not match on "Form" and "Focus," these words are looked up in the system's dictionary to discover associated definitions (Def, signified by $=$) and inference rules (Drul, identified by $=>$). As it applies each inference rule or definition, the system rewrites the structure and makes the comparison again. Table 10–3 summarizes the steps taken by the system, show-

Table 10–3. Computation of Similarities Between SR1 and CA1

Depth 3 comparison: Focus ON retina vs. Form OBJ image, ON retina

Diff:	Focus vs. Form OBJ image
Def:	Focus = Form OBJ (Point OR image)
Diff:	Form OBJ (Point OR image) vs. Form OBJ image
Drul:	(X1 = X2 R (X3 OR X4)) => (X1 = X2 R X3)
	or (X1 = X2 R X4)
Result:	Form OBJ image, ON retina
Diff:	0

Depth 2 comparison: Bend OBJ (Rays ASSOC light), PURPOSE 3 vs. Bend OBJ light, PURPOSE 3

Diff:	Rays ASSOC light vs. light
Drul:	X1 ASSOC X2 => X2
Result:	Bend OBJ light, PURPOSE 3
Diff:	0

Depth 1 comparison: Is SUBJ function, OBJ 2 vs. Is SUBJ function, OBJ 2

Diff:	0 = case 1

ing the inference rules used successfully and the result of applying each until, for this example, the SR is transformed to match the CA.

In the depth 3 comparison, the first result is the difference between "Focus" in the SR and "Form OBJ image" in the CA. The definition of "Focus" is next shown to be equivalent to the structure "Form OBJ (Point OR image)," so this equivalence serves as a deduction rule that allows the definition to be substituted for the word. The difference between "Form OBJ (Point OR image)" and "Form OBJ image" still remains. Because a definition containing or-ed elements implies a set of alternative definitions, the deduction rule used is true and applicable (where X1, X2, X3, X4, and R are positional variables that can stand for any term). The result of applying this rule is the reduction of the differences in depth 3 to zero.

In the depth 2 comparison both SR1 and CA1 include the triple "Bend PURPOSE 3." The number 3 refers to the depth 3 structures that have already been found to be transformationally equivalent. In Table 10–2 the depth 2 structure for the SR1 was "Bend OBJ 2a, PURPOSE 3," where 2a referred to the structure "Rays ASSOC light." To clarify the comparison task, this structure has been used in Table 10–3 in the depth 2 comparison. The result of this comparison is the difference between "Rays ASSOC light" and "light." The relation ASSOC is symmetrical and also has the property of left collapsibility.[3] Therefore the deduction rule, X1 ASSOC X2 => X2, is applicable and the difference is reduced to zero. Finally, in the depth 1 comparison the two structures are found to match exactly.

The whole computation shows that the SR fits case 1 and should transfer control to the generator, which produces a positive reinforcement and continues with the lesson. Subsequent illustrations will be presented briefly with comment limited to that needed to explain unusual situations.

The next query in the lesson was presented as follows:

> The iris and pupil work together to . . . ?

The canonical answer was

> Regulate amount of light entering the eye.

The student's response was

> Accommodate for light intensity.

Table 10–4 shows the embedded structures in the SR and CA and the detailed comparison of each depth level. The depth 3 comparison failed com-

---

3. Left collapsibility is a property that allows the head of certain linguistic constructions to substitute for the whole construction. It is defined as follows: If R is left collapsible, (X1 R X2) => X1.

Table 10–4. Treatment of SR2

Depth	CA2	SR2
3	Enter SUBJ 2, OBJ eye	NONE
2	Light ASSOC amount	Light ASSOC intensity
1	Regulate OBJ 2	Accommodate FOR 2
	4a. Embedded structures in CA2 and SR2	

Depth 3 comparison: NONE vs. Enter SUBJ 2, OBJ eye

Diff:	CA2
Drul:	NONE
Diff:	Enter SUBJ 2, OBJ eye

Depth 2 comparison: Light ASSOC intensity vs. Light ASSOC amount

Diff:	Intensity vs. Amount
Def:	Intensity = Amount ASSOC (Force OR energy)
Drul:	X1 ASSOC X2 = X1
Result:	Intensity = Amount
Diff:	0

Depth 1 comparison: Accommodate FOR light vs. Regulate OBJ light

Diff:	Accommodate FOR vs. Regulate OBJ
Def:	Accommodate = Adjust OBJ lens, PURPOSE (see AT (Distances MOD different))
Def:	Regulate = bring OBJ (Order OR uniformity)
Diff:	Greater than before
	4b. Comparison of differences

Correct portion:	Light ASSOC intensity
Remainder of CA:	Regulate OBJ (CORRECT SUBJ-1 (Enter OBJ eye))
CASE:	3
Generate:	The iris and pupil work together to ____ intensity of light entering the eye
	4c. Response generation

pletely. The depth 2 comparison used a definition and a deduction rule successfully to discover that intensity of light means amount of light. The depth 1 comparison also failed, so the only correct portion of SR2 was "light intensity," which allows the substitution of the marker CORRECT in CA2 at the point that it called for "amount of light." From the original query and the remainder of the CA the generator is now allowed to give the deepest structure "entering the eye" as a hint and to use the correct portion of the student's response and so generate the following two statements:

Light intensity is part of the answer, try this:

The iris and pupil work together to _____ intensity of light entering the eye. (FILL IN THE BLANK.)

In the example of Table 10–4, the student's use of "accommodate" shows a basic confusion that a tutor should be expected to note and correct.

Although our present design does not allow for this, we have eventual plans for a list of words and concepts significant to the lesson, and when any one of these is used in an incorrect manner, the tutor will first attempt to correct that concept and then return to the frame at hand.

The two preceding examples have illustrated response cases 1 and 3, the completely true and partially true cases. The next illustration exemplifies case 2, where there is no correspondence between the SR and the CA. After appropriate text the following query was presented:

Explain why the process of accommodation deteriorates with age.

The CA:

Lens becomes increasingly rigid with advancing age.

The SR:

The ciliary muscles are losing their ability to contract.

The language processor found no similarity between these two responses. Instead of simply repeating the query, as the present tutorial model allows, it is apparent that the system would be improved by a generation such as "That's not the answer, try again."

The lens becomes . . . ?

Such a generation, taking the subject of the CA as a hint, would be easily possible in this case, but we do not yet know how general such a rule would be.

A case 4 incomplete but correct partial answer is illustrated by the next example. In this case the query was

Despite their need for nutrients, can you think of any anatomical elements in the eye that should be isolated from the blood vessels?

The CA:

Cornea, lens, vitreous and aqueous humors.

The SR:

The vitreous humor.

Because the CA has the syntactic structure of a simple list, the system can easily be expected to count the remaining members and generate:

Vitreous humor is one correct answer, try again. There are three more, _____, _____, _____.

So far we have obtained only a single example of a case 5 response where the SR has more information than the CA. The query was

How does the lens accommodate in human vision?

The CA:

Lens shape changed by ciliary muscles.

The SR:

The ciliary muscles change the convexity of the lens.

The only comparison problem in this pair of responses was to find the correspondence between "Lens ASSOC convexity" and "Lens ASSOC shape." Part of the definition of convexity is "Convexity SUP shape," so convexity implies shape but it is a particular curved shape so it carries more information than the CA required. The tutorial system design calls for generating:

Lens shape changed by ciliary muscles is the correct part of your answer; the rest is irrelevant.

This would be a rather surprising response that might be expected to arouse some bitterness in the student because convexity of the lens is certainly relevant to accommodation. It would obviously be more appropriate to accept this as a case 1 correct response. However, exactly how to recognize and deal with case 5 responses will have to await our obtaining of a larger sample of actual cases.

Discussion and Conclusion

We have discussed the problem of dealing with English constructed responses, presented the design for a tutorial system based on a natural language processor, and illustrated its operation by the analysis of some sample student responses. The PSIII language processor is sufficiently well developed that it can accept definitions, deductive rules, and generated responses using a generation grammar. However, before we use this system for this purpose, many analyses of the type presented must first be made and the tutorial system must be programmed to account for their variations in form and content.

Although the system we are currently building is a large one with 4–8 million words of storage available to it, it is still a moot question as to whether we can supply a sufficiently large vocabulary, grammar, and system of deductive rules to allow relatively free interaction with students. We believe that the design of a tutorial system is basically sound and that our methods for analyzing student responses are basically correct. Nevertheless, we are painfully aware at this stage of our research that there is a long hard path still ahead of us before our designs and techniques coalesce into a programmed system that will allow us to test our basic hypothesis that a tutorial system is superior in teaching effectiveness to other forms of CAI.

REFERENCES

Burger, J. F., Schwarcz, R. M., and Simmons, R. F. 1968. *Users guide and program descriptions for protosynthex III.* Santa Monica, Calif.: System Development Corporation. TM-4068.

Feingold, S. L., and Frye, C. H. 1966. *Users guide to Planit, Programming Language for Interactive Teaching.* TM-3055/000/01. Santa Monica, Calif.: System Development Corporation.

Fillmore, C. J. 1966. *A proposal concerning English prepositions.* Monograph Series on Languages and Linguistics, no. 19. Washington, D.C.: Georgetown Univ. Institute of Languages and Linguistics.

———. 1968. *The case for case.* In *Universals in linguistic theory,* ed. E. Bach and R. T. Harris. New York: Holt, Rinehart and Winston, pp. 1–88.

Schwarcz, R. M., Burger, J. F., and Simmons, R. F. 1970. A deductive question answerer for natural language inference. *Communications of the ACM,* 13, (3): 167–183.

Simmons, R. F., and Burger, J. F. 1970. A semantic analyzer for English sentences. Santa Monica, Calif.: *Mech. Trans. & Computational Ling.*

Simmons, R. F., and Silberman, H. F. 1967. *A plan for research toward computer-aided instruction with natural English.* TM-3623. Santa Monica, Calif.: System Development Corporation.

Simmons, R. F., Burger, J. F., and Schwarcz, R. M. 1968. A computational model of verbal understanding. In *Proceedings of the American Federation of Information Processing Societies, Fall 1968.* Washington, D.C.: Thompson Book Co., pp. 441–456.

Taylor, E. F., ed. 1968. *Eliza; a skimmable report on the Eliza conversational tutoring system.* Cambridge, Mass.: Educational Research Center, MIT.

11

Raven I. McDavid, Jr.

Analysis of Natural Language

It is said that when my distinguished predecessor John M. Manly went to the University of Chicago, President Harper invited him to go riding. "And what time do you ride, Mr. Harper?" "Every morning at seven." "Excellent, Mr. Harper; any night I am up that late, it will be a pleasure."

The story has, I feel, both short- and long-term applications to the purposes of the Austin conference. For the short term I can testify to the physiological difficulty of staying awake long enough to be ready for an 8 A.M. session. For the long term it is well to remember that in any language, natural or otherwise, the meaning of an utterance is at least partially determined by the sociocultural context in which it occurs. The phrase "every morning at seven" meant more than a clock hour to the participants in the conversation at Chicago: To William Rainey Harper it meant a time to get out into the fresh air in preparation for the daily ordeal of a college administrator; for John M. Manly it meant a period of rest after scholarly celebration late into the evening and convivial relaxation afterward. (Scholars and administrators work at different paces.) Because the range of cultural experience in a metropolitan high school is far greater than the differences between two nineteenth-century humanists such as Harper and Manly, the problem of meaning in natural language can hardly be overestimated in preparing computer-directed or -assisted instructional programs for a mass audience. I shall ask a number of irreverent questions that may help us decide which parts of the instructional program may be turned over to computer installations, which assigned to some other kind of programmed materials, and which shall be reserved—at least for the moment—for human instructors, although perhaps sharply different in background and personality from the typical public school teacher we have today.

I am not sure that I can provide for Simmons' paper the traditional evisceration the critic (or respondent) is called on to offer. I have done no immediate work with computers, either for research or for teaching. (I have less than a passionate commitment to any school of generation—Chomskemic, Hallidayley, or Lambent.) I cannot listen to any paper on generative grammar without quickly finding myself disagreeing irreconcilably on the grammaticalness of some of the illustrative sentences before five minutes have elapsed—and I am not about to take the time to construct a grammar of my idiolect. And in contrast with the interest of Simmons in the structure of written responses, I have worked primarily as a social anthropologist, concentrating my research on the spoken language.

On the other hand, the direction of my work has given me a useful if different perspective on language matters. As a scholar I have been concerned with the taxonomy of regional and social dialects of American English and with reactions to their differences. For the last half-dozen years I have been encouraging my students to make studies of the social dialects of particular communities with a view toward preparing teaching materials adapted to local needs. At present a group of us are completing a set of materials on social dialects for the classroom teacher. Tying all these ends together is my continuing work at editing the *Linguistic Atlas,* a collection of field data from the Atlantic seaboard, with a pronouncing dictionary as one of the probable by-products. And I have devised and run a tolerable home-study course in American English.

Now each of these projects has its own potential uses of the computers, most of them at present in the realm of dreams. The pronouncing dictionary will be a relatively simple problem of typesetting by computer tape with a provision for inserting addenda in subsequent printings; the only complication is the phonetic alphabet, but because the transcription will be relatively broad, it should offer few difficulties.

For the *Linguistic Atlas* we must provide a keyboard and a print-out head to take care of a complicated phonetic alphabet in addition to conventional alphabetical and numerical characters: thirty-six vowels, fifty or more consonants, twenty diacritics, with at least the theoretical possibility of all vowel and consonant symbols appearing in two positions, on line and above. Again, after this material is stored, all kinds of correlations are possible, including the direct printing of dialect maps by the computer. Furthermore, computer analysis of the correlation between linguistic forms and social status may make possible a far more sensitive and sophisticated teaching of usage than we now find in our schools.

But if we are to use the full resources of the computer in connection with programs for teaching standard English to speakers (and writers) of non-standard dialects, we must not stop with discovering the points of divergence. We must use the computer to catch divergencies in the speech or writing of the individual student and direct him to the desired response. And here we need recognition devices—for speech and writing—far more sophisticated than now exist.

For speech we need to develop an audio receptor that can respond to vocal signals and indicate the accuracy of the student's response with auditory or visual signals or both, and perhaps with a repetition of the canonical performance. The computer system must be programmed to disregard differences in the phonic quality of the phonemes, in voice quality, in paralanguage, and even in stress and intonation—unless stress or intonation is a part of the problem, in which case these must be the target. Beyond this the program must be adapted to the known contrasts between the language of the student and the target, some standard dialect. In other words, this is a language-teaching situation.

For written responses a whole set of additional problems occurs. Because the computer can detect misspellings, it should be made to distinguish, first, between haphazard errors—caused by visual confusion of words—and systematic confusions—caused by the nature of the student's dialect. It must also be able to discriminate between systematic errors indicative of a non-standard dialect, such as the confusion of graphic *t* and *th,* as found among the Acadians of Louisiana, and such confusions—characteristic of standard dialects in various regions—as *Wales* and *whales, pen* and *pin, cot* and *caught, ear* and *air, boarder* and *border, former* and *farmer* (a common problem in Louisiana and Texas), and the likewise common Texas confusion between King *Arthur* and the *author* of a book, with such by-forms as *aurthor* for both. These confusions arise from the simple fact that forms that contrast in some regions do not contrast in others; my own standard South Midland speech has many contrasts that do not occur in the standard speech of the Upper Midwest. We should therefore have programs in reading and spelling based on a recognition of such regional differences in phonemic-graphemic correspondences. Furthermore, it would be desirable to include in our teaching programs a realization that different reductions of consonant clusters occur in different dialects, even at the standard level; for instance, I regularly say *I didn't mind* /maind/ *it,* but *I can't make up my mind* /main/, with omission of final /-d/.

Inflections—plural and possessive of nouns, third singular present indicative, past tense, present and past participles of verbs—are among the surest touchstones for social dialects. The computer, we are told, can be taught to recognize deviations from the standard. But here, too, it must be able to discriminate between forms that are clearly nonstandard and those that reflect the regional morphophonemics imperfectly adjusted to the conventions of writing. After all, I say *I burned* /bərnd/ *a hole,* but *I burned* /barn/ *my pants,* with assimilation of the final /-d/. And when I add a half and a third it inevitably comes out *five sixths*/siks/, pronounced like the cardinal numeral, although I have never worried about the spelling. I would want our teaching strategies to take care of inflectional problems such as these. And on the syntactic level there are similar problems, notably the omission of the copula *be* with adjectives, nouns, and participles—something often associated with Negro-American dialects but documented in the speech of many educated whites, particularly in the South (excellent examples are available in the speech of the recent presidential candidate from Alabama).

So much for the computer and natural language sentences in teaching situations with which I am personally concerned. Let me finally pick a few nits from Simmons's chapter—reverting to my unsavory past as a humanist.

First of all, I seriously question whether in a live sociocultural setting one can equate

> Mary bought a boat from Tom.

with

> Tom sold a boat to Mary.

In fully natural, that is, spoken, language it is possible that shifting the primary stresses, so that *Tom* or *Mary* is most heavily accented in both sentences, would reduce the discrepancy. But because word order is a part of the apparatus of the English sentence, I would still feel a difference between the two. If we expand a little, the difference is greater. Let us compare

> The Russian spy bought the plans from the CIA agent.

and

> The CIA agent sold the plans to the Russian spy.

Leaving out the rest of the plot (I'm a Durrell fan), one can argue that the subject indicates the initiative in the transaction; it could make a serious difference in court. And I am sure one would probably encounter less trouble at home by saying

> I bought my wife some perfume from a sexy French salesgirl.

than with

> A sexy French salesgirl sold me some perfume for my wife.

Whether or not "deep structure" really exists—and some of the Lower Charles River braves say that it does not—I wonder if it profits us to deepen our structure by blurring our meanings.

A second peccadillo I find in the "case for incomplete but correct partial answer."

The question was "Despite their need for nutrients, can you think of any anatomical elements in the eye that should be isolated from the blood vessels?" The canonical answer was "Cornea, lens, vitreous and aqueous humors." The student's response was "The vitreous humor." The system would be expected to respond "Vitreous humor is one correct answer, try again. There are three more, ———, ———, ———."

But I submit that for this question, as put, the canonical answer and the computer amplification are both in error. Looking at the question as a computer should, I would accept four, three, two, or one of the eyeparts as a correct answer—or even *yes* or *no*. For the question reads not "Name the parts . . ." or "What parts . . . ?" but "Can you think of any parts . . . ?" It is like the story of one of Darrell Royal's tackles a few years back who made the mistake of enrolling in a chemistry course. Flunking a midterm test, he was about to be ineligible for the game with A&M. So Royal went to the instructor and asked him if he could give a makeup exam. The instructor consented and turned in a grade of 100. Royal was grateful but a little embarrassed, so he went to the instructor again and said, "I appreciate your cooperation, but I didn't want this turned into a farce." "It wasn't any farce; I gave him a short oral examination and he answered the questions correctly." "Well, what were the questions?" "I asked him to give the chemical formula for water, and he said H_2O—and that was correct. Then I asked him, 'Can you give me the formula for sulfuric acid?' and he said 'No'—and that was correct, too." Our computers cannot be expected to provide instruction if we have asked the wrong kinds of questions. And the more we approach the conditions of informal natural spoken language, the harder it will be to ask the right questions.

Nevertheless, I can think of many ways in which computers might be effectively used to improve instruction. For the undergraduate engineering courses at Chicago that are catalogued under the name of humanities, they would probably improve the quality of instruction.[1] Every year, my colleagues in charge of these courses complain that some of the young instructors "don't teach these courses in the way we want them taught." If it

1. As one of the uninitiated after only twelve years in the department, I gather that the primary aim of these introductory humanities courses is indoctrination, so that every student will judge every literary work according to a set of canonical principles (presumably Aristotelian) and come up with the same kind of interpretation. They should be at least as amenable to computer-assisted instruction as chemistry or anatomy.

were not for student unrest over impersonality, I would suggest they invest in a computer program and use lower-grade technicians to monitor student output; this would be more likely to achieve the clearly desired uniform product. On the other hand, I despair of finding a computer program that can take a handwritten theme and evaluate it for creativity, organization, and development. But maybe John Carroll and his confreres can solve even that problem. I do not resent the "intrusion" of computers into the relationships between teachers and students; I feel that the inevitable mechanical labors of instruction can usually be done more effectively by machines and should be turned over to machines wherever possible, regardless of the discipline. With increasing enrollments in our schools at all levels, it is incumbent on us to use all available resources to bring to students the best possible instruction our affluent society can provide.

Language Processing: Discussion

The full simulation of a human tutor requires a computer program capable of understanding the student in his own language. Although progress is being made in the solution of some of the problems associated with processing natural language, many critics believe a productive approach to computer aids to learning should begin from some reasonable division of tasks between human teachers and the various automated devices and self-instruction techniques proposed. Clearly, humans will continue to be involved in the instructional process and do many things more effectively than alternatives provided through automation. It is almost as certain that machines will do a number of things more effectively than humans: definitely the tedious and repetitive tasks associated with drill and testing where human patience is taxed by students of low ability; certainly the problem-solving and information-processing aids that make the computer a useful tool to scholars in many areas; and probably the diagnostic help provided through specialized language-processing routines.

Simmons' language-processing idea of translating sentences into a "deeper" structure, that is, abstracting or simplifying the information given by the student, appears a necessary part of classifying ("understanding") answers and must be done in spite of possible blurring of the meaning, which McDavid cleverly demonstrates. No two sentences in English can have exactly the same meaning; however, it becomes necessary to recognize as equivalent any two phrases that are taken by most subject experts to be essentially identical. "Depth" of structure may have inappropriate connotations for some readers—the deeper into the structure one goes, the wider the variety of meanings that are considered equivalent. At the extreme, all sentences have just that single attribute of being sentences, and in that trivial sense are considered to be identical!

Presently, it is necessary to place the burden on the curriculum designer to formulate his questions and construct his synonym dictionaries and transformation rules so that the system will make a useful abstraction of the student answer, that is, work at the "right depth." Simmons is developing tools for handling the constrained dialect of written language on examinations in a particular area of study.

His model for investigation of response processing should be differentiated from those that emphasize another part of the instructional dialogue. Weizenbaum's work with Eliza involves transformation of the student's input in order to produce an apparently relevant reply even when the content is not recognized, as well as controlled movement from one subtopic to another within a limited context of discussion (Weizenbaum, 1966).

This discussion provokes difficult questions: How far away is the present state of CAI from evaluation of a handwritten theme in terms of creativity, organization, and development? How soon could oral examinations involving free response and conversation be introduced into certification examinations and selection procedures for continuing education? Simmons suggests that one should ignore the next five years; the magnitude of problems associated with analyzing and describing the structure of language requires that one look ahead ten or more years to anticipate significant gains.

REFERENCES

Weizenbaum, J. 1966. Eliza—a computer program for the study of natural language communication between man and machine. *Communications of the ACM* 9:36–45.

PART **VI**

Stanford Programs in Arithmetic, Logic, and Russian

Several chapters in Part VI and subsequent parts deal with major demonstrations of computer-assisted instruction already under way for advanced interactive systems that provide interesting models of future educational applications. Among the best known demonstrations are those conducted at Stanford University.

In Chapter 12 Suppes and Morningstar summarize four ongoing programs that have recently been evaluated. The most extensive of these is the drill-and-practice program in arithmetic, which involves the participation of more than 1500 children in grades 1 through 6. The short drills are taken daily by children working at typewriter terminals connected by telephone lines to a central computer at Stanford. The second system described by Suppes and Morningstar is tutorial and involves the teaching of mathematics to first graders in a local school. Curriculum material is presented by audio and visual displays; the student responds on a standard keyboard or uses a light pen to touch one of the answer choices displayed on the cathode-ray tube. A logic and algebra program, using the same system as the tutorial program for first graders, was employed by Suppes with thirty fourth graders at the Brentwood School. The fourth system described by Suppes and Morningstar is a Russian program instituted at Stanford for teaching comprehension of written and spoken Russian and mastery of Russian grammar and syntax. In each case evaluation was based on a variety of measures internal to the programs as well as some external criteria. In some cases comparisons were made with similar groups receiving conventional instruction. The scope and volume of internal data indicated a wealth of relationships, the analysis of which has barely begun, which can be of enormous value to the psychologist and educator. When compared to control groups, the groups taught in the various programs have often proved superior in one way or another.

In reviewing the Stanford programs, Young (Chapter 13) emphasizes the potential contributions of computer-assisted instruction in alleviating a number of broad social problems as well as improving the quality of mathematics education. He cautions against overstandardization, pointing out that diversity of approaches to education should be encouraged. The ability of the skilled teacher to translate an intuitive observation by the student into a learning experience that nourishes the germ of a mathematical idea could hardly be duplicated by a machine.

12

Patrick Suppes and Mona Morningstar

Four Programs in Computer-assisted Instruction[1]

Four of the major programs in computer-assisted instruction developed in the Institute for Mathematical Studies in the Social Sciences at Stanford University will be presented. These programs provide examples of the various methods of integrating a computer system into an educational setting, the specific role the computerized aspect of education can assume, and the range of curriculum taught by such a system.

Drill-and-Practice Program

The most extensive program is a drill-and-practice program in arithmetic that involved, by the end of the 1966–1967 academic year, the participation of more than 1500 students in grades 1 through 6. Although the drill-and-practice program was the most extensive in terms of students and sheer amount of curriculum material, the role of the program in the educational setting was supplementary; that is, the program was designed to drill and review students on concepts previously presented in the classroom

1. The research reported here has been supported by the Carnegie Corporation of New York, the National Science Foundation, and the U.S. Office of Education. The curriculum efforts, as well as the analysis of data, have been a joint enterprise with many people. With respect to the drill-and-practice program we are indebted particularly to Mr. Max Jerman; with respect to the Brentwood tutorial program, Mrs. Jamesine Friend and Mrs. Betsy Gammon; with respect to the logic and algebra program, Mr. Fred Binford and Mr. Roulette Smith; and with respect to the Russian program, Professor Joseph Van Campen and Mrs. Elise Belenky.

by the teacher. Therefore a close temporal relationship between the learning of a concept and drill on that concept was not part of the program design. In fact, the temporal relationship between the material in the program and the mathematics curriculum in the classroom at any given point in time was determined by each teacher, not by our research staff.

For the 1966–1967 academic year the curriculum material, for each of grades 1 through 6, was arranged sequentially in blocks to coincide with the development of mathematical concepts introduced in several text series. There were 20–27 concept blocks for each grade level. Each concept block included a pretest, five days of drill, a posttest, and sets of review drills and review posttests. A brief description of the material in each concept block is shown in Table 12–1.

Table 12–1. Concept Blocks for Grades 1–6—Drill-and-Practice Program 1966–1967

Grade 1		Grade 2	
Block	Description	Block	Description
1.	Counting, how many, 0–9	1.	Addition facts to 10, horizontal
2.	Counting in sequence	2.	Subtraction facts to 10, horizontal
3.	Sums to 4	3.	Addition and subtraction facts to 10, vertical
4.	Sums to 4, vertical, mixed	4.	Addition facts to 10, mixed horizontal and vertical with variables
5.	Differences to 4, vertical, mixed		
6.	Sums to 6, vertical, mixed	5.	Mixed addition and subtraction to 10, mixed horizontal and vertical
7.	Sums to 7, vertical, mixed		
8.	Differences to 7, vertical, mixed	6.	Counting by 1's and 2's, finding what comes before and after
9.	Sums to 9, vertical, mixed		
10.	Sums to 10, vertical only	7.	Addition, 11, 12, 13; horizontal and vertical
11.	Differences to 10, vertical only		
12.	Sums to 10 with variables	8.	Subtraction, 11, 12, 13; horizontal and vertical
13.	Differences to 10 with variables		
14.	Sums and differences to 10, horizontal	9.	Mixed addition and subtraction, horizontal and vertical to 13
		10.	Units of measure, counting, inequalities
15.	Sums and differences to 10, vertical format		
		11.	Addition, 14, 15, 16; horizontal and vertical
16.	Sums and differences to 10 with variables		
		12.	Subtraction, 14, 15, 16; horizontal and vertical
17.	Sums to 10, 3-digit numbers		
18.	Column addition, sums with 10's, no regrouping	13.	Mixed addition and subtraction, 14, 15, 16; horizontal and vertical
19.	Column subtraction, no regrouping	14.	Word problems, units of measure, counting to 200
20.	Mixed addition and subtraction in columns, facts to 10		
		15.	Fractions, ½, ⅓, ¼
21.	Mixed addition and subtraction, inequalities	16.	Addition, 17, 18, 19; horizontal and vertical
22.	Mixed 1- and 2-digit column addition and subtraction	17.	Subtraction, 17, 18, 19; horizontal and vertical
23.	Sums to 10, form $a + b = c + d$	18.	Mixed addition and subtraction, horizontal and vertical
24.	Sums to 10 with variables, form $a + b = c + d$		
		19.	Units of measure, counting, inequalities
25.	Special addition and subtraction		
27.	Special mixed drills		

	Grade 2 (cont.)
Block	Description
20.	Multiplication, 2's and 3's to 9 (i.e., $2 \times 0 = \underline{} \ldots 2 \times 9 = \underline{}$)
21.	C and A laws for addition, subtraction, multiplication
22.	Achievement tests
23.	Mixed drill: fractions, units of measure, inequalities, multiplication
24.	Mixed drill: addition, subtraction, multiplication
25.	Special addition and subtraction
27.	Special mixed drills

Grade 3		Grade 4	
Block	Description	Block	Description
1.	Mixed addition and subtraction, horizontal format, sums 0–18	1.	Addition, 1 and 2 digit, vertical and horizontal
2.	Addition, sums 0–18, horizontal and vertical	2.	Subtraction, 1 and 2 digit, vertical and horizontal
3.	Subtraction, sums 0–18, horizontal and vertical	3.	Subtraction, 2 and 3 digit, vertical format
4.	Addition, no carry, vertical (2 addends, 3 digit) and (3 addends, 2 digit)	4.	Addition, 2 and 3 digit, column addition
5.	Subtraction, no borrow, vertical, 2 and 3 digit	5.	Mixed addition and subtraction, vertical format, limits same as blocks 3 and 4, word problems
6.	Addition, vertical with carry	6.	Measure: length, time, weight, money; some word problems
7.	Subtraction, with borrow	7.	Multiplication, 2's → 9's, horizontal format, levels by products
8.	Mixed addition and subtraction, carry and borrow	8.	Mixed addition, subtraction, and multiplication; addition and subtraction, vertical format; multiplication, horizontal format; limits same as blocks 3, 4, 7; word problems
9.	Measure and word problems and inequalities	9.	CAD laws: days 1–4 apply law, day 5 identify law
10.	Column addition and subtraction, addition, subtraction	10.	Division: ladder form, no remainders, level by products, single-digit divisor, 2's → 9's
11.	Measure, inequalities	11.	Multiplication: 2's through 12's, horizontal format, level by products
12.	Multiplication, horizontal, 2's and 3's	12.	Fractions: identify (to ⅛), simple reducing
13.	Mixed multiplication and division, 2's and 3's	13.	Mixed drill: multiplication, division, fractions; inequalities; word problems; same limits as blocks 10, 11, 12; horizontal and vertical
14.	Division, ladder form, 1 digit into 2 digit		
15.	CAD laws: addition, subtraction, multiplication		
16.	Mixed drill: measure, word problems, inequalities		
17.	Fractions		
18.	Multiplication, horizontal, 2's → 9's		
19.	Mixed drill: multiplication, division, fractions		

Grade 3 (cont.)	
Block	Description
20.	Division, ladder form, 1 digit into 3 digit
21.	Multiplication, vertical, 1 × 2 digit
22.	Achievement tests
23.	Mixed drill: column addition, subtraction, multiplication
24.	CAD laws
25.	Special addition and subtraction drills
27.	Special mixed drills

Grade 4 (cont.)	
Block	Description
14.	Long division: ladder form, 1-digit divisor, 2–4-digit dividend, random divisors
15.	CAD laws: days 1–3 use, days 4–5 identify
16.	Fractions: addition, subtraction, reducing
17.	Measure: time, money, liquid measure, length, weight; some word problems
18.	Multiplication: multiples of 10, inequalities
19.	Mixed drill: multiplication; division; fractions; CAD laws; same limits as blocks 14, 15, 16, 18; some word problems
20.	Long division: ladder form, 1-digit divisor, 2–4 digit dividend, random remainders
21.	Fractions
22.	Achievement tests
23.	Mixed drill: long division; fractions; negative numbers; same limits as blocks 20, 21, 22
24.	Estimation of quotients in division
25.	Special addition and multiplication drills
26.	Special subtraction and division drills
27.	Special mixed drills

Grade 5	
Block	Description
1.	Addition; vertical and horizontal; 1, 2, 3 digit; level 4, carry to 10's; level 5, carry to 10's or 100's
2.	Subtraction, vertical and horizontal, 1 and 2 digit
3.	Mixed addition and subtraction, 3 and 4 digit, mixed borrow, carry
4.	Multiplication, 2's → 12's, level by products, horizontal
5.	Multiplication, vertical, up to 1 × 4 digit, carry, no carry
6.	Mixed drill: multiplication, division, fractions
7.	Division, ladder form, level 3: 1 into 3 digit
8.	Measure

Grade 6	
Block	Description
1.	Mixed drill: ½ column, addition, subtraction, ½ multiplication, some involving decimals
2.	Multiplication: 2's → 12's, level by products, horizontal format
3.	Column multiplication: (1 digit) × (2 digit) through (2 digit) × (3 digit)
4.	Division: ladder form, 1-digit divisor
5.	Fractions: factors, reducing, comparing, simple addition, subtraction
6.	Mixed drill: inequalities, decimals, word problems, exponents, addition, subtraction, multiplication, division
7.	Division: ladder form to 2-digit divisors

Grade 5 (cont.)		Grade 6 (cont.)	
Block	Description	Block	Description
9.	Multiplication, vertical, 2 digit, 2's → 12's	8.	Fractions: addition, subtraction
10.	Mixed drill: column addition, subtraction, multiplication, decimals, CAD laws	9.	Measure: length, time, money, temperature, liquid measure
11.	Division, ladder format, level 3: 2 into 3 or 4 digit	10.	Ratio: per cent
		11.	Division: ladder form, 2-digit divisor
12.	Fractions	12.	Mixed drill: fractions (addition, subtraction, multiplication), ratio, per cent, division, decimals (addition, subtraction)
13.	Measure, decimals		
14.	CAD laws		
15.	Division, ladder format	13.	Fractions: decimals, addition, subtraction, multiplication
16.	Fractions		
17.	Mixed drill: multiplication, division, fractions	14.	CAD laws: days 1–4 apply, day 5 identify
18.	Measure	15.	Multiplication: multiples of 10, horizontal format
19.	Fractions, decimals		
20.	Mixed drill: multiplication, division, decimals	16.	Division: ladder form, 2-digit divisors, 3- to 5-digit dividends
21.	Division, ladder format	17.	Mixed drill: fractions ($+$, $-$, $\times$, $\div$), fractions (column addition), CAD laws, division
22.	Achievement tests		
23.	Mixed drill: summary	18.	Measures: all, including a few metric, area, volume
24.	Estimation of quotients in division		
25.	Special addition and multiplication drills	19.	Ratio, per cent
		20.	Mixed drill: all operations, per cent, decimal multiplication
26.	Special subtraction and division drills	21.	Negative numbers: addition, subtraction, multiplication
27.	Special mixed drills	22.	Achievement tests
		23.	Mixed drill: summary
		24.	Estimation of quotients in division
		25.	Special addition and multiplication drills
		26.	Special subtraction and division drills
		27.	Special mixed drills

Four parallel forms of a test, A, B, C, and D, were prepared for each concept block. The test consisted of an equal number of problems from each of five levels of difficulty. Three of these forms (A, B, and C) were used as pretests and posttests for the block, with each student randomly assigned to one of these forms as the pretest and another as the posttest. A student assigned to a given sequence of forms, for example, form A pretest and form B posttest, received the same sequence for every block. The remaining form and form D were divided into halves to be used as review posttests. For each day of drill, five drills, one at each of the five levels of difficulty, were prepared; a total of twenty-five drills per block. Several sets of review drills for each block were also prepared at the five defined levels of difficulty.

Each student was given his problems individually in the school on a computer-based control terminal connected to the PDP-1 at Stanford via telephone lines. The student responded on a Model-33 teletype with a modified keyboard. After the student signed into the program by typing his assigned student number and his first name, the teletype would print his last name and present the appropriate set of problems. The temporal pace of the problem presentation was determined by the student.

The materials presented to the student for the seven days required for each concept block were

Day 1	pretest
Days 2–5	drill and review drill
Day 6	drill and review posttest
Day 7	posttest

Examples of the format for several types of problems are shown in Figure 12–1. The teletype would print out each individual problem and then position itself to accept the answer in the appropriate place. The student would type in the answer. If his answer was correct, he would proceed to the

GRADE	BLOCK	PROBLEM	GRADE	BLOCK	PROBLEM
1	1	HOW MANY M'S... R M R R M M M R M M R M	4	2	3 6 =2_3
		. . .	4	6	3 YD. AND 2 FT. = ___ FT.
1	2	COUNT. 10 11 ___ 13	4	9	36 X (28 + 34) = (___ X 28) + (___ X 34)
			5	4	___ X 11 = 33
1	4	3 + 1 = ___	5	5	2 9 4 ___X4
2	4	9 + 1 = 5 + ___	5	6	1/3 OF 18 = ___
2	5	7 + N = 9 N = ___	6	4	----- 5 / 9 5
2	9	1 1 +__2	6	5	TYPE THE MISSING NUMERATOR OR DENOMINATOR. 2/3 = ___/9
2	9	1 0 =__3	6	6	TYPE < OR = OR > 3 + 8 ___ 9 + 4
3	1	___ + 35 = 38	6	7	(17 X ___) + 9 = 28722
3	4	2 3 1 4 ±2_1			

Figure 12–1.
Samples of problem formats for grades 1 through 6, drill-and-practice program.

next problem. If he input the wrong answer, the teletype would print out NO, TRY AGAIN and present the problem again. If he made a second error, the teletype would print out NO, THE ANSWER IS . . . and present the problem once more. If the student input the wrong answer for the third time, he would be given the correct answer and the teletype would automatically proceed to the next problem. The student was allowed from ten to forty seconds to respond, depending on the type of problem presented. If a student took more than the allotted time to input his answer, the procedure just described would be followed, but the teletype would print out TIME IS UP, TRY AGAIN in place of NO, TRY AGAIN.

The level of difficulty of the first day of drill was determined by the student's performance on the pretest according to the criteria presented in Table 12–2. The level of difficulty of each successive drill in the same concept block was determined by the student's performance level on the preceding day's drill. Thus, if the student's performance on a drill was 80 per cent or greater, his next drill was one difficulty level higher. A score of less than 60 per cent would branch him down a level for the next drill. Otherwise, the student would remain at the same difficulty level for the next drill.

Whereas the content of the drill was the same for all students in a class with only the difficulty level changing as a function of the preceding day's performance, the content of the review drills differed among students as a

Table 12–2. Branching Criteria

From pretest to drill[a]		From drill to drill	
Per cent correct	Level assigned for drill	Per cent correct on drill D_i	Level assigned for drill D_{i+1}
0–19	1	0–59	Next lower level
20–39	2	60–79	Same level as D_i
40–59	3	80–100	Next higher level
60–79	4		
80–100	5		

a Also from posttest to review.

function of the total past history of each student. The computer individually selected the review drills to correspond to the content of that past block having the lowest posttest score for that student, with the restriction that he was not reviewed for two seven-day blocks in a row on the same past block. The level of difficulty of the review drills was determined by the posttest according to the criteria presented in Table 12–2; the difficulty level remained constant for all four days of review. After a student had received a set of review drills on a given concept block, the score on the review posttest given on the sixth day, replaced the previous posttest on that concept block for determining the concept block and difficulty level for future review drills.

The branching structure for a seven-day sequence of problems is shown in Figure 12–2. Each darkened circle represents a drill; each open circle represents a review drill. To make up for absences, a student could take more than one drill per day, branching accordingly after each drill.

To summarize, the basic features of the drill-and-practice program are

1. Role—drill, a supplement to the teacher's regular classroom instruction.
2. Age group—grades 1 through 6.
3. Curriculum—arithmetic.
4. Individualization:
   a. Temporal pace of problem presentation determined by the student.
   b. Immediate feedback.
   c. Opportunity for second response if first one incorrect.
   d. Level of difficulty of drills changes as a function of individual performance.
   e. Concepts for review selected for each student as a function of his past performance.
5. External materials—none.
6. Number of students—more than 1500 in 1966–1967.
7. Presentation of curriculum—teletype.
8. Response mode—standard keyboard (with some extra mathematical symbols).

Brentwood Tutorial Mathematics Program

The Brentwood program is in direct contrast to the drill-and-practice program. The system was tutorial rather than drill, teaching mathematics to forty-nine first graders during the 1966–1967 academic year. Also, the computerized aspect of learning elementary mathematics was completely integrated with the classroom work; a member of our staff taught all mathematics that was not presented in the computer program. Curriculum material was presented by audio and visual displays; the student responded on a standard keyboard or used a light pen to touch one of the answer choices displayed on the cathode-ray tube (CRT).

There were 400 lessons covering the topics of counting, numerals, addition, subtraction, linear measure, sets and set notation, and geometry. The content and scope of the curriculum were drawn largely from *Sets and*

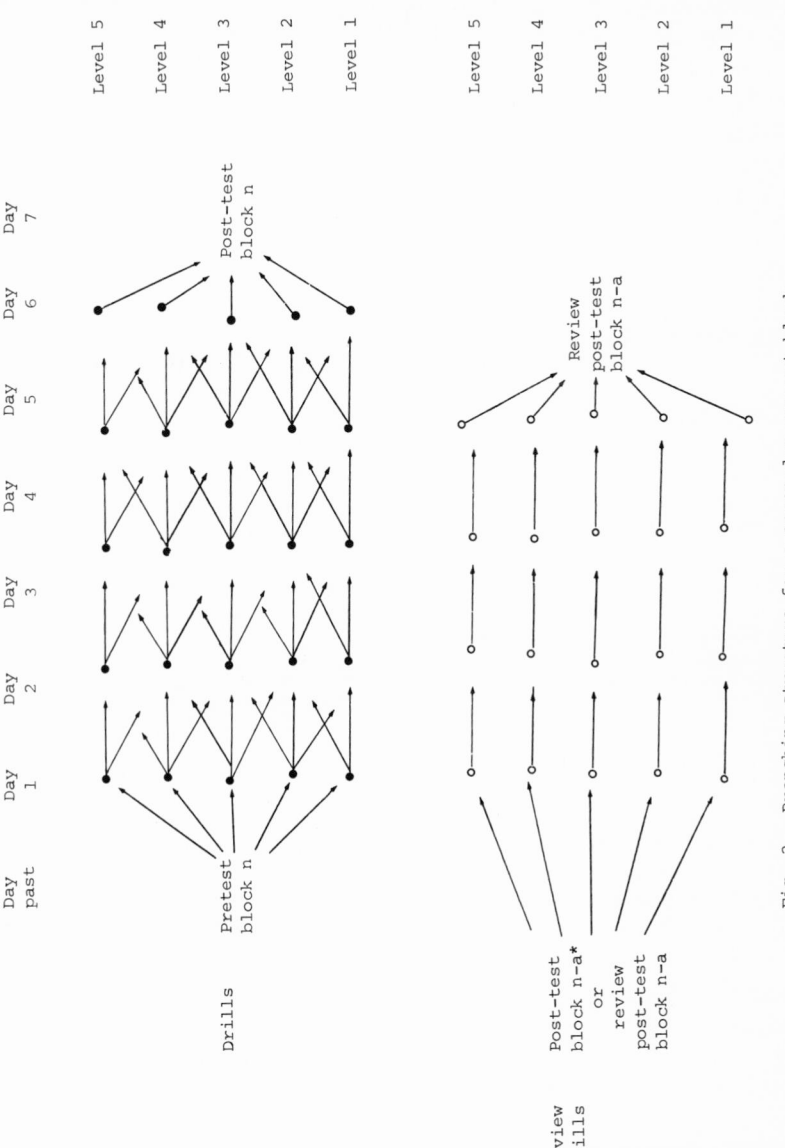

Fig. 2 Branching structure for a seven-day concept block.

*n-a Block with lowest post-test performance

Figure 12–2.
Branching structure for a seven-day concept block. *n-a block with lowest posttest performance.

Numbers, Book 1 (Suppes, 1965), with the addition of some topics such as oral story problems, which cannot, by their nature, be adapted to a textbook format. An outline of the programmed curriculum is shown in Table 12–3.

Table 12–3. Curriculum Outline for Grade 1—Brentwood Tutorial Mathematics Program

| Book | Number of lessons | | | Description |
	Core curriculum	Remedial branches	Drills	
1	8	1	0	Using the machine
2A	7	5	0	Introduction to sets
2B	3	3	0	Matching equal sets
3A	5	4	0	Union of two sets with one member
3B	3	1	2	Union of empty sets
4	11	4	1	Geometry—learning to identify squares, circles, triangles, and line segments
5	7	6	0	Balancing set equations
6A	8	7	0	Introducing the numerals 0, 1, and 2
6B	9	8	1	Introducing N notation with equivalent numerals, introducing the numerals 3 and 4
7A	5	5	1	Sums with N notation (0–4)
7B	5	0	0	Sums with numerals, keyboard responses (0–4)
8	8	2	0	Review
9	8	7	1	Addition
10	9	2	1	Geometry
14A	4	0	1	Measuring line segments
14B	4	0	1	Concave figures, meaning of *half*
15	6	7	1	Balancing addition equations (0–9)
16	7	5	1	Number words, one–six
17A	6	5	2	Number words, zero–ten; sums to nine with three addends
17B	9	1	1	Subtraction
18A	11	6	0	Subtraction combinations through 6
18B	6	2	2	Relating addition and subtraction
19A	12	1	2	Geometry, matching similar figures
19B	11	3	1	Subsets
20A	4	3	2	Review
20B	6	3	2	Subtraction $c - a = b, 7 < c < 9$
21A	11	0	0	Counting and typing to 19
21B	6	2	0	Place value
22	17	6	1	Addition on the number line
23	14	1	1	Counting by 10's
24	19	2	2	Counting by 5's
25	14	2	1	Addition combinations (10–15)

Because the programmed lessons were tutorial, many of the lessons were explanatory, relying on oral explanations synchronized with changing visual displays. The lessons were short (the average length was less than ten problems) and explanations were simple and direct. Generally the problems within one lesson were all of the same type; the first few were accompanied by explanatory audio messages, leaving the remainder as practice problems.

The students received their programmed instruction in a room that contained seventeen student stations and a proctor station for use by the teachers on duty. The student stations were separated by four-foot partitions, which extended far enough from the walls to provide a degree of privacy to the students. When the children arrived in the student station room, they looked for their names on the CRT screen at their assigned stations, put on their headsets, and started their program by touching the light pen to a smiling face displayed on the CRT. After the allotted time for the class, approximately twenty minutes, the students were automatically signed off as they completed their current lesson; the message YOU HAVE BEEN SIGNED OFF appeared on the CRT and the children went into the adjoining classroom, joining a teacher who escorted them back to their homeroom.

Both explanatory and practice problems contained provisional audio messages that were heard only by students who responded incorrectly or who failed to respond within a reasonable time. For example, for one problem, a drawing of a car and a drawing of a truck surrounded by set braces and followed by an equal sign were presented on the CRT; this problem was accompanied by the audio message, "There are two members in this set." After this message, two more sets, one empty and one containing a train and a steam shovel, each preceded by a box, were displayed below the initial set; the choices were accompanied by the audio instructions, "Find another set with two members." At this point a small "p" (for pen) was displayed in the corner of the CRT as a signal to the student to respond. If the student touched his light pen to the box in front of the correct choice, a smiling face was displayed and he heard, "Yes, the sets have the same number of members," and proceeded to the next problem.

If the student did not respond within twenty seconds, he heard, "Which set below has two members?" If the student responded incorrectly, he heard the audio message, "Point to the box next to the set with two members," and saw a sad face. For most problems in the curriculum, students were allowed three chances to produce the correct answer. After three incorrect responses, the correct answer or an arrow pointing to the correct choice was displayed, accompanied by a brief audio message.

For most lessons the number of initial correct responses to the practice problems was accumulated and compared to a criterion. As soon as a student had made the required number of correct responses, he was allowed to skip remaining problems and begin the next lesson. As soon as a student failed criterion, which was, for instance, three incorrect answers if the criterion was seven out of nine problems, he was branched immediately to a remedial lesson containing the same kinds of problems but with a slower development of ideas using simpler vocabulary and sentence structure. If a student failed criterion on a remedial lesson, his program stopped and an automatic call for assistance from a proctor was typed at the proctor station.

This mode of branching permitted students to make their own progress through the curriculum. Thus all students were not required to work on the same concept block at the same time as in the drill-and-practice program. In fact, the faster students were considerably separated in terms of curriculum material from the slower students.

The classroom activity, completely coordinated with the programmed instruction, contained (1) use of physical objects to introduce concepts presupposed by the programmed lessons, (2) work originally planned as programmed lessons, (3) remedial work for individual children, and (4) enrichment material for individual or group use.

To summarize, the basic features of the Brentwood tutorial mathematics program were

1. Role—tutorial.
2. Age group—grade 1.
3. Curriculum—elementary mathematics.
4. Individualization:
   a. Temporal pace of problem presentation determined by the student.
   b. Immediate feedback.
   c. Opportunity for second response if first one incorrect with audio hints to aid problem solution.
   d. Opportunity to advance faster by eliminating some practice problems if student performance met criterion.
   e. Remedial problems at lower difficulty level if student below criterion performance.
   f. Special teacher attention if remedial performance below criterion.
5. External materials—teachers, proctors, all aids normally available in the classroom.
6. Number of students—forty-nine.
7. Presentation of curriculum—cathode-ray tube, film, and audio.
8. Response mode—light pen and standard keyboard.

The students' station room at the Brentwood Laboratory was shared with a reading curriculum program directed by Professor Atkinson (Atkinson and Hansen, 1966; Atkinson and Wilson, 1967). All the first graders not participating in the mathematics curriculum, approximately fifty students, spent about twenty minutes per day at the computer terminals on the tutorial reading curriculum. Both the reading and mathematics programs at Brentwood contained all the individualization inherent in the drill-and-practice program plus the additional features described.

Logic and Algebra Program

The logic and algebra program, similar to the Brentwood mathematics program, is tutorial. However, the teaching of symbolic logic and algebra, unlike the mathematics curriculum for Brentwood and the drill-and-practice program, introduces curriculum materials that are not encountered in a standard elementary school mathematics curriculum. Thirty students in the fourth grade started with sentential logic in December 1966; late in January 1967, the same students started algebraic derivations with logic and algebra presented on alternate days.

The logic curriculum introduced thirteen rules, shown in Table 12–4,

Table 12–4. Rules for Sentential Logic

FC—form a conjunction
P   (1) R
P   (2) S
1.2 FC   (3) R & S

LC—left conjunct
P   (1) R & S (conjunction)
1 LC   (2) R

RC—right conjunct
P   (1) R & S (conjunction)
1 RC   (2) S

CC—commute conjunction
P   (1) R & S
1   CC1 (2) S & R

AA—affirm the antecedent
P   (1) R → S (conditional)
P   (2) R (affirms antecedent)
1.2 AA   (3) S

DC—deny the consequent
P   (1) R → S (conditional)
P   (2) ¬S (denies consequent)
1.2 DC   (3) ¬R

DN—double negation
P   (1) ¬¬S (¬¬is dominant)
1 DN   (2) S
or
P   (1) S (¬¬ is not dominant)
1 DN   (1) ¬¬S

CD—commute disjunction
P   (1) R v S
1 CD1   (2) S v R

DD—deny a disjunct
P   (1) R v S (disjunction)
P   (2) ¬R (denies a disjunct)
1.2 DD   (3) S

FD—form a disjunction
P   (1) R
1 FD   (2) (R) v (S)a

HS—hypothetical syllogism
P   (1) R → Q
P   (2) Q → S
1.2 HS   (3) R → S

CP—conditional proof
P   (1) Q
WP   (2)   R (added premise)
(3)   S
2.3 CP   (4) R → S

IP—indirect proof
P   (1) Q
WP   (2)   R (added premise)
(3)   S
(4)   ¬S
2.3.4 IP   (5) ¬R

a Filled in by student.

including conditional proof and indirect proof, presented in nineteen lessons averaging nineteen problems per lesson. Most of the problems were derivations of one or more steps to be carried out by the use of the thirteen rules. A multiple-choice response mode was used for vocabulary drill, dominance of connectives, strategies, and derivations involving English sentences. Beginning at the end of lesson 9, occasional use was made of the algebraic rules presented in the algebra program. The topics covered in the logic curriculum are presented in Table 12–5.

Table 12–5. Topics Covered in the First-year Logic Program

Lesson number	Rules intro- duced	Vocabular items introduced	Topics covered
1	AA	Conditional, antecedent derive	Deriving conclusions, extraneous premises
2			Additional one-step uses of rule AA
3			Two-step derivations with AA
4	FC	Conjunction	One- then more-than-one-step use of FC, FC and AA used in same derivations
5	LC, RC		Use of LC and RC and their use with AA and FC
6	DD	Disjunction	One- and two-step use of DD, use with the other rules
7	DC	Deny, consequent	Use of DC, its use with other rules
8	DN		DN to add, then to remove dominant double negation
9	HS	Hypothetical syllogism	Use of HS, use of the algebraic rule ND within sentential derivations
10	FD		Use of FD
11			Derivations with all rules presented, use of multiple-choice mode for a review of vocabulary and rule uses
12	CD, CC	Commute	Use of rules CD and CC, in multiple-choice mode English application
13			Review and English examples by multiple-choice mode
14			Dominance in complex cases
15	CP		Technique of conditional proof
16			Special rules for dominance without parentheses
17	IP		Technique of indirect proof
18, 19: Two lessons introducing the multiple-choice mode, inserted into all student's curriculums as soon as the mode was programmed and the lessons coded			

The goal of the algebra curriculum was to teach the students the fundamental properties of the commutative ring of integers with unity and how to use these properties in formal mathematical proofs. The curriculum covered the properties of (1) commutativity of addition and multiplication, (2) associativity of addition and multiplication, (3) additive and multiplicative identities, (4) additive inverse, and (5) the distributive law. A total of fifteen rules, shown in Table 12–6, were presented during the course of twenty-three lessons with from eleven to thirty problems per lesson.

Table 12–6. Rules for the Algebra Program

ND—number definition	MR—associate multiplication right
7ND (1) $7 = 6 + 1$	(1) $12 = (4 \times 1) \times 3$
D—definition	MR2 (2) $12 = 4 \times (1 \times 3)$
(1) $6 = 5 + 1$	ML—associate multiplication left
5D1 (2) $6 = (4 + 1) + 1$	(1) $12 = 4 \times (1 \times 3)$
CA—commute addition	ML1 (2) $12 = (4 \times 1) \times 3$
(1) $4 = 3 + 1$	DL—distributive law
CA1 (2) $4 = 1 + 3$	(1) $A = 4 \times (5 + 6)$
AR—associate addition right	DL1 (2) $A = (4 \times 5) + (4 \times 6)$
(1) $4 = (2 + 1) + 1$	Z—zero
AR2 (2) $4 = 2 + (1 + 1)$	(1) $7 = 7 + 0$
AL—associate addition left	Z1 (2) $7 = 7$
(1) $4 = 2 + (1 + 1)$	IZ—inverse zero
AL1 (2) $4 = (2 + 1) + 1$	(1) $7 = 7$
ID—inverse definition	7IZ2 (2) $7 = 7 + 0$
(1) $5 = 3 + (1 + 1)$	N—negative
2ID1 (2) $5 = 3 + 2$	(1) $2 = 6 - 6 + 2$
CM—commute multiplication	6N1 (2) $2 = 0 + 2$
(1) $6 = 2 \times 3$	IN—inverse negative
CM1 (2) $6 = 3 \times 2$	(1) $2 = 0 + 2$
	6IN1 (2) $2 = 6 - 6 + 2$
	MI—multiplicative identity
	(1) $6 = 6 \times 1$
	6M12 (2) $6 = 6$

The students, as in the drill-and-practice program, were presented problems on a Model-33 teletype. The rules in the logic and algebra program were presented to the student one at a time, followed by a few problems making one-step and then two-step use of the rule. Thereafter, derivations made regular use of the new rule and all previously given rules. All students received the same curriculum. For multiple-choice problems the error message WRONG, TRY AGAIN followed incorrect responses; the student continued to respond until he gave a correct answer. For derivation problems, incorrect syntax or invalid commands from the student were followed by brief explanatory error messages.

Problem 13–5 is a typical example of a sentential derivation. The numbers in parentheses are line numbers; all input by the student is underlined.

Problem 13–5

YOU MUST DERIVE 'K v S' BEFORE USING CP.

DERIVE J → K v S

P	(1)	K v ¬J
		J
P	(2)	J
DD1.2	(3)	K
FD		
		NOT ENOUGH LINE NUMBERS GIVEN.
FD3	(4)	(K) v (S)
CP2.4	(5)	J → K v S
CORRECT		

The problem and the premises (P) on lines (1) and (2) were printed by the teletype. The student then typed DD1.2, which commanded that the *deny-a-disjunct* rule be applied to the disjunction in line (1) using the premise in line (2). The teletype then printed the result of the command including the line number. The error message between lines (3) and (4) informed the student why the rule FD, form a disjunct, was not executed. When the student typed the proper command, FD3, (K) V __ was printed. The student then formed the disjunction he wanted by typing (S). The application of the conditional-proof rule to lines (2) and (4) completed the derivation correctly.

An example of a completed problem from the algebra curriculum is

DERIVE		$7 = (5 + 1) + 1$
ND7	(1)	$7 = 6 + 1$
6D1	(2)	$7 = (5 + 1) + 1$

The ND7 typed by the student on line (1) calls for the number definition of 7. The program responds to this command by typing the line number and the result of applying the ND rule. The number preceding the D on line (2) gives the number to be replaced by its definition; the number following the D states which occurrence of that number is to be replaced. Thus 6D1 asks the program to replace the first occurrence of 6 on the previous line with its definition.

In addition to material on the teletype, the students received a handbook and an instruction booklet. The handbook defined all rules, defined kinds of formulas and dominance of connectives, and listed possible strategy questions. The instruction booklet presented each rule, emphasizing the mechanics of typing the correct information necessary to apply the rule. For each rule several examples were given showing the typed command and the result. Following the examples, from three to six problems were given in which the student was shown the result of an unknown command and told to fill in the missing command.

Although this program contained no branching as a function of performance, the student could proceed through the curriculum at a pace congruent with his ability. For most of the derivations a unique solution did not exist, and each student could develop his own solution strategy. If a student encountered difficulties, a staff member was present to give on-line assistance.

To summarize, the basic features of the logic and algebra program are

1. Role—tutorial.
2. Age group—grade 4.
3. Curriculum—logic and algebra.
4. Individualization:
   a. Temporal pace of curriculum presentation determined by the student.
   b. Immediate feedback.
   c. Opportunity to correct errors immediately.
   d. Student could develop his own strategy for solving problems.
5. External materials—handbook, instructional booklet, attending staff member.
6. Number of students—30 in 1966–1967 (more than 200 in 1967–1968).
7. Presentation of curriculum—teletype.
8. Response mode—keyboard (with some extra logical symbols).

Russian Program

The Russian program was instituted at Stanford in September 1967. This project is directed by Dr. Joseph Van Campen, who has designed a program to teach the standard aspects of a first-year course at the college level: comprehension of written Russian, comprehension of spoken Russian, and mastery of grammar and syntax. Of the three main components of a college-level language course, regular classroom sessions on a daily basis, time in the language laboratory, and regular homework assignments, only the functions of the tutorial classroom sessions have been assumed by the computer program. In addition to their time at the computer console, the students have to spend time in the language laboratory and do homework assignments. The language-laboratory tapes with drill sheets and the homework assignments are prepared by the staff at the Institute.

The twenty-nine students beginning the introductory Russian course during the fall quarter of 1967 were required to spend about fifty minutes per day, five days per week, at the computer console. A total of 135 lessons were prepared, which were presented to the students in a combined audio and teletype format. The students responded on a Model-33 teletype with a special keyboard containing the Cyrillic alphabet.

During the first quarter all errors by the student were corrected immediately. Because typing errors were corrected by the computer just as if they were real mistakes on the student's part, a distorted picture of performance occurred for problems with extensive amounts of typing. To correct this distortion, a change was made in the second quarter that allowed the student to (1) delete as many characters as he wished, replacing them with "correct" characters, or (2) delete the entire answer and retype from the beginning. When he felt the response was correct, the student pressed a special key that instructed the computer to check the given item.

Although the basic curriculum was the same for all students, there were several remedial branches. At given points students were tested on several items of a given type and were given remedial instruction on the points covered if their performance on the test block failed to meet a satisfactory standard. Later in the year routines were provided that produced more specific remedial work based on the type of error, a sophisticated approach to remedial work not present in any of the other programs.

The educational level of the students in the Russian program permitted another unique role for the computer. During the period prior to the final examination, lesson summaries for each new lesson and a final summary covering the material for the entire quarter were given to the students. The computer then assessed the student's performance and told him the rules on which he should concentrate his efforts. At following sessions the student was again tested on the points he had missed and informed where more study was needed. In addition, the student could redo any lesson or portion of a lesson at the computer console.

The language-laboratory tapes provided material for pronunciation practice and also for testing a student's ability to comprehend spoken Russian. A test at the end of the tape either presented a number of Russian sentences for transcription by the student or required the student to respond in writing to oral questions on a paragraph that he had just heard.

To evaluate the pronunciation of the students, a process not possible at this point on the computer, two recordings were made each quarter. The students were counseled immediately after each recording as to what pronunciation errors were made and how to correct them.

To summarize, the basic features of the Russian program are

1. Role—tutorial.
2. Age group—college.
3. Curriculum—Russian.
4. Individualization:
   a. Immediate feedback.
   b. Remedial blocks when performance below standard.
   c. Directed review for examinations.
   d. Could repeat lessons on own initiative.
5. External materials—language-laboratory tapes and tests, homework assignments, individual counseling on pronunciation.
6. Number of students—twenty-nine.
7. Presentation of curriculum—audio and teletype.
8. Response mode—keyboard (with Cyrillic alphabet).

RESULTS AND DISCUSSION

The amount of data collected and the extensive number of analyses performed prohibit a complete presentation of results in this chapter. Consequently, we restrict ourselves to specific examples from each of the programs.

Drill-and-Practice Program

The major emphasis in our analysis of data from the drill-and-practice program was to delineate the factors contributing to problem difficulty. Multiple-regression models with average proportion correct as the dependent variable were applied to the data. Analysis of the pretests and posttests from two blocks of subtraction problems from the fourth grade, 402 and 403, will serve as examples of this technique.

Block 402 contained both horizontal and vertical subtraction problems; all the problems in block 403 were in a vertical format. Two of the independent variables, DIFF and BOR, accounted for characteristics of the numbers shown above the line in vertical problems and to the left of the equal sign in horizontal problems. The two other independent variables, VF and HVC, depended partly on the characteristics of the correct response. Noncanonical horizontal problems, for example, $36 - \_\_ = 30$, were treated as if the missing number were present.

In the following definitions, lowercase letters represent digits. The four independent variables were

1. Differences (DIFF: possible values, 0–4). The value of DIFF for

each problem was equal to the number of columns with the exception of basic borrow problems. The basic borrow problems are those of the form $ab - c = \underline{\hspace{1cm}}$, where the minuend (ab) is a number from 10 to 18. Although these problems have two columns, they involve only one difference and therefore received a value of 1 for this variable.

$$\text{DIFF} \left(\begin{array}{c} a \\ -b \\ \hline c \end{array} \right) = 1$$

$$\text{DIFF} \left(\begin{array}{c} ab \\ -c \\ \hline d \end{array} \right) = 1$$

$$\text{DIFF} \left(\begin{array}{c} abc \\ -de \\ \hline fgh \end{array} \right) = 3$$

2. "Borrows" (BOR: possible values, 0–2). The value of BOR for each problem was the number of times a 1 was "borrowed" from an adjacent column, or, in more recent language, the number of times a regrouping was required.

$$\text{BOR} \left(\begin{array}{c} ab \\ -cd \\ \hline ef \end{array} \right) = \begin{cases} 0 & \text{if } b \geq d \\ 1 & \text{if } b < d \end{cases}$$

$$\text{BOR} \left(\begin{array}{c} ab \\ -c \\ \hline d \end{array} \right) = 1$$

$$\text{BOR} \left(\begin{array}{c} abc \\ -def \\ \hline ghi \end{array} \right) = \begin{cases} 0 & \text{if } c \geq f, b \geq e \\ 1 & \text{if } c < f, (b-1) \geq e \\ 1 & \text{if } c \geq f, b < e \\ 2 & \text{if } c < f, (b-1) < e \end{cases}$$

3. Vertical format variable (VF: possible values, 0, 1, 3). All horizontal problems and vertical problems with one-digit responses received a value of 0. Multicolumn problems with multidigit responses and one-column addition problems with a sum of 11 received a value of 1. One-column addition problems with a multidigit sum other than 11 received a value of 3.

$$\text{VF} \left(\begin{array}{c} ab \\ -cd \\ \hline e \end{array} \right) = 0$$

$$\text{VF} \left(\begin{array}{c} abc \\ -def \\ \hline ghi \end{array} \right) = 1$$

VF probably reflects the likelihood of the mistake of reversing the digits of the correct response. Responses to vertical problems were typed from right to left, whereas responses to horizontal problems were typed from left to right. Thus a student could know the correct answer but err by typing the digits in the reverse order.

4. Horizontal format composite variable (HFC: possible values, 0–3). Horizontal problems were assigned a 1 for each of three characteristics. The sum of the 1's for each problem was the value of HFC. Ones were assigned to problems in noncanonical form, to problems in which the minuend and the subtrahend or the addends were each two or three digits, and to problems with multidigit responses.

$$HFC(a - b = c) = 0$$
$$HFC(ab - c = de) = 1$$
$$HFC(ab - cd = ef) = 2$$
$$HFC(ab - cd = ef) = 3$$

Although the examples given for assigning values of variables to the problems are all subtraction problems, VF and HFC also apply to addition problems. Two other independent variables, not presented here, were defined and, in combination with the four presented, were used in the analysis of all data from addition and subtraction problems in the third, fourth, and fifth grades.

The correlation coefficient (R), the coefficient of determination (R^2), and the regression coefficients for the four variables are shown in Table 12–7 for the pretests and posttests on blocks 402 and 403. When the same

Table 12–7. Regression Coefficients for Grade 4 Subtraction—Drill-and-Practice Program

Block	Test	Form A	Form B	Form C	Constant	DIFF	BOR	HFC	VF	R	R²
402	Pre	64	69	81	−3.49	0.49	0.98	1.28	1.33	0.94	0.87
	Post	75	49	68	−3.63	0.60	0.74	0.86	0.56	0.85	0.72
403	Pre	56	65	77	−2.75	0.06[a]	1.26		0.22[a]	0.89	0.79
	Post	69	43	54	−2.75	−0.01[a]	0.86		0.52[a]	0.70	0.49

a Not significant.

problem occurred more than once in a block, the data for the identical problems were averaged. There were forty-eight problems in block 402 and sixty problems in block 403.

Several of the results presented in Table 12–7 are similar to those obtained for all the addition and subtraction blocks we analyzed. First, the correlation coefficient decreases from pretest to posttest. Second, the regression coefficients for the independent variables, with few exceptions, decrease from pretest to posttest. Finally, the vertical format variable is significant for the block with both horizontal and vertical format (402); it is not significant in the block with only vertical problems (403). This last finding supports the interpretation that VF reflects the likelihood of typing the digits of the response in reverse order, because this error would be more probable in mixed-format blocks than in blocks with all vertical problems.

To provide a description of performance in terms of these variables, the problems in block 402 were classified into similar types. Problems that received the same pattern of values on the four variables were considered identical. Table 12–8 presents the number of problems, the mean observed proportion correct, the predicted probability correct, and the average deviation between predicted and observed for each problem type.

Table 12–8. Observed and Predicted Probabilities for Problem Types, Block 402 —Drill-and-Practice Program

Problem type	Number of problems	Average observed probability	Predicted probability	Average deviation
Horizontal format				
$a - b = \underline{c}$[a] No borrow	4	0.96	0.95	0.01
$ab - c = \underline{d}$ One borrow	2	0.92	0.88	0.04
$\underline{ab} - c = d$ One borrow	3	0.42	0.37	0.05
$ab - c = \underline{de}$ No borrow	3	0.80	0.77	0.03
$ab - \underline{c} = de$ No borrow	6	0.78	0.77	0.01
$ab - c = \underline{de}$ One borrow	3	0.44	0.56	−0.12
$\underline{ab} - c = de$ One borrow	3	0.24	0.26	−0.02
Vertical format				
$a - b = \underline{c}$ No borrow	2	0.92	0.95	−0.03
$ab - c = \underline{d}$ One borrow	1	0.87	0.88	−0.01
$ab - c = \underline{de}$ $ab - cd = \underline{ef}$ No borrow	9	0.75	0.77	−0.02
$ab - c = \underline{de}$ One borrow	9	0.53	0.55	−0.02
$abc - de = \underline{fgh}$ One borrow	3	0.52	0.43	0.09

a Underlined digits are the students' response.

In this block the predicted probabilities were usually lower than the observed ones for horizontal problems but were higher than the observed for vertical problems. In general, the average deviation was low. The exception for horizontal problems was the format $ab - c = \underline{de}$ with one "borrow." For vertical problems the largest deviation occurred for the problem $abc - de = \underline{fgh}$ with one borrow.

Extensive regression analyses of the kind presented here have already been published (Suppes et al., 1968), using the data from our 1965–1966 program. Although it is not possible to enter into details, the analyses of the 1965–1966 and 1966–1967 data were used directly in making revisions in the drill-and-practice program for 1967–1968. Still more extensive revisions are being made during 1968–1969. In fact, for 1968–1969 we are abandoning the block structure described earlier and using concept strands that run across a number of grades. Each student's position, as represented by a vector of grade placements in the strands, depends only on his own work and progress. A preliminary description of the strand approach is to be found in Suppes (1967).

Brentwood Tutorial Mathematics Program

Three approaches were followed in the analysis of the Brentwood data. First, regression models were used to relate structural properties of problems to proportion correct and success latency when performance on a given problem was an average of all students completing that problem. Second, regression models were utilized to identify significant factors in individual performance. Finally, data were compiled to describe performance, in terms of proportion correct, as a function of the problem types defined by the factors found significant in the structural analyses.

Individual models. The students completed 270 lessons. Each lesson contained from 10 to 15 problems. A block, the unit on which performance was measured, contained from 25 to 100 sequential problems on the same concept. When one or two lessons on one concept were interspersed in a series of lessons on another concept, the interspersed lessons were not included in the analysis. Thus no problems in block n were completed prior to the completion of the problems in block n-1. If a sequence of lessons on the same concept contained more than 100 problems, a new block was formed. In this manner thirty-nine blocks were formed on the concepts of addition, subtraction, sets, geometry, counting, numerals, sequences, and miscellaneous. About 70 per cent of the original lessons were used in the final analysis.

Two basic types of models were examined: a temporal model in which the prediction of an individual's performance in a given block was based on his performance in the immediately preceding blocks and a conceptual model in which prediction was based on performance on previous blocks of the same concept. A number of the models we examined are presented in Table 12–9.

Table 12–9. Models for Prediction of Individual Performance—Brentwood Tutorial Mathematics Program

Type	Model[a]	Parameter estimation
I Temporal	$p_{s,i} = \alpha_i + \beta_i p_{s,i-1} + \theta_i p_{s,i-2}$	Group
II Temporal	$p_{s,i} = \alpha_s + \beta_s p_{s,i-1} + \theta_s p_{s,i-2}$	Individual
III Temporal	$p_{s,i,m} = \alpha_{s,m} + \beta_{s,m} p_{s,i-1}$	Modified individual; estimated every four blocks
IV Temporal-conceptual	$p_{s,i,c} = \alpha_i + \beta_i p_{s,i-1} + \theta_i p_{s,i-k}$	Group
V Temporal-IQ	$p_{s,i} = \alpha_i + \beta_i p_{s,i-1} + \theta_i IQ_s/100$	Group
VI Conceptual	$p_{s,i,c} = \alpha_i + \beta_i p_{s,i-k} + \theta_i p_{s,i-j}$	Group
V Conceptual	$p_{s,i,c} = \alpha_{s,c} + \beta_{s,c} p_{s,i-k}$	Modified individual; estimated for each concept

a Where p is proportion correct; s is the student; i is the block, α, β, and θ are parameters to be estimated; m is a set of four blocks; c is a concept; i - k is the block immediately preceding i with same c; and i - j is the block immediately preceding i - k with same c.

Because the difference in an individual's performance at two points in time is a function of the curriculum and of individual differences, three methods of parameter estimation were employed. If one assumes that the major factor in an individual's performance is the curriculum, then group-parameter estimation is most appropriate. For each of the group-parameter estimation models (Table 12–9), one set of parameters was estimated for each block, using the data from all students in the blocks appropriate to the model. Thus, to predict an individual's performance, a different set of parameters was used for each block; for a given block the same set of parameters was used for all individuals.

The individual-parameter estimation technique assumes that differences within the individual are dominant. Under this assumption the performance data on all blocks for a given individual were utilized to estimate parameters. Thus, to predict a given individual's performance, a set of parameters unique to the individual was used for all blocks. For a given block a different set of parameters was used for each student. A more realistic combination of curriculum and individual effects resulted in a modified individual-estimation technique where all data from a given student's performance on a subset of blocks yielded a set of parameters. Thus the set of parameters used to predict an individual's performance was unique to the individual and to a subset of the curriculum. Both temporal (model III) and conceptual (model VII) subsets were employed in the modified individual-estimation procedure.

Because the number of students completing a block decreased rapidly after block 35, only the data from the first thirty-five blocks were used for the estimation of group parameters. All blocks completed by a given student were used in the estimation of parameters for that student. The number of blocks completed varied from twenty-three to thirty-nine.

The regression program used for parameter estimation yielded a chi-square value based on the observed performance data and the predicted value determined by the multiple regression equation for each student for each model. The number of parameters estimated and the total number of predictions for each model are shown in Table 12–10. The average chi-squares in Table 12–10 were calculated by averaging the individual chi-

Table 12–10. Comparison of Models for Predicting Individual Performance—Brentwood Tutorial Mathematics Program

Model	Average chi-square	Number of blocks	Number of individual estimates	Number of parameters estimated
I Temporal group	2.66	33	1199	99
II Temporal individual	4.33	35	1211	120
III Temporal modified individual	2.84	35	1211	598
IV Temporal-conceptual group	2.24	25	858	75
V Temporal-IQ group	2.66	33	1199	99
VI Conceptual group	2.26	20	699	60
VII Conceptual modified individual	1.56	27	938	480

squares for a given block and then averaging these averages to yield an average individual chi-square for each model. It must be noted that these chi-squares are for comparative use only; they are not corrected for number of parameters estimated and therefore should not be utilized for statistical inference.

Of these models the conceptual model with individual parameters for each concept (model VII) had the lowest average chi-square; the temporal model with individual parameters (model II) produced the largest chi-square. This analysis indicates that a student's performance on a given concept depends more on his past performance on the same concept than on his more recent performance on a different concept.

Although the conceptual model with modified individual parameters (model VII) appears to be the best model, the large number of parameters affects the goodness of fit. Two models using about the same number of parameters, the temporal-conceptual (model IV) and the conceptual model with group parameters (model VI), yielded very similar average chi-squares. This result indicates that the most recent performance was as useful in predicting performance as the most recent performance on a concept if the next most recent performance on that concept was used. However, the poorer fit for the temporal model with group parameters (model I) indicates that at least one conceptual factor is important.

The average chi-square for each model within each block provides evidence supporting the use of modified individual parameters. In this comparison the temporal model (III) with modified individual parameters yielded the lowest or second lowest chi-square in twenty-five of the thirty-five blocks, whereas the chi-square for the conceptual model (VII) was one of the two lowest for eighteen of the twenty-seven blocks for which predictions existed. The superiority of model III in this comparison appears contrary to the finding presented in Table 12–10. However, three blocks, two addition and one subtraction, were each more difficult than the other three blocks used in their four-block subset for estimation. Therefore, the observed performance was much lower than the predicted performance for model III, resulting in three of the highest chi-squares for any model in any block. These three large chi-squares contributed 47 per cent of the total chi-square for the thirty-five blocks, contributing disproportionately to the average presented for model III in Table 12–10. However, the superiority of these two models is not as genuine as it seems, because many more parameters were estimated for them than for the other five models.

Of additional note is the comparison between model I and model V. Given the most recent performance in time, the information added by either the next most recent performance or the IQ for the student made no difference in prediction as measured by average chi-square. The average chi-squares for the two models were also similar for all comparisons within blocks.

To summarize these models, conceptual factors predict performance better than temporal factors and, in terms of parameter estimation, modified individual techniques are better than group estimates. These, in turn, are better than individual-parameter estimation.

Group performance. To describe the absolute performance level of the students in the first grade mathematics curriculum, problems were grouped as a function of concept. Within each concept the mean proportion correct was examined as a function of the structural properties of the problems. Some examples of possible curriculum interest are given here. The concepts were (1) sets A, identity of sets and union of sets in canonical form; (2) sets B, identity of sets, union of sets in canonical and noncanonical form, and subtraction of sets; (3) geometry; (4) counting; (5) addition; and (6) subtraction. The mean proportion correct for each concept is shown in Table 12–11. Overall, the students performed best in geometry,

Table 12–11. Average Proportion Correct for Concepts—Brentwood Tutorial Mathematics Program

Concept	Proportion correct	Number of problems
Sets A	0.89	94
Sets B	0.74	62
Geometry	0.94	46
Counting	0.87	275
Addition	0.78	185
Subtraction	0.77	123

the identification of geometric shapes; their lowest performance was on the set problems appearing later in the curriculum (sets B).

Table 12–12 presents the proportion correct for addition problems for two of the factors examined, story versus nonstory and type-of-problem format. Children had the most difficulty with problems in noncanonical format, for example, $3 + \underline{} = 8$.

A more extensive report of the Brentwood tutorial program will be subsequently published. Major aspects of the project have not been covered here, especially the operational or evaluation aspects. We have attempted to give a sense of the kind of detailed questions that can be asked (and answered) about individual student differences and about individual concepts in the curriculum.

Table 12–12. Average Proportion Correct for Addition Problems as a Function of Structural Characteristics—Brentwood Tutorial Mathematics Program

Structural characteristic	Proportion correct	Number of problems
Story versus nonstory		
Story	0.87	29
Nonstory	0.76	156
Type-of-problem format		
Vertical, 2 addends	0.82	9
Horizontal, 2 addends	0.79	64
Horizontal, 3 addends	0.64	12
Vertical, 3 addends	0.54	8
Horizontal, noncanonical	0.29	5

Logic and Algebra Program

We have restricted presentation of the analysis of data for this program to one important example. The rank ordering of seventeen logic and algebra rules of inference, in terms of mean latency, is shown in Table 12–13.

Table 12–13. Rank Ordering of Algebraic and Logical Rules of Inference on the Basis of Mean Response Latency

Rank	Rule	Latency, seconds	Number of occurrences of rule in data
1	ND (number definition)	2.93	2589
2	D (definition)	2.94	4732
3	CA (commute addition)	3.42	2885
4	LC (left conjunct)	4.06	25
5	AR (associate addition right)	4.09	1419
6	AL (associate addition left)	5.36	103
7	CD (commute disjunction)	5.75	41
8	ID (inverse definition)	6.11	361
9	AA (affirm the antecedent)	6.24	482
10	FD (form a disjunction)	6.34	325
11	DN (double negation)	7.12	244
12	CC (commute conjunction)	8.42	41
13	DC (deny the consequent)	9.16	302
14	DD (deny a disjunct)	11.73	219
15	HS (hypothetical syllogism)	11.79	137
16	FC (form a conjunction)	12.63	33
17	RC (right conjunct)	13.07	19

These are the seventeen rules used in the first half of the course. It is probably a fair inference to hold that the mean latency for each of the rules, which is based on summation over the students and occurrences of the rules in the student's proofs, is a good measure of relative difficulty. Perhaps the most important observation to be made about the data of Table 12–13 is that the six algebraic rules of inference are among the first eight rules in rank ordering. The definitional rule ND had a mean latency of 2.93 seconds and the longest latency for any of the algebraic rules was for the inverse rule ID, which had a mean latency of 6.11 seconds. Before a hasty inference is made to the conclusion that algebraic rules of inference are easier than those of sentential logic, it is important to keep in mind that the six algebraic rules each require reference only to a single preceding line, and in the present context this reference to the preceding single line was restricted to the *immediately* preceding line, which simplifies very much the search procedure the student must go through in deciding what rule to apply and where. The greater ease of application of the algebraic rules does suggest, however, that it would be wise to emphasize these rules at the beginning of the course. The data do show, too, that mastery of these algebraic rules is probably easier for students than mastery of the beginning rules of sentential logic.

The number of occurrences of each rule in the data, as summed across students and problems, is also shown in Table 12–13. We believe that the large discrepancy between the mean latency for LC and RC, which are conceptually so closely related, is not to be taken seriously in the present data because there were only twenty-five occurrences of the use of LC and only nineteen of RC. The logical rule CD also had only forty-one occurrences in the data. If we exclude LC and CD, no other rule of logic had a mean latency as short as any of the six rules of algebra. On the other hand, as might be expected, the rule of logic that follows immediately after the algebraic rules, with the exception of LC and CD, is AA, which is classical *modus ponendo ponens* and which had by far the most frequent occurrence in the data. Four of the six algebraic rules had very frequent occurrence, being used a good many times more than even the most frequent logic rule. This circumstance undoubtedly also helped produce the shorter latencies for the algebraic rules.

Russian Program

Although data analysis for the Russian program is not complete, several points of information are available. Thirty students started the autumn quarter in the computer-based Russian section. A total of eight students left the program—one during the first quarter, three between the first and second quarter, one during the second quarter, and three between the second and third quarter. Two new students entered the computer-based section at the beginning of the second quarter. Of the thirty-eight students enrolled for the autumn quarter in the regular Russian section, ten left the course during the first quarter, thirteen between the first and second quarter, and three between the second and third quarter. Four new students entered the regular section at the beginning of the third quarter, one of them a transfer from the computer-based class. Of the thirty students originally enrolled in the computer-based program, twenty-two (73 per cent) finished all three quarters, whereas of the thirty-eight students in the regular class, only twelve (32 per cent) finished the year's curriculum. This finding suggests that the interest of the students was maintained during the computerized teaching.

To evaluate the computerized program, approximately 66 per cent of the final examinations for the autumn and winter quarters were identical for the computer-based and for the regular Russian sections; the complete final examination for the spring quarter was identical for the two groups. The error distribution and the mean number of errors per student for the two groups on the final examination for the autumn, winter, and spring quarters are shown in Tables 12–14, 12–15, and 12–16, respectively. Although no significance tests have been applied to the differences in performance between the two groups, the average number of errors was lower for the

Table 12–14. Error Distribution for the Common Portion of the Autumn Quarter Final Examination—Russian Program

Number of errors	Number of students	
	Computer-based	Regular
3.5	1	
5	2	1
6	3	
7	1	
8	2	
9	3	
11	3	
13		1
15	1	
16	1	1
17	2	
19		1
21	2	1
22	1	1
23		2
25	1	1
27	3	
29		1
30		1
31		2
33	1	
34		1
37	1	
38	1	
41		1
43		1
45		1
53		1
61		1
64		1
65		1
72		1
76		1
79		1
93		1
97		1
120		1
141		1
Total number of students	29[a]	28[b]
Average number of errors	15.8	49.0

a Of the thirty students enrolled, one left during the quarter.
b Of the thirty-eight students enrolled, ten left during the quarter.

Table 12–15. Error Distribution for the Common Portion of the Winter Quarter Final Examination—Russian Program

Number of errors	Number of students	
	Computer-based	Regular
2	1	1
6	1	
6.5	1	
8	1	
9.5		1
10	1	
11		1
12	2	
13		1
14.5		1
16	1	
16.5	1	
18	1	
18.5	1	
19	1	
19.5		1
21	2	
22.5	1	1
23	1	1
23.5	1	
24	1	
24.5		1
25	1	
26.5		1
27	1	
29.5	1	
30		1
30.5		1
32.5		1
33	1	
37.5	2	
38	1	
39.5	1	
41	1	2
47.5		1
Total number of students	27[a]	16[b]
Average number of errors	21.8	24.2

[a] Three of the original students did not enroll, two new students were added, and one student did not finish the quarter.
[b] Thirteen of the original students did not enroll.

computer-based students in all three quarters. Because the selection process resulting from the poorer students leaving the regular course biases the results on the examinations against the computer-based group, the superiority of the computer-based group on the spring examination is more impressive than the difference indicated by the average number of errors.

Table 12-16. Error Distribution for the Spring Quarter Final Examination—Russian Program

Number of errors	Number of students	
	Computer-based	Regular
21.5	1	
24.5	1	
26	1	
27	1	
31.5	1	
32	1	
34		1
35	1	
37	1	1
39		1
40	1	
41		1
42	1	
45	1	
46		1
47.5	1	
50.5		1
51.5	1	
60	1	1
61	1	
63.5		1
67		1
69	1	
69.5	1	
73	1	
74.5	2	1
76.5	1	
80.5		1
81	1	
82	1	
89		1
91		1
92		1
93	1	
106		1
166		1
Total number of students	24[a]	16[b]
Average number of errors	53.0	71.1

[a] Three students did not enroll.
[b] Three students did not enroll, three students enrolled for the first time, and one student transferred from the computer-based section to the regular section.

CONCLUSIONS

We have attempted to describe four programs in computer-assisted instruction and to give a sense of some of the results that have been obtained. The programs and the data flowing from them are complex and continuing.

We shall not yet attempt to give an overall summary of what we judge to be the significance of these programs. We do hope that we have included enough detail to give the reader a sense of our current activities in computer-assisted instruction and the kind of data results and analyses with which we have been concerned.

By presenting some programs being run in elementary schools and one program being run at the university level, we have also hoped to give a sense of the range of possibilities open for the use of computers as instructional devices. It is fair to say that during the early years of the Stanford operation we have concentrated on developing programs that can be run with fairly large numbers of students. This is particularly true of the drill-and-practice program in elementary mathematics. It is interesting to note, however, that even within the context of this program we are still in the process of making radical changes in it. The kind of data analysis reported here has been the source of much discussion among our staff regarding better ways to approach the subject. We feel that it will be still a good many years before even the possibilities in drill and practice are thoroughly developed, particularly as we move toward mathematical and quantitative formulations of the basic curriculum structure. From our current work it is evident that without the kind of empirical information reported here it will not be possible to move to more mathematically and scientifically sophisticated formulations of the curriculum.

So we would like to conclude on the note that we consider none of the programs reported here as being in a final form. Each of them is in process of development and change. What we have attempted to give are some examples that constitute an interim report. It is far too soon to attempt anything like an overall set of final conclusions.

REFERENCES

Atkinson, R. C., and Hansen, D. N. 1966. Computer-assisted instruction in initial reading: the Stanford project. *Reading Research Quarterly* 2:5–25.

Atkinson, R. C., and Wilson, H. A. 1967. *Computer-based instruction in initial reading: a progress report on the Stanford project.* Technical Report No. 119. Stanford University, Calif.: Institute for Mathematical Studies in the Social Sciences, Stanford Univ.

Suppes, P. 1965. *Sets and numbers,* Book 1. New York: Singer.

———. 1967. Some theoretical models for mathematics learning. *Journal of Research and Development in Education* 1:5–22.

Suppes, P., Jerman, M., and Brian, D. 1968. *Computer-assisted instruction: Stanford's 1965–66 arithmetic program.* New York: Academic Press.

13

Gail S. Young

Comments on Social, Psychological, and Mathematical Aspects of the Suppes-Morningstar Chapter

I regard Chapter 12 by Professor Suppes and Miss Morningstar as perhaps the most important one presented at the conference. I do not say this because of the level of the content but because of the problems it considers. Let me explain what I mean.

By and large the other papers that have been presented are aimed either at problems of college teaching or are "internal" to the field of computer-assisted instruction. We are not, however, faced with major manpower problems at the college and university level. Cartter (1965) presented a model of staffing to the American Council on Education several years ago that has convinced me that under present trends before the end of the next decade there will actually be a surplus of Ph.D.'s in most fields. The work of the Conference Board of Mathematical Sciences's Survey Committee, which I chair, on the problems of mathematical manpower has led me independently to the same conclusion for mathematics, which has been regarded as one of the tightest fields (Jewett and Lindquist, 1967). Thus work at the college level in CAI will be valuable to supplement or aid the efforts of an adequately trained staff of adequate size. I do not underrate this, and I am aware of the danger of that last sentence being quoted by a future historian as an example of twentieth-century obscurantism, to the embarrassment of my descendants.

However, Suppes' work is directed at the problems of school instruction. There the situation is entirely different. Let me continue for a few moments not as a mathematician but as an educator deeply worried about the future of our society, or indeed our species, and searching for ways in which we, as educators, can help assure that future. There is no need for me to list the perils that we face. I shall instead concentrate on certain aspects that have particular relevance to our work as educators and then explain the connection I see between these aspects and the work of Suppes.

One of the traditional goals of public education has been to provide the country with a population able to make reasonable choices, based on information, on the problems of our government and our society. Again, this audience knows well how much more difficult that task has become. Perhaps the schools have never done this well. But, with much more to communicate, we must at least do relatively as well as we did in the past.

The schools have also begun to face the educational implications of the changes in employment produced by our new technology. I think it is difficult even for a group such as this to realize how drastic these changes have been. Technology has not brought about a scarcity of jobs, as many had feared, but it has made a part of our population unemployable. Without changes in the level and nature of education that we provide all students, the part of our population that is unemployable will increase. Let me illustrate the problem with something familiar to all of us here, the increased difficulty of repairing our ordinary possessions. Consider, for example, the change from radio to colored television, from Model A's to contemporary automobiles, from wringer washers to automatics, from electric fans to air conditioners. One does not drop out of high school and "pick up" the skills required to repair the new things. Real knowledge is involved. I believe that it is the technological revolution that has been the real impetus behind the widespread adoption of the new science and mathematics program in the schools, as school system after school system has reacted to local advice and pressure.

But the greater education required for current employment is only part of the problem. How many jobs will still exist in anything like their present form twenty years from now? Instead of mastering a trade or a skill and then having a long productive life in it, most people will be faced with the necessity of starting all over again in some new skill at least once in their lifetime. The implications are quite clear. Not only must we give our children the basic training in science and mathematics to enable them to get meaningful jobs now—we must also teach them what is needed to enable them in middle life to resume learning again. No other generation of educators has had to face a problem such as this.

The third task that I see for the schools is one that is not now regarded as one of their primary functions. One of the most neglected statistics of our time is that between a tenth and a twentieth of the population will be hospitalized at some time for psychiatric reasons. What must be the percentage of our population that needs psychiatric treatment but that will stay outside a hospital? There has been, of course, a rise in hospitalizations for emotional diseases. I am not drawing the conclusion from this rise that there is a rise in emotional illnesses. I believe that there is more emotional illness, but my belief is based on the opinion of several experienced psychiatrists, not on statistical evidence, which almost certainly could not be obtained. But that is not crucial. In the United States of 75 or 100 years ago, if there were as much emotional illness, still there was less exacerbation of it by society, and there were easier ways to function than there are now. If a small farmer 75 years ago were, to use a technical term, "nutty as a fruit cake," still he might be a reasonably successful farmer, and his ideas presented little danger to society. The survival of our present society requires an emotionally healthy population. I cannot believe that improvement will take place without the considerable help and involvement of the schools.

That the schools should be concerned with the emotional development of their students is, of course, not new. Perhaps this is the real essence of the work of John Dewey. This is certainly the point of Anna Freud's utopian wish that all teachers be psychoanalyzed. What I am saying is somewhat different, that the schools will have to take on a healing role in mental health.

We are all aware of how far even the best schools are from meeting all these goals. What human resources do we bring to the problem? If we visit a freshman education class for elementary teachers, what we will find is a room full of nice, attractive eighteen-year-old girls who like small children and most of whom are planning to work for several years before getting married and having their own children. Individuals who have been concerned in any way with curriculum development in the past have been aware of the gap between the demands that the new curricula make on the teacher and the training the teacher receives. Some seven or eight years ago the American Association for the Advancement of Sciences and the National Association of State Directors of Teacher Education and Certification jointly sponsored a study of the science and mathematics training of elementary teachers (1963). I well remember how at the final conference one after another of the representatives of each science made an irrefutable case —and I really mean irrefutable—for the necessity of including one semester, one year, or two years of their own field in the curriculum if the student was to be competent to teach the programs in elementary science and mathematics then being put into the schools. The total came to something like sixty hours, an impossible amount to implement in a four-year program, even if the nice eighteen-year-old girls would take such a program. In the case of my own field, we have worked very hard and spent considerable money trying to implement a recommendation of (essentially) twelve hours of training in specialized mathematics for elementary school teachers, a program that in my view is actually inadequate for what the teacher is now called on to do. But in four years of work, we have succeeded only in raising the amount taken by the student to where most prospective teachers now get six hours (Committee on the Undergraduate Program in Mathematics, 1966).

You can see now why the Suppes-Morningstar chapter excites me. Work of this type offers the real possibility of giving more time, both in teacher training and in the school, to meet the demands I have listed and also offers the possibility of making more learning, of certain material, in the time available.

However, I shall not discuss the details of Chapter 12. The work raises in my mind issues fundamental to education—issues that we have almost no data on. It does not surprise me that fundamental issues are most sharply in focus in a discussion of a mathematics program. Ours is the clearest, the most rational, and the most logically connected of all the disciplines; the problems of the subject matter are, then, separated the most cleanly from the problems of learning, of psychology, and of sociology. It is this that makes me believe that work in mathematical education always has implications for other fields.

The first program the authors discuss is the drill-and-review program for first-graders. The authors summarize this briefly on page 233, and I shall not describe it here. I would like to concentrate on the differences between a program like theirs and the handling of the same sort of work in the present classroom.

In the present classroom this sort of routine drill is handled by, for example, sending the class to the blackboard, or by having the students work in their seats and exchange papers for grading with the students in the opposite seats, and so on. Let me contrast the situation with the class at the board and the class at the console. The teacher will say something like "Work the odd-numbered problems on page 15." She will then walk around the room correcting errors, chiding slowpokes, making quick explanations of errors, and rewarding good work by approval and rebuking bad work by disapproval. The rewards and punishments are direct emotional contacts between individuals. There is, however, little individualization of the work. The student who does not understand it so well simply works fewer problems than the others. In the computer program, branching provides a great deal more individualization. Errors are pointed out even quicker than at the blackboard. Explanations are not given as to the nature of error (presumably a later stage of development would make that possible), and reward is simply the internal recognition that one has gotten the right answer.

One could perhaps raise a number of technical questions. Are there better drills for the same material? Is there a better means of communication than the teletype? Does the student receive a grade and a comment on his paper that he can take home to show his parents? But these are not the questions that interest me. Apparently the program is successful; that is, the students do learn the material and do keep up their interest. What sort of things are made possible by such use of the computer?

One such possibility is this: By separating the teaching of mathematics from the drill and review, one could economically schedule the work of a specialist in the elementary schools. One specialist could perhaps teach all the mathematics in a given elementary school, with the computer doing all the drill-and-review work and even all the grading. Such a specialist could teach twice as many children as he could if he were also responsible for the routine work. Under such an arrangement the demands for mathematical training of elementary teachers for the new curricula could be reduced.

Another advantage of such a drill-and-review period is found in the very small amount of time that the program takes. Each day's work is, in this first grade program, about ten problems and takes five to ten minutes in the day. In the course of the year the number of problems is close to that worked under the old method. The computer and the student simply communicate faster than the student and the teacher. Thus this one program frees twenty to twenty-five minutes a day for beginning to meet the other needs I have discussed.

I would now like to ask some questions of a psychological nature. What are we doing to the emotional development of the child by such a program? I think it highly doubtful that we could be doing anything quantitatively significant in five to ten minutes a day, and whatever conceivable damage we did could be more than made up for by proper use of the saved time; but nevertheless the sort of issues I want to raise have not been discussed. I shall take up here only one question, the possible effects on the child of the different systems of reward and punishment.

It was easy to see both the reward and the punishment in the drill situation with a live teacher, but it is only possible to point out the reward in the computer. The computer does not punish. It merely tells you that you have the wrong answer and in the next lesson switches to a lesson at a lower level. This is the feature of the drill that seems to me to have definite psychological advantages to some children. Perhaps for others this is a drawback. We have not had to worry about the role of punishment before, because overpunishment has been the risk, and there was no possibility of removing punishment from the classroom with any human teacher.

The reward from the computer is internal, not social. This must produce a change in personality, although in the doses prescribed here presumably not a great one. Is the direction of the change good or bad? (I ignore the question of what is "good" or "bad.") Would the student tend to be more self-reliant or merely more detached from people? The reward is instant, not delayed. Is *that* good or bad? Does it militate against the child's acceptance of the "reality principle" of Freud? I believe we have no way of answering such questions at the present time. It is the sort of question, however, that we must know how to answer if we are ever to know what the effect of a given educational program is, and certainly before beginning any large-scale use of new teaching methods.

Let me turn now to the Brentwood Tutorial Mathematics Programs. These are considerably more experimental than the program I have just discussed. All the questions I raised about the drill program still apply, but others come up.

I will interpolate quickly for my own clarification a question that I hope Suppes will comment on. I do not understand from Chapter 12 what he sees as the role of the teacher in this program. It is clear from his description that the teacher is actually involved. How much mathematical competence must the teacher have? Must she have the sort of skills that will be required to teach material of this sort directly?

I bring to the discussion the insights and prejudices of a professional mathematician and graduate teacher, and it is hard for me to tell one from the other. Yet I have some confidence that the aims and problems of the teaching of mathematics to talented preprofessionals have relevance for teaching children. I cannot imagine a computer program with enough branches to take care of all but the simplest types of responses. The learning of mathematics, at least, does not seem to me to consist of steady accretion of information in small units. It is not continuous. There are periods of incomprehension, followed by sudden jumps to understanding. In fact, part of the learning of mathematics is acquiring confidence that with continued work the jump will occur. Mathematics as done by humans consists also in sudden combinations of elements that may be logically quite some distance apart. Let me illustrate: Take the familiar formula for the sum of the first n odd numbers, $1 + 3 + 5 + \cdots + (2n - 1) = n^2$. Young children can be led to conjecture this formula. At a more advanced level one can prove it by mathematical induction, although with no particular understanding of why it is true. I suppose all of us in this audience are familiar with the argument using the squares of dots: In passing from a square $(n - 1) \times (n - 1)$ of dots to a square $n \times n$ of dots, one adds precisely $2n - 1$ dots. Now one can certainly devise a computer program that will get the realization of this fact across to students. What is really important, however, and not just from the standpoint of students who will go into very mathematical fields, is to give them some way of learning how to make such jumps themselves. Suppes could very well say we are not very good at doing that with live teachers, but if computer instruction means the abandonment of the hope of doing such things, then this is something to think quite seriously about.

David Paige has produced films for the Educational Development Corporation showing elementary mathematics classes taught by the "discovery" method. In many of these films he himself is not doing the teaching but very good young teachers are. There are always a couple of instances where the teacher misses or misinterprets some remark by a child that, to a professional mathematician, seems very bright. However, a computer would miss all of these. Let me give an example from an anecdote that, if I am correct, was told me by Paige himself. The class was playing a "game" on the set of nonnegative integers. The game consisted in beginning at an integer and moving a certain amount right or left and predicting the integer that would result. Thus, one could begin at 10 and move three numbers to the left arriving at 7. At one point the class was told something like "start at 2 and move five to the left," which, of course, was completely baffling, because they had not heard of negative numbers. Finally a little girl said that it reminded her somehow of Alaska. Paige, if it was he, pushed on this and discovered that the connection with Alaska in the girl's mind was that it was very cold in Alaska and they had temperatures below zero. Now that sort of response is meaningless to the computer and will stay so in any computer I can imagine, but it is an important response to recognize in the student. Where will this sort of recognition be given? I shall push this thought a little further. Just as hand-operated computing devices, such as adding machines and cash registers, have made speed and accuracy in arithmetic less important vocational tools, in place of which has come a greater need for understanding, so the computer itself may replace almost all routine mathematical operations. What will be left for the human will be the need to understand and the need to make creative jumps. If I am at all right about this, I will be most interested in Suppes' ideas as to how to circumvent the difficulties of computer teaching for these.

A perfectly legitimate reply would be to say that in point of fact, whatever methods we use, we are not going to be able to teach very many children to do mathematics in the way I want, that the computer will do a better job for most students than the classroom teacher, and that the sort of teaching I am asking for can be supplied only to a small number of students, and possibly at a much later point in their education. If that is indeed the case, and if I am right in my view about what is needed, then that amounts to a statement that we are not going to be able to give most of our students adequate training in mathematics. Another conceivable reply would be to say that children receiving their mathematical education in this fashion will actually do as well as children who have been taught by teachers trained in the methods of Paige or of Robert Davis of the Webster project, Max Beberman of UICSM, or other such virtuosos. That, of course, can be determined only by experiment. But such experiments must be carried out, despite their difficulty, and not merely for the one field of mathematics, if the computer is actually to serve as a teacher in many disciplines.

One of the problems that we face in designing computer instructional programs is the fact that we know almost nothing about the deeper psychology of learning, even in the clear subject of mathematics. With or without the computer, we do not know the real implications, only the logical implications, of various choices in the curriculum. To illustrate, Suppes' first grade curriculum in this program begins with sets. That is, he is going to introduce the number "2" as the answer to such questions as "How many eyes do I have?" and "How many hands do I have?" In other words "2" means the cardinal number "2." There are other meanings for "2," for example, the answer to the question "How wide is this table?"— the answer being "two feet." This would be to introduce "2" as a real number. It is perfectly possible to introduce this meaning of "2" in the first grade, and indeed the Cambridge Conference (1963) has proposed to introduce the whole real line in grade 1. There are mathematical and logical arguments for either approach.

I had better say what I mean by *mathematical and logical arguments.* Suppose that I am furnished with a description of what the student should know in mathematics at the end of high school. For example, oversimplified, suppose I am told the student should take calculus in the twelfth grade. I can then write a system of theorems and concepts, starting with basic axioms, from which the calculus can be logically and rigorously deduced. Such a system is by no means unique. There are quite different ones possible, and one can discuss them from the standpoint of logical simplicity, of logical clarity, or of how much extra mathematical information is learned. Mathematical education has, by and large, been concerned with how to modify a chosen system to meet the intuitively grasped limitations of young children. Thus the Cambridge Conference would like to begin the first grade with the axioms for an Archimedean-ordered field, but that is clearly impossible. So they begin with the real line, as close as they can reasonably come. Perhaps Suppes would like to begin with the Zermelo axioms for set theory. But that also is clearly impossible, so he begins with sets of fingers and the like. A great deal of wisdom, experience, and creativity goes into such work. I can give no better example than Sections 2 and 3 of the Cambridge Conference report. I would, in fact, urge this as reading for anyone pursuing further the topics of the Suppes-Morningstar chapter and my own comments.

However, this form of curriculum work has been done without benefit of deep-learning theory, largely because this does not appear to exist, aside from the brilliant intuitions of Piaget. We do not know, we can only guess, which approach—the set theoretic or the real line—fits in better with the psychology of most six-year-olds and which one leads ultimately to a deeper understanding of mathematics. Let us suppose that we all decide by intuition and our naive experience that the set-theoretic approach is better, but that later it is proved that the real-number approach is far better. Under the present methods of teaching there would be a period of re-writing textbooks and of retraining teachers and the error could be rectified. If we were in a period of heavy utilization of computers for teaching, and made the same choice, made the same realization of error, but then found that it was impossible to teach the better approach with computers, we would be trapped. Is this sort of concern foolish? I do not think anyone can *prove* that it is.

We are all aware of the effect of ecological blunders, for example, the introduction of rabbits into Australia. We must not start creating our own blunders because of our ignorance of the learning process and because of our ignorance of the effect of various curriculum choices. What Suppes has shown, and shown brilliantly, is that computers can be used as the primary instructional device in elementary mathematics programs. But this leaves completely unanswered all the questions of what to teach and of how the child learns.

If I may continue to make remarks that are not really about Suppes' work but are reflections started by reading Chapter 12, let me speak a little of the biology of learning. We have always disliked the idea of looking at ourselves as a species of animals. If we are forced to consider our animal nature, we try to disguise the consideration by abstractions, such as the "mind-body problem" or speaking about the effect of physiology. But we are no longer able to get away with these comforting evasions. The effect of our being members of a species of animals is showing all too much in our society, and the facts are being forced on our attention by a remark-able series of popularizations in biology, with such books as Desmond

Morris' *The Naked Ape*. I am not aware that any great attention has been given in education to this aspect of us, but I am sure that it needs recognition and that, in fact, many of our unthinking assumptions about education have this biological base. Our species has what appears to be the immense advantage of being relatively free from instinctual, quasi-reflex behavior. We can adapt to an amazing variety of conditions without the necessity for genetical modification because of our long period before maturity in which we can learn and be taught ways to behave. As it seems to me Freud himself hinted, much of the Freudian picture of psychological development can be looked at as the biological machinery to ensure learning. Thus "in nature" the child learns from a parent; in any case, the child always attaches emotions that belong to one or both of his parents onto his teachers. Occasionally we hear the oddity of a child having emotions for a computer that is teaching him. But that seems to me to be absolutely inevitable. That is where the energy for learning comes from. Our natural instincts about teaching call for small classes, a parent figure doing the teaching, opportunities for emotional interchange, as much individualization of instruction as possible, and freedom for the teacher to "express her own personality." Without taking the time to do it here, it seems to me that I can rather easily make out a case for these phenomena fitting our biology. Those societies that have attempted to disregard these assumptions have done it only at considerable damage. I am not saying at all that instruction by computer will be damaging. I am saying that we must be very sure to see that it is not and that we provide by other means what is lost from the computer.

Another biological aspect of our success has been diversity. Indeed, the main reason for sexual reproduction is to assure genetic diversity, but I believe our species has carried diversity as a biological principle much farther than the mere genetic. As applied to teaching, my point is this: If Suppes and I each taught a course in ninth grade algebra, from the same textbook, I could hope that my students would do as well as his on a final examination over the material. But the two classes would have had quite different experiences all the same.

Perhaps in Suppes' class all the students would want to take the maximum of mathematics permitted in the school, whereas in mine they would all be trying to get out of the requirement. That is not necessarily bad. It could be a great disaster if we found out how to be brilliantly successful in teaching mathematics. What would we do for doctors, social workers, and poets? Bad teaching of a subject has a biological function as much as good teaching does. But even if Suppes and I taught equally well, I am sure my students would have a more geometric, less logical, less algebraic, more intuitive course than his. There would be real differences of understanding, whatever a multiple-choice test said to the contrary. When the teaching is done by a computer, we are not getting this diversity, even if we have a number of different programs for the same material. Again, this is not to say that we should not do it. But I do say that we should be as careful as possible about what it is we are actually doing.

It seems to me that in my comments I am calling for three things: A crash program of work like Suppes' work aimed deliberately at the problems I began with, a crash program of depth research in learning theory, and a high degree of caution in the workers in the first program until the second is done. We are being offered a tremendously powerful tool. Let us use it prayerfully and without unthinking faith.

REFERENCES

Cambridge Conference on School Mathematics. 1963. *Goals for school mathematics, the report of the Cambridge conference on school mathematics.* Boston: Houghton Mifflin.

Cartter, A. 1965. A new look at the supply of college teachers. *Educational Record* 46: 267–277.

Committee on the Undergraduate Program in Mathematics. 1966. *Forty-one conferences on the training of teachers of elementary school mathematics, a summary.* Report No. 15. Washington: Mathematics Assoc. of America.

Jewett, J., and Lindquist, C. 1967. *Aspects of undergraduate training in the mathematical sciences.* Report of the Survey Committee, vol. I. Washington: Conference Board of the Mathematical Sciences.

National Association of State Directors of Teacher Education and Certification. 1963. *Guidelines for preparation programs of teachers of elementary school science and mathematics.* Washington: American Association for the Advancement of Science.

Stanford Programs in Arithmetic, Logic, and Russian: Discussion

Maintaining diversity in the mathematics curriculum may be difficult for potential authors and publishers faced by the considerable cost of computer-based curriculum preparation and for potential users who find limited alternatives available on the particular computer system to which they have access. Will interesting curriculum ideas fail to be developed because they cannot be readily implemented on a computer-based system? Does costly CAI curriculum development take money away from important noncomputer projects? Will subject-matter experts be attracted to the new technology and ignore important problems of mathematics education that are better handled without computers? Probably computer-based mathematics exercises will be as varied and numerous as those in the textbooks and perhaps even more so. Most likely they will be used as adjunct material for regular textbooks. Computers will also be used to assist authors and publishers in the preparation and testing of text materials. Greater variety of opinion, content, and instructional strategy can be incorporated within each package. A single curriculum effort is likely to include the contributions of three or more authors, and both teachers and students will be able to choose alternatives.

A mixture of computer and noncomputer media, and different modes of computer use, will result from reasonable examination of the costs of each along with its benefits for mathematics instruction. For example, now that drill and remedial testing programs in mathematics have been demonstrated to be successful, it is time to ask whether the same objectives could be achieved with less expensive or more interesting alternatives. The answer will be complicated by the fact that contributions of the computer to individual learning depend on student characteristics—background, skills, motivation, and attention—as well as on the characteristics of the mathematics competency to be acquired and the learning strategy employed. As compared to the standard classroom, the Stanford programs have shown greater gains for students with lower-level intellectual skills and poor motivation. This outcome should be taken as a challenge by the regular classroom teachers to show that they can adapt their instructional strategy to the characteristics of the students, particularly those who ordinarily have difficulty.

Young's critique raised the question of the role of teachers in tutorial programs. In the discussion period Suppes indicated that there was no clear answer to this question, because the "teacher(s)" had assumed differing—from active to nonexistent—roles in each of Stanford's programs. In the math tutorial program the Stanford staff did the teaching rather than regular classroom personnel. In the logic and algebra program there was no competent teacher to assist the students, and this program was aimed only at the bright students. In the Russian program, no systematic instruction was given; the professor was available to provide individual assistance.

A number of other efforts are worth the attention of readers interested in mathematics instruction using computers. The proceedings of a conference on CAI in mathematics education held at Pennsylvania State University in September 1968 included a variety of samples and opinions (Heimer, 1969). At this conference Uttal discussed his current work on the generation of exercises and remedial sequences in analytic geometry (Uttal et al., 1969). Rosenbaum and others (1967) at System Development Corporation have incorporated on-line use of the computer as a statistical tool into a tutorial program in statistics. The approach proposed by Feurzeig and Papert (1968) at Bolt Beranek and Newman is particularly interesting because the computer is used by elementary school students as an on-line tool for testing algorithms of their own construction. A simple programming language provides a means for describing mathematical concepts and procedures, and on-line interaction may be important to the students for learning the language and debugging the procedures. A system for college students has been developed and used by Culler (1967) at the University of California at Santa Barbara.

REFERENCES

Culler, G. J. 1967. Appendix: user's manual for an on-line system. In *On-line computing*, ed. W. J. Karplus. New York: McGraw-Hill, pp. 303–324.

Feurzeig, W., and Papert, S. 1968. Programming languages as a conceptual framework for teaching mathematics. Paper presented at a NATO conference on major trends in programmed instruction research, 13–17 May 1968, at Nice, France.

Heimer, R., ed. 1969. *Computer-assisted instruction and the teaching of mathematics*. Washington, D.C.: National Council of Teachers of Mathematics.

Rosenbaum, J., Feingold, S. L., Frye, C. H., and Bennik, R. D. 1967. *Computer-based instruction in statistical inference, a final report*. Technical Memorandum TM-2941/100/00. Santa Monica, Calif.: System Development Corporation.

Uttal, W. R., Pasich, T., Rogers, M., and Hieronymus, R. 1969. *Generative computer-assisted instruction*. Communication 243. Ann Arbor: Mental Health Research Institute, Univ. of Michigan.

PART VII

Simulation of Science Experiments

The use of the computer to simulate laboratory instruction in chemistry or physics is particularly attractive because it offers a possible means of improving instruction in large science classes at the high school and college levels. In Chapter 14 Lagowski discusses the logistical problems of university laboratory sections for which computer-assisted instruction provides a promising alternative. He presents a number of examples of laboratory simulation, ranging from spectroscopy to titration experiments. In each case the student manipulates the simulated apparatus, varying the parameters and observing the results. Although feasibility studies completed by Lagowski and others demonstrate the practicality of such simulated laboratory experiments, major evaluative studies are still in progress, and it is too early to determine whether or not the amount and kind of learning that take place are as effective as in a real laboratory.

In Chapter 15, a critique of Lagowski's paper, Lambe analyzes the important differences between the simulated and real laboratory and points out a number of problems in attempting to use computers for science teaching in a university setting. An analysis of current costs in an undergraduate science laboratory yields a figure just under $2.00 per student-hour for laboratory instructional cost. Lambe argues that computer-assisted instruction must offer more than merely an artificial substitute for the actual laboratory, particularly because current costs for CAI run closer to $5.00 per student-hour, if laboratory simulation on computers is to be a really significant new form of instruction. The essential features of a laboratory simulator are outlined, together with suggestions on their implementation.

14

Joseph J. Lagowski

Computer-assisted Instruction in Chemistry[1]

Interest in the use of teaching machines, exemplified in the most sophisticated instance by specially adapted high-speed digital computers, has until recently been primarily centered on research in the learning process and/or on the design of hardware and software.[2] Computer systems have now been developed to the point where it is feasible to use such devices with relatively large classes. As a result, definition of the problems involved in the implementation of CAI techniques to supplement classic instructional methods for large classes and their solution have become important considerations. This chapter is addressed to the problems of adapting CAI techniques for the large lower-division chemistry courses. Many of the factors that must be considered are common to other science-oriented courses at the same level; indeed, much of the rationale for using CAI techniques is valid for nearly all college- and university-level courses at the present time. It should be emphasized that although this discussion may appear to be cast in a static context, the state of the art is rapidly changing because innovations

1. I should like to acknowledge the Research and Development Center for the College Instruction of Science and Mathematics for financial assistance in certain aspects of this program and L. O. Morgan, its director, for constant personal encouragement. The expert assistance of the staff of the Computer-Assisted Instruction Laboratory has been of much help in various phases of our work. Finally, I want to acknowledge the work of S. Castleberry, W. C. Bard, C. E. Rodriquez, and Joan D. Bateman on the programs that are reported here.
2. See, for example, *Programmed Learning and Computer-Based Instruction,* John E. Coulson, Editor, published by Wiley, New York, 1962, which is a report on a conference on application of digital computers to automated instruction.

in hardware and software are a characteristic of computer technology and experience in using instructional modules with larger and larger groups is being gained continually. Thus this chapter may be looked on as a progress report on the present status of CAI techniques in chemistry instruction.

The Nature of Modern Chemistry Instruction

In the eighteenth century a teacher could, in a very informal way, discuss chemistry with the few students who were interested in the subject. To prove a point in the discussion, the small group might go to the instructor's private laboratory to observe the results of an experiment that was most often performed by the instructor himself. Even when the number of students increased, the pattern changed only slightly; formal lectures were held with relatively detailed demonstrations being conducted in conjunction with the lectures. Often those students with a consuming interest in chemistry could not obtain laboratory instruction as we know it today. Thus Benjamin Silliman, one of the earliest successful chemists in the United States, described his effort to obtain laboratory experience as a student in the following way:

> A small working laboratory was conceded to us by the indulgence of our hostess Mrs. Smith, and we made use of a spare cellar kitchen in which we worked together in our hours of leisure from other pursuits.[3]

Chemistry subsequently attained a degree of success that has led to the problems we are discussing here. In addition to the directly useful benefits, a knowledge of chemistry became essential to the understanding and interpretation of many other subjects. More students were attracted to the study of chemistry with the result that instruction had to become more efficient; increased course organization was inevitable.

Immediately after the Civil War, the rigid classic collegiate curriculum was liberalized to allow a choice of electives by the student, and science courses were introduced as part of the regular offerings. In 1895 the Committee on College Entrance Requirements chaired by A. F. Nightingale outlined recommendations for work in high school chemistry, which admonished that

> All colleges must give admission credit for [chemistry]. In addition to this each college must provide definite means for advancing the entrant to an extent corresponding to his previous knowledge of the subject. . . . In any case no

3. Edgar F. Smith, *Chemistry in America,* D. Appleton & Co., New York, 1914, p. 182.

pupil who offers chemistry for entrance, and receives definite credit for it, should be placed in the same class with beginners who had no such credit.[4]

Moreover, the report states

Without laboratory work school chemistry is wholly valueless for the purposes just mentioned. . . .

The experiments must be performed by each pupil individually.[5]

Thus, some 70 years ago, began the structure of chemistry instruction that is still used today with little alteration. Typically, lower-division chemistry courses in a large university consist of lectures (in which demonstrations may or may not be conducted), small group discussion periods, and laboratory work. Large enrollments have forced many universities to discontinue group discussions for lack of adequate personnel; another casualty under these conditions is the laboratory portion of the course for nonscience majors. Thus the student has come to play a less and less active role in his education. With computer techniques it may be possible to reverse this trend by providing a system that will (1) engage the student in decision-making processes and (2) allow students to proceed at their own pace; such a system can be used to provide a degree of individualized instruction to students in large classes.

Irrespective of personal feelings on the subject, the day of the leisurely scholar-teacher is past, and we shall not, because we cannot, return to it. A recent survey of B.S. degrees shows that only 20 per cent of the institutions accredited by the American Chemical Society granted 51 per cent of the 3349 B.S. degrees earned in chemistry. These figures, of course, do not reflect the large number of students enrolled in lower-division chemistry courses whose majors are not in chemistry.

The Problem

Basically, a major problem in the teaching of chemistry on all levels today concerns human logistics. Whether the classes are large or small, colleges and universities are faced with presenting increasingly sophisticated concepts to a rising number of students; the available teaching facilities, both human and technical, are increasing at a less rapid rate than the student population. Typically, the logistics of teaching a course such as general chemistry becomes geared to convenience.

It is apparent that we no longer can afford the luxury of employing teachers—whether they be on the permanent staff or teaching assistants—

4. Arthur F. Scott, Education and Training of Chemists in the U.S. I. *Chemical and Engineering News,* 29 March 1965, p. 86.
5. Ibid.

to engage in nonteaching functions. Many chores such as grading and record keeping as well as certain remedial or tutorial functions do not really require the active participation of a teacher, yet it is the person hired as a teacher who performs them. Much of this has been said before in various contexts; however, it should now be possible to solve some of the problems using modern computer techniques. In chemistry, as in all subjects, there is a body of information that must be *learned* by the student but that requires very little *teaching* by the instructor. Successful methods must be found to shift the onus for learning this type of material onto the student, thereby permitting the instructor more time for teaching. Thus computer techniques, in our opinion, should be treated as resources to be drawn on by the instructor as he deems necessary, much the same as he would regard books. With some classes certain CAI materials might be very useful; in others these materials might be unnecessary and their use might do more harm than good. Consequently, we would argue for the generation of CAI modules that are essentially independent of each other so that they could be used by individual instructors in a variety of ways; the logical coupling of the modules occurs because of their unique arrangement in a given course and allusions to them by the instructor at the proper time. This rather detailed discussion of the use of CAI techniques as *supplemental* to rather than as a *supplantation* of the human teacher is made for a specific reason. The average instructor who has had little or no experience with computers may be awed by the way the subject matter of a good instructional module comes across in a typical student-computer interaction. It must be emphasized that in all instances the computer is merely performing the operations that have been programmed into it by a human. If the human is imaginative and has a mastery of *both* his subject and the vagaries of programming in a given language for a specific system, the instructional modules will reflect this; on the other hand, a pedantic approach to a subject and/or to programming of the subject will also be faithfully reflected in the module. Thus, just as it is impossible to improve a textbook by changing the press used to print it, a CAI system will not generate quality in a module. Indeed, compared with other media, CAI methods often amplify pedagogically poor techniques out of proportion.

Laboratory Simulation

It is commonly accepted that the role of laboratory work in undergraduate chemistry courses (especially those in the lower division) is to provide the student with opportunities (1) to use equipment and gain some degree of experience with laboratory techniques and (2) for decision making based on experimental data as well as for manipulation of these data. Thus a technique may be taught in the laboratory (for example, titration) and then belabored—apparently endlessly—to show the student how it may be used to obtain experimental results directed toward a variety of ends. For example, it is not uncommon to have students do acid-base titrations, equivalent weight determinations, oxidation-reduction titrations, complexometric titrations, and analyses of various elements using titration methods. All these experiments involve a basic titration technique, yet the student spends five laboratory periods doing essentially the same thing but for a slightly different reason each time. Direct laboratory experience is necessary to acquire manipulative techniques; however, CAI methods can be devised to provide experience in decision making and in the manipulation of experimental results.

The logistics problems associated with laboratory instruction in chemistry impose an artificial constraint on the type of experiments that can be performed by the student. Laboratory instruction in lower-division chemistry courses has not kept pace with the theoretical concepts introduced in the lecture portions of the same course for several reasons. (1) The number of students involved has increased to the point where use of physical facilities must be severely restricted to accommodate everyone; schedules are crowded and logistics demand that experiments must be performed that require no more than three to four hours of laboratory time—a very artificial situation in the real world of chemistry. (2) Generally, funds are not available for the equipment required to perform experiments that would illustrate the more sophisticated concepts taught in the lecture portions of the course. (3) Many experiments, although simple in principle, require several periods for their completion and cannot be performed for lack of time available to the student. The lack of time can often be traced to the factors described in point (1) and/or to the student's own schedule.

Computer simulation can be used to advantage to alleviate many of these problems.

Examples of Simulation Programs

Decision-making experiments. Many experiments conducted in general chemistry laboratories are designed to provide experience with certain techniques; often these experiments are performed in the context of also illustrating a principle and/or giving the student experience in decision making.

For example, schemes that illustrate the qualitative analysis of mixtures have been popular in the past for the first laboratory course in chemistry. Such schemes (1) demonstrate separation techniques (precipitation, filtration, centrifugation, and so on), (2) illustrate chemical principles (solution equilibria, solubility products, and so on), (3) provide a means for students to make decisions based on their individual observations, and (4) familiarize students with the behavior of ordinary chemical substances. Unfortunately, qualitative analysis has been gradually eliminated from many courses of instruction, not because any of the objectives mentioned are unimportant but because of the pressure of time. Many instructors cannot afford the luxury of a full semester devoted to this practice, especially because after the student has mastered a given separation technique, he still spends an afternoon or two in the laboratory collecting the results of numerous short experiments for the purpose of making decisions.

Using computer techniques it has been possible to simulate the standard sulfide qualitative analysis scheme, thereby permitting the student to continue to gain experience in decision making and the application of chemical principles *after* he has acquired an understanding of the techniques involved, without spending time in the laboratory. The logic of a portion of the qualitative analysis scheme appears in Figure 14–1; space limitations prevent inclusion of the entire program, but a part of the dialogue for one member of the silver group is shown in Figure 14–2. In this program the student has at his command a list of analysis actions ("add," "filter," "wash," "heat," "flame test," etc.) that correspond to common laboratory operations; the results of these analysis actions on his unknown are then either typed out or displayed on colored slides. The programs will permit student errors that lead to erroneous results; however, when the analysis is complete, it is possible to recognize the error and the student can repeat the relevant portion of the scheme.

The dialogue shown in Figure 14–2 illustrates several points in this type of laboratory simulation. First, it is possible to minimize the "cookbook" approach to laboratory work that is encouraged by many experiments. Often it is difficult to get a student to consider the reasons for, or the principles involved in, a particular experimental technique. Computer simulation provides a means for incorporating such considerations explicitly. Under normal laboratory conditions a student would need nearly constant attention by an instructor to accomplish the same ends.

Experiments that are basically repetitive with respect to technique but that are performed to provide each student with individualized results occur in quantitative analysis where gravimetric, titrametric, and instrumental techniques as well as the corresponding principles are illustrated. These experiments are well suited to computer simulation.

Experiments requiring complex equipment. Early in their careers many students are capable of handling the results of experiments that require apparatus too complex for their manipulative expertise. Indeed, acquiring a working knowledge of much of the apparatus used to obtain re-

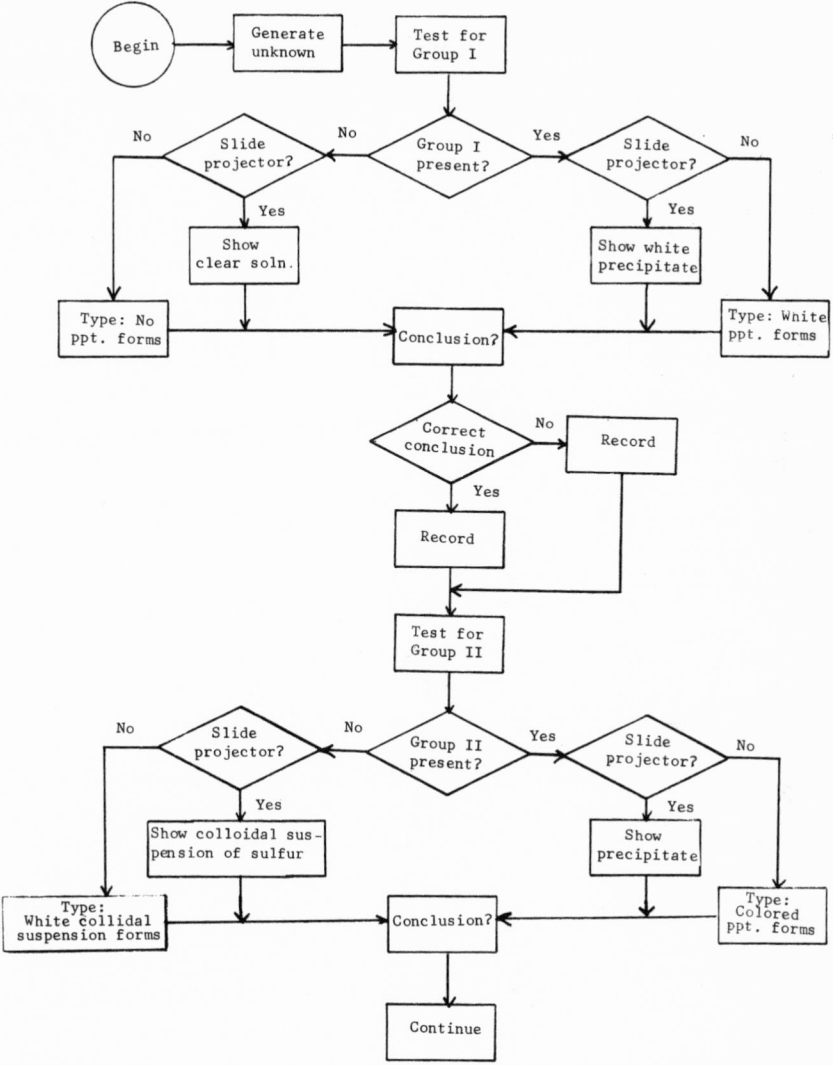

Figure 14–1.
A flow diagram of the logic involved for a portion of the group separation scheme.

sults that are commonly quoted in beginning chemistry courses would require more time than is available; such experiments suffer the additional disadvantage that the equipment is usually available only for research purposes.

Emission spectroscopy is a very good example of an area from which

Figure 2

Computer: Observation. A yellow precipitate forms. Specify an analysis action.

Student: Conclude,

Computer: You do not have sufficient information at this point to make a conclusion. Answer again. Specify an analysis action.

Student: Add.

Computer: Reagent?

Student: NaOh

Computer: O.K. Concentration?

Student: 6M,

Computer: Good. How much?

Student: 8 drops.

Computer: The precipitate dissolves. Specify an analysis action.

Student: Conclude.

Computer: You still shouldn't make any conclusions. Specify an analysis action.

Student: Add.

Computer: Good. Reagent?

Student: HAc,

Computer: O.K. Concentration?

Student: 6M

Computer: Good. How much?

Student: Until acidic.

Computer: Good. A yellow precipitàte forms again. Specify an analysis action.

Student: Conclude.

Computer: O.K. What is your conclusion?

Student: Lead is present.

Figure 14–2.
Sample dialogue from a portion of the qualitative analysis program for the silver group. This student has reached the point in the analytical scheme where lead has been detected as a white precipitate ($PbCl_2$) and he is in the process of conducting a confirmatory test. The white precipitate has been dissolved and the student is working with the filtrate; potassium dichromate ($K_2Cr_2O_7$) has been added and the next computer reply appears at the beginning of this figure.

modern general chemistry courses draw considerable material but for which a representative experiment is not usually included in the laboratory portion of the course. We have simulated a spectroscopic experiment in which the student is required to calibrate an emission spectrometer using a standard substance, collect spectroscopic data for several unknowns (pure substances and mixtures) using this spectrometer, and identify the unknowns. The student is expected to write his experiment in the usual manner. Prior to performing the experiment, the student is required to pass a short quiz (computer-generated, -given, and -graded) on the nature of the basic components of a typical spectrometer; if he does not do sufficiently well on the quiz, he is not allowed to begin but is referred to study material. (A diagram outlining the basic logic for this experiment appears in Figure 14–3.) Thus early in his course of study the student is required to understand the principles on which a spectrometer works, and he makes decisions concerning the data he will collect and the manner in which he will treat his data without becoming involved in the (often idiosyncratic) vagaries of the operation of a spectrometer. Presumably, the student will be exposed to the latter in a more advanced laboratory course when and if this experience is important to his professional development.

There are many experiments that fall into this category, such as X-ray defraction experiments, the Mulliken oil-drop experiment, the Rutherford scattering experiment, and J. J. Thompson's discharge experiments.

Time-compression or time-expansion experiments. Computer techniques can be used to simulate experiments that take either unacceptably long or very short periods of time to perform. For example, there are many kinetics experiments that require relatively simple equipment (which is acceptable from a financial standpoint for large numbers of students); however, they require periodic sampling for ten to twenty-four hours (which is unacceptable in a class with a tight schedule). Experiments involving radioactive substances also fall into this category; in this instance the cost of equipment as well as the time available to do the experiments are important factors.

Computer simulation of a kinetics experiment has been successfully accomplished (Figure 14–4). With this program a student makes decisions concerning experimental parameters (for example, method of analysis, how often to take data, how long to take data), collects his data, and determines one of several kinetically important parameters of the system he is studying (which, incidentally, is randomly chosen for him by the computer). Thus computer simulation can be used to compress the time required for an experiment that might take several days or expand time for an experiment that might take only a fraction of a second. In either case the experimental data could be handled by the lower-division student, but the

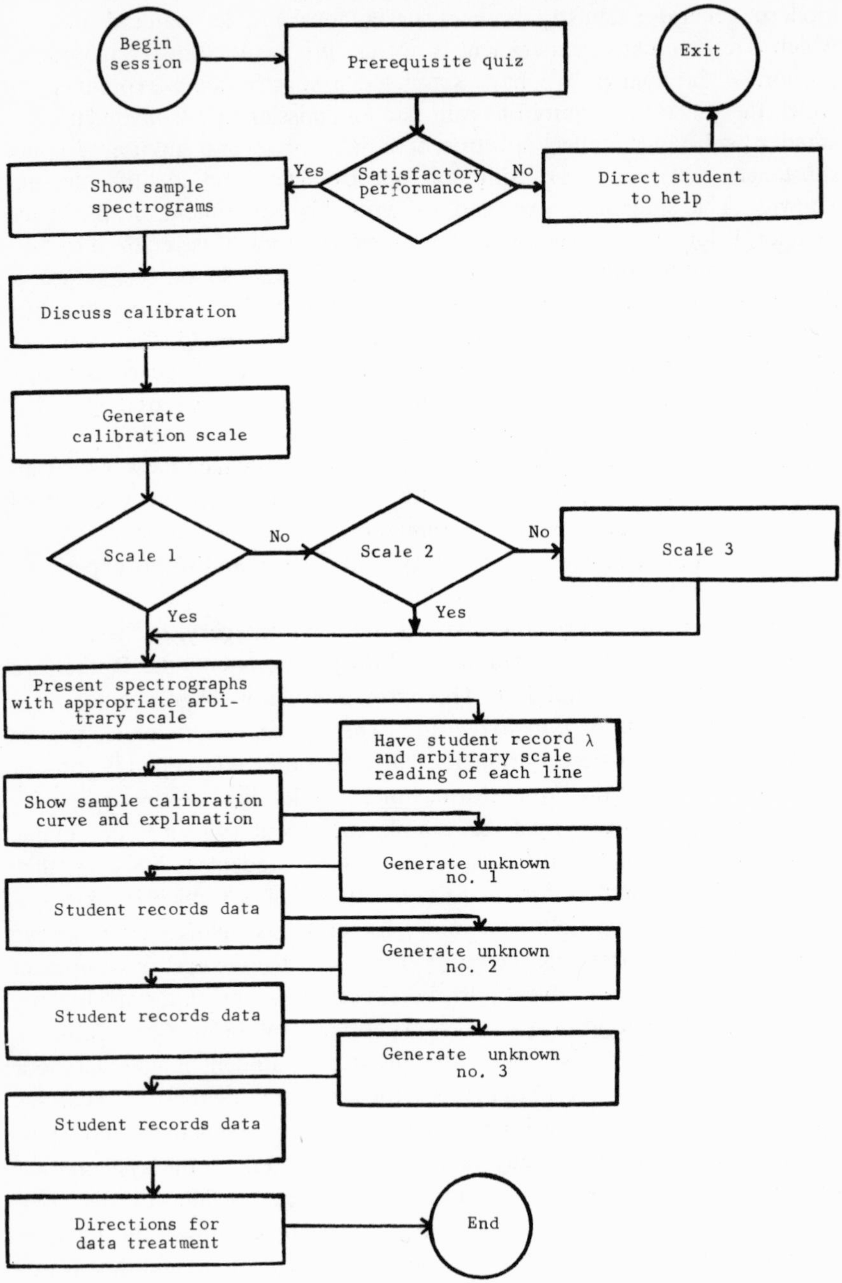

Figure 14–3.
The flow diagram of the logic involved in a simulated spectroscopy experiment.

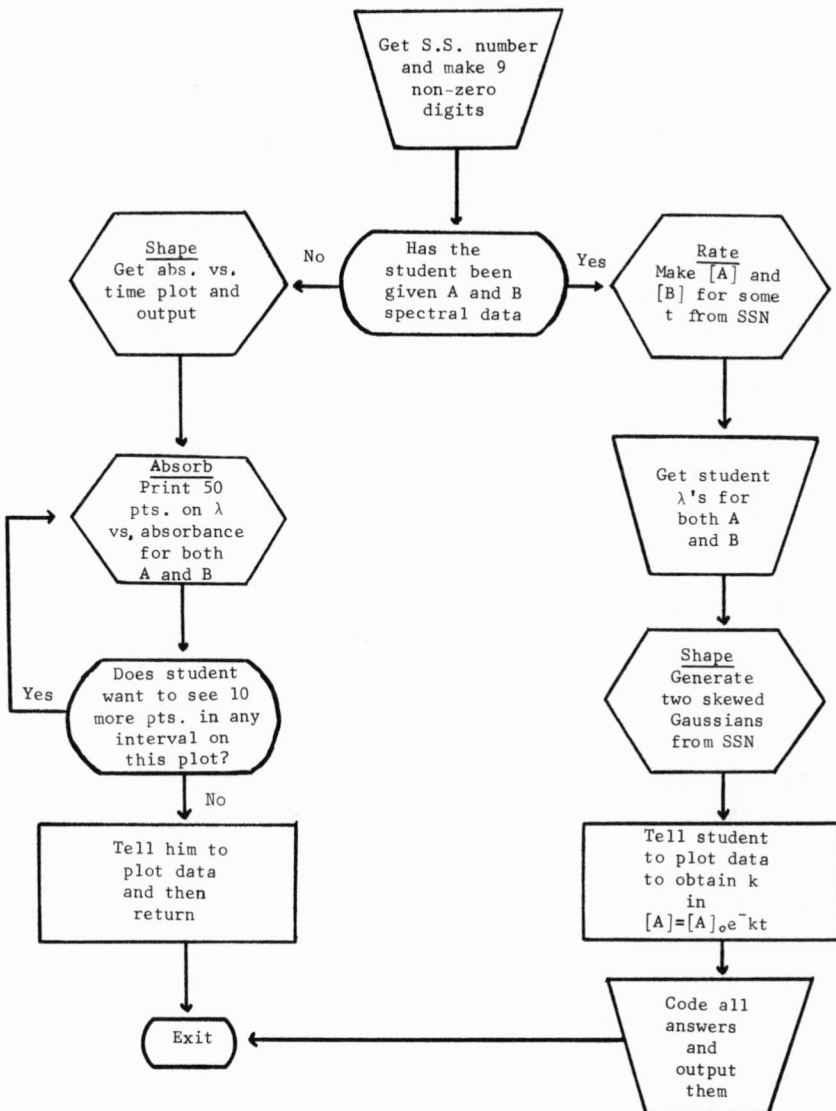

Figure 14–4.
The flow diagram of the logic involved in a simulated kinetics experiment.

manipulation of the apparatus and/or the detailed planning of the experiment might be beyond his capabilities.

Advantages of computer simulation. Computer techniques judiciously used in conjunction with live experiments can lead to a more meaningful laboratory. Actual laboratory time can be gained if, for example, qualitative analysis is supplemented by computer-simulated experiments; this time can be used to expose the students to experiments that normally could not be performed. Using simulation, students can be exposed to relatively sophisticated experiments early in their training. In addition, some experiments can be extended into areas that would be impractical in a real laboratory. For example, it would be a simple task to incorporate some of the more exotic elements in the qualitative analysis scheme; at present many of these elements are eliminated from the scheme because they or their compounds are hazardous and/or too expensive. It should even be possible to have a student develop his own analytical scheme for a given group of elements and then analyze an unknown mixture using his scheme. This approach would be prohibitive in the usual chemistry laboratory course.

A series of individual simulated experiments could serve as a vehicle for demonstrating the unity of experimental work when directed toward a given goal. Thus simulated experiments involving qualitative analysis, certain quantitative techniques, molecular weight determinations, and spectroscopy could be organized with the object of identifying and characterizing unknown substances. An attempt to do this in actual practice would undoubtedly involve more time, equipment, and space than would be available in the normal freshman laboratory. However, the equivalent in computer-simulated experiments could probably be accomplished in several afternoons.

Computer-simulated experiments, especially those that reflect the constitution of matter, could be used to advantage in conjunction with the lecture portion of a chemistry course. At the discretion of the lecturer, pertinent experiments could be performed by the students before or after discussion of the theory, depending on the circumstances.

Finally, it would be expected that considerable savings in terms of space, equipment, and expendable supplies would accrue from laboratory simulation techniques.

Evaluation. At present evaluation of the success of computer-simulated experiments is difficult. The usual criteria are not applicable to many of the simulated experiments discussed here because the equivalent live experiments are not normally performed by the student; some of these experiments are done as lecture demonstrations. Thus control groups at the same level of development are not available. We can only compare the performance on written examinations of students who have performed simulated experiments with those who (1) have not, (2) have read about the experiment, or (3) have observed them in lecture demonstrations. Comparison with group 1 would be a useless exercise, and many would question the validity of comparison with groups 2 and 3. Perhaps the best procedure would be to compare the overall performance of a group of students who have had a course that was entirely computer-supplemented with a group that has had a classic course by using a common instrument. Such a comparison is not possible because a completely supplemented course in chemistry does not yet exist. Indeed, some might argue that when the comparison is made it may be more of a reflection of the so-called Hawthorn effect than of the validity of computer techniques! It might be anticipated that the influence of the Hawthorn effect could be minimized by a continual program of evaluation of students who have been exposed to a series of courses, all of which have heavy CAI supplementation.

Although evaluation of simulated experiments for which there is no live counterpart in the student's experience is meaningless, it is possible to test whether the student has attained the very specific behavioral objectives that the author of the program incorporated, for example, the ability to interpret spectra.

A more indirect method of evaluation involves the use of an attitude scale to ascertain the effect CAI techniques have had, for example, on study habits and the *subject* of chemistry.

There is, however, one factor that represents a positive gain when computer-simulated techniques are used. Students invariably use less real time to do the computer-simulated experiments than to do the corresponding live experiments. Two examples concerning this point are available. The average student requires about 12 hours of laboratory time to complete the general cation unknown in the qualitative analysis scheme. Using computer simulation techniques, the same unknown was done in an average of 4.5 hours. In another experiment using the cations of the silver group, the average completion time for the unknowns done in a live laboratory was 131.8 minutes, whereas computer-simulated unknowns were completed in an average of 66.7 minutes. There was no noticeable difference in performance as measured by a common instrument between students who did the unknown by computer and a control group that performed the live experiments.

A word of caution is necessary at this point. It is now possible to inundate the student with a combination of live experiments and computer-simulated experiments so that he could not possibly keep up with the laboratory reports for these experiments, let alone have sufficient time to digest their implications or attend to his other courses. It has always been easily possible to overwork students using normal teaching methods; computer techniques can translate this into a student nightmare if care is not exercised.

Tutorial-Drill-Remedial Programs

Chemistry (and many of the other sciences) serves as an admirable vehicle for the development of CAI programs that will provide the student with practice in manipulating quantitative concepts. In their general form many of these concepts are not difficult to grasp; however, students often have difficulty with specific examples that reflect these concepts because they have not had sufficient experience in working with them. Much of chemistry can be divided into modules that quantitatively deal with a simple idea; these subjects can be formed into a larger unity by the lecturer using a general discussion. It is important that the student recognize the generality of these ideas as well as being able to handle specific examples. Computer techniques can provide for an almost infinite number of the latter because it is possible with some languages to operate mathematically on student responses. Students have classically gained experience in some of these areas by solving numerical problems, which then must be graded and/or accepted solutions posted. The onus for interpreting his method with respect to the grader's method then falls on the student, especially in a large class.

Many of the basic concepts associated with chemistry are common to other sciences. Learning research has shown, however, that very little transfer of learning from one subject area to another occurs unless a specific effort is made; generally the instructor has little time to engage in such efforts. CAI modules could be used as vehicles for transfer, not only by explicit programming for this objective but by placing the modules in the appropriate place in the schedules of more than one subject, for example, as a tutorial and drill module in one subject and as a remedial drill in another.

For example, programs in which the student is actively engaged in balancing equations, solving problems of stoichiometry, and determining the nature and quantity of the species present in solution using the principles of equilibria can serve many useful functions, depending on the format in which they are set as well as the level of the student when he is first exposed to them. Thus a given program can have many of the aspects of tutorial work if a beginning student uses it in conjunction with his first exposure to this subject in lecture. The same program can be used as a source of drill material in studying for an examination or as a remedial program for a student who indicates (by his response on conventional examinations or computer-generated quizzes) that he needs additional practice. Programs developed in this category can even be used for review of certain principles in more advanced courses.

Prerequisite Skills Programs

Often students have difficulty in chemistry courses because of a deficiency in certain peripheral subjects such as simple mathematical skills. Such skills are not really germaine to chemistry, but they frequently prove to be stumbling blocks for students. Thus, for example, a facility for using logarithms when discussing some of the concepts of solution chemistry (for example, for pH) is desirable; however, students are often ill-prepared or do not recognize the principles involved in the context of chemistry. CAI programs on the use of logarithms using chemical examples can prove to be very useful. These programs may contain diagnostic questions couched in chemical terms as well as remedial material to alleviate deficiencies that are uncovered. Such programs move the onus for understanding peripheral material to the student from the chemistry instructor.

Quizzes

Many of the types of programs that are discussed here involve some aspect of quizzing to judge whether a student is sufficiently versed in some aspect of a given subject to continue in the program. Obviously, records of performance on these short quizzes could be incorporated into the overall measure of a student's performance.

There is, however, a more direct approach to quizzing using computer techniques. We have investigated the possibility of creating a minimal-level quiz covering certain important subjects such as balancing equations, stoichiometry, and nomenclature. A program has been written that randomly generates a quiz, presents it item by item to the student, grades the quiz, tells the student whether he has achieved the minimal level of attainment set for this material, and keeps a record of the results. The student may take this quiz as often as is necessary to pass at the minimal level; each quiz item is randomly generated (*not* chosen from a list) by the computer so that it is highly improbable that any two quizzes would be the same. Obviously, an understanding of the subject matter of these quizzes can be obtained from any source, not just from CAI material.

Future Developments

We have demonstrated that individual, sophisticated CAI programs that have a professionally acceptable content can be written and successfully used by students (see Table 14–1). It is now imperative that an attempt

Table 14–1. Chemistry Programs Developed at The University of Texas

Program description	Type[a]	Language[b]	Visuals[c]
1. Quantitative analysis[d]	SE	CII	CS, CRT
2. Titration	SE	APL, MAT	ET, CRT
3. Kinetics	SE	APL	ET
4. Equation balancing	Q	CI	ET
5. Stoichiometry	RD	APL	ET
6. Gas laws	RD	APL	ET
7. Equation balancing	RD	APL	ET
8. Atomic structure	RD	APL	ET
9. Spectroscopy	SE	CII	CS, CRT
10. Mulliken oil-drop experiment	SE	CII	CS, CRT
11. Charge on the particle	SE	MAT	CS, CRT
12. Determination of e/M for electron	SE	CII	CS, CRT
13. Heat, work, energy, kinetic theory	TD, Q	CII	CS, CRT
14. Law of constant composition, law of multiple proportions, percentage composition	SE, TD	CII	CS
15. Chemical formulas, combining volumes, stoichiometry	SE, TD, Q	CII	CS, CRT
16. Metric system	RD, Q	CII	CRT
17. Electron distribution and periodicity	TD, Q		CS, CRT

a SE, simulated experiments; RD, remedial drill; Q, quiz; TD, tutorial drill.
b CI, Coursewriter I; CII, Coursewriter II; APL, A Programming Language; MAT, Mathematical Algorithm Translator.
c CS, colored slides; CRT, cathode-ray tube; ET, electric typewriter.
d Several of the qualitative analysis groups have also been written in Coursewriter I.
Note: The programs described in this chapter and outlined in Table 14–1 were developed for the following systems: (1) IBM 1401–1026 System using IBM 1050 typewriter terminals incorporating a computer-controlled image projector, (2) IBM 1440 System using terminals similar to those described in (1), (3) IBM 1800/1500 Instructional System using 1510 cathode-ray terminals with electronic light pen and 1512 image projectors, and (4) IBM 360/50 System using 1050 or 2740 typewriter terminals.

be made to supplement an entire chemistry course with such programs to (1) determine the impact of CAI techniques on the traditional methods of teaching (that is, lecture, laboratory, and discussion periods) and (2) evaluate the students' reactions to and performance in such a course.

15

Edward D. Lambe

Simulated Laboratory
in the Natural Sciences

The natural scientist knows why experimental work should accompany his courses. The concepts, the theories, the problem-solving techniques that he lays before his students have meaning only insofar as they represent the natural universe. Without raw experience the neophyte can find the presentation of science too persuasive, too neat—he may come to accept and to believe the theory of science with superstitious zeal. Because scientists generally believe that, in the face of the real complexity of events, the miracle is that any adequate symbolic representation can be discovered, they deeply desire to confront the learner with the mystery of reality at the earliest possible time. This is the intent of undergraduate laboratory experience.

In such a context a "simulated laboratory" is a nonconcept, a contradiction in terms. Many (perhaps most) science teachers recoil from the idea. The response is automatic until it is realized that most undergraduate laboratory experience exposes a student to an elaborate simulation of nature rather than to nature itself. A "real" confrontation of nature is clearly improbable within massive lock-step instructional patterns—the time and materials required to meet any given goal are much too variable. In particular, this is true of the laboratories that accompany the large beginning natural science courses. These laboratories typically serve 100 to 1000 students in a single course, meet about once each week for two or three hours, and process about a dozen "experiments" each semester. Such experiences are highly distilled from nature—so much so that many ask if they retain any significant relation to nature at all. But they live on. Boredom, even misery, notwithstanding, it seems better to give something than nothing at all.

But any science department chairman can tell you that these laboratories create monumental logistic problems. What is worse, they are a focus of academic gripes—from students, teaching assistants, faculty, and administration alike.[1] In the immediate future, laboratory simulation using electronic computers would have to be miraculously successful to solve any significant portion of the academic and managerial headaches associated with laboratory instruction. Nonetheless, it is useful to assess the force of economic arguments in favor of electronic simulation, if only to know how seriously to pursue the question of this form of simulation.

The Price of Instructional Laboratories

The instructional laboratory means different things to different disciplines. In some contexts it means a small group (20 to 30 students) as against a large one (larger than 100 students), for example, a problem-solving laboratory (others might call this a recitation). In some contexts it implies a variety of special activities; for example, practice teaching is sometimes conceived as laboratory work in education. For the purposes of this discussion, *laboratory* is taken to mean an activity in which each n-student group (where $n \leqq 5$ and is most probably 2) is to manipulate apparatus and materials in surroundings that provide access to special facilities. Such laboratories are offered as a matter of course in many undergraduate courses in chemistry, biology, earth sciences, and physics.

Conventional laboratory costs come in two guises: capital construction costs and operating costs. A laboratory that can handle about 25 students costs roughly $50,000 ($40 per square foot times 1200 square feet) to build[2] and (for example) another $50,000 to equip—about $100,000. If we depreciate the value of this furnished space to zero in ten years (clearly a wildly optimistic estimate of practice, considering the appearance of most older laboratories), capital costs come to $10,000 per year. This laboratory supports about 25 (students) $\times$ 6 (hours per day) $\times$ 5

---

1. All the national commissions on undergraduate instruction in the natural sciences have revealed considerable anxiety about laboratory instruction. A recent survey of physics departments indicated a very strong belief that the Commission on College Physics should work hard on the problem. *CCP Newsletter #17*, October 1968, contains a review article "Toward a New Lab Style"; articles by J. W. G. Ivany and M. R. Parlett ("The Divergent Laboratory") and J. A. Soules ("The Instrumented Laboratory") will appear in the December, 1969, issue of the *American Journal of Physics*.

2. Private communication from Assistant Vice Chancellor M. C. Gassman, State University of New York, October 8, 1968.

(days per week) × 30 (weeks) or 22,500 student-hours of instruction during the academic year. Use during the summer may bring the number up to about 25,000 student-hours, yielding a cost of about 40 cents per student-hour. [Note, in passing, that if $50,000 buys for each laboratory 25 different experimental setups (1 per week) each setup costs $2000; if 10 sets are bought for 25 students, each can cost $200. In current practice this is probably a generous allowance, particularly for undergraduate laboratories.]

Let us (again generously) suppose a technician, paid $10,000 per annum in wages and benefits, devotes full time to the maintenance of this laboratory: Add another 40 cents per student-hour. If each graduate student (paid $3000 per annum) teaches two sections (50 students) as his main load, he provides 50 (students) × 2 (hours per laboratory session) × 30 (laboratory sessions) or 3000 student-hours of instruction during the academic year: Add $1 per student-hour.[3] Thus the total cost per student-hour becomes

Capital	$0.40
Technical support	0.40
Instruction	1.00
	$1.80

Personally, if I had to choose between $1 and $2 per student-hour for laboratory instructional cost, I would choose the dollar.

In the immediate future laboratory simulation that relies on computers similar in capability to the IBM 1500 System now in experimental use in about two dozen institutions in this country will cost $4 to $5 per student-hour. The difference between $2 and $4.5 is not so great that the question of substitution should not be considered for some future time, particularly in view of the fact that all conventional laboratory costs will escalate steadily, perhaps as much as 5 to 10 per cent per year. Computer costs, on the other hand, tend to decline in cost per unit operation, optimistically as much as 50 per cent in three years. Within a reasonable time the computer-simulated laboratory may be cost-competitive if the two kinds of laboratory can be shown to have a reasonable hour-for-hour equivalence.

Minimal Requirements for Simulation

To the extent that laboratory work is conceived as allowing the student to experience raw nature, simulation has no apparent role. If the student

3. This accords reasonably with the figure of $60 estimated to be the per-student annual cost of an instructional laboratory by the President's Scientific Advisory Council Panel in the report "Computers and Higher Education."

is to learn to judge the character of a real precipitate, to get a sense of hotness, or mass, or hardness, simulation will not do. *Simulation,* as used here, implies that real elements and real effects are abstracted by pictures, or symbols. The question of simulated laboratory becomes the question of what values attach to a laboratory-like manipulation of elements and whether such manipulation has a value independent of the detailed "feel" of the elements. Such acts may manifest a "process of science" that involves the formulation of hypotheses, the utilization of theory, observation, measurement, and conclusion—all sustained and guided by informed judgment and creative imagination. Process is in this way at least partially separated from the presence of real objects and quasi-natural circumstances.

For now, both modesty and skepticism are reasonable attitudes toward the possibility of teaching process. It is far easier to recognize that a brilliant chain of reasoning and observation has led to an unexpected conclusion than to find systematic ways to cause others to develop such chains. This large question seems too difficult to answer or even to formulate clearly at this time. However, some insight into laboratory objectives, and some data, may be available if we can formulate a simple set of procedures that has a laboratory-like character. If this quasi-laboratory looks interesting enough to students, if programming is feasible, and if sensible data reduction schemes can be found, it may be worthwhile to go on. The formulation assumes processing and control functions currently available on terminal-oriented computers at the University of Texas and at Stony Brook.

To begin, the experiments must have a reasonably unambiguous goal or set of goals. Examples are quantitative measures: the mass or charge of an electron or the identity of incompletely described substances. Goals of this required specificity are generally a part of elementary laboratory exercises because of the necessity of an unambiguous criterion for the determination of zeroth-order success.

Next, the student needs "his own things"—apparatus and substances. These must be described in some terse format, presumably a combination of pictures, drawings, works, and numbers. What comes to mind is a small Cenco/Fisher catalog. From this store of elements the student selects the glassware, chemicals, timers, balances, carts, and so on that he needs for his experiment. For some items that he buys from the store, quantity may need to be specified.

He must as well be able to command an acceptable set of operations. At least three classes of operations are necessary:

1. State-setting operations on the elements chosen by the student. For apparatus, such state-setting operations are normally reversible, and where there are independent sets, commutative, for example, range-setting

switches, mode selection, and on-off. There may occasionally be a set of "destruct" operations, for example, dead short across dry cell terminals. For substances, operations will generally be irreversible and noncommutative: crushing, mixing, dyeing, dissolving, and so on.

2. Conjunctive (or assembly) operations that act on pairs of elements. These operations assemble the apparatus and materials in configurations that permit data collection—circuit elements must be connected, timing microswitches placed at appropriate locations along a travel path, chemicals placed in beakers, and so on. These conjunctive operations need stratification—permissible, neuter, incompatible, "destruct."

3. Data-initiating operations—a set of release or activate procedures that immediately precede data-record requests. They might frequently be the same operations as those of previous categories, for example, "close switch" or "connect first and last elements" in an electric circuit problem. However, this is not always the case: for example, "release cart" and "excite oscillation."

There are some additional features that it would be convenient to have and that can be provided at some cost. One is a student calculation feature, enabling him to manipulate his collected data in a convenient and natural way. This need not have high priority, because it is easy to simulate calculation with either a slide rule or an electric calculator at the terminal. Of greater consequence is an internal configuration calculator so that the student may choose his own values for the experimental variables under his control. This internal calculator would then compute the appropriate "measurement" values. Without such a feature the quantitative variation of experimental variables must be obtained by selection from a list for each entry of which the appropriate data measurements are stored.

Student Command Repertoire

To proceed through such a simulator, the student needs to be able to choose fairly freely from a list of commands. For obvious reasons this list must be structured as simply and as generally as possible, so that control of the listing readily becomes natural and repeatable from one laboratory to the next. The list of commands can be inferred directly from the foregoing discussion:

1. ENTRY. This may be a statement of immediate experimental objectives, specifying the conclusion to be judged. It may only be a convenience to present this statement on the terminal (it can be part of the written material for the laboratory) unless the specific objectives for a given student are partially determined by an online assessment of his previous history.

2. $\left.\begin{array}{l} \text{SELECT from} \\ \text{RETURN to} \end{array}\right\}$ STORE.

> The student chooses items for his experiment, most reasonably from a printed catalog with pictures and necessary description (apparatus functions and options, materials composition, and so on). The select operation sets up the lists of objects on which he can operate; the list can be rewritten by item cancellation (return to store) and reselection. Presumably this list will be complete before set and assembly operations begin. It may be a pedagogical and programming simplification to assume for all experiments a core collection of equipment, equivalent to the items at the student bench.

3. $\left.\begin{array}{l} \text{Set} \\ \text{DISPLAY} \\ \text{Change} \end{array}\right\}$ STATE.

> Apparatus or substances are each characterized by a specific set of state and assembly operations. The display state is, first, a list of items, selected by the student. A second column lists the features of the item that the student has chosen to specify (set) and a third lists the way in which he has set them. Change is, of course, cancellation of previous setting and reset. This list constitutes the active set of elements that the student now assembles into working order.

4. $\left.\begin{array}{l} \text{Set} \\ \text{DISPLAY} \\ \text{Change} \end{array}\right\}$ ASSEMBLY.

> Again, the display feature is the main apparent feature of this set of operations. The active graphic features of the CRT are almost indispensable as a shorthand for describing to the student what he has done with what. The array of elements is now one that will (hopefully) produce one or more pieces of data.

5. Initiate. The student activates the assembly. Internally this is a judge step—for element selection, state, and assembly operations. A consistent, acceptable set provides student access to the data store appropriate to his experimental variable settings. For unacceptable combinations corrective messages must be provided that lead to revision of his assembly.

6. $\left.\begin{array}{l} \text{QUERY} \\ \text{DISPLAY} \end{array}\right\}$ DATA.

> Each of the pieces of data expected by the student are called for, one by one. In this list he accumulates the information that dictates next steps and leads to his conclusion.

7. CONCLUDE. The student announces he is ready to speak to the laboratory objectives—internally, another judge operation. When the answer provided is finally acceptable, a laboratory score statement might appear on the screen.

8. EXIT. The begin-again opportunity.

9. PROGRESS CHART. A summary of the selection and operation steps as they have been taken by the student. This chart may be consulted at any time.

10. BACK-UP. The "goof" button. Permits the student to backtrack along his progress chart and rewrite it from the point he chooses.

11. HELP. The primary function of this call is to get the student out of logical loops and cul-de-sacs. In first order it simply provides successively detailed portions of the sequence of required steps.

There are a few program functions that would appear to be useful but not clearly essential and therefore to be omitted, at least at first:

A. TABLE.   Listings of useful (or required) constants of nature and mathematics.

B. THEORY.   Appropriate summaries of the theoretical background of the experiment.

C. CALCULATE. On-line programming capability for the reduction of data and the like.

D. PLOT.   On-line display of data.

Although each of these capabilities can be provided to the student off line, it may be important for the construction of the student progress chart to have him indicate when he is exercising any of these options and to time each separate activity.

The Major Question: Assessment

Such a categorization of laboratory-like manipulations is useful if it gives the right kind of flexibility to teacher and student. But the crucial question is whether the categorization permits a reasonable professional judgment to be made of good and not-so-good performance by an assessment of the separate features. The nature of the scoring procedures is the crucial question to be asked of those experimenting with the simulated laboratory.

For example, did the student make an optimal selection of elements for the goal described? Did he make this selection on the first pass or on a later trial? Is it worse to select too many elements, or too few, or the wrong ones?

Was he sufficiently conscious of all element functions and characteristics so that they were all set, at least before data was expected? How many incompatible assembly operations were demanded, and how serious is each? Was the ordering of set-assembly operations optimal? Was the number minimal? What are the characteristics of backtracking—when is it acceptable (reasonable evidence of learning) and when floundering?

We have to begin with intuitive judgments and then refine and amend them on the basis of experience. This process will require several iterations before a value set that bears reasonable correspondence with intuitive judgments of good performance can be established. In the meantime the analysis that accompanies a serious attempt of this kind provides a mirror in which to scrutinize our standard performance in, and expectations of, student laboratory. If this mirror can materially assist in improving the effectiveness of this instruction, it will be valuable even if, when it is all done, everyone agrees that a simulated laboratory is even worse than anything we are presently about.

Simulation of Science Experiments: Discussion

Discussion focused on two major questions: What things about laboratory work, especially in the sciences, are desirable or undesirable? How are results achieved by various laboratory formats and content to be evaluated?

Perhaps computer-based laboratory exercises will be especially important in providing more suitable experiences for nonscience students. Presumably simulated laboratories will become more economical than equipment-based laboratories, and experience in manipulation of equipment may be less important for nonscience students. A conceptual laboratory without specific apparatus should be less threatening to these students, and during a short course the experience could more closely approach the professional work of scientists in the area being studied.

Evaluation of such intended outcomes will not be possible until objectives are more clearly defined and measurement techniques are devised. The interesting work by Lagowski at The University of Texas is only a small step in this direction.

It may be that other modes of instruction, such as a filmed demonstration of a laboratory exercise, will be as effective or more so than a regular laboratory or a computer-based simulation. Three classes of laboratory objectives were mentioned in discussion; two of them appeared to be better handled by approaches other than direct laboratory experiences. Acquisition of concepts and principles and understanding of procedures for derivation or illustration of relationships can be handled by films or even by printed, static presentations. Formulation and testing of processes, that is, practice in some kind of problem-solving skill, can be handled by simulation, perhaps in a computer environment. Only the class of objectives labeled "manipulation" appear to require the equipment-based simulation of the real world, which we call a science laboratory.

It may be useful to identify four dimensions of simulation, which isolate (1) object, (2) fidelity of representation, (3) generality of practice, and (4) role of an automated tutor in laboratory exercises. These are considered again in Part VIII on complex man-machine systems.

1. What is it that is to be simulated? The object of study may be a set of processes in the real world, even an open and poorly defined system, or a single process with clearly defined boundaries. Lambe has provided a useful list of functions.

2. How faithful is the simulation to the real situation? At first it may appear that fidelity is itself a good thing. However, because the instructional function of a simulation may be to present an abstraction or simplification as well as to provide experience, an instructional situation need not be as faithful to the real world as would be desirable in a research setting.

3. How wide a range of situations can a simulation handle? Generality may be important in a simulation, especially when a student is a trainee or practitioner faced by real-world problems. A very specific simulation provides limited practice because a student's attention is focused on a rather narrow range of possibilities. Generality is important to the extent that the performance of the trainee in novel situations is a significant objective.

4. What teaching goal is assumed by the computer program? The conversation between student and simulation program may include comments inserted by the program to correct student errors as they occur or redirect him if he leaves the optimal path toward a solution, a "debriefing" at the end of the session to point out all his errors at once, or no diagnosis at all if the student is expected to go elsewhere to find answers to his questions.

It was also suggested that another reason for use of simulation procedures is in assessment of current abilities of college students in order to place them in appropriate-level courses in engineering and the sciences. Tasks involving design and test of procedures may be quite significant in the aptitude being tested. Furthermore, additional information is obtained about the examinee's ability to use representations of objects and relationships.

Although a satisfactory measure might be obtained without computerization of the examination procedure, it might be that a test of such skills could be made significantly shorter if a computer were programmed to make decisions during the testing period; time spent by examinees becomes important if the institutional testing program for selection and placement is already overcrowded.

Finally, the participants ended discussion on two points: whether the increasing automation of science laboratories should have implications now for the objectives and procedures of laboratory instruction and whether the increasing availability of models that adequately describe the processes in science has implications for the essential purposes and strategies of science education.

PART VIII

Complex Man-Machine Systems

The simulation of complex man-machine systems for training purposes has become an important instructional technique, especially in military and aerospace programs. The preparation of flight controller teams for mission control and monitoring of the Project Apollo manned space flights involves intensive training on a complex, computer-driven, real-time simulation system. In Chapter 16 Shelley and Groom first describe this system, which is designed to duplicate the actual flight controller mission environment with a high degree of realism. Then they suggest some possible implications of this kind of training for the development of educational systems in general. Although the Apollo Flight Controller Trainer System is highly complicated and expensive, several principles embodied in it can be applied on a more modest level in the design of educational technology for general purposes. Simulation of a space flight for training purposes of necessity involves very expensive equipment, extensive computer programming, and a high degree of fidelity because of the critical character of the mission itself. The objective of the instruction is to ensure that every member of the flight controller team can process all kinds of information very rapidly, making quick decisions accurately as part of the total complex man-machine system.

In his critique of the Apollo training system and its educational implications in Chapter 17, Licklider points out that the essential features of the system involve (1) providing each student with his own data base and his own displays and controls, together with a language through which to employ them; (2) placing each student into interaction with other students; and (3) maintaining instructional supervision by computer-aided monitoring. He argues that this general paradigm is so important for education that much greater effort should be exerted to overcome the current, prohibitively high costs and to develop the urgently needed educational applications. The motivational force of interaction for the involved student is potentially very great in this type of system, provided significant features of the process are properly simulated. Although realism may be worth its high cost in training flight controller teams, the motivation of interacting with a well-programmed computer where the right things have been abstracted for simulation will be more valuable for learning in an educational setting.

16

Carl B. Shelley and Vaughn Groom

The Apollo Flight Controller Training System Concept and Its Educational Implications

The recent Apollo flight to the Moon represented one of the most complex man-machine systems ever devised. The purpose of this chapter is to describe the training of one segment of the population in this system, the Apollo flight controller team, and to suggest some possible implications of this training for development of educational systems. Such implications are generally derived from the design and use of the Apollo Simulation, Checkout, and Training System (ASCATS)—a complex, computer-driven, real-time simulation system. This system was designed to duplicate the actual flight controller mission environment with a high degree of realism while maintaining maximal operational flexibility in its use as a teaching system. This objective has been accomplished.

ASCATS, which is complicated and somewhat expensive, embodies several principles that might be applicable on a more modest level to specific classroom situations. The first part of the chapter will describe the design and use of the ASCATS flight controller training concept. Some of the implications of this concept for education will be explored in the second part.

Apollo Flight Controller Training Concept

The Apollo flight controller team is a group of persons responsible for mission control and monitoring of the Project Apollo manned space flights. As a member of this team, the individual flight controller interacts with his environment of people and equipment largely in terms of mission objectives, mission rules, and flight control procedures. In addition to the implicit objectives associated with a safe flight for the crew, each flight has a set of specific *mission objectives,* which, in effect, define the purpose of the flight. To accomplish these objectives, *mission rules* and *flight control procedures* are developed as guidelines for the flight. As an example of a mission rule, consider the following. The environmental control system of a typical spacecraft provides two thermal control coolant loops, a primary and a backup. A mission rule might state that if the primary coolant loop fails, the spacecraft is to return to earth as soon as it is in proper position with respect to the best landing area. The rule is, in effect, a decision based on a preconceived situation. Such rules form the basis for real-time decisions in contingency situations. The flight control procedures, on the other hand, define how certain activities carried out by the flight controllers are to be accomplished—in other words how they will interface with each other, the equipment, and the astronauts. We are, therefore, led to a training requirement with three prime objectives:

1. Test the flight controllers' knowledge of mission objectives, rules, and procedures.
2. Develop flight controller proficiency in the execution of the flight plan within the context of the mission objectives, rules, and procedures.
3. Validate the mission rules and procedures.

These training objectives will be discussed in terms of the flight controller task, general training requirements for the flight controller, and the design and use of ASCATS.

The flight controller task. The individual flight controller is a member of a team of specialists numbering between 75 and 150, depending on the particular mission, whose responsibility during a mission is basically that of monitoring spacecraft data and initiating actions that support the flight crew in the accomplishment of mission objectives. This task must be accomplished under either normal or contingency situations. The activities of team members, under the leadership of the flight director, may involve such routine things as keeping track of the use of spacecraft consumables, executing spacecraft switching functions, and transferring navigation "updates" from the Real-Time Computer Complex in Houston to the onboard computer in the spacecraft. However, it may also be necessary for the team to carry out an alternative flight plan, as was the situation during the fifth Apollo mission when problems with the spacecraft required that an alternative sequence of events be performed. The fact that such contingencies must be provided for is fundamental to the task definition, and thus to the qualifications and training requirements, for the members of this team. In this perspective, then, it is necessary that the flight controller be able to interact with available data and other team members so as to adapt and modify the mission profile in near real-time within the framework of mission objectives, rules, and procedures.

Consider first the environment of this interaction. The worldwide Manned Space Flight Network (MSFN) serves as a two-way data acquisition system for gathering spacecraft telemetry and tracking information and for providing ground information uplink to the spacecraft. MSFN provides data to and accepts data from the Mission Control Center (MCC), located in Houston. Within MCC the flight controller interacts with the system through a console terminal (see Figure 16–1) driven by computers that process the incoming data from the network. The console may include two or three television monitors as well as various combinations of event lights, alphanumeric displays, push-button keyboards, and voice communication key sets. Other devices in the flight controller's environment include teletype systems, strip chart recorders, and group displays such as X-Y plotboards and projection plotters.

Each console television monitor can be used to access any of twenty-eight channels of digital-to-television displays for which computer-generated dynamic data are optically mixed with a static background to provide a composite picture. Approximately forty additional channels of closed-circuit television providing reference data, coordination information, and so on are also available on the television monitors. Telemetered indications of discrete events such as lift-off are displayed by the event lights, and the digital displays show such things as elapsed mission time. The push-button keyboards can be used to initiate actions involving requests for television displays and printed summary messages, event overrides, and control of certain mission program subroutines in the support computers.

Insofar as the interaction of the flight controller and the available data is concerned, it should be noted that the flight controller has considerable choice as to the data he monitors. In fact, the data base available has been custom-designed, within limits, in accordance with the flight controller's desires. He has specified which data he wants to monitor and how he wants them displayed. For example, one flight controller may be assigned the responsibility for a specific subsystem of the spacecraft. Suppose that his console as configured at that time included two television monitors and two event light modules. Based on his knowledge of the given subsystem, he decides what data he wants displayed from the computer support system. This decision may require that the data associated with one module of event lights be displayed by television instead. Both the hardware and software have a degree of flexibility to accommodate the necessary changes.

LOC	DESCRIPTION
01	PRECISION 14 TV MONITOR
02	BLANK PANEL
03	STATUS REPORTING
04	EVENT INDICATOR
05	VOICE COMM POSITION—180
06	PRECISION 14 TV MONITOR
07	PRECISION 14 TV MONITOR
08	EVENT INDICATOR
10	EVENT INDICATOR

LOC	DESCRIPTION
11	EVENT INDICATOR
12	LAUNCH TRAJECTORY SELECT
14	MANUAL SELECT KEYBOARD
15	SWITCH MODULE
16	INDICATOR/SWITCH
17	EVENT INDICATOR
18	SWITCH MODULE
19	INDICATOR/SWITCH

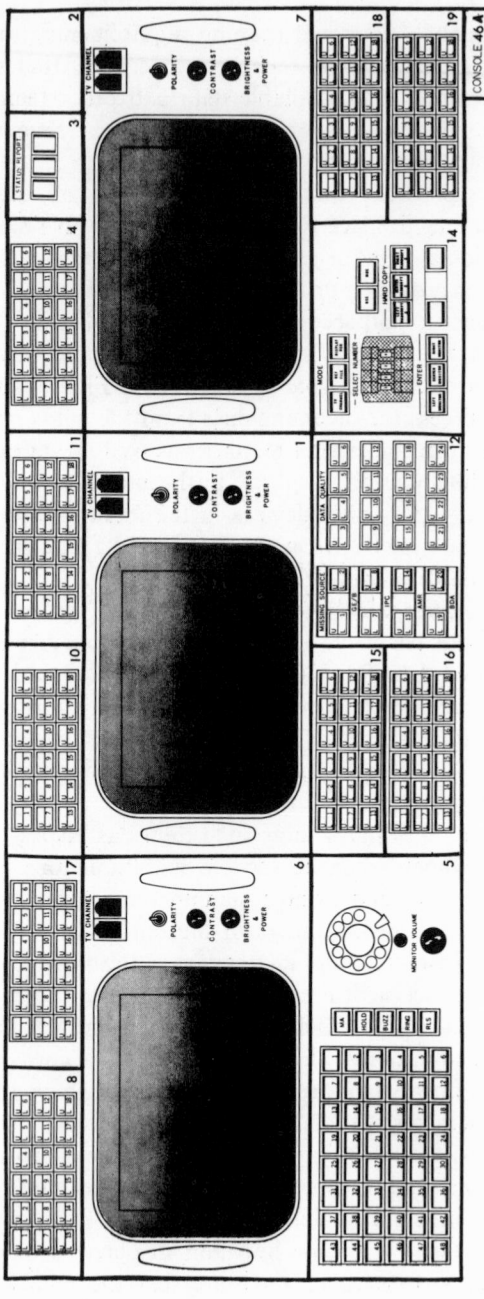

Figure 16–1.
Typical flight controller console.

Additionally, the flight controller may specify in some cases the spacecraft instrumentation in order to ensure that certain data he regards as important are telemetered. By selecting the data he will monitor, the flight controller has defined some of the details of his mission task and has, to a large degree, established his "classroom" data base.

In terms of the preceding description of the mission data environment, the flight controller's task now becomes one of proper management of his available data base such that he can readily discern anomalies in spacecraft or related performance areas. He must interact with other members of the team to ensure a coherent approach to the solution of existing problems or to the normal conduct of the mission. He must apply his knowledge of mission objectives, rules, and procedures to the task of solving problems in different ways, that is, deriving different solutions for the same problem and determining the best solution. In general, he must analyze the progress of the spaceflight and redirect it as necessary.

General training requirements for the flight controller. The mission environment of the flight controller has been briefly described. The qualification requirements that must be satisfied for an individual to function properly in this environment will now be examined.

To begin with, it should be recognized that not only the data base but also the framework of mission rules and procedures under which the team will operate is largely determined by the flight controllers. Definition of these rules is normally a part of the flight controller's full-time office job. Consequently, qualifications and training requirements are not so much related to fitting the flight controller into some predefined mold as they are to giving him a basis for defining the details of his task within certain broad guidelines.

Flight controller qualifications should also be considered in the light of the fact that members of the team are usually specialists in some area. The flight controller must therefore be an expert in the particular spacecraft system related to his specialty. He must have knowledge of the support capabilities of MCC and MSFN, which are involved with the data flow he monitors and controls. A thorough understanding of the mission rules and flight control procedures is necessary, as well as the flight objectives reflected in the primary and alternative flight plans. He must be familiar with flight crew procedures so that information may be passed efficiently via voice communications between the ground and the spacecraft.

Finally, and most important, the flight controller must be able to think clearly and rapidly while under pressure. The nature of the environment associated with space flight control is such that real-time thinking is an absolute necessity.

With a general knowledge of the qualification requirements, the problem now becomes one of training the individual and evaluating his performance to determine if he is or is not qualified to perform flight controller duties. However, the activities of the flight controller are so interrelated with other members of the team that it is extremely difficult to devise criteria for the evaluation of the individual flight controller. (Studies are currently under way in an attempt to do this.) The lack of such formal criteria has made it necessary to emphasize team performance as the basis for determining mission readiness. What kind of training is best suited to exercise the flight controller as a team member—to provide a realistic environment that requires his participation in decision making based on the mission rules and procedures? How can it be determined before an actual mission whether flight controllers have chosen the right data to be displayed or whether the mission rules are even workable? How can the flight controller's performance be evaluated? The answers to these questions seem to culminate in an instructor-controlled high-fidelity simulation, with the flight control team occupying the same positions within MCC as they occupy during the flight. However, a large amount of "background" training for the team members is required prior to their simulation training to enable them to obtain maximal benefit from the latter. This presimulation training is oriented toward self-directed study and the development of mission rules and procedures, mission handbooks, flight plans, and flight crew procedures. Also involved is formal classroom study of subjects such as orbital mechanics as well as spacecraft, MCC, and MSFN systems. (Much of this formal classroom study can and will be replaced with programmed instruction texts for the remainder of Project Apollo.)

The simulation phase of flight controller training is of most interest and will be described in the following paragraphs with reference to the ASCATS currently in use.

General ASCATS design philosophy. A detailed description of ASCATS is much too lengthy for the purpose of this chapter; however, the underlying philosophy of this system can be explored. The initial, and foremost, tenet of the ASCATS design philosophy is concerned with placing the flight controller in a controlled environment that provides not only data of the same kind he interacts with during a mission but also a procedural interface with other team members and the flight crew identical to that existing during a mission. This means that data simulating spacecraft and MSFN activities are generated external to MCC and provided to the MCC computing complex in the same manner as mission data. Depending on the simulation mode, the spacecraft data may be generated for the flight controllers by a computer controlled by a mathematical model of spacecraft systems or by elaborate spacecraft flight crew trainers. The activities and data associated with the acquisition of the spacecraft signal by various sites in MSFN are also simulated by computer for the flight controllers. When the math model of the spacecraft is used, all the simulated data are generated by an IBM System/360 Model 75 computer augmented by a Univac 494 system. Use of the spacecraft flight crew trainers requires seven additional DDP 224 computers. The reasons for requiring separate operational modes are obvious in terms of equipment scheduling; in-house simulations with the math model are used to bring the flight controller team to a certain level of proficiency before including the flight crew and their trainers. A similar approach is used to develop flight crew proficiency prior to the integrated training.

The second tenet involves a closed-loop concept that allows the flight controller to take actions and observe the effects of such actions as he would be able to do during a mission. He is able, for example, to send commands to the simulated spacecraft, with the model or the trainer returning indications in the telemetry stream responsive to the command. The system, in fact, provides reinforcement to the flight controller for each action initiated that affects the environment.

Being able selectively or consecutively to control the environment in terms of mission phases is a third tenet of the ASCATS design philosophy. It is not desirable to simulate an entire ten-day mission on an hour-for-hour basis. Therefore, means are provided to exercise high-activity phases of the mission, such as launch and reentry, as well as to start the simulation prior to certain maneuvers that should be practiced. Also, to maintain continuity in the training exercises, capability is provided to restart the simulated environment in the proper configuration if it is interrupted unexpectedly.

Flight controller training, by nature, must involve contingency operations. Therefore, a fourth tenet of the ASCATS design philosophy is the simulation of various contingency situations. The importance of this aspect of team training has been stressed previously. Controls are made available to the simulation instructors that enable them to fault certain simulated spacecraft functions to cause indications of such things as stuck valves or leaking propellant. The flight controllers are not aware of the types of failures that will be used in a given simulation exercise. The team is then evaluated as to its effectiveness in isolating the problem and in making decisions that correct the malfunction or offset its possible effects on the mission objectives.

The final tenet of the ASCATS design philosophy to be discussed deals with the establishment of both an overall and a detailed monitoring and control capability for the simulation instructor. Such capability is needed to provide the instructor with control of the environmental stimuli in order to gauge and pace the progress of the flight controller. In ASCATS, five simulation instructors occupy four consoles that selectively parallel the flight controllers' consoles in addition to providing environmental displays independent of a selected flight controller console. Visual observation of the flight controllers is maintained from these instructor stations. An additional eight to ten instructors and five to seven consoles, depending on the simulation mode, adjacent to the simulation computing complex are used for controling the simulation environment. The student/instructor ratio is approximately 15 and is estimated to be "about right" for effective monitoring and control of the simulation for *team* training. As previously mentioned, individual flight controller monitoring and evaluation was considered extremely difficult because of the interactions with other personnel. Also, there are approximately twenty major areas and numerous minor areas of specialization within the framework of the flight control team. It was estimated that a student/instructor ratio of 4 or 5 would be required for individual controller evaluation because of the large number of flight controller specialization areas. The exorbitant cost and effort required to provide such detailed individual evaluation was a deterrent to the implementation of such a capability. Instead, the position taken was one that allowed for variation in individual performance as long as the team performance remained satisfactory. Therefore, ASCATS evolved as a team training system. However, it inherently would provide, with regard to equipment, a limited capability for individual evaluation with the major constraint being the ability of the simulation instructors to master a large number of specialization areas to qualify themselves to conduct the training.

Training exercises with ASCATS. The preceding paragraphs have briefly described the flight controller environment, the ASCATS simulation of this environment, and the instructors' capability for controlling the environment and monitoring the flight controller performance. The next topic of discussion should, logically, be the use of ASCATS as a training and educational device. In this respect the questions of quality and quantity of required ASCATS training must be examined. These two factors are dependent on each other and on the complexity of the function for which skills are to be developed. For example, a greater training effort is required for a manned lunar landing mission than for an earth orbit mission simply because the mission complexity is higher for the former. Additional factors affecting the quality and quantity of training include the amount of classroom training and/or on-the-job training personnel have received and the general experience level of the flight control team. It is in this determination of the amount of training required that a somewhat subjective evaluation of the flight control team begins. The determination is, in general, based on the judgment of the flight director and the simulation supervisor.

The quality of the simulation training is dependent on the quality of the simulation preparation effort by the instructors. The simulation instructor must develop a mission profile that will require meaningful action by the flight controllers as a team or individually. Such a profile must be presented as a variation in some portion of the flight controllers' data base in order properly to exercise detection of spacecraft malfunctions by the controllers. Additionally, the problem created by the spacecraft malfunction, in general, will be one that the flight controller will be able to resolve or procedurally bypass within the context of existing mission rules, objectives, and procedures. Alternatively, the problem may be one that emphasizes the need for an additional rule or procedure or one that emphasizes conflicts between existing rules and procedures. Numerous rewrites of the rules and procedures indicate that the quality of the training is quite high in this respect.

It is apparent that the quality and complexity of individual simulations may vary considerably, depending on the individual instructor's efforts in preparing the exercise and its inherent complexity. In all cases, however, the presentation of the problem is identical. Specifically:

1. The problem is indicated by some abnormal change in the flight controller's data base. This requires the controller to exercise his knowledge of spacecraft performance, support system performance, and data base manipulation in order to isolate the symptoms and identify the malfunction. The controller receives no instruction relative to the existence of a problem.

2. The problem requires the controller to make decisions that will either resolve the situation producing the malfunction or bypass its effect. This requires the controller to exercise his knowledge of mission rules, where applicable, or to exercise his judgment in the absence of a mission rule.

3. The problem may or may not require a modification to the planned flight profile. This determination is made after the malfunction has been identified and depends on the corrective action taken. This decision is based quite heavily on the malfunction's impact on desired mission objectives, other existing malfunctions, and mission objective priorities.

4. The flight controllers are allowed to take whatever action they deem necessary to correct the situation without any assistance from the simulation instructors. Because ASCATS realistically reinforces any action taken by the controllers, it is generally believed beneficial to allow this action, even if incorrect, as a means of illustrating to the controller its consequences.

After a mission simulation using ASCATS, a debriefing or group critique of the exercise is held. The general method of evaluation involves a discussion of the team's performance based on instructor observations and flight controller self-critique. Performance is evaluated in terms of five criteria: (1) correct analysis of simulated functions, (2) corrective action accomplished satisfactorily, (3) adherence to mission rules, (4) adherence to flight control procedures, and (5) achievement of flight plan objectives.

Although evaluation in terms of these criteria seems to be a relatively simple matter, it is in fact quite difficult. The problem lies in assigning a "degree-of-difficulty" rating to the individual exercise because there are few clear-cut decision boundaries that can be recognized. Instead, the flight controller may have several rather obvious options available to him as solutions to the problem confronting him, or he may have somewhat more subtle options from which to choose. In either case the degree of difficulty is largely established in terms of the best solution to the problem (within the framework of rules, procedures, and objectives) rather than in terms of the malfunction causing the problem. Because the best solution generally refers to that action that results in the optimal mission profile in terms of mission objective accomplishment, it tends to become subjective because the weighting factors associated with mission objective accomplishment are subjectively assigned. The result is that flight controllers in general arrive at a course of action that is an adequate solution but that may or may not be the *best* solution. Determination of the adequacy of the solution therefore leads to a subjective analysis of flight controller performance with heavy reliance being placed on the judgment of the flight director in ascertaining the "state of readiness" of the flight control team.

The preceding discussion relating to evaluation of the problem solution leads directly to the quantity of simulation training required. It is a relatively simple matter to isolate the high-activity phases of a mission in order to determine which phases should be simulated. It is not so simple to identify clearly all the options available within these phases should contingency action be required. As a result, no attempt is made to train for all contingency situations but rather for representative contingency situations that exercise the flight controller's thinking processes such that he receives training in techniques of attack and resolution, insofar as problem solving is concerned. Here again, however, the determination that the flight controllers' thinking processes are adequate is a subjective one, relying quite heavily on the judgment of the flight director, simulation instructors, and the flight controllers themselves. This determination is aided somewhat by the significant experience level that has been attained in a large number of the personnel involved. This experience level also allows a fairly accurate forecast of training requirements to be made. The mechanics of determining the quantity of training required is therefore one of subjectively estimating the number of times each phase should be simulated in order to instill in the flight controller skill in attacking representative problems. A typical training profile is shown in Table 16-1.

The schedule for conducting flight controller training is largely determined by the availability of support systems such as computer software. In general, however, it has been observed that the flight controller work

Table 16–1. Apollo 11 Simulation Summary

Mission phase simulated	Number of times performed	Total time (hours)
Launch	23	13
Translunar injection	11	28
Translunar coast	2	7
Lunar orbit insertion/Abort	8	31
Lunar descent	33	60
Lunar surface	4	13
Lunar ascent	9	44
Transearth injection	1	2
Reentry	8	24
Total		222

load of simulations plus office work is best accomplished with an average of two to three simulations (ten hours each) per week initiated perhaps seventy-five to ninety days prior to the actual flight. Additional simulation training interferes with office work dealing with development and revision of mission rules and procedures, whereas less simulation training results in a deterioration of skills through lack of use. These numbers, of course, apply to individuals who are already familiar with flight controller functions and primarily need integration into a team. Simulation training is not administered to personnel who are not familiar with flight control functions because experience has shown that they are unable to cope with the complexity of the environment.

ASCATS training problems. It has generally been indicated in the preceding discussion that ASCATS is a most useful system for training flight controllers. However, this system, and concept, is constrained by the very characteristic that makes it useful for such training. Namely, the computer software required for such a system is extensive, as could be suspected from the number and size of computers involved, and its development is complicated by the dynamic nature of the mission profiles to be simulated. For example, it takes as much as a year to develop a complete software package for the system; however, the mission profiles are not generally accurately defined at this time. ASCATS software has been developed in modular fashion to allow maximal flexibility in responding to profile changes, spacecraft changes, and so on, but there are situations in which training must be conducted with an obsolete environmental configuration because of lengthy software response time. Of course, these problems can generally be eliminated after initial software development if the environment remains relatively stable.

ASCATS, because it is complicated and requires the use of extensive support facilities, is relatively expensive. Training time must be rigidly regulated, with little time for experimentation. For example, it has not been practical to take a single flight controller, place him at a console, and give him specialized training in which he can experiment with various actions affecting spacecraft operation. In other words, ASCATS does not lend itself to part-task training.

Summary. ASCATS is a team training system designed to provide for the flight controllers an environment that is as realistic as possible. It does this by presenting a real-time simulated mission interface to MCC, through which the flight controllers exercise their monitoring and control functions. Nearly all the training carried out in this environment is designed to provide the flight controllers with normal and contingency situations that give them the opportunity to integrate their individual and team skills through real-time decision making. Their performance rating, in accomplishing these functions, is a subjective determination based on the judgment of recognized authorities in the specific areas of responsibility. This method of training has proved valuable and has resulted in flight control teams that are generally better trained than would otherwise have been possible.

One important characteristic of the space program has been the spin-off of useful knowledge and techniques into other application areas. It is hoped that the area of education can profit as well. The remainder of this chapter will discuss some possible educational implications suggested by the preceding description of ASCATS and its use.

Some Implications for Education

From the preceding description it is evident that the tasks for which flight controllers must be trained are complex, involving extensive interactions of men, equipment, and data. The requirement of a high-fidelity simulation, therefore, results in a training environment that is also complex. In addition to the complexity of the training, there is the close relationship between the flight controller's job and his training requirements; the mission environment of the flight controller is well defined, and the implications for training simulations are quite clear.

The school setting, however, is not characterized by the same degree of complexity with its attendant high cost. In addition, the direct application of schooling to specific occupational tasks is difficult, especially for elementary and secondary schools. Not only are the vocational goals vague for many students, but often the specific tasks associated with these vocations are not well defined. Also, unlike the flight controller, the student usually does not have the opportunity to direct his education in accordance with vocational experiences or to restructure vocational tasks based on what he is learning. On what basis, then, can implications of the specialized flight controller training be developed for the more general educational environment?

Flight controller training and the use of the computer. To answer the preceding question, it should be noted that for both flight controller training and education in the schools there are interactions among the common elements of students, teachers, and subject matter. Therefore, the following identification of some of the characteristic ways in which the computer has actually been involved in these interactions for flight controller training simulations will be the basis for suggesting similar computer applications to the interactions in more familiar educational situations.

1. The computer provides flight controllers with a data base that gives them the capability to monitor and control both their mission and training environment. Significantly, the flight controllers themselves have been involved in the definition of this data base and its display.

2. The realism of the training exercises, made possible by the computer generation of simulated data, provides challenging and interesting problems that are highly motivating to the participants. The associated problem-solving activity not only makes practice in problem solving possible but helps the flight controllers to integrate past learning and to direct their future study.

3. The computer provides the simulation instructor with the capability to monitor, evaluate, and control the training environment. For a given training session the instructor establishes the problem constraints under which the flight controllers operate. Based on the evaluation of their performance, the constraints of the current or succeeding training exercises can be manipulated by the instructor in accordance with observed strengths and weaknesses.

4. Individual flight controllers are specialists in different areas. The computer-based training system makes it possible to provide exercises that integrate these individual skills into the total team performance necessary for accomplishing the mission objectives.

In flight controller training, then, computers are involved in the interaction of students, instructors, and subject matter in a way that utilizes the computers' information-processing capabilities. The flight controller operates in terms of data expected from the mission environment, and the simulation instructor interacts with an environment that not only includes the data available to the flight controllers but data indicating flight controller activity and the status of the simulation system as well. Such an emphasis on the availability of flexible data gathering and representation techniques for both student and instructor expedites the exercise of human judgment during training sessions.

Computer augmentation of problem-solving activities in the schools.

What do the uses of the computer in flight controller training, as identified in the preceding four points, suggest regarding the more common educational environment? For the purpose of this chapter the answer is not sought in terms of new or unique principles of learning. Certainly drill and tutorial interactions were involved in learning situations, for example, before the computer was introduced, as described in Chapter 12 by Suppes and Morningstar. Similarly, present implications are sought with reference to the kinds of worthwhile teaching techniques that might be enhanced by the use of a computer in ways suggested by the computer's involvement in flight controller training.

Lagowski, in Chapter 14, has pointed out one such use—the computer simulation of chemistry experiments. This can be regarded as a special case of a more general type of learning activity, often referred to as problem solving. One general way of thinking about the characteristics of problem-solving activities suggests the following (Mills and Dean, 1960):

1. A difficulty is recognized.
2. The problem is clarified and defined.
3. A search for clues is made.
4. Various suggestions are made and are evaluated or tried out.
5. A suggested solution is accepted, or the thinker gives up in defeat.

This characterization of the nature of problem-solving activities seems to be quite descriptive of the flight controller's training environment. The uses of the computer in this environment, in turn, suggest applications of the computer to problem-solving activities in more general educational situations. For convenience in discussing these applications a distinction will be made between computer-assisted instruction and computer-augmented instruction (Allen and Bushnell, 1967). It is not intended for this distinction as used in the present context to be a rigorous one but rather to indicate a difference in emphasis. Computer-assisted instruction, as exemplified by drill and tutorial programs, will describe the use of a computer to dispense programmed sequences of instruction in response to student performance. Computer-augmented instruction, however, will emphasize the use of the computer as an aid to the student for computation or in problem-solving activity as characterized above. Of course, features of both computer-assisted and computer-augmented instructional programs could be combined in a single instructional system if desired.

It should also be noted that although simulation techniques have been justified for flight controller training in the first part of this chapter, and are illustrated in examples in the second part, they are not the only techniques suitable for engaging learners in problem-solving activities. However, a simulation does offer several advantages. The process being simulated is useful as a way of organizing various aspects of the problem. A simulation suggests ways the data base can be presented in terms of the general features of the problem. A meaningful context in which to learn specific skills can be provided in a simulation exercise—a result cited by Guilford and Tenopyr (1968) as being important if a student is to be able to use the concepts being taught. Finally, there are positive motivational advantages in the use of a simulation.

The learning and motivational benefits of the meaningful use of problem-solving activities in the classroom are emphasized in a book edited by Michael entitled *Teaching for Creative Endeavor* (1968). The usefulness of this emphasis is stressed for students from kindergarten through college in a wide range of subjects including science, social studies, and language arts. One of the comments regarding such teaching for creativity reflects the interactions identified earlier: "Instruction could be improved by a substantial factor if the teachers could read the chapters in textbooks in advance and would allow pupils to perform the activities suggested, to collect their own data, to draw their own inferences, to make their own predictions, to test their own predictions against the reality of the world, and then to allow them to read the chapter to see whether the authors agree with what the children themselves have found on their own initiative" (Fischler, 1968, p. 114). Although the author is referring in this instance to the study of the natural sciences, the comment captures the spirit of the expressions of contributors from other subject matter areas represented in the book.

Teachers have often encouraged individual and group projects as a way of establishing appealing problem-solving situations to integrate and direct the learning of their students. But in the large classes with which most teachers are confronted, the meaningful use of such projects is limited by the difficulties involved in planning, administering, and evaluating them. In contrasting discovery learning and reception learning, Ausubel has pointed out that "problem-solving methods of instruction are incomparably more time-consuming than the method of verbal presentation" (1961, p. 22). The following examples are illustrations of some of the possible uses of a computer in problem-solving activities to make such projects not only less time-consuming but more manageable in general. The purpose of these examples is to bring out in a general way some of the interactions among students, teachers, and subject matter that lend themselves to organization and control through the implementation of a computer in ways related to the four points identified for flight controller training. After the examples have been presented, implications will be considered for the design and development of such programs.

Examples of some possible computer-augmented projects. Suppose a high school teacher decides to organize a study of the principles of optics around the design of a telescope. At a simple level he may wish the design to be based on combinations of specific lenses. For a more powerful integration of the principles he may choose objectives of a more general sort, so that the student must also design the lenses involved. With the usual classroom resources, the administering of such projects often becomes quite complex, especially if the project is to be a nontrivial one in terms of its pedagogical value. It is often difficult to vary the characteristics of the basic problem among individuals or groups to ensure that each is indeed working through the project rather than using the results of other students' work. The expense of maintaining a large inventory of components for the telescopes is usually prohibitive, and there is the problem of having suitable work space. The teacher is likely to have difficulty monitoring the work and providing useful guidance to the students. Also, an excessive amount of time may be necessary for the manipulation of the apparatus in comparison to the time spent on activities that are important for the actual integration of theoretical principles. Although the manipulative experience is useful if one is learning how to actually build a telescope, it can interfere with the learning objectives of the project.

By involving a computer in the preceding project, several of these problems can be overcome. Each individual's project can be similar in its basic objectives but differ in the parameters required for the algorithms used for modeling various optical relationships. Thus unique solutions can be required for each individual, with additional variations possible for examination purposes. Problems associated with terminal utilization replace the more rigid restraints of material and space. Records of terminal activities summarized by the computer prepare the teacher for an active role in aiding the goup. Based on the student's progress, certain constraints can be changed to either simplify or extend the complexity of the problem. Finally, one of the most important advantages of such a computer-augmented project is that certain activities that ordinarily consume much time in the real world, but that have limited value insofar as the learning objectives are concerned, can be eliminated from the simulation. In other words, the degree of "fidelity" of the simulation, either physical or psychological (McCormick, 1964), can be manipulated in accordance with the objectives of the problem-solving activity.

A project such as the one described is applicable on an individual basis or for small groups. A simulation approach can be used to encourage more group integration than occurs with many computer-assisted instruction programs. For flight controllers, team training is conducted out of necessity. But what are the advantages of such group activity in the normal school situation? The benefit here seems to be largely motivational. Teachers sometimes comment that they wish they could get students to work as hard and to display as much enthusiasm in the classroom as they often do when involved in such activities as the yearbook staff or the school paper. Certainly students are grouped together in the classroom but the characteristic motivational aspects of a team relationship are difficult to achieve. Part of this problem, as in the previous example, may be administrative. If so, the computer has a contribution to make toward focusing group effort by giving the teacher and student a monitor and control capability beyond that available in the usual classroom situation.

As an example of a more complex project requiring interaction among groups consider an industrial arts electronics class in which it is desired to organize a class project around the computer-augmented design of a radio receiver. Different groups in the class are made responsible for different stages of the system. One group, for example, might be required to "build" the audio amplifier; and another, the I-F stage. What is involved here is student interaction with simulation models that allow the manipulation of prescribed components to give a variety of idealized operations and outputs. Admittedly, such an idealized situation does not involve the range of problems associated with actually building a radio receiver. But if the goal is to integrate theoretical principles or to motivate a study of the principles in a way that can be monitored and controlled by the instructor, such a lack of this kind of realism is not critical. The use of a computer for such a purpose does not preclude projects in which electronic equipment is actually built if those skills are part of the instructional objectives.

In addition to accomplishing the tasks related to a specific stage of the radio receiver, the students are also involved with problems of interfacing between stages. The design required by a given group is dependent on the output of the stages designed by other groups. Experience in communicating with other people as data sources becomes part of the project. In other classroom situations the use of exercises such as management games is another way to involve students in such experiences.

The effective use of the computer in group projects is going to require an examination of some questions about the nature of individual learning in a team setting. For example, if each member is concerned with some part of the overall problem, how much is he likely to learn about the problem's other aspects? To what extent does the opportunity of team members to interact make the overall learning effort more efficient than in cases in which such interaction is minimized? In what ways can measures of team performance be indicative of individual performance?

Uses of computers in projects or other problem-solving activities need not be restricted to scientific subjects. Classroom courses such as consumer mathematics, for example, are often a part of the secondary school curriculum with the intent of helping students become thoughtful and informed consumers. The intent often miscarries in its implementation, however, with the course ending up as a place for students who are unable or unwilling to take algebra and related college preparatory mathematics courses. Such classes are difficult to motivate. They are also unattractive to the better students who could profit from consumer education but who do not wish to waste their time with extensive remedial work. In this situation, activities that involve the computer simulation of realistic consumer situations associated with such things as buying on the installment plan or acquiring insurance are appropriate. The concreteness of such problems would likely be motivating to the students, and individual differences are better accommodated through the control of remediation and problem difficulty. Students with a variety of background preparation could participate under a set of constraints commensurate with their abilities.

Some implications for program design and development. The preceding examples have illustrated in a general way some of the things involved in the implementation within the school environment of features identified earlier with the use of the computer in flight controller training. Another way to explore the implications of these features is to compare, in terms of program design and development, some of the aspects of computer-augmented instruction programs to those more oriented toward a tutorial approach. To establish a context for such a comparison, assume some set of instructional objectives that could, with minor adaptation, serve equally well for the definition of a simulation or a tutorial program. (This is not to say, of course, that all situations lend themselves to both approaches.) Along what general lines would design and development differ for these programs? Realizing that there are variations in characteristics within both types of programs, three such differences in emphasis will be considered.

First of all, there is a difference in the amount of subject-matter content for display at the terminal station. The actual program size, of course, would depend on features of the author language and whether all the content was coded into the program or presented at a peripheral device, such as a slide projector, to supplement the display at the terminal CRT or typewriter. The program size, in turn, has implications for requirements related to entering and storing the program on the system. It is likely that a simulation program designed to meet instructional objectives similar to those for a given tutorial program would often be significantly smaller, because the resulting problem-solving activity is geared to help the student organize his use of a variety of available external subject-matter resources.

In the second place, some of the ways of accommodating individual differences may be simpler for computer-augmented instruction programs than for the tutorial type. Tutorial programs may involve rather detailed logic for processing and evaluating student responses in order to provide alternative learning paths according to certain built-in individualization rules. Actually, the programming necessary to support such rules seems not to be as much a problem as the prescription of the rules themselves (Suppes, 1967). In a simulation program, on the other hand, individualization is emphasized in terms of providing the student with a data base and a specific problem as a framework for self-directed learning. Such a system gives him the opportunity to choose the data to be displayed, the form of its representation, and the external sources of information to aid him as he encounters particular aspects of the problem. There are fewer restrictions on possible learning paths. The student can "cut and try" solutions and has the opportunity to learn from incorrect responses or even discover novel ones. The learning process is likely to be more stimulating than in a corresponding tutorial interaction because the learning environment is responsive to the student's needs, both in terms of the control he has over the data and the control exercised by the teacher as he evaluates student progress and uses his judgment to modify the problem in ways that simplify, emphasize, or enrich. With a tutorial program the teacher may have some options in its use, but not the degree of immediate control of problem constraints he could have with a simulation program. Such control is especially useful for making possible problem-solving activities at different educational levels for the same basic problem.

Guilford and Tenopyr (1968) emphasize the efficacy of discovery learning for the retention of knowledge. Tutorial programs can be used in this way, but although the Socratic approach involved may lead a student step by step to the point where he "discovers" the solution, he may not be able to reconstruct the process by which he got there or transfer the principles to another problem-solving situation (Willoughby, 1968). The point here is not that simulation techniques can replace the need for tutorial programs but that providing for individualization is not necessarily restricted to the tutorial program approach. As Rubin comments, "learning through inquiry does not imply that the student must acquire all his knowledge through self-discovery. What it does imply is something profoundly important in learning: that periodically the student ought to use his aggregation of data, however accumulated, in attacking problems so that he gives meaning to his information and order to his conceptual understanding and his rational insights" (1968, p. 76).

As a third aspect of program development it would seem that simulation systems can be designed in a more modular fashion than is possible for tutorial programs in general. Subroutines for accessing and representing data could be common across several different simulation applications. A package of basic routines could be prepared with features that permit user modification or definition of the simulation models. Tutorial programs, on the other hand, are designed with fewer options for user modification of the system to fit specific situations. Another point to consider is that the use of a data base, such as provided by a simulation system, lends itself to the development of a consistent language for communication with the system in much the same way that the flight controllers and instructors control their system through the entry of special formatted statements from their terminals. Such a language might involve a set of operators geared to data manipulation much in the same way that languages such as APL (Falkoff and Iverson, 1968) provide operators for computational purposes. Such a user control language would standardize some of the student responses and give some consistency in the use of the computer for a variety of problem-solving situations.

Some implications for the school curriculum. The implications of the flight controller training simulations have been discussed so far in terms of the development and implementation of computer programs for education in general. But the uses of the computer in the ways described have their own implications for the school curriculum as well. Two such implications should be noted.

The first of these implications involves data management skills associated with the problems and techniques related to the gathering, representing, manipulating, and interpreting of data. These skills not only have immediate application to the functioning of the student in his current educational environment, especially if computer-augmented instruction is involved, but also cut across vocational boundaries in that they have potential use in whatever vocation a student eventually enters. That such skills are important for education in problem solving has been emphasized by Guilford and Tenopyr (1968), who stress that students should not only have *practice* in solving a wide variety of problems but have *training* in the basic abilities associated with the productive performance of problem-solving tasks.

Computer-augmented problem solving could be one way to involve students in interactive experiences that teach efficient data management methods as well as provide them with opportunities to explore methods on their own. As a specific example, consider the simulation of the data structures associated with the ordinary library. If a series of realistic problems related to the use of library facilities were provided along with a computer simulation of features related to document retrieval, much of the orientation to library use could be controlled and monitored efficiently with a minimum of disruption of the actual facilities. This is just one of the many areas related to data management techniques that are scattered throughout the school curriculum and that might well be integrated into a simulation package.

The second implication for the school curriculum is related to the fact that the flight controller participates in the definition of mission rules and the organization of the data with which he interacts. Thus he not only shapes his working environment but to some extent his training environment as well. The extent to which a student should be permitted to participate in defining his learning experiences in a particular area of study involves, of course, many factors. Beyond the identification of those factors is the point that computer-augmented instruction can make it possible to overcome some of the limitations of the usual school setting that make it difficult for the student to obtain information about his interests and learning needs.

Would computer-augmented composition of music (Gill, 1963; Smith and Smith, 1966), for example, provide the depth of experience in the area of music theory that would enable the student with a nominal musical background to determine if he were interested in going into the subject more deeply? Would the opportunity to become involved with general problems from major subject-matter areas through simulation be useful to the student for making decisions about investigating these subjects further? Beyond making it possible for the student to gain insight into his interests, it might be feasible to help the student decide what courses to take to meet his educational needs, especially at the more specialized levels of study. For example, a student entering a graduate program could be given the opportunity to interact through simulation with the kinds of problems he is interested in as one basis for his selection of course offerings. One such problem area in psychology could be in experimental design in which a simulation program could help the student become familiar with design errors, statistical techniques, and other information that he could then use in the selection of topics for study.

Concluding Comments

A good teacher will lead a class in a variety of activities as he seeks to encourage learning. In some situations he may use a drill, whereas in others a tutorial type of interaction may seem more appropriate. He may wish to direct a variety of stimulating problem-solving activities to serve either as a vehicle for teaching specific subject matter or as a way of providing a context in which students may gain experience in problem solving itself. All these approaches tend to become increasingly hard to use to their maximal effectiveness as the size of the class increases. Because of its information-processing capabilities, the computer can be a useful tool to aid the teacher in the management of the various aspects of the educational environment associated with any of these activities.

The different modes of instruction mentioned involve the student, teacher, and subject matter in different kinds of interactions. The use of ASCATS, as described in the first part of this chapter, is an example of an existing application of the computer to problem-solving kinds of interaction. The second part of the chapter points out some of the implications for involving the computer in similar interactions in the classroom environment as well as implications for the nature of the interactions themselves.

Although it has not been within the scope of this chapter to discuss cost and other problems associated with the implementation of computers in the classroom, one point is worth considering. For a given set of instructional objectives, simulation and other types of computer-augmented instructional programs for problem-solving activities are not only quite powerful in their potential, but they may be simpler and cheaper to develop and implement than tutorial programs designed to satisfy very similar objectives. In addition, the use of computers to augment instruction in the ways described makes it feasible to fit into the rather closely constrained school environment a range of problems whose power as organizers, integrators, and motivators of learning would not otherwise be consistently used.

REFERENCES

Allen, D. W., and Bushnell, D. D. 1967. Developing EDP systems: issues and recommendations. In *The computer in American education,* eds. D. D. Bushnell and D. W. Allen. New York: Wiley, pp. 226–238.

Ausubel, D. P. 1961. In defense of verbal learning. *Educational theory* 11:15–25.

Falkoff, A. D., and Iverson, K. E. 1968. The APL/360 terminal system. In *ACM symposium on experimental systems for applied mathematics.* New York: Academic Press.

Fischler, A. S. 1968. The natural sciences. In *Teaching for creative endeavor,* ed. W. B. Michael. Bloomington: Indiana Univ. Press, pp. 101–114.

Gill, S. 1963. A technique for the composition of music in a computer. *The Computer Journal* 6(2):129–133.

Guilford, J. P., and Tenopyr, M. L. 1968. Implications of the structure-of-intellect model for high school and college students. In *Teaching for creative endeavor,* ed. W. B. Michael. Bloomington: Indiana Univ. Press, pp. 25–45.

McCormick, E. J. 1964. *Human factors engineering.* New York: McGraw-Hill.

Michael, W. B., ed. 1968. *Teaching for creative endeavor.* Bloomington: Indiana Univ. Press.

Mills, L. C., and Dean, P. M. 1960. *Problem-solving methods in science teaching.* Science Manpower Project Monographs. New York: Teachers College, Columbia Univ.

Rubin, L. J. 1968. Creativity and the curriculum. In *Teaching for creative endeavor,* ed. W. B. Michael. Bloomington: Indiana Univ. Press, pp. 74–89.

Smith, K. U., and Smith, M. F. 1966. *Cybernetic principles of learning and educational design.* New York: Holt, Rinehart and Winston.

Suppes, P. 1967. On using computers to individualize instruction. In *The Computer in American education,* eds. D. D. Bushnell and D. W. Allen. New York: Wiley, pp. 11–24.

Willoughby, S. S. 1968. Secondary school mathematics. In *Teaching for creative endeavor,* ed. W. B. Michael. Bloomington: Indiana Univ. Press, pp. 115–130.

17

J. C. R. Licklider

A Critique of the Apollo System and Its Educational Implications

Chapter 16 by Shelley and Groom is essentially two chapters. The first deals specifically with the training of flight controllers and with the Apollo Simulation, Checkout, and Training System (ASCATS), not with education in school or education in general. The second deals with ways in which computers might augment education in school and does not owe any large debt directly to ASCATS or, for that matter, to space missions or space technology. The paucity of flow from "Chapter 1" to "Chapter 2" is disappointing, but the description of the training of flight controllers provided by the first is clear, and the ideas about *computer-augmented instruction* (as distinguished from *computer-assisted instruction*) presented in the second are good.

Economics

ASCATS is a large, complex system of computers and consoles connected to flight trainers and the Manned Space Flight Network. It affords each student (flight controller) his own data base and his own displays and controls and places at his service a comprehensive array of mission-oriented and training-oriented computer programs, together with a "language" through which to command them and interact with them. It puts each student into interaction also with other students and under computer-aided monitoring by instructors in a situation or process controlled through computers by instructors. Is the foregoing a valuable paradigm for school systems to adopt, or is it in principle not, or do economic considerations preclude it insofar as schools are concerned? Shelley and Groom do not examine the economics further than to admit that ASCATS is expensive. I would argue that the paradigm is so important for school education that many more people (than are) should be working, even now, to overcome the cost obstacle. It is not enough that the cost of a unit of information processing tends to halve in about two years. Something special is required to develop educational applications, and something even more special is required to make them affordable.

Team Training

ASCATS provides team training but not part-task training on an individual basis. Is that a great shortcoming? Within the Apollo context, Shelley and Groom appear to regret the restriction to team training—but only mildly. Within the school context, the shortcoming would be severely regrettable. The shortcoming stems not from the nature of computers or simulations but from the nature of the flight controllers' tasks. Computer-augmented instruction in schools need not be (and should not be) limited to team training.

Training or Education?

In the first part of their chapter (description of ASCATS and the training of flight controllers) Shelley and Groom use the word *training,* whereas in the second part (discussion of educational implications) they use the word *education*. What about the educational implications of that fact? I think they stem from this—that it is easier to train than to educate. I think that the ratio of difficulty of education to training will increase as complex computer systems are introduced and that, as a consequence, the tendency to substitute training for education will increase. I think that it would be very bad to permit this substitution to occur; much thought and work will be required to prevent it. I mean, of course, the substitution of the process of training for the process of education, not merely the substitution of the word *training* for the word *education*.

Motivation

Shelley and Groom emphasize the motivational quality of interacting with a well-programmed computer. Let me emphasize it again; it deserves great emphasis. Interaction—affecting outcomes and being affected by them; making responses to stimuli and having your responses stimulate someone or something else, whose responses then stimulate you—is one of the main keys to motivation. In this connection, however, Shelley and Groom stress realism. I think that realism per se is not very important. The important thing, in addition to interaction, is to include within the simulation the significant features of the situation or process simulated. Thus, the other important thing is abstraction. Realism is very expensive. Abstraction reduces costs. But it is not easy to abstract the right things. If you do not know what is significant or how to abstract it, realism provides insurance, but it is expensive insurance. In ASCATS the insurance provided by realism was probably worth the cost. In the school it will not be. The motivating force of interaction, on the other hand, will be more valuable in the school than in ASCATS.

Participation in Formulation

As Shelley and Groom point out, the student flight controllers contributed to the definition of the mission rules and procedures, to the specification of their own data bases, displays, and controls. They helped to invent the game they played. That fact had motivational significance. The motivating quality of participation in formulation is well known in school educational circles, but it will be difficult to implement the idea effectively in the school context until schools have computer-augmented instruction.

Criteria

Shelley and Groom's treatment of criteria does not make me happy, but in the ASCATS context it may not be essential to handle the criterion problem precisely. It is probably fairly easy to tell whether an Apollo mission is a success or a disaster, and an Apollo mission is likely to be considered a success if it is not a disaster. In the school context, on the other hand, there are few missions that have such clear and immediate outcomes, and the problem of criteria is therefore more difficult. But good criteria are necessary. They are especially necessary in computer-based games and simulations that are inherently complex and unrepeatable. The experience of participating in computer-based games and simulations tends to become an end in itself. It is so reinforcing, so energizing—such an experience—that questions of "who actually learned what about what?" tend to be pushed into the background in favor of planning to make the next "run" even more elaborate and more involved. Perhaps this is part of the problem that arises when "education for life" is made more and more like life: It becomes more and more difficult to make sure that it is education.

Monitoring of Performance

The computer can, of course, record many aspects of the student's performance and facilitate monitoring and evaluation by the instructor. Moreover, the computer can make it possible actually to use the wealth of data in determining what the student should do next. These ideas existed before ASCATS. However, in ASCATS they have probably been implemented more fully than they have been implemented in computer-assisted-instruction and computer-managed-instruction systems.

Programming

In ASCATS the flight controllers evidently do no programming; they interact with programs prepared (partly to their order, but with a very long time from order to delivery) by specialist programmers. Taking advantage of flexibility built into the programs by the specialist programmers, the flight controllers do what they can to adapt the programs to the needs and concepts that are current at the time of actual use. Problems of constraint surely arise, but perhaps the flight controllers' ideas do not change enough from day to day to make them wish they could get in there and rewrite some of the programs overnight in order to try out a new technique during the next simulation test. In the school situation, however, at least during the early years of computer-augmented instruction, there should be a continual flow of new and different—and sometimes better—ideas about method, technique, and content. The only way to achieve the desired rapid evolution will be to permit quick "spontaneous variation" through on-the-spot program modification and effective "natural selection" through competitive comparison and evaluation. I think I see how to set up such an accelerated Darwinian process in a graduate school or even in an undergraduate college. To set one up in a secondary or a primary school, graduate students or professional programmers would have to be brought in en masse. In any event, computer-augmented-instruction systems should themselves be computer-augmentable. They should be amenable to on-line modification and should provide good facilities for their own improvement through on-line programming.

Complex Man-Machine Systems: Discussion

Discussion of the benefits of simulation as a mode of computer-assisted learning expanded along a number of dimensions: fidelity, abstraction, selected incidents, compression or expansion of time and space, and student manipulation of the underlying model. The last one in the list, student interaction with the designer's representation of the real world, is itself an interesting and potentially powerful use of interactive systems.

The Apollo simulation has been constructed to approximate as closely as possible the flight controllers' actual experiences during a mission. The expensive fidelity is worth the cost if use of the simulation identifies inconsistencies in the flight plan or associated rules and provides an environment in which to test the skills and emotional reactions of the operators.

A less faithful representation of the flight that focused on essential component skills would almost certainly be a more cost-effective training device, not only through savings in computer time and additional hardware construction but by a reduction in training time as well. However, given the cost of each mission, the time scale during which training and checkout must be completed, and the requirements of human safety, the best strategy has been to work as near to the real situation as possible.

Because the purpose has been to imitate the real mission without risking lives of the flight team or loss of the equipment, ASCATS should not be expected to explore simulation as a cost-effective training device.

Examination of the dimensions of abstraction and fidelity expose an interesting relationship between trainer understanding of performance requirements and program control of trainee activity. Those facts, procedures, and skills that are well understood by the designers of the training system are presented via reference manuals, textbooks, training films, and perhaps programmed texts. When the trainer is not yet sure of either what he wants the trainee to be able to do or how competency should be developed, he uses a lecture approach with some discussion. Perhaps it is when the trainer does not even trust himself to talk about the essential skills and attitudes that he simply puts the trainee in the situation or some close approximation.

The control that the trainer has over practice and achievement increases as the fidelity of the practice situation is reduced; typically the abstraction of the situation is increased at the same time. However, the importance of the simulation experience in preparation for the flight would not decrease; in fact, the payoffs probably increase when the trainee comes to the simulation with more intellectual tools and working concepts acquired in advance of the practice session.

The facility for compression or expansion of time and for the representation of geographically distributed events via simulation is one important factor in deciding whether a training exercise requires a computer. Other considerations are complexity of the model and of the feedback to the trainee, who must manage information and make decisions.

For those situations in which fidelity of the model may be neither possible nor desirable, a second phase of activity may be important in a computer-based learning exercise. After the student has performed as a manager or problem solver playing by the rules of the game designed by his professor, he should explore the underlying model in order to understand it as only one of a number of possible representations of the process. He should see that the model was designed to demonstrate or isolate for study some set of concepts or relationships. Other designs lead to other forms of the game, other styles of play, and one student might modify the model for use by another student. He should see that the model is a research tool for exploration of models and hypotheses, not a complete representation of the real phenomena.

Computer simulation in education and training has considerable attractiveness, especially in comparison with the requirements set down for validation of and justification for computer-aided exposition of facts and concepts. It seems to be a good thing to give students experience doing something that appears to be similar to tasks they are expected to perform later. Perhaps validation is not necessary beyond the approval of persons considered expert in that area of training or education. However, the attractiveness of the system can seduce users into attributing effectiveness to nonessential (and costly) attributes. On the other hand, the particular design of a model, for example, in business or social relations, can inadvertently influence a learner in directions not intended by the designer. Objectives and associated values must be an important consideration.

PART **IX**

Guidance and Counseling

Can a machine counsel? This provocative question forms the basis for Chapter 18 by Ellis and Tiedeman. After a general discussion of the similarities and differences between the human counselor and the computer, Ellis and Tiedeman describe the Information System for Vocational Decisions Project in which Harvard University and a number of school systems in New England participate. Thirteen major data files, ranging from the student's own biographical and test data to occupation files and information about educational institutions, are stored in the computer memory from which the student can call forth information as needed in exploring vocational or educational areas and in attempting to reach decisions. A brief description is given of the occupations data file to illustrate the way in which a student can interact with the information stored in the computer. A detailed example of a student exploring his choice of a college is also presented.

Agreeing in general with Ellis and Tiedeman, Super in Chapter 19 comments on other important issues in the use of a computer system for counseling or guidance purposes. Machines may never be able to counsel in the fullest sense of the term, but they will provide a new order of information essential to intelligent planning on the part of the student who is seeking guidance.

18

Allan B. Ellis and David V. Tiedeman

Can a Machine Counsel?[1]

Just about everyone who spends his time trying to figure out what counseling in education is all about agrees that only human beings can counsel. These men—school counselors, professors of guidance, counseling psychologists, and the like—disagree with each other on all the other matters in their profession, and this makes the one thing they agree about that much more powerful. Indeed the power of this agreement and the common sense on which it is based make the question "Can a machine counsel?" a very strange thing to ask. By it we seem to be wondering whether or not something can be human and nonhuman at the same time, and it must be difficult to imagine how we can take our question seriously. To make matters worse, we are willing to admit, for the duration of the next few paragraphs at least, that people are correct when they say that only human beings can counsel. But we do not consider this any contradiction because we go along with the consensus only to suggest that the answer to a question can be unrelated to the posing of it. We assert—and those who recall the works of G. E. Moore, Russell, Wittgenstein, and the other philosophers of language will know this is not a new idea—that the trouble with questions is that they seem so strongly to demand answers. People tend to judge questions by whether or not they can answer them or on their willingness to live with the answers. But questions are good for other things, of course, besides the answers to which they lead.

Our intention with the question of this chapter is to gain perspective on our feelings about the activity of counseling. One thing a question can do,

1. The work presented herein was supported in part by Grant No. OEG-1-6-061819-2240 of the U.S. Office of Education under terms of the Vocational Education Act of 1963.

of course, is lead to other questions, and we hope to get from our perspective a better sense of what those other questions are that must be considered when coming to terms with our idea of counseling. Because of what machines are, we accomplish our task best, we think, by using the word *machine* the way we do in our question.

Machines execute procedures and each machine is the embodiment of the procedure it executes. This is an important relationship that exists for all machines; people are just not in the habit of speaking about machines in this way. It means, of course, that knowing in detail what a particular machine does—how it works—is enough to know what procedure it is executing. The thing that counts about a machine is the way it behaves and this behavior is prescribed by the procedure it executes. All automation, far from being magical as some suppose, is nothing more than the physical expression of well-formed procedures.

When we say that a machine is the embodiment of the procedure it executes, we are saying, in effect, that a statement of a procedure *describes* the machine needed to carry out that procedure. Thus *mechanizing* means thinking about procedure, not about hardware, and after we state a procedure explicitly, we should not really be surprised that a machine can be built to execute it.

To make things simpler in this chapter, we shall confine ourselves to computers instead of machines in general. This poses no real restriction, however, because a computer is a device whose job it is to accept descriptions of other machines and to imitate the behavior of those machines. This description is called a computer program and is usually thought of as a set of instructions for what the machine is to do. But a computer program is more like a blueprint that the computer uses to build itself into the particular machine needed to execute the particular procedure described by the program. It is as though the computer were armed with pliers and screwdriver, rebuilding itself to conform step by step to the elements of our procedure. Having done this, the computer becomes the machine our program described, and it will then function as that machine.

A computer without a program will do nothing, whether or not it is plugged in, because computers are not like other machines. In a sense the computer is not a machine at all in its own right, and yet it can become many machines. For example, one may build an address printing machine, or he may write a program that will turn a computer into an address printing machine. In either case the results will be the same with the exception that even though both machines would be operationally equivalent they would be different from each other in one crucial respect: The computer can do other things tomorrow. Whereas the power of most machines is in what they do, the power of the computer rests in what it can become, and the essential idea of a computer is that it is an incomplete machine ready to be completed in an infinite number of ways, each way producing a different machine. Thus a computer program is at the same time an explicit statement of a procedure and the blueprint of a machine needed to carry it out, and whether or not a computer can execute a given procedure depends primarily on how well we understand the components of that procedure and how imaginative we are in conceiving procedures in terms of the basic elements of which they are comprised. Centering our attention on a computer, therefore, has the advantage that we depict a machine in terms of such a procedural statement and thus maintain a clearer attitude about machines and their relation to procedures.

Now this attitude about machines is helpful to us because, contrary to first impressions, the form of our question does not impose any preconceived notions on our exploration of counseling. We hope, with this attitude, to avoid the kind of commitment that led Christopher Columbus, for example, to think that Watling Island was the East Indies or the kind of vision that led Abel Tasman to discover two islands in the southern hemisphere and at the same time to sail completely around the continent of Australia without ever noticing it was there.

One thing this attitude about machines—and its subsequent application to the activity of counseling—frees us from is a concern about the physical aspects of machines. If there is such a thing as a counseling machine, we need not worry about whether or not it must have arms and legs. Furthermore, we are freed from the somewhat more general worry of whether or not such a machine should be able to smile or frown or nod sympathetically. We may discover later, of course, that these or similar characteristics are necessary parts of our notion of the act of counseling, but our question does not impose this on us and therefore we do not start out needing to believe that such is the case. In this spirit our question represents a point of view about problems. As with all points of view we do not expect resolution from it but rather some insight into the topography of the problem under consideration. This is why the answer to the question, even if it happens to come out of our analysis, is secondary to the analysis itself.

Imitation and Meaning

We begin this analysis by considering the meaning of the question "Can a machine counsel?" To do this, we first look at the procedure adopted by the late Alan M. Turing in his consideration of a similar question. In 1950 Turing, who was an eminent mathematician and logician in England, published an article entitled "Computing Machinery and Intelligence" in which he proposed to examine the question of whether or not a machine can think. His first step was to replace this question by another "which is closely related to it and is expressed in relatively unambiguous words." He said:

> The new form of the problem can be described in terms of a game which we call the "imitation game." It is played with three people, a man (A), a woman (B), and an interrogator (C) who may be of either sex. The interrogator stays in a room apart from the other two. The object of the game for the interrogator is to determine which of the other two is the man and which is the woman. He knows them by labels X and Y, and at the end of the game he says either "X is A and Y is B" or "X is B and Y is A." The interrogator is allowed to put questions to A and B thus:
>
> C: Will X please tell me the length of his or her hair? Now suppose X is actually A, then A must answer. It is A's object in the game to try to cause C to make the wrong identification. His answer might therefore be, "My hair is shingled, and the longest strands are about nine inches long."
>
> In order that tones of voice may not help the interrogator the answers should be written, or better still, typewritten. The ideal arrangement is to have a teleprinter communicating between the two rooms. Alternatively the question and answers can be repeated by an intermediary. The object of the game for the third player (B) is to help the interrogator. The best strategy for her is probably to give truthful answers. She can add such things as "I am the woman, don't listen to him!" to her answers, but it will avail nothing as the man can make similar remarks.
>
> We now ask the question, "What will happen when a machine takes the part of A in this game?" Will the interrogator decide wrongly as often when the game is played like this as he does when the game is played between a man and a woman? These questions replace our original, "Can machines think?" (Turing, 1950, p. 433).

Now, our interest in Turing's approach is in determining if such a procedure for establishing the meaning of the question will work for us. Can we make use of the idea of an imitation game?

Clearly there are two kinds of imitation possible, and even though Turing was never explicit about their differences, it is possible to think about the imitation game in terms of one or the other. The first of these two kinds of imitation we shall call *imitation 1* for lack of some better term, although the word *simulation* comes very close to our intended meaning. Imitation 1 consists in the machine *becoming* the thing imitated. Our question, in these terms, becomes, "Can a machine *be* a counselor?"—the implication being that the inner workings of the machine would be identical to a counselor, not a particular counselor or even counselors in general. We mean that these inner workings would be such that the resultant behavior would be counseling.

If we replace our question with some test or other, perhaps one like

Turing's, that would indicate whether or not a machine is making a successful imitation 1 of a counselor, we are quickly in trouble. Aside from the formidable difficulties of constructing the test itself, we are faced with the problems posed by all the new questions that arise out of imitation 1. Because imitation 1 requires that the machine *become* a counselor, we must expect it to experience all the relevant conditions in which counselors find themselves. If the counselor cares, the machine must care. If he experiences the dilemma of the counselee in order to mirror its form and substance, then so must the machine. If it is important that the counselor empathize with the client, then too must the machine empathize, and so on through the range of human conditions essential to the counselor when he counsels.

You no doubt see what we get ourselves into by adopting imitation 1 as our meaning to the question. We are forced to expect the machine to feel what a counselor feels, and this feeling must arise *in the same way* in the machine as in the human being. But this is a contradiction, making the question nothing more than a word game. To expect something to undergo a human experience is to expect it to become human to that extent. On what grounds, for instance, can we say that a machine that feels and loves and cares is not by that very fact human to some degree? We confuse ourselves with this not because we are led to consider machines to be human, even though they are not flesh and blood and do not live and die and breathe, but because our words deceive us into thinking we ask something meaningful, when in fact all we have done is wonder if something that can become human can do human things. In light of these difficulties we reject imitation 1 as our approach.

The second kind of imitation, which we will call *imitation 2,* is essentially the approach adopted by Turing in his imitation game. Imitation 2 consists in the machine *behaving like* the thing imitated, and in our case there is some hope in this approach. Our question, in these terms, becomes "Can a machine *behave* the way counselors do?" That is, no matter what the real state of the machine, can it give the appearance of being a counselor?

An imitation counseling game in this case would become a test to see if a machine could do as well as a human counselor in exhibiting all those behaviors that make up the relationship between the client and the counselor. For instance, can the machine *exhibit* concern? Can it seem to be honest and trustworthy? Can it generate confidence? Can the machine make utterances that are relevant and of a kind that assist the individual in dealing with his problem? Compared to imitation 1, this approach seems much more manageable, although we probably do not know enough about the act of counseling to be able to catalog all the things that must be exhibited by this brand of counseling machine.

We see on closer inspection, however, that imitation 2 is much more troublesome than imitation 1 precisely because it seems reasonable. It does not clearly reveal its weaknesses and faulty assumptions and thus can too easily lead us astray. One objection is that imitation 2 is based on deceit. We believe a counselor behaves in order to reveal himself, and this revelation is the mechanism by which he helps the counselee to gain insight. To mirror the counselor's behavior without the substance behind it would be to violate one of our basic premises of what counseling is. Beyond this, imitation 2 ignores the fact that counseling behavior has its effect only when the client's perception of that behavior is appropriate. For example, not only must a counselor exhibit honesty—the client must perceive this honesty and believe it. But regardless of its behavior, how do we convince someone that his counselor-machine is honest or concerned or even relevant?

Now these are severe handicaps and yet they are not the worst things about imitation 2 when applied to counseling. Foremost among the difficulties with imitation 2 is its assumption that the things a human being does when he counsels are essential to the notion of counseling itself. This is not necessarily the case and we miss the opportunity to consider what is essential when we accept this form of imitation as appropriate. To see what we mean here, consider a mountain climber. In preparing to climb a good-sized mountain, he will, of course, pack a lot of things in his knapsack including a supply of food. Food is a very important thing on a climb of long duration, but we must be clear about the reason for this. Food is important when you climb a mountain not because it is in any way essential to the notion of mountain climbing but precisely because human beings climb mountains and human beings must eat at regular intervals. If we built a robot to climb a mountain, no food would be needed.

It may be the same with counseling. Perhaps things such as honesty are important in counseling only when human beings counsel. It may be that such things are irrelevant to counseling by machine. Imitation 2 does not allow for this possibility and thus gives up the chance we get by the use of the word *machine* to consider what behavior is or is not essential to our view of counseling. We would therefore have to give up the perspective we gain by our question with imitation 2. On this ground, as well as on the basis of its other weaknesses, we discard imitation 2.

Neither kind of imitation will do, it seems, and the expectation that our question can be answered through an imitation game such as Turing's must be abandoned. In saying this, we seem to do nothing more than confirm the suspicions you must have had at the onset, that the question "Can a machine counsel?" is a strange and fruitless one to pose. But we do not give up the enterprise because we discard Turing's approach. Indeed, we learn a very important thing from our consideration of the imitation game—a fact that helps us construe our question properly. This is that all our difficulties with both kinds of imitation stem from the assumption that a machine can counsel only if it can mimic a human counselor. If we think of our question in a different way—one in which, although we maintain the notion of imitation, we need not expect a machine to ape a counselor—then we can proceed without running such a risk of heresy.

The idea that *imitation* need not mean "copying" is not new. Aristotle, for instance, begins his *Poetics* with a consideration of imitation, and Oates and O'Neill tell us he "is seeking to give a secondary meaning to the term." They say that Aristotle uses the word to mean the process that takes place when an artist creates his work of art. "It is through *mimesis* [imitation], that form comes to be imposed upon the artist's material, broadly conceived" (1938, p. xxiii). That which art imitates is nature—or more accurately, the *process* of nature—and even though the objects of nature are natural and the objects of art are artificial, these objects of art "are produced as nature would have produced them" (McKeon, 1947, p. 621). Art imitates nature in the processes of production as well as in the objects produced.

The difference between art and nature to Aristotle rests in the difference between internal and external causation. He considers nature to be "a cause of motion internal to the thing moved, while art is an external cause employed by the artist to impose on matter a form first conceived in his mind" (McKeon, 1947, p. 621). This distinction is important to our purpose because it is in the play between the internal and the external imposition of form that we can begin to characterize our beliefs about the act of counseling and thus the role, if any, a machine can have in this act.

The artist wishes his audience to undergo an experience and as a result to become more sensitive not to the objects of art themselves but to the natural phenomena that the process of their creation mirrors. The artist differs from others not so much because he can draw or sculpt or write the language well but because he can experience in a natural phenomenon that which the rest of us can experience only through his artistic expression of that phenomenon. Thus the artistic process—the imitation—is a way of experiencing the world, and the object of art is an effort to communicate this experience.

Artistry and Counseling

But this meaning of *imitation* can be used also, we feel, to describe generally the act of counseling, and the mission of the counselor can be thought of as much like that of the artist. The counselor's material is his client's predicament, and the manner in which he establishes and develops the relationship between the client and himself and their subsequent creation together of the basis for resolution of this predicament constitute the counselor's mode of imitation. The counselor's intent is not merely the resolution of difficulty but rather the revelation of the *process* by which such resolution becomes possible. He accomplishes this through a kind of enactment in which form comes to be imposed on the client's predicament first by the counselor's external representation of the process of resolution and, eventually, through insight, by the client's internal experiencing of the process.

This internalization is the goal the counselor seeks to reach through the essentially artistic activity of revealing, by way of the counseling relationship, the processes of resolution. Should the relationship become more important to either of them, then the counselor has failed, just as the sculptor fails if his model of man obscures the experiencing of men from which the sculpting stems.

Now, what all this means, of course, is that counselors are themselves imitators. When we wonder if a machine can counsel, therefore, we shall confuse the issue by expecting the machine to mimic the human counselor because in expecting this we forget that a human being is one kind of medium and a machine is another. Because machines and human beings are different media, expecting one to act like the other is much like expecting a poet literally to paint a portrait with words. We must let the machine stay a machine but recognize that the activity of counseling by human beings is a means to an end, this end being some desired condition in which the client will eventually find himself. Our interest thus centers on the possibilities of a machine achieving this same end even though it does so in a manner clearly different from human beings.

In this way we come to the heart of our question "Can a machine counsel?" By it we mean to ask: Is it possible to create a machine environment such that an individual who functions in certain specifiable ways within this environment can be said to have been counseled? We do not ask if a machine can copy what human beings do when they counsel but rather if we can achieve an identity of goals between a counselor and a machine.

The Goals of Counseling

Having settled on this meaning of the question—and thus gained the perspective we need—we are faced with the problem of answering it. To deal with this problem, we shall first consider what it is a machine must accomplish (notice we do not say "what is must *do*") for the answer to our question to be yes. That is, the primary concern here must be with the *basis* on which the question is to be answered. Following this, we can assess the possibilities that such a machine can exist.

Because we pose the question in order to gain perspective on our beliefs about what counseling is, we shall at this point present these beliefs, although we shall be general about it and hardly as explicit as might be desirable. Notice, however, that even though we speak about a particular idea of counseling, the approach to the question is not bound to any specific technique or form of counseling. As a way of viewing the problem, it is general. Thus we recognize the diversity of opinion that can be tolerated within this approach, and we offer one notion of counseling not to argue its merits here but to provide a case in point from which to evolve a basis for an answer to our question.

Counselors, we assert, deal with problems of a particular kind in the manner generally proposed earlier. That is, they deal with these problems by concerning themselves, and hopefully the client, with the processes by which such problems in general may be resolved. In this way some specific problem and the resultant condition in which it leaves the counselee are used by the counselor as the material with which to fashion an understanding of the process of problem solving. This, of course, is the reason the giving of advice is not enough by itself to amount to counseling.

Now, to be more specific about this, we argue that you should send a person to a counselor, instead of some other kind of psychologist, when that person has a problem[2] related to his career. The word *career* and the word *problem* are two poor choices of words because in their meanings in ordinary language they do not say all we intend to say. Usually *career* is used in a far too limited way and *problem* in a far too general way to suit our needs here; but they both, nonetheless, contain the grains of meaning we seek. A brief explanation of our intentions with these two words will clarify the situation.

By *career* we do not mean just a person's job, or occupation, or vocation, or even his life's work. These are all parts of our meaning, of course, but we include much more. In saying that we include more, however, we do not mean to suggest that a career is something that is pieced together or that it is in fact definable by whatever may be included in it, anymore than we would say that the motion of a motion picture is definable in terms of the frames that make up the film or anymore than we would think of electrical current as the piecing together of electrons. Motion and flow are not inherent in the objects that move or the liquids that flow, but rather they

---

2. We use the strong word *problem* here even though we consider that a problem is not the only thing that can be an appropriate motivation for seeking counsel. Curiosity, for example, may well be equally appropriate, as may be the kind of involvement an individual exeriences when in a game-playing mode.

are the impressions that moving and flowing things leave behind. Thus, although motion, for instance, may be implied by objects that move, it is not in the strictest sense made up of those objects.

In this sense *career* is like *motion*. We view *career*—and this is not a very new idea—as the time-extended working out of self. This working out of self provides the context and the opportunity both for the "expression of hope and desire and limitation upon life" (Tiedeman and O'Hara, 1963, p. iv). By the working out of self, the continuity we call career is created, and although purposive behavior is central to the process, we do not consider career strictly as a road that *leads* somewhere. It is, instead, a trace of much the same kind as the bread path of Hansel and Gretel. Career is the consequence of passage.

Now the mechanism for this working out of self, and thus for the inscription of career, is the activity of deciding, and this leads to our meaning of the word *problem*. By *problem* we mean some difficulty with deciding. The reason deciding is so important to the process is that it is by the exercise of individual freedom through choice that career becomes the mapping of self instead of just a smoke trail. One difficulty that a person might have in making decisions is the lack of ability to decide: He may not know how to decide. A second difficulty might be that he is not aware of the nature of the decision to be made. Perhaps the most general difficulty a person can have—one for which a counselor is most needed—is the inadequate sense that one *can* decide. At the base of much trouble people have with deciding is the absence of a clear sense that a person can be an agent in determining what happens in his life. Later, we shall say more of this sense of agency and its relation to the development of self.

The specifics of the process of decision making may be characterized by way of a paradigm proposed in 1963 by Tiedeman and O'Hara. In confining the paradigm to the rational form of decision making, they state: "It seems sufficient to suggest a paradigm of the process of reaching a rational decision since such is the differentiated and later integrated condition that the practices of guidance attempt to facilitate" (p. 38). It is through the notion of decision making as depicted in this paradigm that we shall view the counselor's effort to impose form on the client's predicament and thus to reveal the processes by which the imposition of such form can generally be achieved.

According to the paradigm, the process of decision making is divided first into two aspects called *anticipation* and *accommodation*. The anticipation aspect consists essentially of a person's preoccupation with the pieces —facts, alternatives, options, consequences—out of which a decision is to be fashioned and with the aspirations, hopes, expectations, constraints, and the like that will determine the form of the decision. The accommodation aspect—also called the aspect of implementation or adjustment—represents the movement from anticipation to induction; it is the point where imagination meets reality. In the case of both anticipation and accommodation it is possible to speak about "subaspects" or stages.

The first stage of anticipation, called *exploration,* begins with a person's awareness "that a problem does or will exist and that a decision must be reached in order to resolve it in a satisfying manner" (Tiedeman, and O'Hara, 1963, p. 38). In discussing exploration, Tiedeman and O'Hara state:

> In the step of exploration . . . a number of different alternatives or possible goals . . . may be considered. Relevant goals are those which can possibly be attained from the opportunities associated with the problem under consideration. . . . During the exploratory step fields are relatively transitory, highly imaginary (perhaps even fantastic), and not necessarily related one to the other. They may be a relatively unassociated set of possibilities and consequences. . . . In the step of exploration in relation to a problem of career development, a person probably reflects at least upon his aspiration, opportunity both now and in the future, interest, capability, distasteful requirements that still can be tolerated, and societal context for himself and his dependents. These are relevant aspects of the field set by each goal. In short, a person attempts to take the measure of himself in relation to each alternative as he senses it (pp. 38 and 41).

Of *crystallization,* the second stage of anticipation, they assert:

> In [crystallization] the cost of the several goals can be considered in relation to the return from each. The value of alternatives can then be assessed. Relevant considerations are organized or ordered in this process of valuing. . . . The process of valuing gives rise to values which tend to fix the organization or order of all relevant considerations in relation to each of the goals as crystallization occurs. . . . Crystallization normally represents a stabilization of thought. A setting of thought is achieved which is ordinarily of some durability and hence of some reliance. This set readies the person for investment of self along a line that then becomes more noticeable. The situation becomes defined, so to speak, at least for a time (p. 41).

The third stage is that of *choice* and it follows readily on the heels of crystallization. Quoting again from Tiedeman and O'Hara:

> With *choice,* a particular goal, and its relevant field . . . orients the behavioral system of the person of relevance for his problem. . . . This goal may be elected with varying degrees of certainty and its motive power will vary as a result. . . . Furthermore, the degrees of clarity, complexity, and freedom generally available to the person in the solution of this problem and in the pursuit of the indicated decision will also affect the motivating power of the resulting resolution of alternatives (p. 42).

The fourth and final stage of anticipation is called *clarification*. You would expect after a choice had been made, that that aspect of decision making that precedes action would have been finished. But even though the decision is made and held firmly, doubt about the decision will often arise. This is true

in even a short period of waiting (a week or more, say) for the expected situation to begin to unfold . . . doubt experienced in the waiting period causes the individual further to clarify his anticipated position. An elaboration and perfection of the image of the future . . . ensues. . . . *Clarification* not only perfects the image of self in position, but also dissipates some of the former doubts concerning the decision (p. 43).

The three stages of accommodation may be briefly described in the following way (Tiedeman and O'Hara, 1963):

Induction: A general defense of self and a giving up of an aspect of self to group purpose; . . . the individual's goal and field assimilatively become a part of the region . . . of the social system in which the person is implementing his desired solution of his problem. He learns the premises and structures-in-interaction required for continued identification. This process leads to a further perfection of individual goal and field in the social system. . . .

Reformation: The receptive orientation of induction [*gives*] . . . way to [*an*] assertive orientation. . . . The person is well immersed in a relevant group. . . . He has a strong sense of self and actively enjoins the group to do better. . . . Since . . . the person acts both upon the in-group goal and field . . . in order to bring that group into greater conformance with his modified goal and field . . . and upon the out-group to bring their view of his identification into greater consistency with his, the effect, if any, is the modification of group goal and field. . . .

Integration: Synthesis is, of course, the essence of integration. . . . A differentiation in identification has been achieved. The new-found appreciation of self is integrated with its larger field. This new part of the self-system becomes a working member of the whole self-system. In integration, individual and group both strive to keep the resulting organization of collaborative activity. . . . The individual is satisfied, at least temporarily, when integration occurs (p. 44).

Now there is something peculiar about this paradigm; a potential difficulty quite similar to the problems we sometimes get into when we use language. A peculiarity of language known to philosophers for some time is that among the things we use language to talk about is language itself. Bertrand Russell, for example, has shown that it is a case of bad "philosophical syntax" to assert something like "The golden mountain does not exist" and from that suppose you are attributing some kind of existence to the very thing whose existence is denied in the sentence. As language does sometimes, the paradigm of decision making turns back onto itself in a way we must be clear about. Not only does the paradigm depict the decision process, it also by this depiction prescribes how one should relate to that process. That is, in enunciating the aspect of accommodation, the paradigm argues that one of the things to which one must accommodate is the decision process itself. But integration is the development of meaning that is independent of language as the instrument of that meaning. Thus the language of decision making, even though it is the medium through which understanding of the process comes, must be thrown off before the accommodation is complete.

This throwing off—perhaps making invisible is a better thing to say—of the instrument of meaning gets us back to the play between the external and the internal imposition of form we spoke of earlier. Accommodation to decision making itself is the most general kind because it represents internalization of the *processes* of resolution. First, the language must be established for the individual (induction); then it must itself become an object of analysis (reformation); and finally it must dissolve, as the individual goes past it to meaning (integration).

By way of the essentially artistic activity described earlier, the counselor must take his client through these phases not with respect to a particular problem so much as with respect to the process itself. He must establish the client's proficiency in the language of the process, develop his awareness of this language and its effects, and, in the end, facilitate the individual's internalization of this process. In doing this, we argue that the counselor leaves the client with a sense of agency as a logical consequence. The state in which one believes himself to be a significant agent in determining what happens to him comes not from convincing him about it but from the internalization of the decision process.

Reconsideration of the Question

Having said all of this—briefly and with hardly enough explanation—about our views of counseling, we can now pursue the terms under which an answer to the question we pose in this chapter might reasonably be formulated. In the most general sense, before we would be willing to say that a person has been counseled by machine, this machine would have to accomplish at least three things. First, it would have to reflect the elements of decision making in such a way that the language of the process was exposed to the client. Naturally this exposure of the language must lead to the development of the individual's proficiency in its use. Second, the machine must encourage the development of awareness of the process and the relation of self to problems as viewed by that process. That is, the process must become a mechanism for the manipulation of this relationship between self and predicament. Finally, the machine must allow and foster the individual's accommodation to the decision process both in terms of specific predicament and, more important, in terms of the process in general. Remember, because we seek *identity of goals* between machine and counselor, we need not expect this act of counseling to be carried out the same way by each.

But this is easy enough to say and, even though the idea of identity of goals enhances our perspective and subsequent analysis, we have no reason yet to suppose that a machine can accomplish anything resembling what we need. To repeat the point we made in the first paragraph, however, we really do not have to bother with what it would take specifically for a machine to counsel. What we are hoping for with this essay is that the reader will be encouraged to ask our question about his view of counseling. In our case we should go back and examine the many roads we have opened for ourselves. We should wonder, for instance, what a human counselor can do to achieve the ends of counseling as they have emerged from our attempt at the question. Are certain techniques more defensible than others? Are the honesty or the concern or the objectivity of a counselor important techniques or essential conditions of counseling? Are there pedagogical issues central to the achievement of the goals of counseling?

Even though such questions must be dealt with carefully and fully before we will know enough to talk in any but a superficial way about machines and counseling, we shall nonetheless attempt an answer here. For two other reasons, the answer will be bad. First, it will be an answer by example, which is the coward's way out. Second, it is a weak example. But some of our previous argument will at least be clarified by this attempt at an answer.

There is an old oriental saying that if a man has one hundred miles to walk, he is wise to consider himself half way there only when he has walked ninety miles of the journey. By such reckoning our example is hardly more than a glance in the direction we wish to go. For our example we shall describe a project on which we have worked for about two years.

In June 1966 the U.S. Office of Education granted Harvard University's request for funds to conduct a project (contract number 1–6–061819–2240) called the Information System for Vocational Decisions Project (ISVD). Preliminary work on this project is described in Ellis and Wetherall (1966) and in Ellis et al. (1968). Cooperating with Harvard in this project is the New England Education Data Systems (NEEDS), a nonprofit facility that provides computer data processing and research service to sixty-two school systems in New England. The responsibility of Harvard and NEEDS is to create a working model of a computer-based information system that can become part of the vocational and educational guidance efforts of school systems, government employment agencies, trade schools, skills training centers, and even industry. In the development of the first model, the Newton, Massachusetts school system is the main focus. This working model is to be delivered on or before 1 July 1969, which is three years and one month from the day the ISVD project began.

The theory underlying the ISVD project deliberately plays on a potentially useful distinction between *data* (facts) and *information* (facts interpreted in relation to use). The task of the information system is to enable the individual to transform data into information. This is to be done by teaching him to interpret the data in the light of his own knowledge, experience, and intention, so that his organization and use of the data represent his own personal relationship to them in the process of decision making. We presume that only when data are used in this way can they be described as information in which the individual is concerned. The information so generated can then, in turn, serve as data in the making of future decisions. Given that the quality of decisions is directly related to the kind, quality, and comprehensiveness of the *information* (that is, data in relation to personal intention) considered by the individual during the process of decision making, then a fundamental task of guidance is to identify, evaluate, and classify needed data *and to make them readily available to students in usable forms and at needed times and places.*

Throughout the individual's passage from point to point in the decision-making process, he continues to engage in the act of turning data into information. This is a major concern of the project, because, in the real world, data are never complete and neither is information. Often it is precisely this incompleteness that makes decisions necessary in the first place. In any event, the quality of the choice depends on the quality of the data. Before one attempts to make a decision, therefore, he must first understand the incompleteness of the data and information with which he is dealing.

Accepting data and information on these terms leads naturally to the condition that one is more likely to take responsibility for the choices he makes, because they are not totally determined by external factors. If they were, then choice would be either irrelevant or superfluous. Furthermore, to create information on which to base decision, one must *actively* process data rather than passively be guided by them, and therefore the individual must become a significant agent in the choice process. That is, the incompleteness of data implies that the individual is *responsible* for his decisions in both meanings of the word: He is the one who makes the decisions, not someone or something external to him; he is the one who enjoys or suffers the consequences. This is one way to define *freedom,* and it is to this notion that the project is dedicated. It will achieve this goal by developing in the student the ability to engage in this kind of decision making relative to his career choice. That is, the project will place the student among resources, enhance his access to them, teach him the stages in decision making, and have him engage the resources in a controlled setting so that he can develop the skills of processing data and making decisions.

An additional factor in the decision-making procedure that this project proposes is called *monitoring* and consists in keeping track of the student as he goes from stage to stage through the paradigm time and again. Aside from the usual reasons for monitoring a student's behavior—to analyze his performance, select from alternative courses of action, and generally maintain an account of his interaction with a system—the project expects to present to him the facts of this monitoring so that he may use them as additional data. These facts become a kind of meta-data that the student processes. The idea of data and meta-data is analogous to the philosophical notion of being and becoming. Not only does the individual act, but he becomes aware of his patern of action. The desired result is a higher order of understanding of both the decision-making act and the panorama of career choice in which decision points are linked. Career becomes a time-extended set of choices, and decision at any given point is enhanced by an overall awareness of the road being traveled.

What the project proposes, then, is a model of decision-making behavior that requires a setting capable of providing feedback and of generating feedforward, the individual's feedforward, that is. It is an interactive setting in which an individual engages one or more data files in certain specifiable ways as a means of determining alternatives and of selecting from among them on bases understood to himself.

The setting we seek is one that will develop in the student the ability to engage in the decision process as depicted by the paradigm described earlier. Some of us call this setting a reckoning environment because we want students to do more than just make up their minds. We want them to figure up, measure, estimate, compare, judge, make calculated guesses, and in the end decide *and* take responsibility for their decisions. This, of course, is what *deciding* means, but often people equate decision making with choice making and thereby miss the inherent notion of the process and its extension over time. What is left, usually, is the mistaken idea that a person decides by making up his mind, and thus we hear about the *moment* of decision as though it all happens at a point in time that is discrete and unbounded by thought and reflection. To make it clear that it is precisely this misconception and the resulting inflexibility we wish to challenge in ISVD, we have come to refer to the setting for vocational decision making that we are creating as a vocational reckoning environment.

After we recognize the obvious fact that data and information are never complete, it becomes wise—often vital—to place the condition on choice that it be made with the best possible data available. We must ask of the data: Are they *accurate?* How *complete* are they? Do they reflect the full *complexity* with which we must deal? Can we get them *in time* to explore alternatives adequately? A library is unsatisfactory in this area, because the time involved in searching is often more than the individual can afford. Certainly large amounts of data—occupational descriptions, for example—can be stored, indexed, cross-referenced, and made generally available in a library, but that is only part of what is needed. The computer, on the other hand, is capable of all this and of providing fast access so that search time need not hamper decision making. Furthermore, the computer can interact with the student and thereby help him to ask relevant questions about the world of work. The project looks to the computer, therefore, as a device to store large amounts of occupational data and to make them immediately and selectively available to the individual as he proceeds through the decision-making process. With this kind of accessibility, the individual can feel he is among resources, and as he becomes more integrated into the reckoning environment, the data become more like extensions of him and less like external quantities; that is, they move toward becoming information.

Along with the student himself there are two additional components within the ISVD reckoning environment. The first of these is an extensive collection of data about the world of work, military service, and education. Facts about jobs, colleges, trade schools, military specialties, and the student himself are just a few of the types of data to be stored and made available to him. These data are organized into five major data files: occupational, military, educational, personal and family living, and student characteristics. Naturally, although each of these files is separate from the other, they all reference each other so that a student may follow a question through all its aspects.

Between the student and the data we intend to place a guidance machine. The function of this third and final element of the ISVD reckoning environment is to facilitate students' access to data and vice versa. That is, not only do we wish to provide a means for the student to gain convenient access to data, but we wish to keep track of such access as well. In this way, not only can an individual get facts with which to make decisions, but he can also gain a sense of the way he goes about making decisions.

One way to describe the ISVD reckoning environment is shown in Figure 18–1. We in ISVD call our machine a guidance machine and we shall use this term for the rest of this chapter even though our intention here is to suggest that its behavior approaches counseling.

Figure 18–1.
Schematic diagram of the ISVD reckoning environment.

Now, it is the purpose of ISVD to create a sufficiently explicit description of the behavior of a guidance machine so that a computer can behave as though it were that machine. Our efforts to create a description of a guidance machine fall into two categories. The first is the development of "necessary software." This consists of a fairly elaborate set of computer programs that permits certain basic and generally required functions to be performed. We need, for example, to operate in a time-shared setting so that more than one student can use the system at any one time. Furthermore, we must provide the ability to create, maintain, edit, and retrieve data files. A programming language to allow both string manipulation and list processing, programs for statistical analyses, routines to permit content analysis, and the general facility of keeping track of who is on the system and what needs to be done next are some other examples of the kind of necessary computer software with which we must be concerned.

The second category, and perhaps the more interesting one, is the development of ISVD software. These are the programs that enable our time-shared computer to behave like a guidance machine, and it is here that any substantive contributions of ISVD rest.

The chart shown in Figure 18–2 depicts in a general and incomplete way the overall organization of the ISVD software. This software may be divided into four parts, each of which plays a role in the student's development of a sense for the decision process.

The first of these parts consists of the ISVD data files. In the chart these data are represented in the bottom two lines. Thirteen such data files are included thus far, and our plan is to increase this number as time goes on.

Even though the thirteen data files that are presently going into ISVD are different from each other in a number of respects, they are essentially alike in overall structure. A brief description of one of the data files, therefore, will provide an indication of what the rest are like. The one we shall describe is the occupations data file.

The occupations data file contains about fifty facts on each of about 850 occupations. These facts relate to such things as wages, education, physical

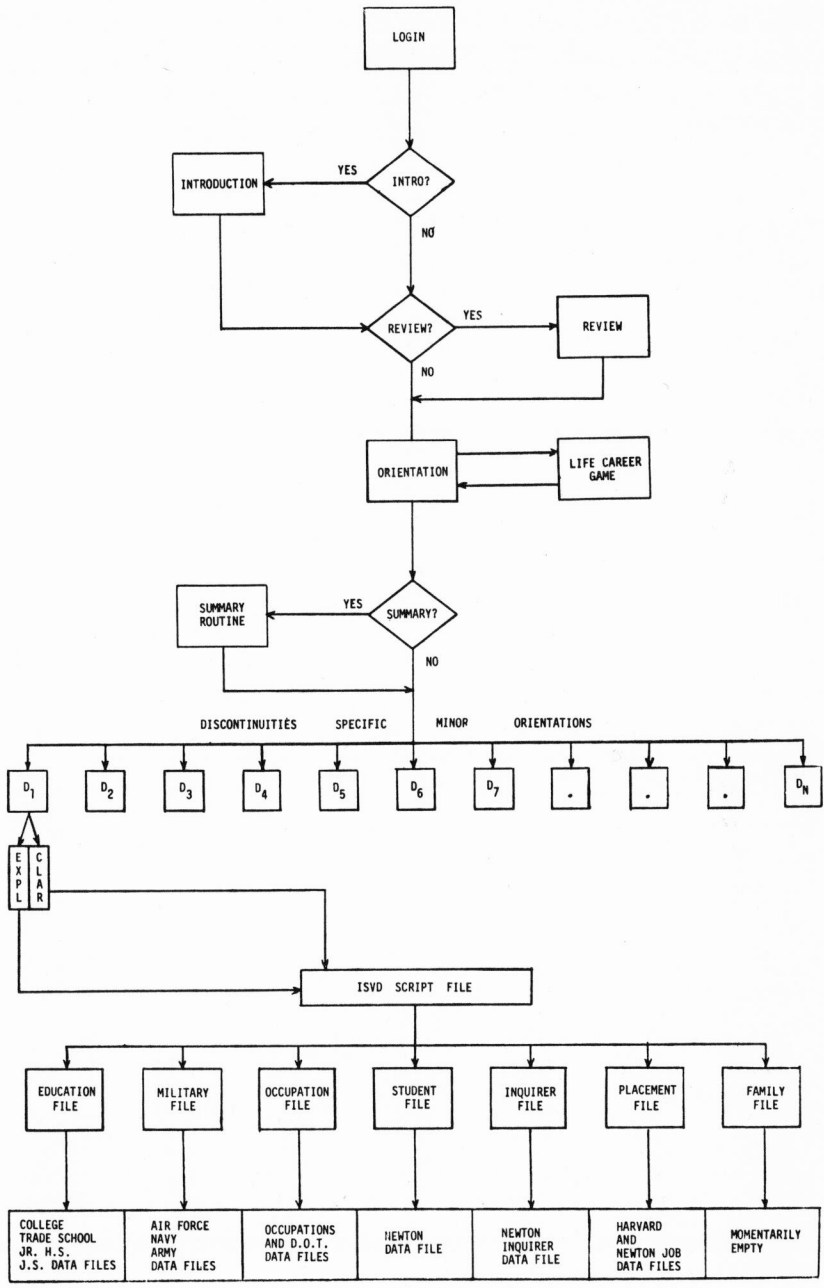

Figure 18–2.
An overview of ISVD.

demands, worker traits, high school courses needed, and the like. The fifty or so facts about each occupation are grouped together to form a record. We call these level-zero records and, of course, there is one level-zero record for each occupation.

In addition to these records, we have made provision for including hierarchical records—level-one, level-two, and so forth—which may be thought of as summary records. The level-one records in the occupations data file, for instance, are used to represent simultaneously many different *logical* organizations of the data without concern for their *physical* organization. One set of such records might be used to characterize the records in terms of the Roe categories (1956), whereas another set might represent someone else's taxonomy.

Besides these two kinds of records, the occupations data file contains a fairly extensive collection of incomplete, but completable, English sentences of the form "The salary of X is Y" or "To be an X requires Y years of education." If a student should ask something like "How much do doctors earn?" or "How long do I have to go to school to become a plumber?" then the variables X and Y in these template sentences would be replaced by the appropriate facts and presented to the student. The use of these template sentences—and paragraphs—need not be as trivial as the example offered here.

The present version of ISVD—called Prototype I—contains in its thirteen data files several million data potentially relevant to career choice. This part of the ISVD software, although in no sense complete, is nonetheless sufficiently extensive to allow nontrivial exploration.

As extensive as these data are, however, the single, most significant component of ISVD software is that network of routines we call *scripts*. Not unlike the manuscript of a play (from which it was given its name), a script is a set of rules describing how the guidance machine is to act. Scripts contain such things as the text to be presented to a student via either a video-display device or a printer, commands to activate a tape recorder or motion picture projector, commands to display a 35-mm slide, instructions for how to process the student's responses, and rules for any computation or storage or retrieval of data.

Some scripts deal with the concepts underlying the decision process and are called teaching scripts. These scripts superficially resemble the usual computer-aided-instruction material. Preference scripts are a second kind. They are used to assist the student in his consideration of the factors on which choice may be based. The taking of a preference script has the effect of processing the associated data file, leaving behind only those records that conform to the stated preferences. Finally, direct access scripts are used to retrieve specific bits of data from the files.

A third part of the ISVD software is called the *access routine*. Exploration, clarification, and review access routines serve to engage the student in behavior representative of the decision paradigm. They are used like filters between the student and his access to data and in this way are supposed to develop his proficiency and his awareness of the decision process. In access routines must rest the artistry that is inherently that of counseling.

To show what we mean here, we shall give an example of how an access routine works. The example deals with the discontinuity of college choice, and even though this excerpt is an actual interchange between an individual and a computer, we do not wish to give the impression that this program functions perfectly or even well enough to be impressive. To us it has been nothing more than a test case. In the example the computer's output is uppercase and the student's input is uppercase and lowercase.

WHAT WOULD YOU LIKE TO DO TODAY.

I want to think about colleges to apply to next year.

SINCE WE KNOW THAT YOU HAVE NOT EXPLORED YOUR COLLEGE CHOICE WITH THE SYSTEM BEFORE, THE FIRST THING WE WOULD LIKE TO FIND OUT IS IF YOU HAVE THOUGHT ABOUT THIS CHOICE ENOUGH TO HAVE SOME ALTERNATIVES IN MIND. IF YOU DO, TYPE THE NAMES OF EACH OF THE ALTERNATIVE COLLEGES. IF NOT, TYPE IN THE WORD NO.

Harvard University, Boston College, and Berkeley.

GOOD. WHAT KINDS OF THINGS DID YOU DO IN EXPLORING COLLEGE CHOICE. DID YOU READ ANY COLLEGE CATALOGUES OR TALK WITH YOUR GUIDANCE COUNSELOR. MAKE AS COMPLETE A STATEMENT AS POSSIBLE.

I read the catalogue for Harvard and Boston College. I talked to my guidance counselor, and had a couple of interviews with the Dean at Harvard. My father went to Berkeley so that's why I'm interested in going there.

THESE ARE THE ACTIVITIES THE MACHINE HAS RECOGNIZED OR ANALYZED FROM YOUR STATEMENT. YOU HAVE DISCUSSED THE MATTER WITH MEMBERS OF THE FAMILY, SPOKEN WITH A GUIDANCE COUNSELOR, READ SOME COLLEGE CATALOGUES, SPOKEN WITH COLLEGE OFFICIALS.

HERE ARE SOME OTHER THINGS THAT MAY BE A GOOD IDEA TO DO IF YOU HAVEN'T ALREADY. YOU COULD HAVE DISCUSSED THE MATTER WITH A TEACHER. NOW THEN, LOOK AT THE LIST OF EXPLORATION ACTIVITIES THAT YOU PER-

FORMED OUTSIDE OF THE SYSTEM. HERE IS THE LIST OF YOUR PRESENT ALTERNATIVES.

HARVARD UNIVERSITY, BOSTON COLLEGE, AND BERKELEY. NOW TYPE IN THE ACTIVITIES THAT YOU FEEL HELPED YOU MOST IN MAKING UP YOUR MIND OR GAVE YOU SOME ALTERNATIVE COLLEGES TO THINK ABOUT. PLEASE TYPE THEM IN ORDER OF IMPORTANCE.

The interviews and talking with my dad.

GOOD. BEFORE WE GO ON TO EXPLORE COLLEGE CHOICE, WHAT ARE THE FACTORS THAT YOU THINK ARE IMPORTANT IN CONSIDERING WHICH COLLEGES TO APPLY TO.

Grades, class rank.

ANYTHING ELSE.

Tuition costs, test scores.

HERE ARE SOME OF THE FACTORS THAT OTHER STUDENTS FOUND IMPORTANT (1) CURRICULUM CHOICE (2) COURSE SELECTION (HIGH SCHOOL SUBJECTS) (3) GRADES (4) CLASS RANK (5) TEST SCORES (PSAT, SAT, CEEB, ACT) (6) EXTRA-CURRICULAR ACTIVITIES (7) FUTURE VOCATIONAL PLANS (8) GOAL IN GOING TO COLLEGE (9) POST COLLEGE EDUCATION AND/OR TRAINING.

HERE IS YOUR LIST.

GRADES, CLASS RANK, TUITION COSTS, TEST SCORES. LOOK AT BOTH LISTS AND THEN TYPE IN ALL FACTORS FROM BOTH LISTS THAT YOU CONSIDER IMPORTANT IN THINKING ABOUT COLLEGE CHOICE.

High school courses, grades, class rank, test scores, tuition costs, future vocational plans.

FINE. THERE ARE SEVERAL WAYS THAT YOU CAN GO ABOUT THINKING ABOUT COLLEGE CHOICE WITHIN THE ISVD SYSTEM.

YOU CAN GO THROUGH SOME CONCEPT SCRIPTS WHICH ARE DESIGNED TO GIVE YOU SOME FACTS ON TOPICS RELEVANT TO COLLEGE CHOICE. OR YOU CAN PLAY THE LIFE CAREER GAME. USING THE DATA OF A MAKE BELIEVE STUDENT WHO IS LIKE YOU IN SOME WAYS YOU GO THROUGH THE PROCESS OF SELECTING A COLLEGE FOR HIM.

IF YOU HAVE SPECIFIC COLLEGES IN MIND, YOU CAN GET DATA ON THEM BY ACCESSING THE EDUCATION DATA FILE.

IF YOU LIKE, YOU CAN LET THE SYSTEM GUIDE YOU THROUGH A STATEMENT OF PREFERENCES TO COME UP WITH A LIST OF COLLEGES THAT MOST NEARLY MATCHES YOUR PREFERENCES. OR YOU CAN ELECT TO FIRST GO THROUGH A UNIT ON DECISION-MAKING, A UNIT THAT TRIES TO HELP YOU UNDERSTAND YOURSELF AND OTHERS IN RELATION TO MAKING DECISIONS. WHAT WOULD YOU LIKE TO DO.

Access the education data file.

YOU HAVE ACCESSED THE EDUCATION DATA FILE. FOR DEMONSTRATION PURPOSES ONLY, THE FOLLOWING SCHOOLS HAVE BEEN IMPLEMENTED. HARVARD COLLEGE (MEN), GOUCHER COLLEGE (WOMEN), BERKELEY UNIVERSITY (LARGE STATE SUPPORTED SCHOOL), BOSTON COLLEGE (RELIGIOUSLY AFFILIATED), AND CARNEGIE INSTITUTE (TECHNICAL TRAINING SCHOOL). THE FOLLOWING FOUR VARIABLES HAVE BEEN IMPLEMENTED . . . COSTS (INCLUDING TUITION, ROOM AND BOARD, AND OTHER FEES), REQUIRED ENTRANCE EXAMS, CRITERIA USED IN SELECTING STUDENTS AND REQUIRED HIGH SCHOOL COURSES.

NOW THEN YOU CAN QUERY THIS MICRO DATA BASE IN ANY WAY THAT YOU WANT.

PLEASE DO NOT USE QUESTION MARKS. IF YOU WISH TO STOP AT ANY TIME, TYPE IN THE WORD STOP.

YOU MAY BEGIN.

How much does it cost to go to Harvard.

TUITION AT HARVARD IS 2000 PER YEAR INCLUDING LAB AND HEALTH FEES. ROOM AND BOARD IS 1170 DOLLARS. NONRESIDENT STUDENT FEE IS 25 DOLLARS. BOOKS AND SUPPLIES ABOUT 70 PER YEAR. PERSONAL EXPENSES ABOUT 375 DOLLARS INCLUDING ROOM SUPPLIES, CLOTHING, CLEANING AND LAUNDRY, RECREATION, AND OTHER PERSONAL EXPENSES (EXCEPT TRAVEL).

How does that compare with Boston College.

BOSTON COLLEGE'S TUITION IS 1600, ROOM AND BOARD IS 1050 DOLLARS. OTHER COSTS INCLUDE BOOKS AND SUPPLIES ABOUT 100 DOLLARS, LAB FEE 100 DOLLARS AND 30 DOLLARS FOR WOMEN BOARDING STUDENTS FOR HEALTH FEES.

What high school courses should I take for Boston College.

NO SPECIFIC NUMBER OF UNITS IS REQUIRED HOWEVER THE FOLLOWING MINIMUM IS REQUIRED. ENGLISH(4), ALGEBRA(2),

PLANE GEOMETRY(1), FOREIGN LANGUAGE(2), TRIGONOM-
ETRY(½) (FOR STUDENTS PLANNING TO MAJOR IN MATH,
BIOLOGY, CHEMISTRY, OR PHYSICS), BIOLOGY, CHEMISTRY, OR
PHYSICS(2) (FOR STUDENTS PLANNING TO MAJOR IN THE
ABOVE SCIENCES AND FOR APPLICANTS TO THE SCHOOL OF
NURSING), ACADEMIC ELECTIVES (5).

What specific entrance exams are required.

BOSTON COLLEGE REQUIRES THE SAT AND THREE ACHIEVE-
MENT TESTS. ENGLISH, LEVEL I OR II MATHEMATICS, AND ONE
OF THE CANDIDATE'S CHOICE.

Does Berkeley require the SAT.

APPLICANTS WHO ARE INELIGIBLE, DUE TO GRADE AVERAGE,
OR TO UNIT OR DISTRIBUTION DEFICIENCIES, OR WHO HAVE
GRADUATED FROM AN UNACCREDITED SECONDARY SCHOOL,
MAY QUALIFY FOR ADMISSION BY CEEB EXAMINATIONS. THE
THREE ACHIEVEMENT TESTS REQUIRED FOR THOSE APPLYING
FOR ADMISSION ARE . . . ENGLISH, ONE TEST IN SOCIAL
STUDIES OR FOREIGN LANGUAGE, ONE TEST IN MATHEMATICS
OR A SCIENCE. REQUIREMENTS FOR CALIFORNIA RESIDENTS
. . . TOTAL SAT SCORE OF AT LEAST 1000, AND TOTAL SCORE
ON THREE ACH OF AT LEAST 1650 WITH NO SINGLE ACH LESS
THAN 500.0. REQUIREMENTS FOR OUT-OF-STATE RESIDENTS
. . . TOTAL SAT SCORE OF AT LEAST 1100 AND TOTAL SCORE
ON THREE ACH OF AT LEAST 1725.0.

What are the costs there.

TUITION AT BERKELEY IS 980 DOLLARS PER YEAR OF THREE
QUARTERS FOR OUT-OF-STATE STUDENTS. NO TUITION FOR
CALIFORNIA RESIDENTS. ROOM AND BOARD VARIES BETWEEN
600 AND 940 DOLLARS. INCIDENTAL FEE OF 242 DOLLARS.
ASSOCIATED STUDENTS MEMBERSHIP FEE 11 DOLLARS. BOOKS
AND SUPPLIES ABOUT 80 TO 110 DOLLARS.

How do they choose their students.

BERKELEY SELECTS ITS CANDIDATES ON THE BASIS OF A CAN-
DIDATE'S SECONDARY SCHOOL RECORD AND CEEB SCORES.
ALUMNI RELATIONSHIP AND GEOGRAPHICAL DISTRIBUTION
NOT RELEVANT.

How about Harvard.

HARVARD CHOOSES ITS CANDIDATES ON THE FOLLOWING
CRITERIA. SECONDARY SCHOOL RECORD, SCHOOL'S RECOM-
MENDATION, AND CEEB SCORES. ALSO, CHARACTER, PER-
SONALITY AND EXTRACURRICULAR PARTICIPATION ARE

STRONGLY EMPHASIZED. SPECIAL TALENTS AND INTERESTS ALSO CONSIDERED.

How much does it cost to go to Goucher.

THERE IS A COMPREHENSIVE FEE OF 2950 DOLLARS PER YEAR INCLUDING TUITION, ROOM AND BOARD, AND LAB FEES. STUDENT ACTIVITY FEE OF 13 DOLLARS, HEALTH FEE 50 DOLLARS, AND GYMNASIUM OUTFIT 27 DOLLARS. OTHER COSTS INCLUDE BOOKS AND SUPPLIES ABOUT 100 DOLLARS.

What kinds of courses should I take.

16 UNITS REQUIRED, THE FOLLOWING RECOMMENDED . . . ENGLISH(4), MATHEMATICS(3), (2 IN ALGEBRA, 1 IN GEOMETRY), ONE FOREIGN LANGUAGE(3), HISTORY(2), LABORATORY SCIENCE(1). THE COMMITTEE ON ADMISSIONS MAY ALLOW ENTRANCE CREDIT FOR WORK IN ELECTIVE SUBJECTS NOT LISTED.

How do they pick their students.

GOUCHER COLLEGE BASES ITS CANDIDATE SELECTION ON THE SECONDARY SCHOOL RECORD, THE SCHOOL'S RECOMMENDATION, AND TEST SCORES. OTHER IMPORTANT FACTORS ARE PERSONAL CHARACTERISTICS, EXTRACURRICULAR PARTICIPATION, AND INDIVIDUAL INTERESTS. ALUMNAE RELATIONSHIPS AND GEOGRAPHICAL DISTRIBUTION CONSIDERED.

I think that I would like to stop now.

WOULD YOU LIKE A SUMMARY OF YOUR EXPLORATION OF THE EDUCATION DATA FILE.

Yes.

FINE.

YOU GOT DATA ON THE FOLLOWING VARIABLES FOR HARVARD COLLEGE . . . COSTS, INCLUDING TUITION AND ROOM AND BOARD, HOW THE SCHOOL SELECTS ITS STUDENTS.

FOR BOSTON COLLEGE YOU GOT DATA ON THE FOLLOWING VARIABLES . . . COSTS, INCLUDING TUITION AND ROOM AND BOARD, WHAT HIGH SCHOOL COURSES ARE RECOMMENDED OR REQUIRED FOR ENTRANCE, WHAT ADMISSIONS TESTS YOU SHOULD TAKE.

YOU HAVE FOUND OUT ABOUT

WHAT ADMISSIONS TESTS YOU SHOULD TAKE, COSTS, INCLUDING TUITION AND ROOM AND BOARD, HOW THE SCHOOL SELECTS ITS STUDENTS, FOR THE UNIVERSITY OF CALIFORNIA

AT BERKELEY. FOR GOUCHER COLLEGE YOU EXPLORED THE DATA ON THE FOLLOWING VARIABLES . . . COSTS, INCLUDING TUITION AND ROOM AND BOARD, WHAT HIGH SCHOOL COURSES ARE RECOMMENDED OR REQUIRED FOR ENTRANCE, HOW THE SCHOOL SELECTS ITS STUDENTS.

YOU DIDN'T EXPLORE THE AVAILABLE DATA ON CARNEGIE INSTITUTE.

NOW THEN. WOULD YOU LIKE TO GO BACK AND FIND OUT ANYTHING MORE ABOUT THESE SCHOOLS.

No.

WOULD YOU LIKE TO GO INTO CLARIFICATION NOW.

Yes.

OF THE FOLLOWING COLLEGES THAT YOU HAVE EXPLORED, WHICH WOULD YOU CONSIDER APPLYING TO.

HARVARD UNIVERSITY, UNIVERSITY OF CALIFORNIA AT BERKELEY, BOSTON COLLEGE, GOUCHER COLLEGE.

Boston College, maybe Berkeley, and Harvard.

ARE THEY LISTED IN ORDER OF PREFERENCE THAT IS, IS YOUR FIRST CHOICE FIRST ETC.

No.

PLEASE TYPE THEM IN ORDER OF PREFERENCE.

Harvard University, Boston College, Berkeley.

YOU HAVE DECIDED TO GO INTO CLARIFICATION CONCERN-ING YOUR PREFERRED ALTERNATIVE HARVARD UNIVERSITY. YOU HAVE ACCESSED THE EDUCATION DATA BASE AND GOTTEN SOME OF THE AVAILABLE DATA ON HARVARD UNI-VERSITY.

IN EXPLORATION, YOU STATED THAT YOU CONSIDERED THE FOLLOWING TO BE IMPORTANT FACTORS IN CONSIDERING COLLEGE CHOICE . . . GRADES, CLASS RANK, TEST SCORES, COURSES, GOAL.

NOW THEN, YOU SHOULD HAVE A FAIRLY GOOD IDEA OF WHERE YOU STAND IN RELATION TO THESE FACTORS AS WELL AS WHERE STUDENTS ADMITTED TO HARVARD UNIVERSITY STAND. RIGHT.

No.

WOULD YOU LIKE TO GO BACK TO EXPLORATION TO FIND
OUT HOW YOU COMPARE WITH HARVARD STUDENTS.

No.

WOULD YOU LIKE TO CHOOSE ANOTHER ACTIVITY.

Sure.

WHAT WOULD YOU LIKE TO DO.

Find out about jobs.

HOW WOULD YOU LIKE TO DO THIS.

I would like to access the occupation data base.

O.K.

The fourth part of the ISVD software consists of those routines that form
the backdrop of the system. These elements perform the task of getting the
student to the appropriate place in the system. When a student "logs on"
the system, he is given an introduction should he need one. He is then asked
what he wishes to do. The backdrop routines process his answer and determine which discontinuity (in the chart, D_1, D_2, and so on) he is dealing
with. Another routine then determines whether he is in exploration or
clarification with respect to this discontinuity and passes him through the
appropriate access routine. From there the student will be provided access
to the relevant scripts for his situation and these scripts will in turn provide
the needed access to the data bases.

This description is an oversimplification, obviously, but it makes the
point of how we intend the guidance machine to function. That is, it indicates in a general way how we hope to develop—through scripts—the student's proficiency with the elements of decision making and—through
access routines—the student's awareness of the process underlying these
elements. These are two of the three things that we earlier asserted a
machine or a human being must accomplish to be said to be counseling.

The third requirement we listed was that the machine must allow and
foster the individual's accommodation to the decision process. This, of
course, is the heart of the matter.

In our development of the first prototype of ISVD we have dealt with
this third requirement least of all. It is clearly the most difficult issue we
face, and although we have certain hunches about it, we are not yet as
clear as we would like to be. One hunch concerns the monitoring function,
and we have already described how we wish to use the monitoring of student interaction with the system as a means to reveal the process and his
relation to it.

Another hunch concerns the Life Career Game and other games we plan for the system. The Life Career Game developed by Boocock (1967) and others allows a person to develop and go through a life plan for any number of fictitious people. By using this game, we hope to have the student experience some of the more realistic concomitants of choice. We place the game where we do in the chart to indicate that it is not merely a component of the ISVD system. We think of it as a point of view about the system in general. That is, a student can use the ISVD either for real (with his own interests) or for someone he pretends to be. The two major gains with the game are the objectivity one has by dealing with someone else's predicaments and the extension over as much as twenty (simulated) years that the game provides. As strong as these hunches are, however, we do not have enough experience yet to tell much about them.

One small force for accommodation to the system and thus to the decision process it reflects is the ISVD command language. With this simple language a student can take over control of the system flow, moving about in the system the way he wishes. This is very much the kind of behavior characteristic of the integration stage of accommodation, and in this way we see the *possibility* that one can indeed accommodate to a machine-based system and thus to the process embodied by that system. We recognize that this is somewhat of an overstatement, and we would be more careful about it if our intention were to argue that ISVD's guidance machine can indeed counsel. We have no such intention.

We describe ISVD to provide a sense of what ISVD can become rather than of what it is today. Relating to the question of this chapter, ISVD is not a case in point because it can prove or disprove anything about this question. On the contrary, in this case ISVD would be irrelevant. We describe ISVD to show a little bit of the relationship that exists between a process and its mechanization. It is here that ISVD is significant.

It is, of course, common sense to say that something must be proceduralized before it can be mechanized and the significance of ISVD is that it clarifies what this means. That is, when thinking about whether or not a machine can counsel, do not be deceived into assuming that the thing that must be proceduralized is the *act* of counseling. If you assume this, you inherit all the difficulties of imitations 1 and 2. But if you wonder, instead, what an environment might be like that has the effects of counseling in terms of what one who functions in this setting is thereby encouraged to become, then even if you decide no machine could ever be a part of this environment, you will have been left with a clearer notion of what your concept of counseling demands.

Now everything we have said in our attempt to answer the question, we recognize, is weak on at least two counts. First, of course, our assertions and our analysis of them need much more consideration if they are to become in any sense firm and sturdy. Second, not only is our example a long way from ideal, but there may be no ideal to be reached. We have not gone far enough to know for sure if we can go farther.

These are important limitations, but even though we have taken the question seriously enough to attempt an answer, our intention is to offer in the question a fresh look at some assumptions about counseling that are rarely challenged. We expect quarrels over our answer because we know it is simpleminded and a bare first attempt. We hope, however, that these quarrels will not discourage the reader from seeing in our strategy an opportunity to start from scratch with the problem of what counseling is all about and of how machines may enter into the procedures of counseling when the goals of counseling and for the machine are consonant.

REFERENCES

Boocock, S. 1967. The life career game. *The Personnel and Guidance Journal* 46:328–334.

Ellis, A. B., and Wetherell, C. S. 1966. *The computer and career decisions.* Technical Memorandum No. I. Cambridge, Mass.: Information System for Vocational Decisions, Harvard Univ.

Ellis, A. B., Pincus, M. E., and Yee, P. 1968. *Getting a guidance machine to understand English.* Project Report No. 14. Cambridge, Mass.: Information System for Vocational Decisions, Harvard Univ.

McKeon, R. ed. 1947. *The works of Aristotle.* New York: Random House.

Oates, W., and O'Neill, E., Jr. eds. 1938. *The complete Greek drama,* vol. 1. New York: Random House.

Roe, A. 1956. *Psychology of occupations.* New York: Wiley.

Tiedeman, D. V., and O'Hara, R. P. 1963. *Career development: choice and adjustment.* New York: College Entrance Examination Board.

Turing, A. M. 1950. Computing machinery and intelligence. *Mind* LIX (236): 433–460.

19

Donald E. Super

Of Tiedeman, Ellis, and Machines that Become Media When Given the Right Messages

Let me begin by restating, as briefly and as simply as I can, the Tiedeman-Ellis theses and their system, after which I shall examine them critically and suggest modifications or additions that may emerge as necessary or desirable.

The Theses

The first points made by Tiedeman and Ellis have to do with the essential characteristics of the machine. These are two in number: It executes procedures planned for it, and it therefore forces one to analyze the procedures that it is to execute.

This focus on procedures leads to consideration of the consequent role of the machine. The imitation of counselors is one possible definition of its role. Two types of imitation are considered: becoming a counselor and behaving like a counselor. By the latter is meant appearing as counselors appear rather than producing the effects that counselors produce. The latter meaning, incidentally, almost slips into the definition through the examples, but that it is not intended is made clear by the later discussion.

The counseling process is examined in order to help evaluate the adequacy of *imitation* as the counseling role of a machine, when imitation is defined as acting or appearing as a counselor. Three statements of the Tiedeman-Ellis definition of counseling are important. (1) The counselor acts in order to reveal himself, this being the mechanism for helping the client to gain insight (p. 351)—a definition that leads the authors to reject this concept of imitation, for acting like a counselor, mimicking him, hides rather than reveals the substance, be it person or machine, behind the behavior. (2) The counselor acts in order to reveal the process of solving problems or resolving conflicts by using it with the client and by thus supplying the format for the client to experience it and through this experience to develop insight (p. 353). Let me inject my thinking here to note that this definition does not lead Tiedeman and Ellis to comment on the acceptability of imitation or simulation as a definition of the computer's role in guidance. (3) The counselor acts to secure client internalization of the decision or resolution process by revealing, through the counseling relationship, these processes of resolution. The nature of the counseling relationship and how it operates to achieve this objective, however, remain undefined in Chapter 18.

The objectives of counseling emerge as the important consideration, objectives that may be attained in different ways by humans and by machines. Tiedeman and Ellis consider a career the "working out of self," or, as I prefer to put it, the "implementation of a self-concept." It is a person's attempt to function in everyday life as the kind of person he believes himself to be. They view counseling as helping with the process of making the decisions with which a person is confronted during the course of his career, and they draw on the Tiedeman-O'Hara model of career processes to define decision making. Their terminology is distinctive, but the concepts underlying it are basically the familiar constructs of problem solving.

Restating their question to avoid the inadequate construct of imitation, Tiedeman and Ellis ask, "Can a person be counseled by a machine?" They identify three conditions that the machine would have to meet for this to be possible. First, the machine would have to reflect the elements of decision making in a way that exposes the process. Second, the machine must encourage awareness of the process and of the implications of its applications to oneself. Third, the machine must foster accommodation to the decision process.

Finally, they reassert the principle that human and machine do not necessarily act in the same way to attain these objectives.

The System

The Tiedeman-Ellis system is described in terms of its immediate operating theory and method or content.

The theory or operating principles of the ISVD are (1) that decisions are made with data that have been transformed into information (that is, assimilated by the individual who examines them in the light of his own situation), (2) that data and information are never complete, (3) that recognition of the incompleteness of data and information comes from engaging in this process of relating data to self and self to data, and (4) that this recognition leads, in turn, to acceptance of responsibility for making choices.

Some of the methods and contents of ISVD are conventional and need not be considered in my summary: These are the data files (impressive in their coverage of educational, military, occupational, personal, and other resources) and the backdrop or routing routines. The scripts deserve specific mention because they are designed to meet the first Tiedeman-Ellis requirement for a counseling machine: teaching decision making. The access routines of exploration, clarification, and review are based on the career-decision paradigm and aim to meet the second requirement, developing awareness of underlying decision processes. Monitoring and games-playing routines are suggested as possible means of fostering accommodation to the decision process, but the authors are less sure that they will accomplish this and think that other methods may be needed.

CRITIQUE

There are a number of points made in Chapter 18 with which it would be a pleasure to express agreement, partly because they are nice points in the older sense of that word and partly because doing so would help to emphasize the sense of colleagueship that my co-workers at Teachers College and I have enjoyed with David Tiedeman and his teammates at Harvard for nearly a decade of both programmed and accidental interaction. But I shall skip these, along with minor points of doubt or disagreement, in order to focus on a few more important issues that merit our attention.

The Role of the Machine

Imitation is such an issue because of its near-synonym, simulation. The distinction made between imitation 1 and imitation 2 is, it seems to me, more rhetorical than real. The machine is not, after all, likely to become a counselor, a human being, although it might indeed behave like a counselor in the sense of doing things counselors do. But I doubt whether we wish to linger on this aspect of the topic.

Counseling

Imitation 2, the machine as mimic, does require consideration, as Tiedeman and Ellis reject this concept because they believe that one cannot equate doing what counselors do with counseling. Their reasons for this lie partly in logic and partly in their definition of counseling, which, you will remember, was threefold. Counseling as they see it involves (1) self-revelation by the counselor to the client to help him get insight, (2) supplying the format of experience in problem solving in order to reveal the underlying processes, and (3) establishing and using a counseling relationship in order to help the client to internalize the conflict-resolution or problem-solving processes.

The first part of the definition would, I believe, be unacceptable to most counselors and to most psychotherapists. It is a widely held axiom of counseling that the counselor should not inject himself into the counseling process by talking about himself, his experiences, his problems, or his ways of solving them. He should, it is equally widely held, be a genuine person, warm, accepting, and capable of feeling and of expressing relevant feelings. But the word *relevant* is the key, and to the best of our knowledge most of the counselor's self is not relevant to the client.

The third part of the definition is often stressed in discussions of counseling and of psychotherapy and has been identified as a probable major determinant of outcomes. Unfortunately, research has so far failed to confirm any of the hypotheses put forth as to the significant dimensions of the counseling relationship, and Tiedeman and Ellis understandably leave us without any understanding of the nature of this magic and mystical construct.

I believe that we must reject both of these definitions, those involving both self-revelation and the counseling relationship, not only because they are unsound and do not lead to operations but also because they pertain more to psychotherapy than to counseling. This last distinction is, admittedly, a difficult one to make, and many of those who have devoted attention to it have concluded that it is a spurious distinction. As this is not a conference on counseling, I shall not seek to dispose of that issue here. Instead, let me point out that regardless of whether or not I am correct in my understanding of counseling, the rejection of these two definitions on the first two grounds leaves only the third, and that if it is indeed a sufficient definition, imitation 2, simulation of counselor behavior, is clearly possible. This leads us back to the second part of the authors' definition, one that might have been supplied by a behavior-modification theorist: Counseling consists of setting up conditions that lead the client to act in certain desirable ways. In this type of counseling the immediate objective is to teach the counselee how to make decisions involving himself by guiding him through the steps of decision making. This is done by helping him to examine personal and situational facts in ways that enable him to assimilate and use them. The focus is on a problem such as educational, vocational, or marital choice, on the facts that bear on it, and on the implications of these facts for decisions.

If, in addition, we take into account the authors' definition of a career, decision making is learned by making decisions under guidance. We must add that counseling is a process in which self-concepts are clarified, modified, and implemented by examining the self and what it does and may do in a given situation. The behavior-modification definition of counseling is thus implicitly supplemented by a client-centered or phenomenological definition. Both are currently widely used by counselors.

The combining of these definitions may appear on the surface to be difficult or even self-contradictory. This it would be were each element in the combination considered to be applicable to every step in the total process of counseling. But this does not appear to be the case, for the establishment of conditions for decision-making experiences is simply one aspect of the situation, accompanied by acceptance of the counselee as a worthwhile person and by the provision of opportunity for the expression and clarification of feelings. The structuring characteristic of behavior modification differs from that of nondirective counseling in that in the former the confrontation of facts is counselor-planned rather than client-determined or accidental. It is true that in ISVD the client decides which facts to confront and when to confront them, thus giving him some sense of agency. Both approaches, however, involve structuring. And the ISVD behavior-modification approach does not seek to set goals, for it modifies the client's method of goal setting and of planning goal attainment, leaving it to him to determine what the objectives are and how they shall be attained.

The System

Construct validity. Does the theory or operating principle of the ISVD follow from or agree with the more general theoretical position taken by Tiedeman and Ellis on counseling by men and by machines?

It does *not* follow from, or make operational, the first part of their definition of counseling. In teaching the process of decision making by dealing with facts in relation to self and situation, ISVD reveals its method but not its substance—what it does but not what it is. One cannot say that the counseling machine reveals itself to the counselee; it has no self, no personality, to reveal.

Neither does it follow from, or make operational, the third part of the authors' definition, for it is difficult to think of the counselee as having a relationship with the machine. One may grant that people do, in a very limited sense, have relationships with machines: For one man, a car is a powerful extension of the self, whereas for another man it is merely a means of getting from one place to another. But the viewing of such relationships as comparable to the therapeutic transference, or to the collaborative rapport of vocational counseling, would be to stretch analogies to the point of hiding important differences. To elaborate on a point made by Tiedeman and Ellis concerning simulation, the machine cannot care for the client no matter what messages it gives him and no matter how much the client admires the machine. If the client bites the machine that feeds him, the machine is likely neither to give him another sandwich nor to slap him.

The second part of the Tiedeman-Ellis definition of counseling, that which appears to be acceptable, emerges as that which is consistent with, and in fact basic to, the operating principle of their system. Counseling, according to this part of the definition, involves supplying the format for experience with facts, and for their conversion into personally meaningful and useful information, while teaching the processes of problem solving; the ISVD software seeks to do just this.

Tiedeman and Ellis make an assumption, in connection with their system, that goes considerably beyond this and that appears to me to be a nonsequitur. They state that the recognition of the incompleteness of data leads to the acceptance of responsibility for making choices. I submit that it can equally well lead to the conviction that there is no point in deciding, for decisions based on incomplete data may prove to be wrong decisions and the resulting disappointment may lead to drifting despair. I think we may better postulate that the experience of examining data for decision making, however incomplete the data may be, will develop the habit of decision making and hence the posture of responsibility.

Method and contents. It is difficult for me to comment critically on the method and contents of ISVD, partly because of the level of abstraction at which they are necessarily described (when I would like as counselor and as system developer to deal with some of the specifics) and partly because some of them are programming problems rather than counseling problems. In the first category, for example, are questions concerning the content of the data files and the scripts: What goes into the family data file, and what are the principles underlying a "preference script" and guiding its writing? In the second category are the backdrop routines, and I am willing to take *routine* for granted. But let me select two or three issues that I can discuss.

The *access routines* are described as exploration, clarification, and review. The last is a routine of a different type from the first two, presumably a teaching device, but the first two constitute only two of the four stages of the aspect of the Tiedeman-O'Hara paradigm called *anticipation*. *Exploration* is the first stage, *clarification* is the last, and omitted are the two middle stages of *crystallization* and *choice*. No explanation of, or even comment on, this omission is offered, and none is self-evident. Indeed, these are two important processes, for *crystallization* is defined as evaluating the costs of alternatives seen in exploration and stabilizing or settling on one of them, and *choice* is defined as establishing a goal that, in clarification, is questioned, elaborated on, and confirmed. Is no help given by ISVD with crystallizing and choosing, do these processes take place and become clear to the counselee without access routines, or are they superfluous verbal refinements of the other two processes?

I am tempted to comment on the example given of an access routine. The occasional use of the technical jargon of ISVD, the level of abstraction of some of the material, and the seeming lack of dynamic quality in the facts supplied cause me some concern. But this is no place in which to edit text, and the dynamics of an audio-visual program are hardly conveyed by verbal transcriptions, and so I shall refrain from such comment after having merely raised the question.

Accommodation is the other aspect of the decision paradigm, and, the authors point out, they do not seek to deal with it because of uncertainties as to how to operationalize it. *Monitoring* may, as they suggest, provide the means: To carry this thought a bit farther, review routines, or the feeding back of periodic summaries of the counselee's trace, may be accompanied by opportunities for the client to evaluate his earlier explorations and choices. The system may ask pertinent questions about the recorded exploration and choice and suggest possible explanations, permitting further reaction by the counselee. *Games playing* also has appeal as a possibility, but my impression from limited evidence is that career games lose some of their appeal when played in computer-accompanied solitude. I can only agree with Tiedeman and Ellis that this problem needs further work.

CONCLUSIONS

As one who has been working on another system for computer assistance to guidance and counseling, interacting periodically with Tiedeman and Ellis about these and other projects, I have found their present statement of their theory and method most helpful. Other researchers have been more empirical in analyzing the work of the counselor and developing a computer system to do it, more logical in their analysis of the task of counseling, or more limited in their conceptualization of the task of presenting information to the student; these men are unique in their effort to develop relevant theory and to devise a system to make it operational. Although I have pointed out what appear to me to be some defects in their theory and have raised some questions concerning their methods, I believe that they have made, in Chapter 18, a major contribution toward clarifying what it is that counseling machines and counseling humans seek to achieve and toward outlining the methods by which these goals may be achieved. In ISVD itself we shall, I am confident, in due course see a system well designed to try out the adequacy of their formulations and the effectiveness of their operations.

Can a machine counsel? Tiedeman and Ellis do not argue that theirs will. They do not even think it will prove whether or not a machine can counsel. I am inclined to be more optimistic than they are. But, as they point out, the important objective that they seek to accomplish, and toward which they are well on their way, is to demonstrate that counseling objectives can be defined, that means of achieving them suitable to a machine can be devised, and that these procedures can indeed be put into a machine. The accomplishment of this is only a matter of time and of the successive improvement of models; machines may never be able to counsel, but they will in fact help to do so.

Guidance and Counseling: Discussion

At the risk of oversimplifying the exchange between two leaders in the field of computer-aided counseling, it might be useful to point out two options. Because counseling as a process is not well understood and the products are not always known, one can elect (1) to model what "good" counselors appear to do or (2) to provide information resources and processing tools that the student can use to acquire certain habits and attitudes.

Construction of a model of the human counselor is a relevant way to explore the traditional process of counseling, as has been shown by Loughary and others (1966) and by Starkweather (1967), but it is not the most effective way to introduce useful tools into counseling. On the other hand, simply providing students with the resources and file management tools is not sufficient. Some model of how the student is expected to think and act is required.

Because the example of student use of ISVD does not appear to be consistent with the discussion in the first part of Chapter 18, it is difficult to understand some of the rationale presented by Ellis and Tiedeman. Perhaps the restraints of present programming systems have not permitted the designers to move from previous styles of student-machine interaction to those that they now intend.

The view of the computer as a human-like counselor should not be discounted. In some situations a patient, friendly, responsive and amoral computer program—even though offered only as a mechanical aid—may help develop favorable attitudes in students who are unable to relate to their regular counselors. For example, numerous school systems will face for some time the problem of white counselors, many of whom are unable to serve adequately the guidance needs of black youths.

The computer also seems to play a useful role in counseling because of its ability to acquire information from interviewees more completely and perhaps at less cost than the human counselor. Some people appear more willing to talk to a machine, or to the clerk operating the keyboard, than directly to a medical doctor or counselor. Furthermore, the procedure carefully prepared by a panel of experts may on the average be more successful than the strategy adopted by the average doctor at the moment.

REFERENCES

Loughary, J. W., Friesen, D., and Hurst, R. 1966. Autocoun: a computer-based automated counseling simulation system. *Personnel and Guidance Journal* 45(1) September: 6–15.
Starkweather, J. A., Kamp, M., and Monto, A. 1967. Psychiatric interview simulation by computer. *Methods of Information in Medicine* 6(1):15–23.

20

Emmanuel G. Mesthene

Computers and the Purposes
of Education

It used to be that technical conferences could do their work free of the need for intervention by philosophers or social commentators. If they can no longer do so—that is, if the trend to include them is anything more than a fad—it is surely because our modern technologies are having and are seen to be having consequences that are far more than technical. Our technologies today are so powerful, so prevalent, so deliberately fostered, and so prominent in the awareness of people that they bring about changes not only in the physical world—which technologies have always done—but also in our institutions, attitudes and expectations, values, goals, and our very conceptions of the meaning of existence. This means that decision making relating to technology can no longer—as it once could—take place without deliberate consideration of those wider ramifications of technology. This lesson has not yet been well learned by many people at the technical heart and the political periphery of technology.

Let me touch on those widening ramifications of technology for a few moments. What the power, prevalence, and prominence of science and technology are doing is to push to the fore certain characteristics of society that are then seen as somehow fundamental to and definitive of society, that is, as setting its basic structure and character and as differentiating it from other societies, past and present, in which science and technology have not been so prominent.

There are a number of fundamental social traits that are thus gaining prominence as a result of the resources and emphasis that advanced societies put on the development and application of science and technology. One such trait is *possibility*. The first-order effect of technology is to expand the menu of options or choices available to society by literally creating new possibilities or by altering the cost-benefit ratios of realizing existing possibilities. This "freeing" of possibilty, that is, the expanding of society's menu, prepares the ground for social change and for changes in social values.

Another trait of society that is being pushed into prominence by the emphasis on science and technology is *institutional flux,* the mixing up of institutions. For example, government, industry, and universities were once largely separate from each other but are now becoming increasingly interdependent and indistinguishable. A third trait concerns *values.* The alteration of the material conditions of experience by new technology affects the process of valuation and therefore creates a strong tendency for value change in society. I have discussed these three kinds of change in more detail elsewhere (Mesthene, 1968) and will not pursue them further at this point.

A fourth prominent characteristic of technological society deserves special attention. That is the importance that society attaches to the generation and uses of *knowledge*. The term *knowledge* as I employ it in this connection is a quite general term that encompasses a number of elements. It includes, of course, the actual content or body of knowledge that exists at any given time as well as the methodology of knowing, that is, the process of scientific inquiry. In other words, it denotes what we know—what the natural and social sciences discover—and how we know. The term also encompasses the institutional forms of knowledge: knowledge organizations, such as universities, research organizations, and research and development and planning divisions or departments in government and industry as well as the less formal but not less significant institutional forms that go with the professionalization of knowledge, such as professional associations, or even less formal groupings such as what we call the scientific community.

Further, I include in the term *knowledge* the various techniques, many of them of recent origin, that we associate with the uses of knowledge, such as techniques of information handling, communication, technology transfer, linear programming, systems analysis, and so on. Finally, the term encompasses the attitudes of commitment that go with the generation and use of knowledge: the receptiveness to knowledge, the ability to suspend judgment and act on probabilities, the willingness to commit resources to education and research, the readiness to act according to rational criteria, the confidence that knowledge can move the world, and the expectations, sometimes overdone, that this confidence inspires.

So construed, knowledge of course encompasses technology also. At the same time, I see technology as a condition without which knowledge probably would have very little social importance. That is, I would argue for the proposition that technological innovation is the cause of the social importance that accrues to knowledge. The enhancement of the social role of knowledge is in fact one of the foremost ways in which technology affects society.

Now, knowledge can be a rather heady thing, especially for intellectuals, of course, and even more so for public officials or for industrial managers who want to exploit knowledge—and intellectuals—for political purposes or for profit. That is where the danger is. There is a long and venerable tradition in the West that the scientific investigator is free—indeed, is duty bound—to advance knowledge in every area and as fast as possible and to pursue the truth wherever it may lead. It has been a concomitant of that tradition that the *uses* of knowledge are not the scientists' or scholar's concern and that the intellectual not only has no responsibility for what the practical man or the politician does with knowledge but that, indeed, the knowledge enterprise would suffer if such concerns were allowed to influence it.

The prominent role of knowledge in our society has reversed this classic situation. The enterprise of knowledge is now likely to suffer—as is society in general—if scientific research is pursued without reference to its wider social ramifications. This is a difficult lesson to learn, because all of us have been brought up in the traditional scientific ethos. It is even more difficult to assent to, because the concern with social consequence can be so easily turned into a distortion of the scientific enterprise for invidious purposes. This is what explains the reaction of the early nuclear scientists: although it was clear after the bomb that science could not be pursued independently of its political implications, the scientists felt *they* had to assume the principal political responsibility because they were pure of heart. However naïve the conclusion, the premise recognized a real danger.

What was true of nuclear physics and nuclear technology continues to be true of science and technology generally and of educational technology as well, although the similarities are less clear in educational technology because the situation is so much more complex. Let me try to explain why.

The great social prominence of knowledge and technology, and the inadequate understanding as yet of what it implies, has given rise to a world view that serves as context for the conduct of scientific and technical work at the present time and that puts it in a public fishbowl, so to speak, that technical people can ignore only to their detriment. This world view holds that technology is an unalloyed blessing for man and society. Technology is seen as the motor of all progress, as holding the solution to all our social problems, as helping to liberate the individual from the clutches of a complex and highly organized society, as the source of permanent prosperity; in short, as the promise of utopia in our time. This view has its modern origins in the social philosophies of such nineteenth-century thinkers as Saint-Simon, Karl Marx, and Auguste Comte. It tends to be held by many scientists and engineers, by military leaders and aerospace industrialists, by people who believe that man is fully in command of his tools and his destiny, by the devotees of systems analysis, by those whom young people refer to as members of the Establishment with a capital E, and, in general and quite widely, by many of the contemporary high priests of educational technology.

An early article that Oettinger (1966) wrote soon after our program at Harvard was underway sounded a good deal like the world view I have just described. It was called "A Vision of Technology and Education." Oettinger's vision included most of what I have heard here these two days, as well as a nationwide, perhaps worldwide electronic information network in which was stored all of man's knowledge in all branches of science, thus making it accessible to people anywhere and everywhere. Suitable terminals and computer consoles were located in schools, offices, and homes. Individual students could be connected instantly with the world's major libraries. They had at their fingertips audio-visual recordings of instruction and lectures on specialized topics prepared by the country's best teachers, as well as teaching programs designed in the light of individual differences of age and capacity.

Would such a vision, if realized, advance or distort the purposes of education? What would be its implications for a teacher's qualifications, training, and attitudes? What would happen to the teacher-student relationship, to the present balance between teaching subject matter and guiding or counseling students, and to the differential abilities of children? Would the problem of general as against vocational education persist? Might the transition from school to work be facilitated, as former students continued to have access to the same information system with which they interacted during their years of formal training? Would such a system meet the growing need for life-long education in a world of widespread change? What would it imply for traditional relationships between school and family, school and community, school and government? What might happen, for example, to the baby-sitting function of the school or to local control of educational policy?

Our program put together a research group under Oettinger's direction to explore those questions and to test the assumptions and implications of the vision. The group began its work with a close look at conditions currently prevailing in secondary education, excluding the extremes both of the small number of avant-garde experimental schools and of the probably equally small number of schools in what might be labeled a "hopeless" category. This exclusion of avant-garde experimental schools is important, because it shows that the objectives of Oettinger's study were quite different from that of many other technical people. Given both the current state of educational technology and especially the current organization of the school system, the group concluded that the average high school a decade hence is unlikely to be very different from that of the present time, in respect either to effective utilization of educational technology or to successful preparation of youth for the demands of a technical society.

Technological devices already introduced into schools in recent years have had only peripheral impact, partly because educational technology is as yet much more primitive than is generally appreciated, so that fragile, unreliable, and expensive devices often gather dust in a classroom corner after an initial wave of enthusiasm has subsided. Knowledge about how to apply the technology is even more primitive, in a number of respects. Teachers are often afraid that expensive equipment will be damaged and try to master the problem by defining a code of behavior toward machines that is reminiscent of the world of George Orwell's *1984*. Even when the machines work and classroom attitudes are attuned to their use, attempts to graft the new techniques to old curriculums have proved spectacularly unsuccessful and largely unrelieved as yet by imaginative technical and curriculum innovation tailored to the new demands and possibilities of education. As Charles Silberman pointed out somewhere, most teachers handle classes of four in exactly the same way that they handle class of forty and then wonder how true it can be that lower teacher-student ratios make for better teaching.

A major claim for educational technology is that it serves the individual needs of students better than the one-teacher/thirty-students organization of the traditional classroom. Oettinger argues, however, that an instructional program geared to allowing each student to proceed at his own pace implies a dispersion rate, even of an initially highly homogeneous group of students, so high as to create problems of administration, scheduling, and guidance that only computer techniques as yet undevised and modes of school organization as yet unimagined could be expected to cope with them. It is unlikely that the next ten years will see improvements on these fronts sufficient to advance significantly the ideal of individualized instruction.

The primitive state of educational hardware and software, however, emerged as the lesser obstacle to the rapid and effective introduction of technology into the schools. The biggest barrier is institutional. The school system of this country may well be among the most resistant to innovation of all social institutions in the United States and the most successful in persisting in that posture. At one extreme, it has all the bureaucratic rigidity of a military service or government agency with practically none of the countervailing centralized authority that ultimately makes the military and the government move. At the other extreme the school system is characterized by most of the fragmentation and frustrations of small-scale organization—such as that of small business, for example—without its correlative freedom of response, initiative, and flexibility. In Oettinger's words, "the educational establishment in the United States seems ideally designed to resist change."

Oettinger and his colleagues thus began with a tendency to share the belief—prevalent in the Office of Education and in the "ed biz" and not infrequently fed by enthusiastic researchers—that the salvation of education in the United States by a combination of computers and systems analysis lies just around the corner. They have since come to a more sober view.

They have found that a number of contemporary processes and devices do have promise but that they are badly in need of hospitable soil. Progress is possible toward limited objectives in the direction of individualization, but as yet only under carefully controlled experimental conditions. Educational technology does not yet promise to revolutionize formal education, because the educational enterprise is not ripe for a technological fix. Bridging the gap between limited success in the laboratory and useful impact in practice hinges first on understanding and then on removing institutional barriers to this transition. Current attempts to integrate technology with the educational enterprise are dominated by faddish orthodoxy and the artificial dissemination of innovations of unproved and often dubious merit. There is a serious danger, therefore, that the continuing adoption of change in form will serve to block change in substance.

From these findings, Oettinger has concluded that technology can bring substantial improvement to education only after we have learned much more about how learning occurs, how educational institutions work and change, how informal educational agents—television, peer groups, apprenticeship training—interact with and affect formal schooling, and how, even, to make existing technical devices work. We need also to look to the people involved. Dr. Strangeloves are not necessarily the best educators of the future. Mechanical teaching aids are unlikely to help teachers who are ill-prepared even for the jobs they are now doing; there is no such thing as teacher-proof technology. Moreover, industrial designers attuned to different markets may believe too readily that selling educational devices to educators is not much different from selling refrigerators to housewives.

Finally, funding policies and R&D strategies must change if we want significant technological change in education. We must find institutional ways to support good ideas longer and encourage more risk taking than either private or governmental programs now allow, and we must be able to follow through in depth with a small number of promising alternatives in genuine competition with each other. Buckshot research in education has no more to recommend it than shotgun marriage.

You can see from all this that Oettinger did not concern himself principally, or importantly, with technical evaluation of educational technology or with a critique of various experimental projects now going on in California, Illinois, Florida, Pittsburgh, and elsewhere. The question he addressed was, rather: What are the probable social impacts of this technology and of such projects if and when they get out of the laboratory stage? What promise do they hold for educational reform, what are the obstacles in the way, what unwitting harm may they bring both to education and to the further pursuit of educational technology? What he found, basically, is that the social, political, economic, and ideological context in which development of educational technology is being carried out, promoted, applied, and exploited gives much less cause for optimism than the promise of the technology itself (Oettinger and Marks, 1969).

Educational technologists by and large do not understand this and are probably convinced that they do not need to understand it. I have not found the contributors to this book to be an exception. Most of the chapters and accompanying discussion revealed dedicated and enthusiastic pursuit of knowledge and technical improvement reminiscent of Galileo's valiant fight against the medieval church. Bitzer's passionate avowal that dollars constitute the only bottleneck to progress in educational technology reminded me, moreover, of the bigger-higher-farther-faster-at-any-cost philosophy that even the most "gung-ho" military services outgrew years ago. This is the twentieth century, not the sixteenth, and what's good for educational technologists is not necessarily good for education.

Let me identify some of the pitfalls. One is the danger of forcefeeding. I see some tendencies to say, "Let us ignore what we don't know about how people learn, how they think, in what directions they need to be developed," and let us instead concentrate on making mathematical models of parts of the process that are susceptible to such treatment. This attitude can be mistaken for scientific humility. It is more likely to lead to forcing scientific technique beyond its limits, which is no longer science, but scientism.

Another danger is that of premature exploitation. Manufacturers who will sell an experimental drug as a tested cure are not unknown—nor are public officials, anxious to move a logy establishment, who will advertise scientific possibility as operational readiness and wind up doing more harm than good by believing their own propaganda. Nor, I regret to say, is the technical man unknown who can be tempted to oversell his product to such overanxious buyers only to let himself in for an awful letdown when the product fails to live up to the impossible, cure-all claims made for it. Scientific dedication may be unchanged since Galileo, but the equally traditional scientific caution tends often these days to be thrown to the winds.

A third danger lies in the seductiveness of rigor. The implicit claim of most of the presentations is a modest one: We are trying only to do better and faster what is now being done less well and more slowly. But much of what we are doing now in education may be wrong, and if technology helps us do it very efficiently, it may lead us beyond the point where we can detect and correct our errors.

This leads me to perhaps the most dangerous pitfall of all, which is the unconscious reinforcement of the values of efficiency and achievement that can result from technical improvement of present educational processes. At a conference held at the Jewish Theological Seminary in New York in August 1968, Thomas Green of Syracuse University distinguished four kinds of education according to the predominant values that each served. Managerial education, he argued, is marked by its emphasis on serving the economic and other institutions of society. Traditional education is devoted to the preservation of social memory. Humanistic education has the primary function of developing the individual capacities of men according to their own best potentialities. Religious education, finally, is bent on nurturing a form of consciousness in which the individual sees himself in relation to dimensions of existence that transcend the self.

The value of Green's observations lies in reminding us that there is more to education than the promotion of efficiency or the imparting of occupational skills. Education also has the functions of socializing individuals, of shaping their values, of preparing for citizenship, of conserving traditions, and of imparting some sense of awe before the wonders of the universe. The application of technology to the improvement only of the instrumental function of education may thus become an obstacle to a society that is trying to redress the balance between the goals characteristic of the heyday of achievement and economic productivity and the greater pluralism in our values and our culture that we are now beginning to seek. If that happens, we could find that we have contributed to technical richness at the cost of moral poverty.

Obviously, I am not saying that you have to engage in sociological analysis or an exercise in philosophical synthesis every time you make a technical calculation. You cannot do that, and you will only mislead if you try. I am saying that you should not judge the value of your inventions by internal criteria only and conclude that they are good just because they work. The power of truth—of technology, science, knowledge—is very great these days. Those who seek after it, therefore, have a duty to measure their contribution in the context of truths that often transcend the two-valued logic of the computer.

REFERENCES

Mesthene, E. G. 1968. How technology will shape the future. *Science* 161:135–143.

Oettinger, A. G. 1966. A vision of technology and education. *Communications of the ACM* IX:489.

Oettinger, A. G., and Marks, S. 1969. *Run, computer, run.* Harvard Studies in Technology and Society, no. 1. Cambridge, Mass.: Harvard Univ. Press.

Index

70 71 72 73 10 9 8 7 6 5 4 3 2 1